*Nature's Remedies
are the best.
H. Lindlahr M.D.*

PHILOSOPHY

OF

NATURAL THERAPEUTICS

HENRY LINDLAHR, M. D.

SECOND EDITION

Published by The Lindlahr Publishing Co.
(Not-Incorporated)
515-529 South Ashland Boulevard
CHICAGO
1919

CONTENTS.

iii

"Ho, ye who suffer! Know ye suffer from yourselves. None else compels — no other holds ye that ye live or die."— *Siddartha*

ANNOUNCEMENT

The term Natural Therapeutics has been adopted to designate that system of natural living and healing which I have evolved and demonstrated in many years of institutional work and outlined in former publications.

While the pioneers of Nature Cure inaugurated the great world wide movement for simpler and more rational ways of living and of treating human ailments, their teachings and methods were very limited in scope as compared with our present comprehensive system of Natural Therapeutics which covers not only the original theories and practices but includes all that has been found good in up to date drugless and bloodless therapy.

As the term "Nature Cure" became more generally adopted by the public and the healing professions it did not stand for anything definite in the way of a school or scientific system. Unfortunately it came to pass that many who did not have the educational training or legal qualifications claimed to be practicing Nature Cure.

The time has come when order and unity must be evolved out of this chaos of theoretical teachings and practical methods.

On the fifteenth of September, 1918, came into existence the Lindlahr College of Natural Therapeutics. This marks the first attempt that has been made in this or in any other country to establish a truly eclectic system of natural living and healing on a strictly scientific basis and in compliance with the provisions of the

Medical Practice Act of a sovereign commonwealth of the United States of America. This means that the Board of Directors of the Lindlahr College of Natural Therapeutics will earnestly endeavor to comply with the provisions of the Medical Practice Act of the State of Illinois insofar as they pertain to the establishment and maintenance of professional schools for drugless healing. We realize that only in this way the movement itself as well as its accredited representatives can secure legal recognition and the merited confidence of the American public and of the world at large.

DO YOUR BIT

A DUTY AND A PLEASURE

We invite the earnest cooperation in this great work of all those who have awakened to the necessity for more rational living and for radical reform in healing methods.

While we are freeing the world at large from the curse of militarism and making it safe for Democracy, let us also do our bit to liberate the individual from the more dangerous and permanent menace of the unholy trinity of ignorance, selfishness and self-indulgence, the arch enemies of health, happiness and success.

"Freely we have received, freely give." These words embrace the highest law of the universe—the law of Love and Service. Only as we give cheerfully and freely the best that is in us can we prosper and progress ourselves.

Surely you cannot render a greater service to your relatives and friends than by teaching them how to help themselves to the greatest blessings in life; how to achieve health, strength, beauty and efficiency.

Be not dismayed by ignorance, indifference, opposition and ridicule. No honest, unselfish effort is ever lost; some seed will fall on good ground and produce an abundant harvest.

Thus you will become an active factor in Nature's great evolutionary scheme and thereby work out your own salvation physically, mentally, morally and spiritually here and hereafter, ever and forever.

THE AUTHOR.

Chicago, October 2, 1918.

TO THE PROGRESSIVE PHYSICIANS
OF THE AGE

THERE are two principal methods of treating disease. One is the combative, the other the preventive. The trend of modern medical research and practice in our great colleges and endowed research institutes is almost entirely along combative lines, while the individual, progressive physician learns to work more and more along preventive lines. The slogan of modern medical science is, "Kill the germ and cure the disease." The usual procedure is to wait until acute or chronic diseases have fully developed, and then, if possible, to subdue them by the use of drugs, surgical operations, and by means of the morbid products of disease, in the form of serums, antitoxins, vaccines, etc. The combative method fights disease with disease, poison with poison, and germs with germs and germ products. In the language of the Good Book, it is "Beelzebub against the Devil."

The preventive method does not wait until disease has fully developed and gained the ascendancy in the body, but concentrates its best endeavors on preventing, by hygienic living and by natural methods of treatment, the development of disease. Thus it endeavors to put the human body in such a normal, healthy condition that it is practically proof against infection or contagion by disease taints and miasms, and against the inroads of bacteria and parasites.

The question is, which method is the more practical, the more successful and more popular? Which will stand the test of "the survival of the fittest" in the great struggle for existence?

The medical profession has good reason to be alarmed by the inroads made in its work by irregular, unorthodox systems, schools and cults of treating human ailments; but instead of raging at the audacious presumption of these interlopers, would it not be better to inquire if there is not some reason for the astonishing spread and popularity of these therapeutic innovations?

Their success undoubtedly is based on the fact that they concentrate their best efforts on preventive instead of combative methods of treating disease. People are beginning to realize that it is cheaper and more advantageous to prevent disease than to cure it. To create and maintain continuous, buoyant good health means greater efficiency for mental and physical work; greater capacity for the true enjoyment of life, and the best insurance against failure and poverty. Therefore, he who builds health is of greater value to humanity than he who allows people to drift into disease through ignorance of Nature's laws, and then attempts to cure them by doubtful and uncertain combative methods.

It is said that in China the physician is hired and paid by the year; that he receives a certain stipend as long as the members of the family are in good health, but that the salary is suspended as long as one of his charges is ill. If some similar method of engaging and paying for medical services were in vogue in this country the trend of medical research and practice would soon undergo a radical change.

The diet expert, the hydrotherapist, the physical culturist, the adjuster of the spine, the mental healer and Christian scientist, pay little attention to the pathological conditions or to the symptoms of disease. Each of these, in accordance with his theory of disease and cure, regulates the diet and habits of living on a natural basis, promotes elimination, teaches correct breathing and wholesome exercise, corrects the mechanical lesions of the framework of the body, or establishes the right mental and emotional attitude, and, in so far as he succeeds in doing this, builds health and so diminishes the possibility of disease. The successful doctor of the future will have to fall in line with the procession and do more teaching than prescribing.

I realize that many of the statements and claims made in this volume will seem radical and irrational to my colleagues of the allopathic school of medicine. They will say that most of my teachings are contrary to the firmly established theories of medical science. All I ask of them is to judge not too hastily; to observe, to think and to test, and I am certain that they will find verified in actual experience many of the teachings of the Nature Cure philosophy. Medical science has been forced to abandon innumerable theories and practices which were at one time as firmly established as some of the pet theories of today.

By none of the statements made in this book do I mean to deny the necessity of combative methods under certain circumstances. What I wish to emphasize is that the allopathic school of medicine is spending too much of its effort along combative lines and not enough along preventive lines. It would be foolish to deny the necessity of surgery in traumatism and in abnormal conditions which require mechanical means of adjustment or treatment.

Such necessity, for instance, will exist in certain obstetrical cases as long as women have not learned to live, or are not willing to live, in such a way as to make surgical intervention at childbirth unnecessary. It is also true that so long as people persist in violating the laws of their being, thereby making their bodies prolific breeding grounds for disease taints, germs and parasites which are bound to provoke inflammatory, feverish processes (Nature's cleansing and healing efforts), combative measures will have to be resorted to by the physician, and precautionary measures against infection will have to be observed. These, however, should be in harmony with Nature's endeavors, not contrary and suppressive; they should tend to conserve and not to destroy.

Natural dietetics, fasting, hydrotherapy, osteopathy, chiropractic, naprapathy, and mental therapeutics, are combative as well as preventive, but if properly applied they do not in any way injure the organism or interfere with Nature's intent and Nature's methods. This cannot be said for much of the surgical and medical treatment of the old school of medicine. We criticize and condemn only those methods which are suppressive and destructive rather than curative.

In many instances the warnings and teachings of Nature Cure philosophy have already been verified, and have had to be heeded and accepted by medical science. The exponents of Nature Cure protested against the barbarous practice of withholding water from patients burning in fever heat, and against the exclusion of fresh air from the sickroom by order of the doctor. The cold water and no drug treatment of typhoid fever, the water treatment for other acute diseases, as well as the open air treatment for tuberculosis, were forced upon the medical profession by the advocates of Nature Cure. For more than half a century the latter have been curing all inflammatory, feverish diseases, from simple colds to scarlet fever, diphtheria, cerebro-spinal meningitis, smallpox, appendicitis, etc., etc., by hydrotherapy, fasting and other natural methods, without resorting in any case to the use of poisonous drugs, antitoxins or surgical operations.

For many years before the terrible after effects of X-Ray treatment, and of extirpation of the ovaries, of the womb and of other vital organs, became so patent that the physicians of the regular school could no longer ignore them, Nature Cure physicians had strongly warned against these unnatural practices, and called attention to their destructive after effects.

As long as seventeen years ago, when the X-Rays were in high favor for the treatment of cancer, lupus, and other diseases, I warned against the use of these rays, claiming that their vibratory velocity was too high and powerful, and that they were therefore destructive to the tissues of the human body. Since the failure of the X-Rays and since the discovery of Radio-activity, the rays and emanations of radium and other radio-active substances are widely advertised and exploited as therapeutic agents, but these rays also are far beyond the vibratory ranges of the physical body in velocity and power. Therefore, it remains to be seen whether their injurious after effects do not in the long run outweigh any beneficial effects.

The destructive action of these high power rays, as well as that of inorganic minerals, is very slow and insidious, manifesting only in the course of many years. This new field of therapeutics, therefore, has not yet passed the stage of dangerous experimentation.

Inorganic minerals also prove injurious and destructive to the tissues of the human body because they are too slow in vibratory velocity, and too coarse in molecular structure.

It is the intent and purpose of this volume to warn against the exploitation of destructive combative methods to the neglect of preventive constructive and conservative methods. If these teachings contribute something toward this end they will have fulfilled their mission.

Literary Construction

The language of this volume has purposely been kept simple, that it may be easily intelligible to the layman;

at the same time, sufficiently technical terminology had to be employed in order to express the subject matter accurately and to meet the demands of the trained scientist.

Division of Subject Matter

"Nature Cure Philosophy and Practice" represented only a brief outline of fundamental laws and principles and of their practical application in the treatment of human ailments. A more complete presentation necessitated a separation of philosophy from practice. This I have accomplished by devoting Volume I of the new series entirely to an exposition of philosophy and principles, and the second volume to instructions for right living and to diagnosis and treatment of disease. Therefore it is necessary to study the two volumes in conjunction.

THE AUTHOR.

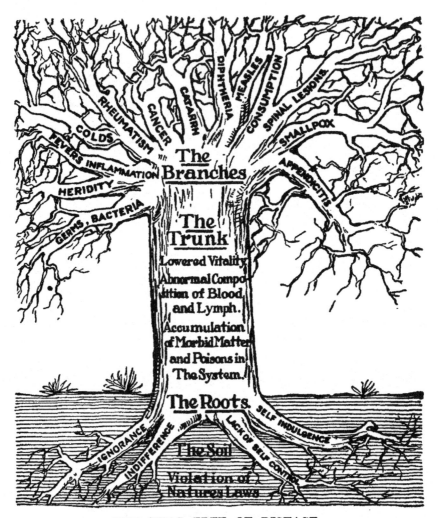

THE UPAS TREE OF DISEASE

EVIL IS NOT AN ACCIDENT, NOT AN ARBITRARY PUNISHMENT, NOT ALWAYS
AN "ERROR OF MORTAL MIND." IT IS THE NATURAL AND INEVITABLE RESULT
OF VIOLATION OF NATURE'S LAWS. IT IS INSTRUCTIVE AND CORRECTIVE IN
PURPOSE, AND WILL REMAIN WITH US ONLY AS LONG AS WE NEED ITS SALU-
TARY LESSONS.

NATURAL THERAPEUTICS

CHAPTER I

MISSING LINKS

ABOUT ten years have elapsed since I began to formulate and give expression to the principles of Nature Cure philosophy in the Nature Cure Magazine and, a few years later, in "Nature Cure Philosophy and Practice."

In the preparation of the present volume, former writings have been carefully re-edited and amplified in many directions. In doing this work I was aided by ten years of added practical experience in an extensive institutional practice and by the labors of a capable scientist recently graduated from one of the best medical colleges in this metropolis.

He brought to bear in his critical examination of Nature Cure philosophy not only his practical experience with Nature Cure gained through many years of faithful work in our institutions, but also his knowledge and experience resulting from intelligent study of up-to-date medical theories and methods. He enjoyed, as I did, the rare privilege of studying side by side the allopathic and the natural methods of healing.

It speaks well for Nature Cure philosophy that, notwithstanding the most careful scrutiny of the early editions, we did not find it necessary to change one single important proposition advanced in these teachings.

However, since producing the earlier formulations, much confirmatory evidence as to their truth and their

wonderful simplicity and efficiency has accumulated from
many sources. Some of the missing links in the chain of
evidence have been discovered.

The fundamental principles of Nature Cure philosophy,
which radically differ from allopathic theory and practice,
and which are destined to revolutionize the chaotic teachings of the old schools and to establish in their place an
exact science of medicine, are the following:

Every acute disease is the result of a purifying, healing
effort of Nature.

The inflammatory processes back of all acute and subacute diseases are identical in nature and purpose and in
the way they run their courses through the five stages of
inflammation.

The bacteria found associated with acute, subacute
and chronic diseases are not the **primary** causes and insti-
gators of these abnormal processes, but rather the product
of pathogenic conditions and the agents through which
Nature breaks down complex, disease-producing (pathogenic) substances into simpler compounds suitable for
neutralization by alkaline elements and for elimination
through the organs of depuration.

The primary cause of germ activity is the morbid soil
in which bacteria breed and multiply. Basing our practice
on these fundamental propositions, we do not endeavor to
''kill the germs'' with poisonous drugs, vaccines, serums
and antitoxins, but instead we endeavor through natural
ways of living and natural methods of treatment to purify
the organism of the systemic waste, morbid encumbrances
and disease taints which furnish the soil for the development and multiplication of disease germs.

Many who carefully studied the former editions of these
writings were probably not entirely satisfied with the
evidence presented in proof of these fundamental laws
and principles. When I described the processes of inflam-

mation solely from the viewpoint of the teachings of Pasteur and Metchnikoff, they may have wondered why the white blood corpuscles should destroy the disease germs if the latter were scavengers of morbid matter and disease taints.

As regards another mooted problem, many inquiries, running somewhat as follows, have come to me from readers and from students of the Nature Cure writings:

"You say that scabies (itch), lice, crab lice and many other so-called contagious diseases develop in the form of 'healing crises' under circumstances where infection or contagion is improbable or impossible. If this be true, where do the germs or parasites come from? In the case of scabies, lice, crab lice, etc., do you believe in spontaneous generation?"

In my former writings I anticipated and answered these questions by saying: "If our bodies contain the morbid soil, we need not worry about the microbes of disease; they will come from somewhere, because the spores of germs are present everywhere. Our bodies are alive with them."

At that time, however, I could not have answered the questions: "What are these spores of disease germs, these seed germs of bacteria? Where do they come from?"

Lately the solution of this problem also has come to me in an unexpected manner. Until a few weeks ago I was not aware of the fact that a French scientist, Antoine Béchamp, as far back as the middle of the last century, had given a rational, scientific explanation of the origin, growth and life activities of germs and of the normal living cells of vegetable, animal and human bodies. This information came to me first in a pamphlet entitled "Life's Primal Architects", by E. Douglas Hume, of London, England. Thus was I led to an investigation of Béchamp's work at first hand. Especially have I made a careful study of his last work, entitled "The Blood", in which the master summarizes the microzymian theory of cell life.

The French scientist demonstrated in his lectures at the University of Montpelier and at the Sorbonne, the ancient seat of learning in Paris, as early as 1864, that cells and germs are not the smallest individual living organisms, as taught by Pasteur and his followers, but that they are in turn made up of infinitely more minute living beings which he named microzyma. This term translated into the English vernacular would mean "minute ferment bodies".

According to the teachings of Béchamp, cells and germs are associations of microzyma. The physical characteristics and vital activities of cells and germs depend upon the soil in which their microzyma feed, grow and multiply. Thus microzyma, growing in the soil of procreative germ plasm, develop into the normal, permanent, specialized cells of the living vegetable, animal or human organism. The same microzyma feeding on morbid materials and systemic poisons in these living bodies develop into bacteria and parasites.

I shall cite here only one of the many experiments made by Professor Béchamp and his collaborators, which prove positively the correctness of his deductions. Beer yeast becomes active and multiplies normally only in a sugar solution. While feeding on sugar and digesting it, it decomposes the sugar into alcohol, carbonic acid and small amounts of acetic acid. When Béchamp added creosote or other antiseptic substances to the fermenting fluid the normal activity of the yeast germs gradually subsided. They deteriorated and decomposed, their detritus gradually changing into bacteria.* The bacteria in their turn, when they had consumed the decaying materials on which they had subsisted, disintegrated until there was nothing

---

* The experiment was conducted under conditions which made impossible invasion of bacteria from without.

left but the original microzyma. Thus he proved that
microzyma are at the beginning and at the end of all
organized beings. He found the chalk of Sens and other
calcareous rocks alive with microzyma, which started
processes of fermentation in blood, milk and other fer-
mentable substances. When we consider that these geological microzyma are the remains of fossil organisms
which lived in remote prehistoric ages we must come to
the conclusion that these primal architects of life are
practically indestructible and must be endowed with life
in its most primitive form.

How wonderfully the discovery of microzyma confirms
the claims of Nature Cure philosophy, according to which
bacteria and parasites cannot cause and instigate inflammatory and other disease processes unless they find their
own peculiar morbid soil in which to feed, grow and
multiply!

The translator of Professor Béchamp's last book, entitled "The Blood", comments as follows:

"The experimental facts learnedly elaborated by Professor
Béchamp and his collaborators make patent the absurdity of all
pretended prophylactics against disease save **one**, and casts all
rational minds back to the one sure and only protection—sound
hygiene!

"We are mocked by quarantines, vaccines, inoculations and
other devices for '**conveying**' the products of labor into the pockets
of official doctors. We are gulled by them to the fullest extent of
our willingness, to be gulled. The opponents of a truly rational
medicine are many and powerful, as evidenced by the suppression,
for more than a generation, of Béchamp's admirable discoveries
beneath a 'conspiracy of silence', and these opponents of the art
of healing are entrenched in nearly all medical schools, in richly
endowed research institutes, in expensive manufactories of animal
poisons for poisoning men and animals (under the ignorant belief
that they are benefiting us), and in all medical officialdom!''

Knowledge of the researches and teachings of Béchamp
came to me but recently, after the manuscript of this
volume had been practically completed. It was most
gratifying to discover at the last moment this **missing**

link which corroborates so wonderfully my own experience
and teachings.

Béchamp's profound revelations were soon superseded
by the plausible theories of Pasteur and Metchnikoff,
which fully justified the suppressive poison treatment of
the allopathic school of medicine. Pasteur compared the
human body to a barrel of beer and pronounced it, like
that beverage, at the mercy of extraneous organisms.
As these produce good or bad beer—a liquid diseased, as
it were, or healthy—so on entering animal bodies microorganisms create disease, each after its own order. It
only needed Professor Metchnikoff's theory of phagocytosis and the alleged discovery of "obsonins" or natural antitoxins in the blood, by Sir Almroth Wright and
Dr. Bulloch, to furnish the medical profession with a
delightfully simple theory as to the origin of disease comprehensible to the least intelligent. Upon this basis rests
the entire structure of modern medical theory and practice.

The microzyma evidently is one of the missing links in
the chain of evidence in proof of the Nature Cure philosophy of health, disease and cure. The other one was
discovered by Dr. Thomas Powell of Los Angeles. As far
as I know, he was the first one to advance the claim that
the so called white corpuscles or "phagocytes" instead
of being valiant germ fighters and germ eaters are in
reality particles of morbid, pathogenic matter; that instead of destroying the disease germs they are, in the
inflammatory processes, destroyed by the germs. It is
interesting to note that Béchamp already ridiculed the
idea of "phagocytosis." In his book "The Blood" he
says: "—although their master (Pasteur) had declared
that the cellules (leucocytes) were not living, his disciples
imagined that the leucocytes (under the name of phagocytes) were living like amoeba and able to perform movements called amoeboid. And it was imagined that these

phagocytes formed themselves into troops to pursue and devour the microbes. There was thus a **phagocytosis,** which was trumpeted forth as **providential.** The precise knowledge of the blood reduces to its just value this latest form of the struggle against the microzymian theory.''

Later on I shall explain more fully Béchamp's reasons for opposing the idea of phagocytosis.

Dr. Powell's discovery of the true nature of the so called leucocyte together with our knowledge of the activity of the microzyma furnishes for the first time in medical history a rational and consistent explanation of the process of inflammation. Inflammation always starts with obstruction in the capillary circulation, caused by ''white blood corpuscles'' and other colloid or pathogenic matter. The obstruction causes the white blood corpuscles in the blood stream to be forced out into the neighboring tissues (''emigration of the leucocytes''). Stagnation causes them to disorganize and putrefy. This morbid soil develops the microzyma of the normal cells into various kinds of ''disease germs'' or bacteria.

According to this theory, then, the microzyma are the spores or the seeds of disease germs which grow and thrive in morbid matter only. Thus the chain of evidence which proves the ''disease germ'' as constructive and the white blood corpuscle (or phagocyte) as pathogenic material, is complete, and Nature Cure philosophy throughout stands justified in theory and practice.

Dr. Thomas Powell's theory of the pathogenic nature of leucocytes is absolutely verified by the clinical records of our patients. This conclusive evidence of the true character of the ''phagocyte'' and of the correctness of natural treatment is given in Chapter IX.

An interesting confirmation of the truth of Nature Cure philosophy and practice comes from the battle fields of Europe. Ever since I began to teach and practice Nature

Cure I have advocated the exposure of wounds to air and light with no antiseptic treatment whatever.

We have cured during the last seventeen years, the worst kind of wounds, many of which under antiseptic treatment had entered upon advanced stages of necrosis. The treatment in all such cases consisted of exposing the wounds freely to air and light, and in keeping them clean and fresh by frequent wash with diluted lemon juice.

For many years I have been denounced as a dangerous ignoramous and quack for this and other radical deviations from orthodox theory and practice. During the last few years, however, reports have come from the battle fields of Europe, according to which the wounds of soldiers, who were left exposed out of doors and did not receive hospital care and antiseptic treatment, healed much quicker and more perfectly than those who received the ordinary surgical treatment.

Of late medical men have frequently lectured on this wonderful discovery in several Chicago colleges. This, of course, upsets completely the allopathic theory of the danger of germ invasion and of the necessity of antiseptic treatment, and it confirms absolutely the truth of the Nature Cure teachings as to the true character of germ activity.

The natural treatment of wounds will be discussed more fully in Vol. II of this Series.

What the Electron Is to the Atom, the Microzyma Is to the Cell

What a wonderful correspondence this theory of the origin of cell life bears to the latest scientific opinions concerning the constitution of the atom! As all elements of matter and their atoms are made up of electrons vibrating in the primordial ether, so all cells and germs are made up of microzyma. As the electrons, according to their numbers in the atom and their modes of vibration, produce upon our sensory organs the effects of various elements of matter, so the microzyma, according to the medium or soil in which they live, develop into various cells and germs, exhibiting distinctive structure and vital activities.

New Light on Heredity

Modern biology teaches us that all permanent, specialized cells present in the complicated adult body are actually contained in the original procreative cell which results from the union of the male spermatazoon and the female ovum. Science, however, has failed to explain this seeming miracle—how it is possible that all the permanent cells of the large adult body can be present from the beginning in the minute procreative cell and in the rudimentary body of the fetus.

Béchamp's theory of microzyma brings the rational and scientific explanation. If these microzyma are as minute in comparison to the cell as the electrons are in comparison to the atom, and the atom in comparison to the visible particles of matter, then the mystery of the genesis of the complex human body from the procreative cell, as well as the mysteries of heredity in its various phases, are amenable to explanation.

If the microzyma are the spores, or seeds, of cells, it is possible to conceive that these infinitesimal, minute living organisms may bear the impress of the species and of racial and family characteristics and tendencies, finally to reappear in the cells, organs and nervous system of the adult body.

CHAPTER II

WHAT IS NATURE CURE?

IT is vastly more than a system of curing aches and pains; **it is a complete revolution in the art and science of living.** It is the practical realization and application of all that is good in natural science, philosophy and religion.

About seventy years ago this greatest and most beneficent of reformatory movements was inaugurated by Priessnitz in Grafenberg, a small village in the Silesian mountains. The originator of Nature Cure was a simple farmer, but he had a natural genius for the art of healing.

His pharmacopeia consisted not in poisonous pills and potions, but in plenty of exercise, fresh mountain air, water treatments in the cool, sparkling brooks, and simple, wholesome country fare, consisting largely of black bread, vegetables, and milk fresh from cows fed on nutritious mountain grasses.

The results accomplished by these simple means were wonderful. Before he died, a large sanitarium, filled with patients from all over the world and from all stations of life, had grown up around his forest home.

Among those who made the pilgrimage to Grafenberg to become patients and students of this genial healer, the simple-minded farmer-physician, were wealthy merchants, princes and doctors from all parts of the world.

Rapidly the idea of drugless healing spread over the civilized world. Hahn the apothecary, Kuhne the weaver, Rikli the manufacturer, Father Kneipp the priest, Lahmann the doctor, Adolph Just the teacher, and Turnvater

18

Jahn, the founder of physical culture, became enthusiastic pupils and followers of Priessnitz.

Each one of these men enlarged and enriched some special field of the great realm of natural healing. Some elaborated the water cure and natural dietetics, others invented various systems of manipulative treatment, earth, air, and light cures, magnetic healing, mental therapeutics, curative gymnastics, etc., etc. Von Peckzely added the Diagnosis from the Iris of the Eye, which reveals not only the innermost secrets of the human organism, but also Nature's ways and means of cure, and the changes for better or for worse continually occurring in the body.

In this country, Dr. Trall of New York, Dr. Jackson of Danville, Dr. Kellogg of Battle Creek, and others caught the infection and crossed the ocean to become students of Priessnitz.

Quimby, the itinerant spiritualist and healer, became successful and renowned by the application of the natural methods of cure. At first his favorite methods were water, massage, magnetic and mental treatment. Gradually he concentrated his efforts on metaphysical methods of cure, and before he died he evolved a complete system of magnetic and mental therapeutics.

Quimby's teachings and methods were adopted by Mrs. Eddy, his most enthusiastic pupil, and by her elaborated into Christian Science, the latest and most successful of modern mental healing cults.

Dr. Still of Kirksville, Missouri, made a valuable addition to natural methods of treatment by the development of osteopathy, a system of scientific manipulation of the framework of the body. Later developments of manipulative treatment are chiropractic, originated by Dr. D. D. Palmer of Davenport, Iowa; neurotherapy, evolved by Drs. Arnold and Walter of Philadelphia, Pennsylvania; naprapathy, founded by Dr. Oakley Smith of Chicago,

Illinois; and spondylotherapy, developed by Dr. Albert Abrams of Los Angeles, California.*

Thus the simple pioneers of Nature Cure, every one of them gifted by Nature with the instinct and the genius of the true healer, who is born, not made, laid the foundation for the world wide modern health culture movement.

They were neither blinded nor confused by the conflicting theories of books and authorities, nor by the action of a thousand different drugs on a legion of different symptoms, but **applied common sense reasoning to the solution of the problems of health, disease and cure.**

They went for inspiration to field and forest rather than to the murky atmosphere of the dissection and vivisection rooms. They studied the whole and not only the parts; **causes as well as effects and symptoms.** Realizing that man had lost his natural instinct and strayed far away from Nature's ways, they studied and imitated the natural habits of the animal creation rather than the confusing doctrines of the schools.

Thus they proclaimed the "**return to Nature**" and the "**new gospel of health**", which are destined to free humanity from the destructive influences of alcoholism, meat eating, the dope and tobacco habit, of drug poisoning, vaccination, surgical mutilation, vivisection, and a thousand other abuses practiced in the name of science.

When parents learn how to create children in accord with natural law, how to mould their bodies and their characters into harmony and beauty **before** the new life sees the light of day, when they learn to rear their offspring in health of body and purity of mind in harmony with the laws of their being, then we shall have true types of beautiful manhood and womanhood, then children will

---

* For details regarding Manipulative Treatment, see Vol. II.

no longer be a curse and a burden to themselves, to those who bring them into the world or to society at large.

These thoughts are not the mere dreams of a visionary. When we see the wonderful changes wrought in a human being by a few months or years of rational living and treatment, it seems not impossible nor improbable that these ideals may be realized within a few generations.

Children thus born and reared in harmony with the law will be the future masters of the earth. They will need neither gold nor influence to win in the race of life; their innate powers of body, mind and soul will make them victors over every circumstance. The offspring of alcoholism, drug poisoning, and sexual perversion will cut but sorry figures in comparison with the manhood and womanhood of a true and noble aristocracy of health,—an aristocracy, not of degenerated and vitiated blue blood, but of pure and wholesome red blood.

CHAPTER III

CATECHISM OF NATURE CURE

THE philosophy of Nature Cure is based on sciences dealing with newly discovered and rediscovered natural laws and principles, and with their application to the phenomena of life and death, health, disease, and cure.

Every new science embodying new modes of thought requires exact modes of expression and new definitions of words and phrases already in common use. Therefore I have endeavored to define, as precisely as possible, certain words and phrases which convey meanings and ideas peculiar to the teachings of Nature Cure.

The student of Nature Cure and kindred subjects will do well to closely study these definitions and formulated principles, as they contain the pith and marrow of our philosophy and greatly facilitate its understanding.

(1) **What is Nature Cure?**

Nature Cure is a system of man-building in harmony with the **constructive** principle in Nature on the physical, mental and moral planes of being.

(2) **What is the Constructive Principle in Nature?**

The constructive principle in Nature is that principle which builds up, improves, and repairs, which always makes for the perfect type, and which is opposed to the destructive principle in Nature, whose activity in Nature is designated as evolutionary.

(3) **What is the Destructive Principle in Nature?**

The destructive principle in Nature is that principle which disintegrates and destroys existing forms and types,

22

and whose activity in Nature is designated as devolutionary.

(4) **What is Normal or Natural?**

That is normal or natural which is in harmonic relation with the life purposes of the individual.

(5) **What is Health?**

Health is normal and harmonious vibration of the elements and forces composing the human entity on the physical, mental and moral planes of being, in conformity with the constructive principle in Nature applied to individual life.

(6) **What is Disease?**

Disease is abnormal or inharmonious vibration of the elements and forces composing the human entity on one or more planes of being, in conformity with the destructive principle in Nature applied to individual life.

(7) **What is the Primary Cause of Disease?**

The primary cause of disease, barring accidental or surgical injury to the human organism and surroundings hostile to human life, is **violation of Nature's laws.**

(8) **What are the Effects of Violation of Nature's Laws on the Physical Human Organism?**

The effects of violation of Nature's laws on the physical human organism are:

1. **Lowered vitality;**

2. **Abnormal composition of blood and lymph;**

3. **Accumulation of waste matter, morbid materials and poisons.**

These conditions are identical with disease, because they tend to lower, hinder or inhibit normal function (harmonious vibration), and because they engender and promote destruction of living tissues.

(9) **What is Acute Disease?**

What is commonly called "acute" disease is in reality the result of Nature's efforts to eliminate from the organism waste material, foreign matter and poisons, and to repair injury to living tissues. In other words, **every socalled acute disease is the result of a cleansing and healing effort of Nature.**

(10) **What is Chronic Disease?**

(a) Chronic disease is a condition of the organism in which lowered vibration (lowered vitality), due to the accumulation of waste material and poisons, with the consequent destruction of vital parts and organs, has progressed to such an extent that Nature's constructive and healing forces are no longer able to react against the disease conditions by acute corrective efforts (healing crises).

(b) Chronic disease is a condition of the organism in which the morbid encumbrances, having gained the ascendancy, prevent acute reaction (healing crises) on the part of the constructive forces of Nature.

(c) Chronic disease is the natural consequence of the inability of the organism to react by acute efforts, or "healing crises", against conditions inimical to health.

(11) **What is a "Healing Crises"?**

A healing crisis is an acute reaction, resulting from the ascendancy of Nature's healing forces over disease conditions. Its tendency is towards recovery, and it is, therefore, in conformity with Nature's constructive principle.

(12) **Are all Acute Reactions Healing Crises?**

No; there are healing crises and disease crises.

(13) **What is a "Disease Crisis"?**

A disease crisis is an acute reaction resulting from the ascendancy of disease conditions over the healing forces of the organism. Its tendency is, therefore, toward fatal termination.

(14) **What is Cure?**

Cure is the readjustment of the human organism from abnormal to normal conditions and functions.

(15) **What Methods of Treatment are in Conformity with the Constructive Principle in Nature?**

Those methods which

1. Establish normal surroundings and natural habits of life in accord with Nature's laws;

2. Economize vital force;

3. Build up the blood on a natural basis; that is, supply the blood with its natural constituents in right proportions;

4. Promote the elimination of waste material and poisons without in any way injuring the human body;

5. Correct mechanical lesions;

6. Arouse the individual in the highest possible degree to the consciousness of personal responsibility and to the necessity of intelligent personal effort and self-help.

(16) **Are Medicines in Conformity with the Constructive Principle in Nature?**

Medicines are in conformity with the constructive principle in Nature in so far as they, in themselves, are not injurious or destructive to the human organism and in so far as they act as tissue foods and promote the neutralization and elimination of morbid matters and poisons.

(17) **Are Poisonous Drugs and Promiscuous Surgical Operations in Conformity with the Constructive Principle in Nature?**

Poisonous drugs and promiscuous operations are **not** in conformity with the constructive principle in Nature, because:

1. They suppress acute diseases or reactions (crises), the cleansing and healing efforts of Nature;

2. They are in themselves harmful and destructive to human life;

3. Such treatment fosters the belief that drugs and surgical operations can be substituted for obedience to Nature's laws and for personal effort and self-help.

(18) **Is Metaphysical Healing in Conformity with the Constructive Principle in Nature?**

Metaphysical systems of healing are in conformity with the constructive principle in Nature in so far as:

1. They do not interfere with or suppress Nature's healing efforts;

2. They awaken hope and confidence (therapeutic faith), and thereby increase the inflow of vital force into the organism;

3. They teach the law of cause and effect and thus awaken and strengthen the consciousness of personal responsibility.

They are **not** in conformity with the constructive principle in Nature in so far as:

1. They fail to assist Nature's healing efforts, but ignore, obscure and deny the laws of Nature and defy the dictates of reason and common sense;

2. They substitute in the treatment of disease a blind, dogmatic belief in the wonder-working power of metaphysical formulas and prayer, for intelligent cooperation with Nature's constructive forces and for personal effort and self-help;

3. They weaken the consciousness of personal responsibility.

(19) **Is Nature Cure in Conformity with the Constructive Principle in Nature?**

Nature Cure is in conformity with the constructive principle in Nature in that

1. It teaches that the primary cause of weakness and disease is disobedience to the laws of Nature;

2. It arouses the individual to the study of natural laws and demonstrates the necessity of strict compliance with these laws;

3. It strengthens the consciousness of personal responsibility of the individual for his own status of health and

for the hereditary conditions, traits and tendencies of his offspring;

4. It encourages personal effort and self-help;

5. It adapts surroundings and habits of life to natural laws;

6. It assists Nature's cleansing and healing efforts by simple natural means and methods of treatment which are in no wise harmful or destructive to health and life, and which are within the reach of everyone.

(20) **What are the Natural Methods of Living and of Treatment?**

1. **Return to Nature** by the regulation of eating, drinking, breathing, bathing, dressing, working, resting, thinking, the moral life, sexual and social activities, etc., establishing them on a normal and natural basis.

2. **Elementary remedies,** such as water, air, light, earth cures, magnetism, electricity, etc.

3. **Chemical remedies,** such as scientific food selection and combination, homeopathic medicines, simple herb extracts, and the vitochemical remedies.

4. **Mechanical remedies,** such as corrective gymnastics, massage, magnetic treatment, structural adjustment and, in cases of accident, surgery.

5. **Mental and spiritual remedies,** such as scientific relaxation, normal suggestion, constructive thought, the prayer of faith, etc.

CHAPTER IV

WHAT IS LIFE?

IN our study of the cause and character of disease we must endeavor to begin at the beginning, and that is LIFE itself; for the processes of health, disease and cure are manifestations of that which we call life, vitality, life elements.

While endeavoring to fathom the mystery of life we soon realize that we are dealing with an ultimate which no human mind is capable of solving or explaining. We can study and understand life only in its manifestations, not in its origin and real essence.

There are two prevalent but widely differing conceptions of the nature of **life** or **vital force**— the **material** and the **vital.**

The former looks upon life or vital force with all its physical, mental and psychical phenomena as manifestations of the electric, magnetic and physicochemical activities of the physical material elements composing the human organism. From this viewpoint, life is a sort of "spontaneous combustion" or, as one scientist expresses it, a "succession of fermentations" or chemical changes.

One of the latest and most pretentious works dealing with life and its phenomena of growth, reproduction, decline and disintegration is a book entitled "Senescence and Rejuvenescence", by Charles Manning Child, published by the University of Chicago Press. I have studied this work carefully and must confess that after its perusal I was as wise as I was in the beginning concerning the vital principles involved in the processes of growth, organization and differentiation and those of disorganization or dedifferentiation, as the author calls it.

He very interestingly describes phenomena but fails to explain causes. While tracing the relationship of the phenomena of life, he tries to prove that life has no place in the scheme of things.

The vitalistic conception of life regards vital force as the primary force of all forces, coming from the great central source of all life. This force, which permeates, heats and animates the entire created universe, is an expression of divine intelligence and will, the "logos", the "word" of the great Creative Intelligence. It is this divine energy which sets in motion the whirls in the ether, the electric corpuscles that make up the atoms and elements of matter.

These electrons are positive and negative forms of electricity. Electricity is a form of energy. It is intelligent energy; otherwise it could not act with that same wonderful precision in the electrons of the atoms as in the suns and planets of the sidereal universe.

This intelligent energy can have but one source: the will and intelligence of the Creator—as Swedenborg expresses it, of "the great Central Sun of the Universe". If this supreme Intelligence should withdraw its creative energy, the electric charges (forms of energy) and with it the atoms, elements, and the entire material universe, would disappear in the flash of a moment.

From this it appears that crude matter, instead of being the source of life and of all its complicated mental and spiritual phenomena (which assumption, on the face of it, is absurd), is but an expression of the Life Force, itself a manifestation of the great Creative Intelligence which some call God, others Nature, the Oversoul, Brahma, Prâna, The Great Spirit, etc., each according to his best understanding.

It is this supreme Intelligence and Power acting in and through every atom, molecule and cell in the human body, which is the true healer, the "vis medicatrix naturae" which always endeavors to repair, to heal and restore the perfect type. All that the physician can do is to remove obstructions and to establish normal conditions within and around the patient, so that "the healer within" can do his work to the best advantage.

Here the Christian Scientist will say: "That is exactly what we claim. All is God! All is mind! There is no matter! Our attitude toward disease is based on these facts."

Well, what of it, Brother Scientist? Suppose, in the final analysis, matter is nothing but vibration, an expression of Divine Mind and Will. That, for all practical purposes, does not justify me in denying and ignoring its reality. Because I have an "all mind" body, is it advisable for me to place myself in the way of an "all mind" locomotive moving at the rate of sixty miles an hour?

The question is not **what matter is** in the final analysis, but **how matter affects us.** We have to take it and treat it as we find it. We must be as obedient to the laws of matter as to those of the higher planes of being.

Life Is Vibratory

In the final analysis, all things in Nature, from a fleeting thought or emotion to the hardest piece of diamond or platinum, are modes of motion or vibration. Until a few years ago physical science assumed that an atom was the smallest imaginable part of a given element of matter; that although infinitesimally small, it still represented solid matter. Now, in the light of more recent evidence, we have good reason to believe that there is no such thing as solid matter; that every atom is made up of charges of negative and positive electricity acting in and upon an omnipresent ether; that the difference between an atom of iron and one of hydrogen, or of any other element, depends solely upon the number of electrons it contains and upon the velocity with which these vibrate around one another in the ether.

Thus the atom, which was thought to be the ultimate particle of solid matter, is found to be a little universe in itself in which electrons revolve around one another like the sun and planets in the sidereal universe. **This explains what we mean when we say life and matter are vibratory.**

Over two thousand years ago Pythagoras taught that all matter was made up of three elements, viz., a primordial substance, motion, and number. It is interesting to note how up-to-date modern science verifies the teachings of this ancient Greek philosopher. In the language of modern science the primordial substance of Pythagoras is the all-pervading ether, motion is electricity, and numbers are the number of electrons vibrating in the atom.

As early as 1863 John Newlands discovered that when he arranged the elements of matter in the order of their atomic weight, they displayed the same relation to one another as do the tones in the musical scale. Thus modern chemistry demonstrates the verity of the ''music of the spheres''—another ''visionary concept of ancient mysticism''. The atoms of matter in their relation to one another are constructed and arranged in exact correspondence with the seven primary tones in the musical scale and therefore with the laws of harmony. Therefore the entire sidereal universe is built on the laws of music.

That which is orderly, lawful, good, beautiful, natural, healthy, vibrates **in unison** with the harmonics of this great ''Diapason of Nature'': in other words, it is in alignment with the constructive principle in Nature.

That which is disorderly, abnormal, ugly, unnatural,

unhealthy, vibrates **in discord** with Nature's harmonies. It is in alignment with the destructive principle in Nature.

What we call "inanimate Nature" is beautiful and orderly because it plays in tune with the score of the symphony of life. Man only can play out of tune. This is his privilege, if he so chooses, by virtue of his freedom of choice and action.

Dr. J. D. Buck expressed these thoughts most beautifully in an essay entitled "The Music of the Spheres":

"Modern science has rediscovered enough of the wisdom of Pythagoras and the old Initiates to discern that all light, all color, all sound, and every form in nature depend upon and are determined by different vibrations. The form of every living being, the crystallizing of every snow-flake as of every physical substance, the veining of every leaf, the pencilling and fragrance of every flower, no less than the forms of thought and the subtle play of human emotions, are all dependent upon vibration, they all conform to the laws of harmony, and belong to the Music of the Spheres. Nay, every atom of matter in the Universe is set to music, and whether dancing in light or coalescing in the deep, dark bowels of the earth, is part of the universal diapason of Nature. For the universe is not dead, but literally breathing and pulsating with life, and the law of that life is harmony.

"Every atom, as every sun and star, through ceaseless motion, under the law of eternal harmony, is striving for equilibrium. Man suffers only because he is out of harmony with himself, with Nature, and with the Eternal source of Being. Every pain is the cry of an organ out of tune; every sin and every crime is but the attempt of a soloist to ignore the score of the orchestra to which he belongs and to which he is indissolubly bound. It is these discords that drown out the Music of the Spheres, and we are so intent upon our own discords, and so bound up in our own performance, that we are deaf to the symphony of life set before us, and when called to account console ourselves with the reflection that we are no worse out of time than the other members of the orchestra.

"Nature is full of music, as it exists only through the

laws of harmony. Man only is discordant and out of tune.

"It is not alone the movement of matter over matter that results in sound, or the friction of moving bodies with the elements of our atmosphere that may become audible. The basic foundation of the Ethers is sound, and long before the appearance of heat and light the immensity of space is filled with resonant vibrations. Both the resistance of the ether and the revolutions of suns are constant and uniform. The human ear is a time organ, and it is because there are no interruptions, nothing to break the sound of revolving planets, that we do not hear the sound they make in revolving space. If the mutual attraction of planets is determined by their size and density, and they are held to their orbit by mutual attraction and repulsion, so also the ratio of movement each to each and of each to all must coincide. But what is this but the movement of different instruments of varying tone as in an orchestra? The symphony of creation must be a fact and not a fancy, and the singing of the morning stars a veritable reality. There is a subjective side to the physical senses, and this only becomes active when the other is suspended.

"We have only to open our souls to the divine harmony, and silence all the discords within, in order to hear and to understand the Music of the Spheres."

We can now better understand the definitions of HEALTH and of DISEASE given in the Catechism of Nature Cure (pages 22-27), as follows:

Health is normal and harmonious vibration of the elements and forces composing the human entity on the physical, mental and moral planes of being, in conformity with the constructive principle of Nature applied to individual life.

Disease is abnormal or inharmonious vibration of the elements and forces composing the human entity on one or more planes of being, in conformity with the destructive principle of Nature applied to individual life.

The question naturally arising here is, normal or ab-

normal vibration with what? The answer is that the
vibratory conditions of the organism must be in harmony with Nature's established harmonic relations in the
physical, mental, moral and psychical realms of human life
and action.

What Is an "Established Harmonic Relation"?

Let us see whether we cannot make this clear by a
simple illustration. If a watch is in good condition, "in
harmonious vibration", its movement is so adjusted that
it coincides exactly, in point of time, with the rotations
of our earth around its axis. The established, regular
movement of the earth forms the basis of the established
harmonic relationship between the vibrations of a normal,
"healthy" timepiece and the revolutions of our planet.
The watch has to vibrate in unison with the harmonics
of the planetary universe in order to be normal, or "in
harmony".

In like manner, everything that is normal, natural,
healthy, good, beautiful, must vibrate in unison with its
correlated harmonics in Nature.

Obedience the Only Salvation

Orthodox medical science attributes disease largely to
accidental causes: to chance infection by disease taints,
germs, or parasites, to drafts, chills, wet feet, etc.

The religiously inclined frequently attribute disease and
other tribulations to the arbitrary rulings of an inscru-
table Providence.

Christian Scientists tell us that sin, suffering, disease
and all other kinds of evil are only "errors of mortal
mind", or the products of diseased imagination (though
this in itself admits the existence of something abnormal
and diseased).

Nature Cure philosophy presents a more rational concept of evil, its cause and purpose, namely: that it is brought on by violation of Nature's laws; that it is corrective in its purpose; that it can be overcome only by compliance with the law. There is no suffering, disease nor evil of any kind anywhere unless the law has been transgressed somewhere by someone.

These transgressions of the law may be due to ignorance, to indifference or to willfulness and viciousness. The effects will always be commensurate with the causes. (See Upas Tree of Disease, page 8.) This places the responsibility for disease and evil in general where it belongs,—on ourselves.

"We are not punished for our sins but by our sins." The great all-wise and all-loving Father-Mother principle does not impose or enforce suffering on its children. We create it ourselves through ignorant or willful violation of the laws of our being. There is no accident, no ill luck nor misfortune,—there is nothing but cause and effect.

The science of natural living and healing shows clearly that what we call disease is primarily Nature's effort to eliminate morbid matter and to restore the normal functions of the body; that the processes of disease are just as orderly in their way as everything else in Nature; that we must not check or suppress them, but cooperate with them. Thus we learn slowly and laboriously the all-important lesson that obedience to natural law is the only means of prevention of disease and the only cure.

The fundamental law of cure, the law of action and reaction and the law of crisis, as revealed by Nature Cure philosophy, impress upon us the truth that there is nothing accidental nor arbitrary in the processes of health, disease and cure; that every changing condition is either in harmony or in discord with the laws of our being; that only by complete surrender and obedience to these laws can we attain and maintain perfect physical health.

Selfcontrol the Master Key

Thus Nature Cure brings home to us constantly and forcibly the inexorable operation of natural law and the necessity of compliance with the law. Herein lies its great educational value to the individual and to the race. The man who has learned to master his habits and his appetites so as to conform to Nature's laws on the physical plane, and who has thereby regained his bodily health, realizes that personal effort and selfcontrol are the master key to all further development on the mental and spiritual planes of being as well; that selfmastery and unremitting and unselfish personal effort are the only means of selfcompletion, of individual and social salvation.

The naturist who has regained health and strength through obedience to the laws of his being, enjoys a measure of selfcontent, gladness of soul and enthusiasm which cannot be explained by the mere possession of physical health. These highest and purest attainments of the human soul are not the results of mere physical well-being, but of the peace and harmony which come only through obedience to natural law. Such is the peace which passeth understanding.

CHAPTER V

THE PRIMARY CAUSE OF DISEASE AND ITS MANIFESTATIONS

WE have learned in the previous chapter that, barring trauma (injury) and surroundings uncongenial to human life, the primary cause of all disease is violation of Nature's laws. Violation of Nature's laws in thinking, breathing, eating, drinking, dressing, working, resting, as well as in moral, sexual and social conduct, results in certain primary and secondary manifestations of disease.

The three primary manifestations of disease coincide with the three primary life requirements of the cell. Biology teaches us that these are innervation, nutrition and drainage. By innervation is meant a copious influx of life force and an adequate nerve supply from headquarters in the brain and spinal cord. Anything, therefore, which obstructs the nerve connection of the cell with the sympathetic and the central nervous systems lowers the vitality of the cells, tissues and organs and of the organism as a whole, and interferes with the transmission of afferent and efferent nerve impulses.

Nutrition, the second life requirement of the cell, necessitates normal composition of blood, lymph and other fluids of the body; therefore, abnormal composition of the vital fluids constitutes the second one of the primary manifestations of disease.

The third life requirement of the cell, according to biology, is perfect drainage. Accumulations of waste and morbid matter interfere with drainage as well as with nutrition of the cell; therefore, is accumulation of waste and morbid matter in the system the third one of the primary manifestations of disease.

The following diagram will illustrate the foregoing statements.

Diagram

Primary Life Requirements of the Cell	Primary Manifestations of Disease
1. Innervation, that is an adequate nerve supply through sympathetic and central nervous systems.	1. Lowered vitality.
2. Nutrition, normal composition of blood, lymph and vital fluids.	2. Abnormal composition of vital fluids.
3. Drainage, that is free and unobstructed drainage through venous and lymphatic circulation.	3. Accumulation of waste and morbid matter which obstructs the venous and lymphatic circulation.

The following diagram will outline the primary manifestations or stages of disease and the secondary stages resulting from them.

TABLE I

Primary and Secondary Stages or Manifestations of Disease

Primary Stages or Manifestations	Secondary Stages or Manifestations
1. Lowered vitality due to overwork, night work, weakening habits, excesses, over-indulgence, over-stimulation, poisonous drugs, ill-advised surgical operations and to wrong thinking and feeling.	1. Hereditary and acquired taints of sycosis, scrofula, psora, syphilis, mercurialism, cinchonism, iodism and many other forms of systemic and drug poisoning.
2. Abnormal composition of blood and lymph due to improper selection and combination of food, and especially to lack of ''organic'' mineral salts.	2. Disease germs, parasites, etc.

3. Accumulation of waste material, morbid matter and poisons (the pathogen of Dr. Powell, see Chapter IX). These accumulations of morbid matter and poisons are caused by lowered vitality, faulty diet, overeating, use of alcoholic and narcotic stimulants, drugs, vaccines, antitoxins, and by suppression of acute disease by poisonous drugs, ice and surgical operations.

3. Fevers, inflammation, skin eruptions, catarrhal discharges, ulcers, abscesses, hemorrhages, etc.—processes which indicate the oxidation and elimination of morbid or pathogenic material.

TABLE II

The Unity of Disease and Treatment

In correspondence with the three primary manifestations of disease, Nature Cure recognizes the following

Natural Methods of Treatment

1. **Return to Nature,** or the establishment of normal habits and surroundings, which necessitates

    (a) Extension of consciousness by popular general and individual education;

    (b) The constant exercise of reason, will and self control;

    (c) A return to natural habits in thinking, breathing, eating, dressing, working, resting, and in moral, sexual and social conduct;

    (d) Correction of mechanical lesions and injuries by means of massage, osteopathy, chiropractic, narapathy, surgery, and other mechanical methods of treatment.

2. **Economy of Vital Force,** which necessitates
   - (a) Prevention of waste of vital force by stopping all leaks;
   - (b) Scientific relaxation, proper rest and sleep;
   - (c) Proper food selection, magnetic treatment, etc.;
   - (d) The right mental attitude, right thinking and feeling.

3. **Elimination,** which necessitates
   - (a) Scientific selection and combination of food and drink;
   - (b) Judicious fasting;
   - (c) Hydrotherapy (water cure);
   - (d) Light and air baths;
   - (e) Manipulative treatment;
   - (f) Correct breathing, curative gymnastics;
   - (g) Such medicinal remedies as will build up the blood on a normal basis and supply the system with the all-important mineral salts in organic form.

In the following chapters I shall endeavor to show how all the different forms, phases and phenomena of disease arising within the human organism, provided they are not caused by accident or external conditions unfavorable to human life, grow out of one or more of the three primary manifestations of disease (Tables I and II). When we succeed in proving that all disease originates from a few simple causes, it will not seem so strange and improbable that all disease can be cured by a few simple, natural methods of living and of treatment. If Nature Cure accomplishes this, it thereby establishes its right to be classed with the exact sciences.

The Primary Stages of Disease

We shall now consider the three primary stages of disease, one by one.

I. Lowered Vitality

HEALTH POSITIVE—DISEASE NEGATIVE

The freer the inflow of life force into the organism, the greater the vitality, the more there is of strength, of positive resisting and recuperating power.

At the very foundation of the manifestation of life lies the principle of polarity which expresses itself in the duality of positive and negative affinity. The swaying to and fro of the positive and the negative, the effort to balance incomplete polarity, constitutes the very ebb and flow of life.

Disease is disturbed polarity or unbalanced chemical equilibrium. Exaggerated positive or negative conditions, whether physical, mental or moral, tend to disease on the respective planes of being. Foods, medicines, suggestions and all other methods of treatment exert on the individual subjected to them either a positive or a negative influence. It is, therefore, of the greatest importance that the physician and every one who wishes to live and work in harmony with Nature's laws should understand this all important question of magnetic polarity.

Lowered vitality means lowered, slower and coarser vibration, which results in weakened resistance to the accumulation of morbid matter, poisons, disease taints, germs and parasites. This is what we designate ordinarily as the "negative" condition.

Let us explain this more fully by a homely but practical illustration: Many of my readers have probably seen in operation in the summer amusement parks the "human roulette". This contrivance consists of a large wheel, board covered, somewhat raised in the center and sloping toward the circumference. The wheel rotates horizontally, evenly with the floor or the ground. The merry-makers pay their nickels for the privilege of throwing themselves flat down on the wheel and attempting to cling to it while it rotates with increasing swiftness. While the wheel moves slowly it is easy enough to cling to it; but the faster it revolves, the more strongly the centrifugal force tends to throw off the human "flies" trying to hold fast.

The accelerated repelling power of the revolving wheel may serve as an illustration of that which we call vigorous vibration, good vitality, natural immunity or recuperative power. This is the positive condition.

The more intense the action of the life force, the more rapid and vigorous are the vibratory activities of the atoms and molecules in the cells, and of the cells in the organs and tissues of the body. The more rapid and vigorous this vibratory activity, the more powerful is the repulsion and expulsion of morbid matter, poisons and germs of disease which encumber and seek to destroy the organism.

This explains why, with advancing age, waste and morbid matter accumulates more readily in the body. Lowered vitality means lowered vibration and this means lowered resistance to the accumulation of waste and morbid materials. This in turn obstructs the inflow and distribution of vital energy. Thus it becomes apparent how the primary manifestations of disease see-saw and aggravate one another.

HEALTH AND DISEASE RESIDENT IN THE CELL

Health or disease, in the final analysis, is resident in the cell. Though a minute, microscopic organism, the cell is an individual living being, which eats, drinks, grows, throws off waste matter, multiplies, ages and declines, just like man, the large conglomerate cell. If the individual cell embodies health, man, the complex cell, is well also, and vice versa. From this it becomes apparent that in all our considerations of the processes of health, disease and cure, we have to deal primarily with the individual cell.

The vibratory activity of the cell may be lowered through the decline of vitality brought about in a natural way by advancing age, or in an artificial way, through wrong thinking and feeling, wrong habits of living, overwork, unnatural stimulation and excesses of various kinds.

On the other hand, the inflow of vital force into the cells may be obstructed and their vibratory activity lowered by the accumulation of waste and morbid matter in the tissues of the body. Such clogging interferes with the inflow of life force and with the free and harmonious vibration of the cells and organs of the body as surely as dust in a watch interferes with the normal action and vibration of its wheels and balances.

From this it is evident that negative conditions may be brought about not only by hyper-refinement of the physical organism, but also by clogging it with waste and morbid matter which tends to interfere with the inflow and distribution of vital force. The "positive nourishing" diet consisting largely of meat, eggs, fats and gluten, clogs the system heavily with pathogenic waste and morbid materials, thereby obstructing the inflow and distribution of the life elements, which is equivalent to lowered vitality or a negative condition. I call attention to this because many people are under the impression that fasting, vegetarian diet or raw food diet and certain eliminating methods of treatment necessarily result in the creation of negative conditions and that negative patients must be kept on a heavy meat diet.

It also becomes apparent that in all cases where negative conditions are caused by clogging with waste and morbid matter, the Nature Cure methods of eliminative treatment, such as pure food diet, hydrotherapy, massage, neurotherapy, etc., must be invaluable means of removing these

obstructions and promoting the inflow and free circulation
of the positive electromagnetic and vitochemical energies.

II. Abnormal Composition of Blood and Lymph

As one of the primary stages or manifestations of disease, we cited abnormal composition of blood and lymph.
The human organism is made up of a certain number of
elements in well defined proportions. Chemistry has discovered, so far, about eighteen of these elements in appreciable quantities and has ascertained their functions in
the economy of the body. These elements must be present
in the right proportions in order to insure normal texture
and functioning of the component parts and organs of
the body.

The cells and organs receive their nourishment from the
blood and lymph streams. Therefore these must contain
all the elements needed by the organism in the right proportions, and this, of course, depends upon the character
and combination of food elements.

Every disease arising in the human organism from internal causes is accompanied by a deficiency in blood and
tissues of certain important mineral elements (organic
salts) and this in turn is caused by an unbalanced diet.
Improper food combinations create an over-abundance of
waste and morbid matter in the system, while failing to
supply the positive mineral elements or organic salts on
which depends the elimination of waste materials and
systemic poisons from the body.

The great problem of natural dietetics and of natural
treatment is, therefore, how to restore and maintain the
positivity of the blood and of the organism as a whole
through providing in food, drink and medicine an abundant supply of the positive mineral salts in organic
form.

III. Accumulation of Morbid Matter and Poisons

This is the third of the primary stages of disease. We have learned how lowered vitality and the abnormal composition of the vital fluids favor the retention of waste and systemic poisons in the body. If, in addition to this, food and drink contain too much of the waste-producing proteins, carbohydrates and hydrocarbons, and not enough of the eliminating positive mineral salts, then waste and morbid materials are bound to accumulate in the system and this results in the clogging of the tissues with pathogenic materials.

Such accumulation of waste and morbid matter in blood and tissues creates the great variety of diseases arising within the human organism. This will be explained fully in the following chapters which deal with the causation of acute and chronic disease.

More harmful and dangerous and more difficult to eliminate than the various kinds of systemic poisons (those which have originated within the body), are drug poisons, especially when they are administered in the inorganic mineral form.

Health is dependent upon an abundant supply of life force, upon the unobstructed, normal circulation of the vital fluids and upon perfect oxygenation and elimination of waste. Anything which interferes with these essentials causes disease; anything which promotes them establishes health. Nothing so interferes with the inflow of life force, with free and normal circulation of blood and lymph and with the combustion of food materials and systemic waste as the accumulation of foreign matter and poisons in the tissues of the body.

This I have endeavored to explain more fully in connection with "Lowered Vitality". Let us now see how health and disease are affected by mental and emotional conditions.

Mental and Emotional Influences

Our mental and emotional conditions exert a most powerful influence upon the inflow and distribution of vital force. Fear, worry, anxiety and all kindred emotions create in the system conditions similar to those of freezing. These destructive vibrations congeal the tissues, contract the minute channels of life and thereby paralyze the vital activities. Emotional conditions of impatience, irritability, anger, fury, wrath, etc. have a heating, corroding effect upon brain and nerve substance and consume it like burning fire. Selfpity has been called the consumption of the soul or psychic phthisis. These mental, emotional and psychical causes of disease and their treatment are more fully described in Volume II.

In like manner, all other destructive emotional vibrations obstruct the inflow and normal distribution of the life forces in and through the organism, while the constructive emotions of faith, hope, cheerfulness, happiness, love and altruism exert a relaxing, harmonizing and vitalizing influence upon the tissues of the body, thus opening wide the floodgates of the vital energies and raising the discords of weakness, disease and discontent to the harmonics of buoyant health and happiness.

Let us see how mind controls matter and how it affects the changing conditions of the physical body. Life manifests through vibration. It acts on the mass by acting through its minutest particles. Changes in the physical body are wrought by vibratory changes in atoms, molecules, microzyma and cells. Health is "satisfied polarity"; that is, the balancing of the positive and negative elements, forces and energies in harmonious vibration. Anything that interferes with the free, vigorous and harmonious vibration of the minute parts and particles composing the human organism tends to disturb and unbalance polarity and natural affinity, thus causing discord or disease.

When we fully realize these facts we shall not stand so much in awe of our physical bodies. In the past we thought of the body as a solid and imponderable mass difficult to control and to change. This conception left us in a condition of utter helplessness and hopelessness in the presence of weakness and disease.

We now think of the body as composed of minute electrons rotating around one another within the atom at relatively immense distances. We know that in similar manner the atoms vibrate in the molecule, the molecules in the microzyma, and these in the cell, the cells in the organ, and the organs in the body—the whole capable of being changed by a change in the vibrations of its particles.

Thus the erstwhile solid physical mass appears plastic and fluidic, readily swayed and changed by the vibratory harmonies or discords of thoughts and emotions as well as by foods, medicines and treatment.

Under the old conception the mind fell readily under the control of the body and became the abject slave of its physical conditions, swayed by fear and apprehension under every sensation of physical weakness, discomfort or pain. The servants lorded it with a high hand over the master of the house and the result was chaos. Under the new conception, control is placed where it belongs. Dictatorship is assumed by the real master of the house, the soul man, while the servants, the physical members of the body, remain obedient to his bidding.

This is the new man, the ideal progeny of New Thought and Higher Philosophy. Understanding the structure of the body, the laws of its being and the operation of the life elements within it, the superman retains perfect poise and confidence under the most trying circumstances. Ani-

mated by an abounding faith in the supremacy of the
healing forces within him and sustained by the power of
his sovereign will, he governs his body as perfectly as the
artist controls his violin, and attunes its vibrations to
Nature's harmonies of health and happiness.

CHAPTER VI

THE UNITY OF ACUTE DISEASE

IN the previous chapter I endeavored to explain the three primary stages of disease, namely: (1) **Lowered Vitality,** (2) **Abnormal Composition of Blood and Lymph,** (3) **Accumulation of Waste, Morbid Matter, and Poisons in the System.**

We shall now consider some of the secondary manifestations resulting from these primary stages. Consulting the table on page 38 we find mentioned as the first one of the secondary causes or manifestations of disease, "**Hereditary and Acquired Taints.**"

On first impression, it might be thought that **heredity** is a primary cause of disease; but on further consideration it becomes apparent that it is an effect and not a primary cause. If the parents possess good vitality and pure, normal blood and tissues and if they apply in the prenatal and postnatal treatment of the child the necessary insight and foresight, there cannot be any inherited disease. In order to create abnormal hereditary tendencies, the parents, or earlier ancestors, must have ignorantly or wantonly violated Nature's Laws; such violation resulting in lowered vitality and in deterioration of blood and tissues.

The female and male germinal cells unite and form the primitive reproductive cell—the prototype of marriage. The human body with its millions of cells and cell colonies is developed by the multiplication, with gradual differentiation, of the germ plasm of the reproductive cell, or rather of its microzyma. Herein lies the simple explanation of heredity which is proved to be an actual fact, not only by common experience and scientific observation but

49

also in a more definite way by Nature's records in the iris of the eye.

The iris of the new born child reveals in its diagnostic details, not only in a general way hereditary taints, lowered resistance and deterioration of vital fluids, but frequently special weakness and deterioration in those organs which were weak or diseased in the parents. Under the conventional (unnatural) care of the infant, these hereditary and congenital tendencies to weakness and disease and their corresponding signs in the iris become more and more pronounced, proceeding through the various stages of infantile diseases through chronic conditions to the final destructive stages.

In the face of the well established facts of disease inheritance we have, however, this consolation: If the child be treated in accordance with the teachings of Nature Cure philosophy, the abnormal hereditary encumbrances and tendencies can be overcome and eliminated within a few years. If the infant organism be brought under the right conditions of living and of treatment, in harmony with the laws of its being, the life principle within will approach ever nearer to the establishment of the perfect type. Hundreds of "Nature Cure" babies all over this country are living proofs of this gladsome message to all those who have assumed or who intend to assume the responsibilities of parenthood.

Natural Immunity

Under Division II of "Secondary Manifestations of Disease" we find mentioned germs, parasites, inflammations, fevers, skin eruptions, catarrhal discharges, ulcers, etc.

Modern medical science is built upon the germ theory of disease and of treatment. Since the microscope has revealed the presence and seemingly entirely pernicious activity of certain microorganisms in connection with certain diseases, **it has been assumed that bacteria are the direct, primary causes of most diseases,** and that they represent definite species of living beings whose natural habitat is the air, earth and water. According to this theory human beings are at the mercy of these invaders;—health and disease, life and death, are largely matters of accident over which we have no control. Basing their prophylaxis and treatment on this idea, the slogan is "kill the bacteria (by poisonous antiseptics, serums, antitoxins, etc.) and you cure the disease."

Nature Cure philosophy takes an entirely different view of the problem. Bacteria develop from microzyma, the primal units of living organisms, but this occurs only under morbid, pathogenic conditions. These microzyma may be the remains of decomposing bacteria entering the system from without, or the microzyma of normal cells may develop into bacteria under pathogenic conditions within the body. According to this conception the cycle of germ life works out as follows: The microzyma of normal, healthy cells under morbid, pathogenic conditions may develop into bacteria (see experiment with yeast cells, page 85). These bacteria feed on and decompose the morbid matter which brought them into being. Thus nature, with the evil, provides the remedy. When the morbid food supply has been exhausted the microzyma devour the protoplasm of their own bacteria until there is nothing left of the bacteria but the microzyma themselves, which seem to be practically indestructible under ordinary conditions, as shown by the finding of living microzyma in calcareous rocks of ancient geological formation. It is undoubtedly true that these morbid microzyma of decomposed bacteria may again develop into disease germs if they enter a living body and find their own peculiar morbid soil on which to feed.

At first glance it may seem that this does not differ materially from the germ theory of the old school of medicine. On closer consideration, however, it will be found that there is indeed a vast difference between the two conceptions which leads to entirely different methods of treatment. According to orthodox belief, disease germs are special creations which of their own accord create disease. If this were true then "killing the germs" would be good practice. On the other hand, if our conception is the right one, then we must prevent the development of morbid conditions and if these exist the treatment must be directed to their removal. Killing the germs will not remove the morbid soil and therefore will leave the way open for the spontaneous generation of bacteria from the microzyma present in all living matter.

Thus the microzymian theory of disease positively confirms the claims of Nature Cure Philosophy that bacteria and parasites are scavengers of pathogenic materials, that inflammation is a purifying, healing process and that therefore acute, febrile diseases are as normal and orderly as anything else in Nature.

Thus it is demonstrated that microorganisms are **secondary** manifestations of disease, that bacteria and parasites live, thrive and multiply **to the danger point** in a weakened and diseased organism only. If it were not so the human family would be extinct within a few months' time.

The fear instilled by the germ theory of disease is frequently more destructive than the microorganisms themselves. We have had under observation and treatment a number of insane patients whose peculiar delusion or monomania was an exaggerated fear of germs, a genuine "bacteriophobia".

Keep yourself clean and vigorous within and you **cannot** be affected by disease taints and germs from without.

Bacteria or their microzyma are practically omnipresent. We absorb them in food and drink, we inhale them in the air we breathe. Our bodies are literally alive with them.

The proper thing to do, therefore, is not to try to kill the germs, but to remove the morbid matter and disease taints on which they subsist and which they reduce to simpler forms suitable for elimination through the organs of depuration.

Instead of concentrating its energies upon killing the germs, whose activities we cannot escape when the conditions are ripe, Nature Cure endeavors to invigorate the system, to build up blood and lymph on a normal basis and to purify the tissues from their morbid encumbrances in such a way as to make germ activity unnecessary. Everything that tends to accomplish this, without injuring the system by poisonous drugs or surgical operations, is good Nature Cure treatment.

To adopt the germ killing process without purifying and invigorating the organism would be like trying to keep a house free from fungi and vermin by sprinkling it daily with carbolic acid and other germ killers, instead of keeping it pure and sweet by flooding it with fresh air and sunshine and applying freely and vigorously broom, brush and plenty of soap and water. Instead of purifying it, the antiseptic and germ killers would only add to the filth in the house.

Bacteriologists are unanimous in declaring that the various disease germs are found not only in diseased bodies, but also in the bodies of seemingly healthy persons.

A celebrated French bacteriologist reports that in the mouth of a healthy infant, two months old, he found almost all the disease germs known to medical science. But recently a celebrated physician, appointed by the French government to investigate the causes of tuberculosis, declared before a meeting of the International Tuberculosis Congress in Rome that he found the bacilli of tuberculosis in 95 per cent of all the school children he had examined.

Dr. Osler, one of the greatest living medical authorities, mentions repeatedly that the bacilli of diphtheria, pneumonia and of many other virulent diseases are found in the bodies of healthy persons.

The inability of bacteria, by themselves, to create disease is further confirmed by the well known facts of natural immunity to specific infection or contagion. All mankind is more or less affected by hereditary or acquired disease taints, morbid encumbrances and drug poisoning, resulting from age-long violation of Nature's laws and from the suppression of acute diseases; but even under the now almost universal conditions of lowered vitality, morbid heredity and physical and mental degeneration, it is found that under identical conditions of exposure to drafts or infection, only a certain percentage of individuals will "take cold" or "catch disease". The fact of natural immunity is repeatedly corroborated by common experience as well as in the clinics and laboratories of our medical schools and research institutes. Of a specific number of mice or rabbits inoculated with cancer, only a small percentage develop the malignant growth and succumb to its ravages.

The development of infectious and contagious diseases necessitates a certain predisposition, or, as medical science calls it, "disease diathesis". This **predisposition to infection and contagion consists in and is explained by the unity of disease as demonstrated in the previous pages.**

Why Epidemics?

When giving these explanations in lectures I am frequently asked the question: "If what you say is true,— if disease arises within the organism rather than through invasion from without,—how do you explain epidemics in which many people become affected at the same time by similar kinds of disease germs?"

The answer to this is: The fact that the majority of people in a certain locality are addicted to the same unnatural habits of living and of treating their ailments produces in most of them the same kind of morbid soil, and this favors the development of normal or diseased microzyma into similar forms of bacteria and the corresponding inflammatory processes.

Certain atmospheric and astrological conditions which we do not fully understand also have much to do with the periodic appearance of epidemic or endemic diseases.

Bacteria: Secondary, Not Primary Manifestations of Disease

We have already learned how lowered vitality weakens the resistance of the system to the attacks and inroads of disease germs and poisons. The development of microzyma into bacteria depends furthermore upon a congenial, morbid soil. Just as the ordinary yeast germ multiplies in a sugar solution only, so the various microorganisms of disease thrive and multiply to the danger point, each in its own peculiar and congenial kind of morbid matter. Thus, the typhoid fever bacillus develops and thrives in a certain kind of effete matter which accumulates in the intestines; the pneumonia germs flourish best in the morbid excretions of the lungs; and meningitis germs in the diseased meninges of the brain and spinal cord.

Dr. Pettenkofer, a celebrated physician and professor of the University of Vienna, also reached the conclusion that bacteria by themselves cannot create disease, and for years he defended his opinion on the lecture platform and in his writings against the practically solid phalanx of the medical profession. On one occasion he supported his theory by a startling, practical test. While instructing his class in the bacteriological laboratory of the University, he picked up a glass containing millions of live cholera bacilli and swallowed its contents before the eyes of the astonished students. The seemingly dangerous experiment resulted only in a slight nausea. Numerous cases are on record of persons in this country who subjected themselves in similar manner to infection, inoculation and contagion with the most virulent kinds of bacteria and disease taints, without developing the corresponding diseases.

A few years ago Dr. Rodermund, a physician in the state of Wisconsin, created a sensation all over this country by smearing his body with the exudate of smallpox sores in order to demonstrate to his medical colleagues that a healthy body could not be infected with the disease. He was arrested and quarantined in jail, but not before he had come in contact with many people. Not a single case of smallpox developed through this "exposure".

During the many years that I have been connected with sanitarium work, my workers and myself, in administering the various forms of manipulative treatment, have handled intimately thousands of cases of contagious diseases, and I do not remember a single instance where any one of us was in the least affected by such contact. Ordinary cleanliness, good vitality, clean blood and tissues, the organs of elimination in good, active condition and last but not least, a positive, fearless attitude of mind, will practically establish natural immunity to excessive and destructive activity of bacteria and disease taints. If infection takes place the organism reacts to it through inflammatory processes and by means of these endeavors to overcome and eliminate microorganisms and poisons from the system.

In this connection it is of interest to learn that the

danger to life from bites and stings of poisonous reptiles and insects has been greatly exaggerated. According to popular opinion, anyone bitten by a poisonous insect or reptile, as the rattlesnake, Gila monster or tarantula, is doomed to die, while as a matter of fact statistics show that only from two to seven per cent of such cases prove fatal. In this, as in many other instances, popular opinion should rather be called "popular superstition".

In the open discussions following my public lectures, I am often asked: "What is the right thing to do in case of snake bite? Would you not give plenty of whiskey to save the victim's life?"

It is my belief that of the "seven percent" who die after being bitten by rattlesnakes or other poisonous reptiles, a goodly proportion "give up the ghost" because of the effects of enormous doses of strong whiskey poured into them under the mistaken idea that whiskey is an efficient antidote to snake poison.

People do not know that the death rate from snake bite is so very low, and therefore they attribute the recoveries to the whiskey, just as recoveries from other diseases under medical or metaphysical treatment are attributed to the virtues of the particular medicine or method of treatment applied, instead of to the real healer, the "vis medicatrix naturae"—the healing power of Nature—which in ninety-three cases in a hundred eliminates the rattlesnake venom without injury to the organism.

To recapitulate: Just as yeast cells are not only the cause but also the product of sugar fermentation, so disease germs are not only a cause (secondary) but also a product of morbid fermentation (inflammation) in the system. Furthermore, just as the yeast germs devour and decompose sugar, so the disease germs consume and decompose morbid matter and systemic poisons. In a way, therefore, microorganisms are just as much the product as the cause of disease and act as scavengers or eliminators of morbid matter.* In order to hold in check the destructive activity of bacteria and to prevent their multiplication beyond the danger point, Nature manufactures her own "antitoxins".

An apt illustration of this we have in the activity of yeast germs. While digesting sugar they change it into alcohol and carbonic acid. As the alcohol accumulates in the fermenting fluid it gradually checks and finally stops the activity of the yeast germs. Thus Nature holds in check the activity of germs by their own waste products.

To this it may be answered, if that is so, then the administration of antitoxin must be good and natural treatment. There is a difference, however. Nature does not check or suppress the activity of bacteria until they have decomposed the disease matter (pathogen) on which they live. The powerful and highly poisonous doses of medical serums and antitoxins check and suppress the inflammatory process before it has run its natural course, and thus, if the patient survives, leave the system in a condition of chronic incumbrance. This will be more fully explained in the following pages.

Whatever tends to build up the blood on a natural basis, to promote elimination of morbid matter and thereby make unnecessary the activity of bacteria and parasites without injuring the body or depressing its vital functions, is good Nature Cure practice. The first consideration, therefore, in the treatment of inflammation must be not to interfere with its natural course. Secondly, the natural method of treatment must keep the inflammatory activities below the danger point and within constructive limits. This the Nature Cure physician accomplishes by careful regulation of the diet, or by fasting, by hydropathic,

---

*This aspect of germ activity will be discussed fully in Chap. X.

manipulative and homeopathic treatment as described in Vol. II of this series.

By the various statements and claims made in this chapter, I do not wish to convey the idea that I am opposed to scrupulous cleanliness and to surgical asepsis. Far from it! These are dictates of common sense. But I do affirm that the danger from infectious diseases lies just as much, or more so, in internal filth as in external uncleanliness. Cleanliness and asepsis must go hand in hand with the purification of the inner man in order to insure "natural immunity."

It will be observed that every statement in this chapter is corroborated by the microzymian theory of Béchamp and by the revelations of Dr. Powell as to the true nature of leucocytosis. These matters are more fully discussed in the chapters dealing with inflammation.

CHAPTER VII

THE LAWS OF CURE

THIS brings us to the consideration of acute inflammatory and feverish diseases. From what has been
said, it follows that inflammation and fever are not primary, but **secondary** manifestations of disease. No form
of inflammatory disease can arise in the system unless
there is present some handicap to health which Nature is
endeavoring to overcome and to get rid of. On this fact
in Nature is based what I claim to be the fundamental law
of cure.

"Give me fever and I can cure every disease." Thus
Hippocrates, the "Father of Medicine", formulated the
fundamental Law of Cure over two thousand years ago.
I have expressed this law in the following statement:
**Every acute disease is the result of a cleansing and healing
effort of Nature.**

This law, thoroughly understood and applied in the
treatment of diseases, will eventually do for medical science what the discovery of other natural laws has done for
physics, astronomy, chemistry and other exact sciences.
It will, by demonstrating the unity of disease and treatment, transform the medical empiricism and confusion of
the past and present into an exact science.

Making a general application of the law, we deduce that
all acute diseases, from a simple cold to measles, scarlet
fever, diphtheria, smallpox, pneumonia, etc., represent
Nature's efforts to remove from the system some form of
morbid matter, virus or poison dangerous to health and
life. In other words, acute diseases cannot develop in a

perfectly normal, healthy body living under conditions favorable to human life. The question may be asked: "If acute diseases represent Nature's healing efforts, why is it that people die as a result of them?" The answer to this is: the vitality may be too low, the injury or morbid encumbrance too great, or the treatment may be inadequate or harmful, so that Nature loses the fight; still acute disease represents an effort of Nature to remove the causes of disease and thus to reestablish normal, healthy conditions.

It is a curious fact that this fundamental principle of Nature Cure and law of Nature has been acknowledged and corroborated by medical science. The most advanced works on pathology admit the constructive and beneficial character of inflammation. However, when it comes to the **treatment** of acute diseases, physicians seem to forget entirely this basic principle of pathology and treat inflammation and fever as though they were, in themselves, inimical and destructive to health and life.

From this inconsistency in theory and practice arises all the errors of allopathic medical treatment. Failure to understand this fundamental law of cure accounts for the confusion on the part of exponents of the different schools of healing science, and for the greater part of human suffering.

Nature Cure philosophy never loses sight of the fundamental law of cure. While allopathy regards acute disease conditions as in themselves harmful and hostile to health and life, as something to be "cured" (we say "suppressed") by drug, ice or knife, the Nature Cure School regards these forcible house cleanings as beneficial and necessary—necessary so long as human beings continue to disregard Nature's laws. While, through its simple, natural methods of treatment, Nature Cure easily modifies the course of inflammatory and feverish processes and keeps them within safe limits, it never checks nor suppresses these acute reactions by poisonous drugs, ice, serums, antiseptics, surgical operations, suggestion or any other suppressive treatment.

Skin eruptions, boils, ulcers, catarrh, diarrhea, and all other forms of inflammatory febrile disease processes are indications that there is something hostile to life and health in the organism, which Nature is trying to remove or overcome by these socalled ''acute'' diseases. What, then, is to be gained by suppressing them with poisonous drugs and surgical operations? Such practice does not allow Nature to carry on her work of cleansing and repair and to attain her ends. The morbid matter which she is endeavoring to eliminate by acute reaction is thrown back into the system. Worse than that, drug poisons are added to disease poisons. Is it any wonder that fatal complications arise, or that the acute process is changed to chronic disease?

Why Does the Greater Part of Allopathic Materia Medica Consist of Virulent Poisons?

The statements made in the preceding pages are a severe indictment of socalled ''regular'' medical science, but they point out the difference in the basic principles of the old school of healing and those of Nature Cure philosophy.

The fundamental Law of Cure quoted in this chapter explains why allopathic medical science is in error, not in a few things but in most things. Their foundation—the orthodox conception of disease, being wrong, it follows that everything built thereon must be wrong also.

No matter how learned a man may be, if he begins a problem in arithmetic with the proposition $2 \times 2 = 5$, he will never arrive at a correct solution even if he continue to figure into all eternity. Neither can allopathy solve the problem of disease and cure so long as its fundamental conception of disease is based on error.

The fundamental law of cure explains also why the great majority of allopathic prescriptions contain virulent poisons in some form or other, and why surgical operations are in high favor with the disciples of the old school.

The answer of allopathy to the question, "Why do you give poisons?" usually is, "Our materia medica contains poisons because drug poison kills and eliminates disease poison." We, however, claim that drug poisons merely serve to paralyze vital force, whereby the deceptive results of allopathic treatment are obtained.

The following will explain this more fully. We have learned that socalled acute diseases are Nature's cleansing and healing efforts. All acute reactions represent increased activity of vital force, resulting in feverish and inflammatory conditions, accompanied by pain, redness, swelling, high temperature, rapid pulse, catarrhal discharges, skin eruptions, boils, ulcers, etc.

Allopathy regards these violent activities of vital force as detrimental and harmful in themselves. Anything which will inhibit the action of vital force will, in allopathic parlance, cure (?) acute diseases. As a matter of fact, nothing more effectively paralyzes vital force and impairs the vital organs than poisonous drugs, ice and the surgeon's knife. These, therefore, must necessarily constitute the favorite means of cure (?) of the old school of medicine.

This school mistakes effect for cause. It fails to see that the local inflammation arising within the organism is not the disease, but merely marks the locality and the method through which Nature is trying her best to discharge the morbid encumbrances;—that the acute reaction is local, but that its causes or "feeders" are always constitutional and must be treated constitutionally. When under the influence of rational, natural treatment, the poisonous irritants are eliminated from blood and tissues, the local symptoms take care of themselves; it does not matter whether they manifest as pimple or cancer, as a simple cold or as consumption.

The Law of Dual Effect

Everywhere in Nature rules the great Law of Action and Reaction. All life sways back and forth between giving and receiving, between action and reaction. The very breath of life mysteriously comes and goes in rythmical flow. So also heaves and falls in ebb and tide the bosom of Mother Earth.

In some of its aspects this law is called the law of compensation, or the law of dual effect. On its action depends the preservation of energy.

The Great Master expressed the ethical application of this law when he said: "Give, and it shall be given unto you. . . . For with what measure ye mete it shall be measured to you again." Luke VI, 38.

In the realms of physical nature, giving and receiving, action and reaction, balance each other mechanically and automatically. What we gain in power we lose in speed or volume, and vice versa. This makes it possible for the mechanic, the scientist and the astronomer to predict with mathematical precision for ages in advance the results of certain activities in Nature.

The great law of dual effect forms the foundation of healing science. It is related to and governs every phenomenon of health, disease and cure. When I formulated the fundamental law of cure in the words, **"Every acute disease is the result of a healing effort of Nature"**, this was but another expression of the great law of action and reaction. What we commonly call crisis, acute reaction or acute disease, is in reality Nature's attempt to establish health.

Applied to the physical activity of the body, the Law of Compensation may be expressed as follows: **Every agent affecting the human organism produces two effects: a first, temporary effect, and a second, lasting effect. The second, lasting effect is always contrary to the first, transient effect.**

For instance: the first and temporary effect of cold water applied to the skin consists in sending the blood to the interior; but in order to compensate for the local depletion, Nature responds by sending greater quantities back to the surface, which results in increased warmth and better surface circulation.

The first effect of a hot bath is to draw the blood to the surface; but the second effect sends the blood back to the interior, leaving the surface bloodless and chilled.

Stimulants, as we shall presently see, produce their deceptive effects by consuming the reserve stores of vital energy in the organism. This is inevitably followed by weakness and exhaustion in exact proportion to the previous excitation.

The first effect of relaxation and sleep is weakness, numbness and death-like stupor; the second effect, however, is an increase of vitality.

The law of Dual Effect governs all drug action. The first, temporary, violent effect of poisonous drugs, when taken in physiological doses, is usually due to Nature's efforts to overcome and eliminate these substances. The second, lasting effect is due to the retention of the drug poisons in the system and their destructive action on the organism.

In theory and in practice, allopathy considers the first effect only and ignores the lasting after effects of drugs and surgical operations. It administers remedies whose first effect is **contrary** to the disease condition. Therefore, in accordance with the law of action and reaction, the second, lasting effect of such remedies must be **similar** to the disease condition.

Common, everyday experience should teach us that **this** is true, for laxatives and cathartics always tend to produce chronic constipation.

The second effect of stimulants and tonics of any kind is increased weakness. Their continued use often results in complete exhaustion and paralysis of mental and physical powers.

Headache powders, pain killers, opiates, sedatives and hypnotics may paralyze brain and nerves into temporary insensibility; but, if due to constitutional causes, the pain, nervousness and insomnia will always return with redoubled force. If taken habitually these agents invariably tend to create heart disease and paralysis and ultimately develop the "dope fiend".

Cold and catarrh cures (?) such as quinin, coal tar products, etc., suppress Nature's efforts to eliminate waste and morbid matter through the mucous linings of the respiratory tract, causing retention of disease matter, thus breeding pneumonia, chronic catarrhs, asthma and consumption.

Mercury, iodin, salvarsan and all other alteratives, by suppression of external elimination, and even more so by their own destructive effects, create internal chronic diseases of the most dreadful types, such as locomotor ataxia, paresis, paralysis agitans, etc.

So the recital might be continued all through the orthodox materia medica. Each drug breeds new disease symptoms which are in their turn cured (?) by other poisons, until the insane asylum or merciful death rings down the curtain on the tragedy of a ruined life.

The teaching and practice of homeopathy, as explained

in another chapter, is fully in harmony with the law of action and reaction. Proceeding upon its basic principle— "Similia similibus curantur", or "like cures like"—it administers remedies whose first, temporary effect is similar to the disease condition. In accordance, then, with the law of dual effect, the second effect of these remedies must be contrary to the disease condition, that is, "curative".

CHAPTER VIII

SUPPRESSION VERSUS ELIMINATION

MY claim **that the conventional treatment of acute diseases is suppressive and not curative** will probably be denied by my medical colleagues. They will maintain that their methods also are calculated to eliminate morbid matter from the system.

But what are the facts in actual practice? Is it not true that preparations of mercury, lead, zinc, silver and other powerful poisons are constantly used to **suppress** skin eruptions, boils, abscesses, etc., instead of allowing Nature to rid the system through these "skin diseases" of scrofulous, venereal and psoric taints?

Some time ago Dr. Wiley, former Government Chemist, published a list of the ingredients of a number of popular remedies for colds, coughs and catarrhs. Every one of them contained some powerful opiate or astringent. These poisonous drugs relieve the cough and catarrhal conditions by paralyzing the eliminative activity of the membranous linings of the nasal passages, bronchi and lungs, the digestive and genito-urinary organs; but in doing so they throw back into the system morbid matter which Nature is trying to get rid of, and add drug poisons to disease poisons.

Equally harmful is suppression by means of the surgeon's knife. It may be a quicker and apparently more effective process to **remove** the inflamed appendix or diseased tonsils than to cure them by building up the blood and inducing elimination of systemic poisons by natural methods. But operative treatment is not eliminative. It does not remove from the system the original cause of inflammation or deterioration of tissues and organs, but it does remove the outlet which Nature had established for the escape of morbid material.

These morbid encumbrances, forcibly retained in the body, weaken and destroy other parts and organs or affect the general health of the patient.

My own observations during nearly eighteen years of practical experience prove positively that the average length of life after a "major" operation, performed on important, vital parts and organs, is less than ten years, and that after such an operation the general health of the patient is, in the great majority of cases, not as good as before. This is confirmed by many other conscientious observers among Nature Cure practitioners as well as physicians of other schools and of allopathy itself.

In the following paragraphs are mentioned some very common instances of suppression and some of their usual chronic after effects (sequelae).

Diarrhea is suppressed with laudanum and other opiates which paralyze the peristaltic action of the bowels and, if repeated, soon produce chonic constipation.

Gonorrheal discharges and syphilitic ulcers are checked and suppressed by local injections, cauterization and by prescriptions containing mercury, iodin, arsenic (salvarsan) and other poisonous alteratives which effectually prevent Nature's efforts to eliminate the venereal poisons from the system.

All feverish diseases are more or less interfered with or suppressed by antiseptics, antipyretics, serum and antitoxins. Professors in colleges and the best books on Materia Medica teach that these remedies lower the fever because they are "protoplasmic poisons"; because they paralyze the red and white blood corpuscles, benumb heart action and respiration and depress all vital functions.

Nervousness, sleeplessness and pain are suppressed by

sedatives, opiates and hypnotics. Every one of the drugs
used for such purposes is a powerful poison which benumbs
brain and nerve action, in that way interfering with
Nature's healing efforts and frequently preventing the
consummation of beneficial healing crises.

Epileptic attacks and other forms of convulsions are
suppressed, but never cured, by bromids which benumb
and paralyze brain and nerve centers. All that these
"sedatives" accomplish is to produce in course of time
idiocy and different forms of paralysis and premature
senility.

However, is he not considered the best doctor who can
most promptly bring about these and similar deceptive
results through artificial inhibition or stimulation by
means of the most virulent poisons found on earth?

Dandruff and falling hair are caused by the elimination
of systemic poisons through the scalp. The thing to do,
therefore, is **not to suppress this elimination** and thereby
cause accumulation of poisons in the brain, **but to stop the
manufacture of poison in the body and to promote its
removal through the natural channels.**

Dandruff "cures" and hair tonics contain glycerin,
poisonous antiseptics and stimulants which are absorbed
by scalp and brain, causing dizziness, headaches, loss of
memory, neurasthenia, deafness, weakness of sight, etc.

Head Lice and similar parasites peculiar to other parts
of the body live on scrofulous and psoric taints. When
these are consumed, the lice depart as they came. The
microzyma theory furnishes the solution to this and similar
problems.

This is confirmed by the fact that these noxious pests
do not remain with all people who have been infected with
them, but only with those whose internal or external conditions furnish the parasites with the means of subsistence.

In a number of instances we have seen healing crises

take the form of lice. At that time the patients were living in the most cleanly surroundings, taking various forms of water treatment every day, so that infection was practically impossible.

In each of these cases the patient recalled having been infested with parasites at some previous time, and remembered that sulphur and molasses, mercurial salves or other means of suppression had been applied.

We prescribe for the removal of lice only cold water and the comb. Even antiseptic soaps should be avoided.

The foregoing statements, more than any other portions of this volume, have brought down upon it violent criticism and condemnation. However, many of our patients who have developed, under natural treatment, such parasitic crises will testify to their reality.

As I am writing this, one of our guests is just recovering from one of these parasitic crises. Before this woman came to us she had lived for many years in her own luxurious home and since she has been with us during the last four months she has not left our institution. She has occupied a room alone and has received several water treatments, including head bath, every day, so that infection was impossible. Still, four weeks ago, the attendant who gives her treatment discovered her scalp covered with nits which within a few days developed into swarms of lice.

The lady was very much alarmed and shed tears of mortification, until she better understood the nature of the phenomenon. I showed her the passage in this volume dealing with psora and parasitic diseases; also her original examination report which, in the section devoted to diagnosis from the iris, had the entry "psora positive, several itch spots", indicating suppression of itchy, parasitic skin eruptions. When told that the psora taint on which these parasites live is the soil of tuberculosis and cancer, she endured her itchy crisis with great equanimity. The pesky little visitors remained about three weeks and then suddenly disappeared as they had come. Nothing was used to combat the parasites except fresh, cold water and the comb.

Lice, crab lice, scabies (itch parasites), belong to the same psoric family. They live on psoric taints, just as bacteria live on other disease taints and systemic poisons.

This patient is now fully convinced of the reality of parasitic crises. This delicate but interesting subject has been treated more fully in Volume II of this series.

The Results of Suppression of Children's Diseases

Sycotic eruptions on the heads and bodies of infants, also called "milk scurf", if suppressed by salves, cream, unsalted butter, or even by warm bathing, are often followed by chorea (St. Vitus' dance), epilepsy, a scrofulous constitution, and in later life by tuberculosis.

Measles, scarlet fever, diphtheria, cerebrospinal meningitis, and other febrile diseases of childhood, if properly treated by natural methods, are curative or at least corrective in their effects on the system, and represent well defined, orderly, natural processes for the elimination of inherited or acquired disease taints, drug poisons, etc. But if arrested or suppressed before they have run their natural course, or before Nature has had time to reestablish normal conditions, then the abnormal conditions become fixed and permanent (chronic).

In addition to this, the poisons, serums and antitoxins employed to arrest the disease process very often affect vital parts and organs permanently, causing the gradual deterioration of cells and tissues, and paving the way for cancer, tuberculosis, chronic affection of the kidneys, etc. in later years.

These simple facts, which can be verified by any unprejudiced observer, account for the "mysterious sequelae" of drug and serum treated acute diseases. These never occur where natural methods of healing have been correctly employed. Among these chronic after effects are deafness, blindness, heart and kidney diseases, nervous affections, idiocy, infantile paralysis, tuberculosis, cancer, etc.

These are merely a few common examples of the results of suppression. They could be multiplied a hundredfold, yet medical science assures us that the causes of cancer and other malignant diseases are "unknown".

Good Nature Cure Doctrine from an Allopathic Authority

The following utterances of the late Dr. Nicholas Senn strongly confirm our claims as to the nature and cure of disease. Coming from the lips of so celebrated a surgeon and physician, these statements should carry some weight with those who, being unable to reason for themselves, are prone to worship at the feet of "authority". The quotations referred to are taken from the report of an interview granted by the doctor to Chicago newspaper representatives on his return from his trip around the world.

[Chicago American, August 5th, 1906.]

GERMS PLANTED BY TIGHT LACING

Over-Feeding and Over-Dressing Given as Causes of Cancer

"Dr. Nicholas Senn brought back from Africa, from whence he returned to Chicago yesterday, confirmations of his belief that cancer is a 'civilized' disease.

"Dr. Senn spent from $2,000 to $3,000 worth of time—at the cash value per hour of his time—on his first day at home for four months, telling a half dozen newspaper men more than all the world, except himself and a score of specialists like him, know about the fearful disease.

He summed up his own learning in the statement that the disease is still incurable except by the knife in its incipient stages and that the best preventive is clean, plain living.

"His investigations of the natives of Africa served to strengthen his conviction that cancer is a product of civilization, 'like apoplexy and scores of other exotic ailments,' Dr. Senn said. He could not find or hear of a case of cancer among the 'Hamites,' as he termed them. And from the fact that he found the disease to be an unknown one to the Esquimaux of Greenland, he is assured that climate has nothing whatever to do with it. Climate did not cause it, and climate will not cure it.

Cancer Caused by Over-Living

" 'The nearer the human race approaches the animals in habits, and particularly in the matter of diet and dress, the freer it is from cancer,' he said. 'Cancer comes from over-feeding and over-living.

" 'Drinking, gourmandizing, unnatural habits of women, like lacing, all those things help to plant the seeds of cancer in the child.

" 'And as we have not learned to cure it, the best thing to do is to prevent it when we can. If children were brought up in simplicity by natural mothers; then if care should be taken to prevent hypernutrition, there would be much less danger from cancer. Cancer itself is an overfed thing—tissue that never matures, for if I could mature the cells I could cure the disease. The thing for people to do who fear they may have inherited it, is to live simply—there are many cases among people with a tendency to obesity to one among those of a scanty habit of living —and particularly to remove all sources of irritation, like bad teeth, tobacco, and clothes that chafe.'

Studies African Race

" 'Besides his hobby, as he calls it, Dr. Senn studied the African generally in his voyage along the East Coast of that continent.

" 'It was a fine trip,' he said, 'with so many things to learn. Ethnologically, I am certain Africans are of common stock. The negro is a negro wherever you find him. From Kaffir to Bushman and pygmy, they are all Hamites.

" 'They are mostly a fine people physically, lean and tall, except the dwarfs. There is little tendency toward obesity; they have no apoplexy, no distended veins as we have in civilization. Hence their freedom from cancer. They live naturally, and are vegetarians mostly, while the Northern Esquimaux are meat eaters, but both races eat naturally to sustain life, hence their immunity from that disease. It is where eating is made an art that cancer is most prevalent.

" 'They are free from many other diseases that pester us also. Tuberculosis is hardly known, and only along the coast, where it has been taken by the whites. The real curse of the coast country is malaria. It is bad all up and down the East shore. I kept away from it myself by taking five grains of quinine and the juice of a lemon once a day on an empty stomach. That is a good remedy for malaria, for in all my running around I have never had it.' "

(Author's Note.—Dr. Senn died January 2, 1908. The papers stated after his death, that the doctor had never been well since the return from his long voyage, that his heart and nervous system had been seriously affected by the altitudes of the Andes and other mountains. I wonder whether the "high altitudes" or the "five grains of quinin" daily, were to blame for the celebrated physician's heart disease and premature death.)

Suppression the Cause of Chronic Diseases

Dr. Senn was right. If men and women lived more naturally, the majority of diseases would gradually disappear.

The primary cause of disease is Violation of Nature's Laws. "Civilization" has become almost synonymous with artificiality of life and unnatural habits. A higher civilization, yet to come, will combine the most exquisite culture of mind and soul with true simplicity and naturalness of living. Excessive meat eating, strong spices and condiments, alcohol, coffee, tea, overwork, night work, fear, worry, sensuality, corsets, high heels, foul air, improper breathing, lack of exercise, loveless marriages, race suicide,—all of these and many other evils of "hypercivilization" have contributed their share to the universal degeneracy of civilized nations commented upon by Dr. Senn.

In order to learn these truths, which have been proclaimed for many years by the advocates of Nature Cure, he was obliged to travel to the arctic circle and to the tropics. While expatiating upon the beneficial effects of natural living in relation to cancer, he might have added that primitive races living in accordance with Nature's laws are also practically free from heart disease, dyspepsia, nervousness, insanity, locomotor ataxia, paralysis agitans, paresis, and a host of other curses of "civilization"; and that the women of these races give birth to their children without the dreadful labor pains which afflict the mothers of "civilized" races.

Dr. Senn, however, failed to recognize a most important cause of the rapid increase of destructive chronic diseases; in fact, he overlooked **the principal factor, which is the suppression of acute diseases by poisonous drugs and surgical operations.**

When the unnatural habits of life alluded to have so lowered the vitality and favored the accumulation of waste matter and poisons that the sluggish bowels, kidneys, skin, and other organs of elimination are unable to keep a clean house, Nature is forced to resort to other, more radical means of purification or we would choke in our own impurities. These forcible house-cleanings of Nature are colds, catarrhs, skin eruptions, diarrheas, boils, ulcers, abnormal perspiration, hemorrhages, and many other forms of inflammatory febrile diseases.

Sulphur and mercury may drive back the skin eruptions, antipyretics and antiseptics may suppress fever and catarrh; the patient and the doctor may congratulate themselves on a speedy cure; but what is the true state of affairs? Nature has been thwarted in her work of healing and cleansing. She has had to give up the fight against disease matter in order to combat the more potent poisons of mercury, quinin, iodin, strychnin, etc. **The disease matter is still in the system, plus the drug poison.**

Proof positive of the retention of drug poisons in the organism is furnished by the **Diagnosis from the Iris of the Eye.** This is explained more fully in Volume VI of this series.

When vitality has been sufficiently restored, Nature may make another attempt at purification, this time, possibly, in another direction; but again her well meant efforts are defeated. This process of suppression is repeated over and over again until blood and tissues become so loaded with waste matter and poisons that the healing forces of the organism can no longer react against them by acute diseases. Then results "the chronic condition", which in the vocabulary of the old school of medicine is only another name for "incurable".

The more skilled the allopathic school becomes in the suppression and prevention of acute diseases by drugs, knife, X-rays, serums, vaccination virus, antitoxin, etc., the greater will be the increase of chronic dyspepsia, nervous prostration, insanity, locomotor ataxia, paresis, cancer, secondary and tertiary syphilis, tuberculosis and many other so called incurable diseases.

Suppression of acute diseases, by drug and knife, is the all important factor in the creation of malignant diseases which Dr. Senn overlooked in his discourses on the causes of chronic destructive ailments. If he had analyzed his experiences in foreign lands in the light of Nature Cure philosophy he would have found that the great scourges of mankind exist only in those parts of the earth where the drug store flourishes.

These statements may seem exaggerated; but allow me to cite a few typical cases of suppression and its effects upon the system, on record in our institutional practice.

Paresis, locomotor ataxia and paralysis agitans are not, as is usually assumed, due to secondary and tertiary syphilis, but **to the mercury or other alteratives administered for the cure of luetic and other diseases.** In less than six months' time we cure the so called specific diseases by our natural methods, provided they have not been suppressed and complicated by mercury, iodin or other poisonous drugs. We never interfere with the original lesion, but assist Nature to discharge the poisons through the channels established for this purpose.

By the natural methods of treatment we moderate the inflammatory processes and keep them within constructive limits. A bonfire is useful to burn up the rubbish on the premises, but it must be watched and tended so it will not destroy the buildings.

Under rational treatment, discharges and ulcers act as fontanels to the system. Not only the specific poison, but much of hereditary and acquired disease matter also is eliminated in the process. After such a cure, blood and tissues are purer than before the infection.

The foregoing statement has nothing to do with the moral aspects involved in acquiring venereal diseases. In this connection we are dealing solely with the question of rational or irrational treatment of the infection after it has been contracted. We do not wish to intimate that it is advisable to cure the body by killing the soul. We must deal with the facts in Nature as we find them. Furthermore, a great many persons, especially women and children, acquire these diseases innocently. Are we not justified in relieving their minds of needless fear and in showing them the way to prevent the dreadful sufferings of the "secondary" and "tertiary" stages brought on by suppressive drug treatment by means of mercury, the iodids, "606", etc.?

These poisonous drugs suppress the initial lesions and diffuse the disease poison through the system. Nature takes up the work of elimination by means of skin eruptions and ulcers in various parts of the body, but these also are promptly suppressed with mercurial ointments and other alteratives. This process of suppression is continued for months and years, until the organism is so thoroughly saturated with alterative poisons that vital force can no longer arouse the body to acute reactions against the original syphilitic taint. This condition of vital paralysis is then termed "cure".

The medical professor, however, knows better. He instructs the students from the lecture platform: "When, after two or three years of mercurial treatment, syphilitic symptoms cease to appear, you may permit the patient to marry—**but never guarantee a cure.**"

Why not? Because the professor is aware that the offspring of such a union may be born with "hereditary" symptoms well known to every physician, and because the patient thus cured (?) may confront the doctor at any time thereafter exhibiting a hole in his palate, ulcers on his body, caries in his bones, or other secondary and tertiary symptoms.

Mercury will work its way into the nerve matter of the brain and spinal cord, causing inflammation, excruciating headaches, nervous symptoms, girdle pains, etc., etc. These stages of acute and subacute inflammation are followed in a few years by sclerosis (hardening) of nerve matter and blood vessels, resulting in paresis, locomotor ataxia, or paralysis agitans.

Neither is it necessary to contract specific diseases in order to fall a victim to these dreadful conditions; mercury, iodin, salvarsan and other destructive alteratives are given in a hundred different forms for a multitude of other ailments.

A few years ago we had under our care a patient in the last stages of locomotor ataxia, who for years had been suffering the tortures of the damned. There had never been a taint of specific disease in her system, but four different times in her life she had been salivated by calomel. This dreadful poison had been administered in large doses for the cure of liver trouble and constipation. She was only fourteen years old when, on account of this, she first suffered from acute mercurial poisoning (salivation).

Another patient who, after fifteen years of "slow and torturous dying by inches", succumbed to the same disease, had absorbed the mercurial poison in his boyhood while attending a boarding school. He was twice salivated by mercurial ointments applied to cure the itch (scabies), a disease which was epidemic at times among the boys. He likewise never had a syphilitic infection.

A young man, insane at the age of thirty, absorbed the infernal poison when four years of age. He had at the time a psoric skin eruption. The family physician, suspecting syphilitic infection from the nurse girl, kept the child under mercury for six months. How do we know that the diagnosis of syphilis was false? Because the iris of the eye revealed "psora" as the cause of the suspicious eruption which reappeared several times later in life, and because the servant girl was afterwards absolutely exonerated by competent physicians.

The subject of venereal diseases, their natural and unnatural treatment, has been fully treated by the author in a booklet entitled, "Who Provides the Victims of the Black Stork? Who Makes the Damaged Goods?"

Proofs by the Diagnosis from the Eye

We have treated many hundreds of cases of so called chronic neuralgia, neuritis, rheumatism, neurasthenia, epilepsy, tuberculosis, cancer and idiocy, due to the pernicious effects of quinin, iodin, arsenic, strychnin, coal tar products and other virulent poisons taken under the guise of "medicine".

How do we know that this is so?

(a) Because the diagnosis from the iris of the eye plainly reveals the presence of these poisons in the system.

(b) Because the drug signs in the iris are accompanied by the symptoms of these poisons in the system.

(c) Because the history revealed the fact that the patient had some time in the past taken the poison revealed in his iris.

(d) Because, under natural living and treatment, diseases long ago suppressed by drugs or knife reappear as healing crises.

(e) Because in these healing crises, drugs indicated by the signs in the iris of the eye are frequently eliminated, each under its own peculiar symptoms.

(f) Because, to the extent that a drug is eliminated from the system by a healing crisis, its sign will disappear from the iris of the eye.

To illustrate:

(a) The diagnosis from the iris of the eye reveals quinin poisoning in the region of the brain.

(b) This enables us to say to the patient, without questioning him, that he suffers from severe frontal headaches and ringing in the ears, that he is very irritable, and so on through the various symptoms of quinin poisoning, or, as the medical men call it, "chronic cinchonism".

(c) The history of the patient reveals the fact that he has taken large amounts of quinin for colds, grippe, or malaria.

(d) Under our methods of natural living and treatment, the patient improves; the organism becomes more vigorous, and the organs of elimination act more freely; the latent poisons are stirred up in their hiding places; healing crises make their appearance. The processes of elimination thus inaugurated develop various symptoms of acute quinin poisoning.

(e) The eliminating crises are accompanied by headaches, ringing in the ears, nasal catarrh, bone pains, neuritis, stronge taste of quinin in the mouth, etc.

(f) Every healing crisis, if naturally treated, diminishes the signs of disease and drug poisons in the eye.

CHAPTER IX

INFLAMMATION

FROM what has already been said on this subject it will have become apparent that inflammatory and feverish diseases are just as natural, orderly and lawful as anything else in Nature; that, therefore, after they have once started, they must not be checked nor suppressed by drugs, ice, surgery or any other agent.

Inflammatory processes can be kept within safe limits, and they must be assisted in their constructive tendencies by the natural methods of treatment. To check and suppress acute diseases before they have run their natural course means to suppress Nature's purifying and healing efforts, to bring about fatal complications, and to change acute, constructive reactions into chronic disease conditions.

Those who have followed the preceding chapters will remember that their general trend has been to prove one of the fundamental principles of Nature Cure philosophy, namely, the **Unity of Disease and Cure.**

We claim that **all acute diseases are uniform in their causes, their purpose,** and, where conditions are favorable, uniform also in **their progressive development.**

In former chapters I have endeavored to prove and to elucidate the unity of acute diseases in regard to their causes and their purpose, the latter not being destructive, but constructive and beneficial. I have pointed out that the microorganisms of disease are not the terrible menace they are commonly thought to be, but that, like everything else in Nature, they serve a useful purpose. I have shown that it depends upon ourselves whether their activity is harmful and destructive, or beneficial: that is, upon our manner of living and of treating acute elimination.

Let us now trace the unity of acute diseases in regard to their general course by a brief examination of the processes of inflammation and their progressive development through five well-defined stages. I shall base our studies on the most advanced works on pathology and bacteriology.

The Story of Inflammation According to the Orthodox Interpretation

Before inflammation can arise, there must exist an exciting cause in the form of some obstruction or of some agent inimical to health and life. Such excitants of inflammation may be systemic poisons, dead cells, blood clots, fragments of bone, and other effete matter produced in the system itself, or they may be drug poisons, or foreign bodies such as particles of dust, soot, stone, iron, or other metals, slivers of wood, etc.; again, they may be microorganisms or parasites.

When one or more of these exciting agents of inflammation are present in the tissues of the body in sufficient strength to call forth the reaction and opposition of the healing forces, the microscope always reveals the following phenomena, slightly varying under different conditions:

The circulation in the affected part or organ seems to be obstructed. Owing to the increased blood pressure, the minute arteries and veins in the immediate neighborhood become dilated. The distention of the blood vessels stretches and thereby weakens their walls. Through these the white blood corpuscles squeeze their mobile bodies and work their way into the neighboring tissues.

In some mysterious way they seem to "sense" the exact location of the danger point, and hurry toward it in large numbers like soldiers summoned to meet an invading army. This faculty of the white blood corpuscles to apprehend the presence and exact location of the enemy (bacteria) has been ascribed to chemical attraction and is called chemotaxis.

The "army of defense" is made up of white blood corpuscles or leucocytes. These wandering cells possess the faculty of absorbing and digesting microbes. They contain certain proteolytic or protein-splitting ferments, by means of which they decompose and "digest" poisons and hostile microorganisms. On account of their activity as germ destroyers, these cells have been called germ killers or phagocytes. In their movements and actions these valiant little warriors act very much like intelligent beings, animated by the qualities of patience, perseverance, courage, foresight and selfsacrifice.

The phagocytes absorb morbid matter, poisons, or microorganisms by enveloping them with their own bodies. It is a hand-to-hand fight, and many of the brave little soldiers are destroyed by the poisons and bacteria which they attack. What we call "pus" is made up of the bodies of live and dead phagocytes, disease taints and germs, blood serum, broken-down cells, in short, the "débris of the battlefield".

We can now understand how the processes just described produce the well known "cardinal symptoms" of inflammation and fever; the redness, heat and swelling due to increased blood pressure, congestion and the accumulation of exudates; the pain due to irritation and to pressure on the nerves. We can also comprehend how impaired nutrition, obstruction and destruction in the affected parts and organs interfere with and inhibit functional activity.

The organism has still other means of defending itself.

At the time of bacterial infection, certain germ-killing substances are developed in the blood serum. Science has named these defensive proteids obsonins and alexins. It is also claimed that the phagocytes and tissue cells in the neighborhood of the area of irritation produce antibodies or natural antitoxins which neutralize the bacterial poisons and kill the microorganisms of disease.

With the Evil, Nature Provides the Cure

Furthermore, the growth and development of bacteria and parasites is inhibited and finally arrested by their own waste products. We have an example of this in the yeast germ, which thrives and multiplies in the presence of sugar in solution. Living on and "digesting" the sugar, it decomposes the sugar molecules into alcohol and carbonic acid. As the alcohol increases during the process of fermentation, it gradually arrests the development and activity of the yeast cells.

Similar phenomena accompany the activity of disease germs and parasites. They produce certain waste products which gradually inhibit their own growth and multiplication. The vaccines, serums and antitoxins of medical science are prepared from these bacterial excrements and from extracts made of the bodies of bacteria.

In the serum and antitoxin treatment, therefore, the allopathic school is imitating Nature's procedure in checking the growth of microorganisms, but with this difference: Nature does not suppress the growth and multiplication of disease germs **until the morbid matter on which they subsist has been decomposed and consumed, and until the inflammatory processes have run their natural course through the five stages of inflammation**; while serums and antitoxins given in powerful doses at the different stages of any disease may check and suppress germ activity and the processes of inflammation **before** the latter have run their natural course and **before** the morbid matter has been eliminated.

Besides that, these powerful poisons may cause permanent injury to the cells, tissues and organs of the body, which frequently results in serious chronic after effects, the "mysterious sequelae" of medical science. There is no excuse for resorting to these doubtful and dangerous agents in the treatment of inflammatory processes when the Nature Cure methods will produce satisfactory results in a simple, natural way.

What has been said in former chapters confirms our claim that all acute diseases are uniform in their causes and in their purpose. From the foregoing description of inflammation it will have become clear that they are also uniform in their pathological development. The uniformity of acute inflammatory processes becomes still more apparent when we follow them through their five successive stages, viz.: **Incubation, Aggravation, Destruction, Abatement** and **Reconstruction,** as illustrated in the following diagram:

I. **Incubation.** The first section of the diagram corresponds to the period of **Incubation,** the time between the exposure to an infectious disease and its development. This period may last from a few moments to several days, weeks, months or even years.

During this stage morbid matter, poisons, microorganisms and other excitants of inflammation congregate in certain parts and organs of the body. When they have accumulated to such an extent as to interfere with the normal functions or to endanger the health and life of the organism, the life forces begin to react to the obstruction or threatening danger by means of the inflammatory processes before described.

From the foregoing it appears that allopathy figures the period of incubation from the time of germ invasion, while according to our conception, incubation is coexistent with the three primary stages or manifestations of disease. (Chapter V.)

II. **Aggravation.** During the period of **Aggravation** the battle between the phagocytes and Nature's antitoxins on the one hand, and the poisons and microorganisms of disease on the other hand, gradually progresses, accompanied by a corresponding increase of fever and inflammation, until it reaches its climax, marked by the greatest intensity of feverish symptoms.

III. **Destruction.** This battle between the forces of disease and the healing forces is accompanied by the disintegration of tissues due to the accumulation of exudates, to pus formation, the development of abscesses, boils, fistulas, open sores, etc. and to other morbid changes. It involves the destruction of phagocytes, bacteria, blood vessels and tissues just as a battle between contending human armies results in loss of life and property. The stage of destruction ends in crisis, which may be either fatal or beneficial.

IV. **Abatement or Absorption.** If the healing forces of the organism are in the ascendancy, and if they are supported by right treatment which tends to build up the blood, increase the vitality, and promote elimination, then the poisons and the microorganisms of disease will gradually be overcome, absorbed or eliminated, and by degrees the tissues will be cleared of "the débris of the battlefield''. This is accompanied by a gradual lowering of temperature, pulse rate and other symptoms of fever and inflammation.

V. **Reconstruction.** When the period of abatement has run its course and the affected areas have been cleared of the morbid accumulations and obstructions, then, during the fifth stage of inflammation, the work of rebuilding begins. The struggle having been more or less destructive to the cells, tissues, blood vessels and organs of the areas involved, these must now be reconstructed, and this last stage of the inflammatory process is, therefore, in a way the most important. On the thoroughness of regeneration of the injured parts depends the final effect of the acute disease upon the organism.

The Story of Inflammation According to the Pathogenic Theory

The theory of inflammation according to Metchnikoff and the pathology of the allopathic school of medicine is certainly a most interesting and romantic story. The campaigns and battles of the tiny heroic defenders of the body, the phagocytes or ''germ-eaters'', against the microorganisms of disease and infectious taints and poisons read very much like the accounts of skirmishes, battles, captures and killings in human warfare between the armies of defense of a country and the invading enemy. It looks, however, as though we may have to relegate this romance of pathology to the realm of fairy tales.

There is one phase of this allopathic conception of inflammation, first advanced by Professor Metchnikoff, which does not fully agree with the Nature Cure idea of the activities of bacteria and parasites, and their effect upon the processes of disease and cure. Nature Cure philosophy teaches that these microorganisms are scavengers which live, thrive and multiply on disease matter only. According to the Metchnikoff theory, the bacteria are the enemies of the body, the creators of disease, which have to be killed and eliminated from the system by the brave little phagocytes and by antibodies and antitoxins secreted by certain cells and glandular structures.

Dr. Thomas Powell of Los Angeles has advanced another theory of the pathology of inflammation which is more in line with the Nature Cure conception of acute disease and of the origin and functions of bacteria and other parasites in the economy of Nature. For the last three years we have examined in our clinical and laboratory work the two theories from all possible viewpoints and closely observed the action of leucocytes and bacteria under varying conditions of health and disease. Our studies along these lines of research have convinced us that the phagocytic theory of inflammation is incorrect and that Dr. Powell's interpretation is the true one. Everyone interested in the subject should study Dr. Powell's work, "Fundamentals and Requirements of Health and Disease".

In the introductory remarks to his exposition of the new theory of inflammation, Dr. Powell says, on page 297:

"It is one of the best known facts of today that not so much as a single one of these facts [relating to the origin, nature and behavior of pathogen—Author's note], momentous as they evidently are, has ever been so much as fairly explained, nor have they been adequately defined."

On this point he evidently was not well informed. A careful perusal of his book and especially of the extracts herein quoted will show that all his teachings as to the fundamental causes of disease, lowered vitality, degeneration of the vital fluids, accumulation of waste and morbid matter (his "pathogen"), are straight Nature Cure philosophy. Everything he says on these subjects has been clearly stated and thoroughly explained in the Nature

Cure literature, first in the Nature Cure magazines which
began to appear in 1907, two years before Dr. Powell copy-
righted and published his "Fundamentals and Principles
of Health and Disease", and later in the first edition of
this volume. Many of the expressions and similes used by
him are almost identical with those employed in Nature
Cure philosophy.

The only, and certainly a very valuable, addition which
Dr. Powell has made to the Nature Cure theory of disease
is his version of the nature and activities of the leucocytes.

Dr. Powell agrees with Nature Cure when he attributes
all disease arising in the human body to the accumulation
in the system of certain morbid materials, the end and
by products of digestion and of the metabolic changes in
the cells and tissues of the body. In my writings I
have referred to these as "acids, ptomains, xanthins and
poisonous alkaloids". Collectively I have referred to
them as "colloids", and to the resulting conditions and
symptoms of disease as "collemia". Uric acid and other
morbid materials mixed with it form in the system a
sticky, mucoid substance which obstructs the capillary
circulation, irritates the nervous system, forms deposits,
and in that way causes all kinds of symptoms and disease
conditions. I chose these names because "colloid" means
glue-like and "collemia" signifies a glue-like condition
of the blood.

All the destructive effects resulting from these collemic,
and later on arthritic conditions (see chapter on Treatment
of Chronic Diseases) are fully described in the Nature
Cure magazines and in the first edition of "Nature Cure
Philosophy and Practice".

Dr. Powell has made a happy selection of the word
"pathogen" (which means "disease-creating") for these
accumulations of morbid materials. It is a more appropriate term than "colloid" and more convenient than

"acids, ptomains, xanthins", etc., or the phrases "waste matter, morbid matter and poisons". Therefore, I shall in further discussions of these subjects employ this word in preference to the older, more cumbrous phrases.

Briefly stated, Dr. Powell's theory of inflammation, in conformity with the foregoing quotations and in comparison with the allopathic version, as described in this volume, works out as follows:

Developments during the period of incubation, as explained on pages 86 to 87, are altogether in conformity with Dr. Powell's description of pathogen and its gradual accumulation in the system. We have only to substitute the word "pathogen" for the phrase, "waste, morbid matter and poisons".

According to Dr. Powell's theory, the period of aggravation (see page 87) is explained as follows: The congestion of blood in the area where inflammation is in process of development is caused by the accumulation of pathogen in the circulation which obstructs the tiny capillaries in the affected parts. The accumulation of pathogen in these parts, aside from the great viscosity of the blood, is due to lowered vitality, lowered resistance, or to some kind of irritation or obstruction.

As a result of this pathogen obstruction in the capillary circulation the blood cannot pass, it surges back and bulges or distends the capillaries and gradually the larger blood vessels. This explains the congestion, which is always the first symptom of inflammation. The capillaries expand in such a way that the leucocytes are forced out into the neighboring tissues. This throws new light on the migration of the leucocytes.

We must remember here that the leucocytes, according to Dr. Powell's theory, are particles of pathogenic matter which have been condensed into globular bodies resembling cells. This condensation of pathogen (following his explanation) takes place in the trabiculae (minute passages) of the spleen and in the lymph glands or lymph nodes. This explains why in many diseases characterized by accumulations of morbid matter in the system, the lymphatic glands and the spleen become considerably enlarged. In such cases the allopathic surgeon cuts out the glands. I have always claimed that this is irrational and destructive practice.

To recapitulate: From the Nature Cure viewpoint the functions of the lymphatic glands and of the spleen consist in condensing morbid materials (pathogen) from the circulation. Enlargement and the ensuing suppuration of these structures, therefore, means that they are overcharged or engorged with pathogenic matter.

A perfect analogy of this is found in inflammation and suppuration of the tonsils and adenoid tissue, which are also important parts of the drainage system of the body. The extirpation of these useful eliminating organs is just as senseless and destructive as the cutting out of lymphatic glands or of any other useful organ of the body. We might as well remove the sewers from a house because they are clogged with refuse. The slogan of the allopathic physician and surgeon is destruction; that of the Nature Cure physician, restoration to health and useful function.

We have left the leucocytes after they had "migrated", or as we now believe, after they had been forced out through the distended capillaries into the surrounding tissues. Next we see them engaged in a life and death struggle with the bacteria. This coincides with the stage of destruction (page 87). According to the old version, the leucocytes were devouring and digesting the bacteria. Now the story reads the other way. The leucocytes, or rather the condensed particles of pathogen, disintegrate into pus under the proteolytic action of bacteria.

Thus the pathogenic conception of inflammation re-

verses the old theory from beginning to end. The leucocytes, instead of being the intelligent and heroic defenders of the bodies, are its deadliest enemies. Instead of pursuing the disease germs and destroying them, the leucocytes or particles of pathogen, forced into the tissues, decompose and form the morbid soil for the development of microzyma into bacteria, which in turn cause the oxidation and disintegration of these morbid products of faulty metabolism.

At once questions like the following arise in the mind of the critical examiner of these conflicting stories: "If leucocytes are particles of pathogen, why have they nuclei and amoeboid motion—why do they resemble so closely the living cells of the body?"

While it is true that these particles of morbid matter in a general way resemble genuine cells in their appearance and activities, this resemblance may be easily explained by the new theory of pathogenesis. We have learned that the more or less cellular form of the particles of pathogen is due to the forcing of the pathogen through the trabiculae of the spleen and the lymph glands, which condenses the pathogen into compact particles.

The pathogenic theory of disease may bring up another question: "Why is it necessary that the spleen and the lymph nodes condense the albuminous pathogenic materials of the blood into the so called white blood corpuscles?" In order to explain this we must briefly consider the processes of nutrition and elimination as they take place in the tissues of the body.

The elements of nutrition in the forms of oxygen and of carbohydrates and protein substances are carried in the salty blood serum through the walls of the capillaries into the intercellular spaces to be absorbed by the cells. This passage from the tiny blood-vessels into the neighboring tissues is called osmosis. By osmosis is meant the passage of a salty fluid through an animal membrane. To illustrate: If a bladder filled with pure water be suspended in a larger vessel also full of pure water, and if salt be then added to the water in the vessel, the salt will penetrate through the membrane of the bladder into the water which it contains.

On the other hand, the carbonic acid and other waste materials excreted by the cells are collected by the capillary vessels of the venous and the lymphatic system and through these carried to the organs of elimination. This passage of the "feces of the cells" from the intercellular spaces into the venous and lymphatic vessels also takes place through osmosis.

From the foregoing it becomes apparent that the freer from pathogenic materials the blood serum and the lymph fluid, the more readily they will pass and repass through the walls of the blood and lymph vessels into and out of the intercellular spaces.

If, on the other hand, the blood is in a mucoid, viscous, sticky condition with excessive amounts of colloid or pathogenic matter in diffuse form, then the passage of the blood serum and lymph fluid through the walls of the capillary vessels and the cells will be greatly impeded and may become impossible. This gives rise to obstruction, stagnation, congestion, colloid degeneration or inflammation.

It is to prevent this mucoid or colloid condition of the blood serum and lymph fluid that the lymph nodules and the spleen condense the pathogenic materials into the comparatively compact leucocytes. It is also reasonable to assume that pathogen in the compact form of leucocytes offers a better soil for the action of microzyma than in the diffuse colloid form.

According to Dr. Béchamp's theory the microzyma in the decomposing leucocytes create the bacteria. This does away with the idea that the leucocytes in a mysterious way (chemotaxis) hunt up the disease germs in the tissue and then destroy them.

May this not explain why in the worst chronic destructive diseases, as in the advanced stages of tuberculosis, we find the leucocytes diminished in number. If phagocytosis were a fact in nature we would expect the opposite condition. That is, in the more advanced stages of the disease the phagocytes should be present in larger numbers. We find, however, that the opposite is the case and that the lymph nodes are engorged and enlarged with leucocytes and other colloid materials. This condition is easily explained by the new version of leucocytosis.

Excessive amounts of pathogenic materials in the circulation cause obstruction in the lung tissues, giving rise to the inflammatory tuberculous processes. Finally the accumulations of pathogen in the circulation become so great that the spleen and lymph nodes, being no longer able to cope with them, become engorged. Thus the number of leucocytes diminishes in the circulation but at the same time the vital fluids become more viscous and pathogenic. This explains the enlargement of the spleen and the swelling and degeneration of the lymphatic glands in such diseases as tuberculosis, typhoid, malaria, etc. These facts, instead of contradicting it, are strong evidence in support of the pathogenic theory of leucocytosis.

Another question that will be asked is, "If the white blood corpuscle is not a living cell, why has it a necleus and amoeboid motion?"

The following quotation from Dr. Powell's work will explain the granular and nucleated appearance of the leucocytes:

"When first formed the leucocytes are neither granular nor nucleated, and are known to science as 'young cells' or 'round cells'. In the progress of time they begin to decay in some one of several ways: Sometimes they succumb to the external assaults of Pasteur's 'microbe generateur du pus', masquerade for a while as pus corpuscles and finally fall to pieces and disappear as such; sometimes they yield to the internal assaults of other microorganisms with which they had come in contact. As this form of decay progresses a 'nucleus' appears; to this other nuclei are soon added. As time advances these foci increase in size as well as number, the constituents thereof becoming susceptible first to one dye and then to another, taking at one stage of the process the stain of eosin, in which case they are called eosinophilia; at another stage they take the color of methyl blue, and so on to the end of the list of the leucocyte stains. Sometimes they undergo fatty degeneration, in which case they are called myelocytes. The myelocyte is simply a leucocyte in process of hydrocarbonization, the dangerous leucocyte being thus changed into a less dangerous thing—namely, fat. In short, there is no lack of evidence of the fact that the leucocyte or so-called white blood corpuscle, is a dead thing, that its destiny is dissolution and that in its downward course it carries disease and destruction to its host, the living organism.

"Those distortions on which the migratory or amoeboid movements of the leucocyte depend, and which have seemed to indicate that it is endowed with life, are chiefly attributable to the action of the carbon dioxide gas that is generated within it as it passed into decay. That is to say, it is the expansion of this gas that gives rise to those protrusions of the leucocyte which are called pseudopodia, while the escape of the gas into the aqueous element of the blood permits it (the leucocyte) to resume its former shape, which it does in obedience to that power that gives rotundity to various things, from the dewdrops to the celestial spheres; the fact that after a leucocyte has sent out a pseudopod its fundus is drawn in that direction, is due to the adhesion of the former to the containing vessel and the subsequent escape of the gas in question; in short, the leucocyte, or so-called 'white blood corpuscle', is not what it appears to be. It has impressed the world that it is a living organism—a living cell—while the fact is, it is not a living cell, but a mortuus corpusculum, or lifeless corpuscle, owing to its motility to the forces not of life, but of death—to adhesion, gaseous expansion and chemotaxis.

"I do not hesitate to affirm that every 'nucleus' and every 'nucleolus' that we see in a leucocyte is simply a collection of residual matter (the earthy remains of that arch destroyer, pathogen) and is to be regarded, therefore, as a focus of decay; that the segmentation of the leucocyte is not a matter of 'vital duplication', as has been supposed, but of progressive disintegration; that the increase of its size is due not to growth, but to accretion or the adherence of particles of kindred material which are floating in the blood stream, as above stated.

"A New Interpretation of Facts"

"The fact that the leucocyte becomes less active in consequence of the lowering of its temperature, is attributable to the consequent increase of the disintegrating process; the fact that it is 'killed', as biologists have declared, by iodin, arsenic and other poisons, is due, not to the destruction of its life, as they have supposed, but to the preservative action of these drugs.

"The leucocytes are not the 'vigilant policemen of the vital domain', as we have been led by their performances to believe, but owe their so-called 'phagocytic' powers to their viscidity, or extreme adhesiveness. That is to say, they (the leucocytes) gather the bacteria by sticking to and flowing around them. This is followed by the destruction, not of the bacteria, but of the leucocytes. The leucocyte is not the destroyer but the thing destroyed."

We understand now that the microzyma develop into bacteria while feeding on the decaying materials of the leucocytes. This is explained more fully in the next chapter.

The ameboid motions of the leucocytes are caused by the expansive action of the carbonic acid which is formed in the oxidation and disintegration of their morbid materials, somewhat like dough is "raised" by the carbon dioxide gas which is a product of fermentation.

The foregoing description of osmotic nutrition and lymphatic elimination throws additional light on the importance and the modus operandi of massage treatment. The lymph stream has not behind it the powerful pressure of the heart pump. Both the venous and lymphatic circulation become sluggish through pathogenic obstruction of the capillary vessels and intracellular lymph spaces. It is readily seen how deep manipulation of the fleshy tissues and systematic kneading and stroking from circumference to center will stir up and accelerate the movement of the venous blood and lymph fluids toward the heart and toward the outlet into the subclavian vein.

The best proof of all is practical experience. A careful examination of our patients' records discloses the fact that in ninety per cent of all the cases that improved under our care and treatment, the white blood corpuscles or leucocytes decreased from 1000 to 4000 or more in number; while the red blood corpuscles showed a proportionate increase. In many cases this increase amounted to several

millions. Practically all of these patients were of the stubborn chronic type.

The few cases that went into decline and ended fatally showed an increase in leucocytes, except in tuberculosis, which in the last stages usually shows a decrease. This is because the lymphatic glands and the spleen are so completely engorged and obstructed with leucocytes and colloid matter that they can no longer condense the pathogen into white corpuscles.

Some cases which at the commencement of treatment showed an exceedingly low number of leucocytes, ranging from 2000 to 3000, increased up to 4000 under natural living and treatment. In these the low number of leucocytes at the beginning of treatment was due to the fact that the lymphatic system and the spleen were in a diseased condition and unable to condense the pathogen. As these organs improved, the number of leucocytes increased. The average number of the so called white corpuscles, after six months of Natural living and treatment, seems to be about 4000. This is 3500 lower than the average adopted as normal by the allopathic school.

Their standard in this case is too high for the same reason that their standard acidity of the urine is too high; namely, because they accept the average as the normal, leaving out of consideration that the average individual is abnormal. People following the conventional habits of living suffer from hyperacidity as well as from excessive amounts of colloid or pathogenic materials because the ordinary diet is too rich in pathogen-producing proteids, starches and fats, and deficient in the acid-neutralizing alkaline mineral elements.

According to allopathic standards, the ratio of the white to the red corpuscles is as 1 to 666. In animals the proportion is considerably lower than in the human.

I firmly believe that with proper prenatal care, natural

management after birth, and rational habits of living throughout life, the average number of leucocytes can be reduced far below 4000.

It may be said, if the foregoing theories are correct, it would be good policy to increase as much as possible the number of bacteria and parasites in the body, and if this be desirable then it would be good practice to expose one's self to infectious diseases. The answer to this is, there is no need of artificially introducing the microorganisms of disease or infectious disease taints, because the presence of pathogenic matter in the system will bring about germ activity, whenever that becomes necessary for the protection of health and life. Pathogenic matter breeds its own destroyers, the same as any decaying, putrefying material generates the fungi, parasites or bacterial microorganisms which decompose and destroy it. Proof of this we see in the putrefying cadaver and in the uncleaned house full of filthy rubbish. The rational way is to keep the system, through right living, free from pathogenic matter, then there will be no need for bacterial scavengers. They cannot live and cause trouble in a clean body endowed with good vitality and governed by a positive mind.

The question, where do the microorganisms of disease come from, I have answered as follows: The spores and seeds of disease germs and parasites are practically omnipresent; they are at the same time the product of disease and the disintegrators of morbid matter. This has been briefly explained in the following chapter which deals with Prof. Béchamp's teachings.

CHAPTER X

THE DISCOVERY OF MICROZYMA

IT may be interesting at this point to enter more fully into the researches and deductions of the great French scientist whose discoveries are destined to revolutionize Biology.

Among the many posts Antoine Béchamp held were those of Professor of Medical Chemistry and Pharmacy in the Department of Medicine at the University of Montpelier and Professor of Organic and Biological Chemistry in the Department of Medicine in the Free University of Lille. He was a contemporary of Louis Pasteur and of Professor Metchnikoff.

Impartial investigators now claim that Pasteur appropriated many of the ideas and discoveries which made him world famous, from the teachings of Professor Béchamp. When these men lived and worked in their respective fields, a battle royal raged in the scientific world as to whether substances such as flesh, blood, milk and saccharinaceous (sweet) fluids remained intact when preserved from all contact with the atmosphere. Pasteur claimed that they did; that organisms in the air were needed to cause in such fluids processes of putrefaction or fermentation.

Pasteur compared the human body to a barrel of beer and pronounced it, like that beverage, at the mercy of extraneous organisms. As these produce good or bad beer—a liquid diseased, as it were, or healthy—so on entering animal bodies microorganisms create disease, each after its own order.

Pasteur looked upon atmospheric germs as individual entities, endowed with specific, well defined functions; it was a special germ ferment that soured milk, a special germ ferment that turned grape juice to wine and wine to vinegar, etc. At that time definite organisms had been noticed in sick animals, particularly tiny rod-like bodies in cattle suffering from anthrax. Pasteur assumed that these were caught from the atmosphere and on this he established the doctrine of specific malignant germs, each dealing out its specific malady.

It only needed Professor Metchnikoff's theory of phagocytosis and the discovery of "obsonins" or natural antitoxins in the blood, by Sir Almroth Wright and Dr. Bulloch, to furnish the medical profession with a delightfully simple theory as to the origin of disease, comprehensible to the least intelligent. Upon this flimsy basis rests the entire structure of modern medical theory and practice.

Unfortunately, the world "and all that therein is" is the reverse of simple, and these crude explanations of disease left room for questions from every viewpoint.

Firstly, the origin of malignant, microscopic entities was left an unexplained problem. If plagues be caused by bacillus which passes into man through the flea from the rat, whence did the rat catch it?

Secondly, if a specific organism produces a specific disease, why should its effects differ in different species? Why, for instance, should the organism associated with anthrax cause splenic fever in cattle and pustules on the skin of human bodies?

Thirdly, the laboratory-made sicknesses of experimental work are not produced by organisms caught from the air, but result from the inoculation of substances taken from diseased bodies.

Fourthly, the postulates of Koch, which formulate rules for the recognition of disease germs, have been disproved by the latter's contradictory behavior. The "Lancet" (March 20, 1909) had to admit—"It must be acknowledged that all these postulates are complied with very rarely, indeed, if ever."

Let us examine now the teachings of Professor Béchamp, concerning these mooted problems. During the course of his researches the French scientist observed fermentative effects in all parts of living bodies. His work on yeasts had taught him that fermentation was nothing more than the chemical changes produced by living organisms in their environment through feeding and eliminative processes. For this reason he had always combated Pasteur's idea of a specific role being attached to a specific ferment and maintained that under changed circumstances the achievement of the ferment might be different.

The fermentative effects he noticed in living bodies were frequently quite dissociated from the presence of bacteria. This gave him cause for reflection, being to him clear proof that all organisms were formed of infinitely minute living beings, all largely occupied, like ourselves, in the business of feeding.

He understood why believers in spontaneous generation had never been satisfied that the intrusion of air borne organisms was the one explanation for varying phenomena.

There was life everywhere. Bodies of plants and animals alike were made up of living particles. This explained the necessity for the application of great heat, as well as exclusion of atmospheric germs, in order to prevent putrefactive changes in living protoplasm. It was essential to **kill the internal life,** as well as to **guard against external.**

Pasteur himself, in one of his own experiments, described a piece of meat kept air proof, as yet having become odorous. This in itself should have shown him tnat either his method had been faulty, or else that alteration can take place apart from air borne organisms.

What was Béchamp's explanation? What did he teach at a time when there was more or less acceptance of Virchow's view of the cell as the structural unit of life, or, so to speak, as the primary individual?

The Professor of Montpelier taught that the cell or the germ was no more than a transitory object, built up by the true entities found within it. To these he gave the name of microzyma, or minute-ferment-bodies. These are the same particles now known as microsomes. Of these primary units of life Edmund B. Wilson, Ph.D., says in his text book "The Cell in Development and Inheritance",— "Their behaviour is in some cases such as to have led to the hypothesis long since suggested by Henle (1841) and at a later period developed by Béchamp and Estor, and especially by Altmann, that microsomes are actually units or bioblasts, capable of assimilation, growth and division and hence to be regarded as elementary units of structure, standing between the ultimate molecules of living matter and the cell" (page 21).

The microzyma of Béchamp are the minute granules that mark the honeycomb structure of the cell and the cell nucleus, and have been distinguished as chromatin granules, owing to the deep shade they take when stained for observation under the microscope.

Before the division of the cell nucleus takes place, the chromatin granules assume the appearance of a thread which breaks into pieces known as chromosomes. These subdivide lengthwise during cell cleavage, thus providing each derivative cell with an equal number of what are supposed to be the prime factors of new life and the transmitters of heredity.

Altmann inquired, "How can a granulum (microzyma) arise without its cell?" Béchamp answered, "Every living cell and therefore every living being is reducible to the microzyma.''

It was Béchamp's contention that processes of putrefaction are wrought by microzyma which, upon the corruption of the body that formed their habitat, are freed to the soil, water and air, and are themselves, either in their infinitesimal form or else in larger shapes as bacteria, the ferments that play so great a role in life and for which the orthodox school of bacteriology provides no explanation.

All the microorganisms that teem in the air, the ground, the rocks, are, according to Béchamp, the remains of animal and vegetable matter. This seems to be proved by the fact that bacteria abound wherever decaying plant or animal life is found, and that they are equally scarce wherever such life is wanting, whether on the bleak tops of a high mountain range or on the sterile tracts of the arid desert.

The following statements epitomize Béchamp's important discovery: The birth of bacteria, as well as of normal cells of living bodies, is from within. These minute beings are nothing more nor less than the products of life's primal architects, the indwelling microzyma or microsomes of cells and of germs.

''The cell'', he wrote, ''is a collection of an infinite number of little beings which have an independent life, a special natural history. The microzyma of animal cells (when living in morbid matter) associate two by two or in larger numbers and extend themselves into bacteria.''

These microzyma are those spores or seed germs of bacteria whose existence I presumed and postulated in my philosophy of the unity of disease and cure.

The fermentation of eggs is a puzzle which the germ theorists endeavor to solve by declaring that the shell is not impenetrable to external bacteria. When impenetrability is absolutely assured by artificial means, and yet change, though in a much lesser degree, takes place, he is driven to fall back on Pasteur's explanation that probably germs of putrefaction originally penetrated into the hen's oviduct.

Béchamp, on the contrary, showed that the same causes which under normal conditions produce the chicken, give rise under abnormal conditions to fermentation and eventually to putrefaction.

According to his demonstrations, the causes of the normal as well as the abnormal processes are the microsomes, or, as he named them, the microzyma.

In this connection I may be permitted to quote from a chapter in this volume, entitled "Vaccination", page 145, the following paragraph concerning an attack of smallpox from which my son suffered.

"As far as I could learn, there was not another case of smallpox in Chicago or vicinity at the time of the boy's illness. If the contagion theory be true, from whom did he 'catch' the disease, and why did not one of the many persons living in the same house become infected?

"My answer is, this acute eliminative process was Nature's way of purifying the little body of inherited scrofulous and other disease taints." (This was written originally for the Nature Cure Magazine in 1909.)

Read also on pages 70-72 the description of lice eruptions during and as a result of healing crises.

The microzyma explain the possibility of contagion and infection from without as well as spontaneous generation of bacteria from morbid soil within the system. While bacteria entering the body from without may instigate disease processes, such germs must have originated in morbid soil somewhere and upon entering a body they cannot live and multiply to the danger point unless they find the morbid materials necessary to their existence. **If all germs**

could suddenly be wiped out of existence the conditions which make them necessary would create them anew.

In 1869 Béchamp said, "In typhoid fever, in gangrene, in anthrax, the existence has been proved of bacteria in the tissues and in the blood and this has been looked upon as a case of ordinary parasitism. It is evident, however, after what we have said, that the diseases before mentioned were not caused by the introduction of foreign germs, but that we have to do here only with a deviation of functions of microzyma, a deviation indicated also by the change that has taken place in their form.

"In cases where bacteria have been noted in the blood, it is not a case of ordinary parasitism, but rather of abnormal development of primitive normal organisms. The bacteria, far from being the cause, are on the contrary the effect of the malady."

The microzyma is a microcosm, the cell its macrocosm, just as man is the macrocosm to the cell, and as the sidereal universe is the macrocosm to man, its microcosm. As the well being of man depends upon normal nutrition and wholesome surroundings, so also the health of the cell and of the microzyma depends upon proper nutrition, drainage and innervation. Thus provided with its essential life requirements, the primary unit of life will develop into the normal cells of the vegetable, animal or human body, not into disease germs and parasites.

This theory as to the origin of bacteria would explain such problems as voiced in the "Lancet" (March 20, 1909). "When a causal organism (bacteria) is injected into an animal often it happens that it gives rise to a disease bearing no clinical resemblance to the original malady" (which produced the bacteria).

This discrepancy, besides betraying the unreliability of experiments on animals, points to the conditions in the body as deciding factors, rather than to the parasitic invaders which, in any case, have not been taken from the air, but from a diseased subject. As Béchamp observes (Les Microzymas, p. 768), "the inoculation of anthrax produces splenic fever in cattle and pustules (on the skin) in human beings, thus demonstrating the control factors of diseased conditions to be inborn, not extraneous."

"Disease is born of us and in us", wrote Béchamp, "and that is as it should be, **because the life of man, and of every other creature, is no more delivered over to chance than the course of the stars.**

"Life would be delivered over to chance if it depended upon primitive microbic germs created for destructive purposes." (Les Microzymas, p. 804.)

What an interesting confirmation this is of the fundamental postulate of Nature Cure philosophy, according to which disease is not an accident, not an arbitrary infliction, but the natural and inevitable result of the violation of Nature's laws.

If it is true that disease is bred in us and of us, health undoubtedly arises in the same way and can be maintained by attention to the well being of the infinitesimal entities that build up our bodies and which, therefore, we may justly call "life's primal architects". The well being of these minute builders and workers depends upon right living; that is, our habits of thinking, feeling, breathing, eating, drinking, exercising, bathing, clothing, as well as our sexual and social activities, must be in harmonious relation with the laws of our being.

In commenting upon Professor Béchamp's teachings, Hume says: "When all is said and done, could Professor Béchamp's microscope, or the most powerful lens of the present day, ever hope to pry into the primal entity of life, the first individual unit of organized existence? Far beyond all searching in its minuteness must such an ele-

ment be, and well does August Weissmann in his Germ-
plasm; a Theory of Heredity', write: 'We are thus re-
minded afresh that we have to deal not only with the
infinitely great, but also with the infinitely small; the
idea of size is a purely relative one and on either hand
extends infinity' (p. 468).

Hume continues in his pamphlet:

"Since from such infinitesimal beginnings the brain of
a Newton, the music of a Beethoven, the beauty of a Lady
Hamilton are evolved, we find ourselves reconsidering the
Platonic theory of Ideation."

The final reality is the idea in the mind of the creator.
Thought forms are the souls of things and matter convo-
lutes to these soul patterns.

So the relation of thought and feeling to health and
disease appears to be not without scientific basis—the
physical reverts to the metaphysical. The ancient Vedic
teaching is proved afresh—"The whole of the universe is
evolved through Sankalpa (thought ideation) alone; it is
only through Sankalpa that the universe retains its appearance." (The Varaha Upanishads of Krishna-Yajur
Veda.)

And so "the eternal thought in the eternal mind"
(Bhagavad-Gita) precludes the disseverance of the thought
from the thinker. If, on the one hand, man, in deep
humility, realizes himself a pigmy in an incomprehensible
universe, on the other hand, his consciousness of his one-
ness with the stupendous whole leaves him appalled by
his dignity and the possibilities of his amazing destiny.
Thus, in the mystery of life's primal architects (microzyma), there may be dimly discerned that unity of Creator
and created which, in the oldest philosophic teachings in
the world found voice in that triumphant cry of faith of
the Vedic utterance:

"That supreme Brahman, the self of all, the great abode

of the universe, subtler than the subtle, the Eternal,—That is thyself, and thou art That.'' (Kaivalya Upanishad.)

I leave it to the reader to decide for himself which theory of inflammation is the more rational, the old or the new. The new version removes the last doubt as to the beneficent character and constructive activity of the tiny organisms which so far have been looked upon as the greatest enemies of mankind. It makes the Nature Cure philosophy of health, disease and cure consistent and rational in all its principles and deductions.

CHAPTER XI

RESULTS OF SUPPRESSION

If the inflammation be allowed to run its course through the different stages of acute activity and the final stage of reconstruction, then **every** acute disease, whatever its name and description, will prove beneficial to the organism, because pathogen and poisons have been eliminated from the system; abnormal and diseased tissues have been broken down and built up again to a purer and more normal condition.

As it were, the acute disease has acted upon the organism like a thunder storm on the sultry, vitiated summer air. It has cleared the system of impurities and obstructions and reestablished wholesome, normal conditions. Therefore acute diseases, when treated in harmony with Nature's intent, always prove beneficial.

If, however, through neglect or wrong treatment, the inflammatory processes are not allowed to run their natural course, if they are checked or suppressed by drugs, ice bags or surgical operations, or if the disease conditions in the system are so far in the ascendancy that the healing forces cannot react properly, then the constructive forces may lose the battle and the disease may take a fatal ending or develop into chronic ailments. Whether we accept the old or the new interpretation of inflammation, the foregoing deductions are true. In either case the inflammatory process is constructive in nature and purpose.

Suppression During the First Two Stages of Inflammation

It may be suggested that suppression **during the stages of incubation and aggravation** need not have fatal consequences if followed by natural living and eliminative treatment. To this I would reply: "Such procedure always involves **the danger of concentrating the disease poisons in vital parts and organs**, thus laying the foundation for chronic destructive diseases."

Furthermore, it is not at all necessary to suppress inflammatory processes by poisonous drugs and other means, because we can easily and surely control them and keep them from becoming dangerous by our natural methods of treatment.

I shall now support with proof and illustrations the foregoing theoretical expositions by following the development of various diseases through the five stages of inflammation. I shall first consider the commonest of all forms of disease, the "cold".

Catching a Cold

According to popular opinion, the catching of colds is responsible for the greater part of human ailments. Very frequently I hear from patients who come for consultation: "All my troubles date back to a cold I took at such and such a time", etc. Then I have to explain that colds are not contracted suddenly and from without but come **from within**; that their "period of incubation" may have extended over months or years or over several successive lifetimes; that a clean, healthy body possessed of abundant vitality **cannot** "take cold" under the ordinary thermal conditions congenial to human life, no matter how sudden the change in temperature.

At first this may seem to be contrary to common experience as well as to the theory and practice of medical science. But follow the development of a cold from start to finish. Nature Cure philosophy will throw light on the question as to whether a cold can be "caught", whether it develops slowly within the organism, and whether this development or "incubation" may extend over a long period of time.

"Taking cold" may be caused by chilling the surface of the body or part of the body. In the chilled portions of the skin the pores close, the blood recedes into the interior, and as a result the elimination of poisonous gases and exudates is locally suppressed.

This "catching cold" through being exposed to a cold draft, through wet clothing, etc., is not necessarily followed by more serious consequences. If the system is not too much encumbered with morbid matter and if kidneys and intestines are in fairly good working order, these organs will assist the temporarily inactive skin to take care of the extra amount of waste and morbid materials and eliminate them without difficulty. The greater the vitality and the more normal the composition of the blood, the more effectively the system as a whole will react in such an emergency and throw off the morbid materials which were not eliminated through the skin.

If, however, the organism is already overloaded with waste and morbid materials; if the bowels and the kidneys are already weakened or atrophied through continued overwork and over-stimulation; if, in addition to this, the vitality has been lowered through excesses or over-exertion, and the vital fluids are in an abnormal condition, then the morbid matter thrown into the circulation by the chilling and temporary inactivity of the skin cannot find an outlet through the regular channels of elimination and endeavors to escape by way of the mucous linings of the nasal passages, the throat, bronchi, stomach, bowels or genito-urinary organs.

The waste materials and poisonous exudates which are being eliminated through these internal membranes cause irritation and pathogenic congestion, and thus produce the well known symptoms of inflammation and catarrhal elimination—sneezing (coryza), cough, expectoration, mucous discharges, diarrhea, leucorrhea, etc., etc.

We may safely assume that these forcible house-cleanings do not occur until it becomes necessary for the system to eliminate excessive accumulations of pathogen. In other words, the chilling of the surface is merely the spark that explodes the combustibles stored within.

Why is it necessary that such elimination must take the form of inflammation? Why can it not proceed in the ordinary way without causing violent acute reaction?

The reason is that the organs of depuration are so constructed that they eliminate only waste materials of comparatively simple chemical composition. Thus, the skin eliminates carbonic acid and salts which are neutralized acids. The kidneys eliminate normally urea and salts; in abnormal conditions, they also eliminate uric acid, indican and a few other kinds of acids and ptomains.

The intestines eliminate little else but undigested food waste. Pathogen, however, is made up of chemically highly complex substances which cannot be eliminated through the organs of depuration. Pathogenic substances must first be broken down into simple compounds chemically adapted for elimination through these organs, and this decomposition is accomplished through inflammation and germ activity.

We now understand that these so called "colds" are nothing more nor less than forms of vicarious elimination. The membranous linings of the internal organs are doing the work for the inactive, sluggish and atrophied skin, kidneys and intestines. The greater the accumulation of morbid matter in the system, the lower the vitality, and the more abnormal the composition of the blood and lymph, the greater the liability to the "catching" of colds.

What is to be gained by suppressing the different forms

of acute catarrhal elimination with cough and catarrh "cures" containing opiates, astringents, antiseptics and antipyretics? Is it not obvious that such procedure interferes with Nature's purifying efforts, that it hinders and suppresses the inflammatory processes and the accompanying elimination of morbid matter from the system? Worst of all, that it adds drug poisons to disease poisons? Such a course can have but one result—converting Nature's cleansing and healing efforts into chronic disease.

From the foregoing it will have become clear that **the** cause of a cold lies not so much in the cold draft, or the wet feet, as in **the primary causes of all diseases: lowered vitality, deterioration of vital fluids, and the accumulation of morbid matter and poisons in the system.**

The incubation period of the "cold" may have extended over many years, an entire lifetime or many successive lifetimes.

What, then, is the **natural cure** for colds? There can be but one remedy: increased elimination through the proper channels. This is accomplished by judicious dieting and fasting, and through restoring the natural activity of the skin, kidneys and bowels by means of wet packs, cold sprays and ablutions, sitzbaths, massage, neurotherapy, homeopathic remedies, exercise, sun and air baths and all other methods of natural treatment that save vitality, build up the blood on a normal basis, and promote elimination without injuring the organism.

Suppression During the Third Stage of Inflammation

Should the inflammatory processes be suppressed **during the stage of destruction,** the results would be still more serious and far-reaching.

We have learned that during this stage the affected parts and organs are involved more or less in a process of disintegration. They become filled with morbid exudates, pus, etc., which interfere with and make impossible normal nutrition and functioning. If suppression takes place during this stage, it is obvious that the affected areas will be left permanently in a condition of destruction.

The following may serve as an illustration. Suppose changes and repairs have been found necessary in a building. Workmen have torn down the partitions, hangings, wallpaper, etc. At this stage of the proceedings the owner discharges the workmen, and the building is left in a condition of chaos. Surely this would be most irrational. It would leave the house unfit for habitation. But such a procedure exactly corresponds to the suppression of inflammatory diseases during the stage of destruction. Such suppression leaves the affected organs in an abnormal, diseased condition and accounts for the "mysterious sequelae" or chronic after effects which so often follow drug or ice treated acute diseases.

Numerous cases of chronic affections of the lungs and kidneys, of infantile paralysis, and of many other chronic ailments are directly traceable to such suppression. The following typical case came under our care and treatment a few years ago.

Suppression by Means of Ice Packs

Several gentlemen of Greek nationality called on me with the request that I visit a friend of theirs who had been confined to bed for about two months in one of our great West Side hospitals. On investigation I found the patient had entered the hospital while suffering from a mild attack of pneumonia. The doctors of the institution had ordered ice packs. Rubber sheets filled with ice were applied to the chest and other parts of the body. This had been continued for several days until the fever had subsided.

As a matter of fact, ice is more suppressive than anti-fever medicines. Continued icy cold applications chill the parts of the body to which they are applied, depress the vital functions and effectually suppress the inflammatory processes.

The result in this case, as in many similar ones which I had occasion to observe during and after the ice treatment, was that the inflammation in the lungs had been arrested and suppressed **during the stage of destruction**, while the air cells and tissues were filled with exudates, blood serum, pus, live and dead blood cells, morbid microzyma, bacteria, etc., leaving the affected areas of the lungs in a consolidated condition.

As a consequence of suppression in the case of this patient, the pneumonia had been changed from the acute to the sub-acute and chronic stages and the doctors in charge had informed his friends that he was now suffering from "miliary tuberculosis", and would probably die within a week or two.

Discouraged by this information, the friends of the patient asked me to take charge of the case. The man was transferred to our institution and we began at once to apply the natural methods of treatment. For ice packs we substituted cold water packs—strips of linen wrung out of water of ordinary temperature wrapped around the body and covered with several layers of flannel bandages. (See Vol. II.)

The wet packs became warm on the body in a few minutes. They relaxed the pores and drew the blood to the surface, thus promoting heat radiation and the elimination of morbid matter through the skin. **They did not suppress the fever**, but kept it below the danger point.

Under this treatment, accompanied by fasting and judicious manipulation, the inflammatory and feverish processes which had been suppressed by the ice packs soon revived, became once more active and were made to run their natural course through the stages of **destruction, absorption** (abatement) and **reconstruction.**

The result of this Nature Cure treatment was that about two months after the patient entered our institution, his friends bought him a ticket to sunny Greece. He withstood the fatigue of the voyage well, and in the congenial climate of his native country his recovery was completed.

I have observed a number of similar cases suffering from solidification of the lungs and the resulting asthmatic or tubercular conditions, which had been "doctored" into these chronic ailments by means of antipyretics and of ice. Frequently such treatment results in the accumulation of fluids in the pleura and lung tissues. Then the allopathic physician resorts to "tapping," but the withdrawal of the fluids only results in quicker accumulation. Under natural treatment these morbid excretions absorb gradually through the lymphatic drains.

Equally dangerous is the ice bag or pack if applied to the inflamed brain or to the spinal column. Only too often it results either in paralysis or in death. In many instances, acute cerebro-spinal meningitis is changed in this way by drug and serum treatment or by the use of ice bags into the chronic, so called incurable infantile paralysis.

I say "so called incurable" advisedly, because we have treated **and cured** such cases in all stages of development from acute inflammatory meningitis to chronic paralysis of long standing.

In our treatment of acute diseases we never use ice or icy water for packs, compresses, baths or ablutions, but always **water of ordinary temperature** as it comes from well or hydrant. The water compress or pack warms up quickly and thus brings about a natural reaction within a few minutes, while the ice bag or pack continually chills

and practically freezes the affected parts and organs. This
does not permit the skin to relax; it prevents a warm reaction, the radiation of the body heat and the elimination
of morbid matter through the skin.

Suppression During the Fourth and Fifth Stages of Inflammation

Let us see what happens when acute diseases are suppressed **during the stages of absorption and reconstruction.**
If the healing forces of the body gain a victory over the
pathogenic conditions which are threatening the health
and life of the organism, then the symptoms of inflammation, swelling, redness, heat, pain and the accelerated
heart action which accompanies them, gradually subside.
The "debris of the battle field" is carried away through
the venous and lymphatic circulation—the drainage systems of the body.

When in this way all morbid materials have been
completely eliminated, in other words, when conditions
have become normal, then the microzyma will regen-
erate and reconstruct the injured and destroyed cells and
tissues.

If, however, these processes of elimination and reconstruction be interfered with or interrupted before they are
completed, the microzyma will continue to create germs
of putrefaction and the affected parts and organs will not
have a chance to become entirely well or strong. They will
remain in an abnormal, diseased condition, and their functional activity will be seriously handicapped.

The After Effects of Drug or Ice Treated Typhoid Fever

In hundreds of instances I have told patients after a
glance into their eyes that they suffered from chronic
indigestion, malassimilation and malnutrition **caused by**

drug treated typhoid fever; and in every case these records in the eyes were confirmed by the history of the
patient.

In such cases the outer rim of the iris shows a wreath of
whitish or drug colored specks or flakes. I have named
this wreath the typhoid or lymphatic rosary. It corresponds to the lymphatic glands and other absorbent vessels in the intestines. It appears in the iris of the eye
when these structures have been injured or are engorged
with pathogenic matter as a result of drug, ice or surgical
treatment. Wherever this has happened, the venous and
lymphatic vessels in the intestines do not absorb the food
materials, and these pass through the digestive tract and
out of the body without having been properly digested
and assimilated.

During the destructive stages of typhoid fever, the intestines become denuded by the sloughing of their membranous linings. These sloughed membranes give the
stools of the typhoid fever patient their peculiar ''pea-
soup'' appearance. In a similar manner the lymphatic,
venous and glandular structures which constitute the
absorbent vessels of the intestines atrophy and slough
away.

If the inflammatory processes are allowed to run their
normal course under natural treatment through the stages
of destruction, absorption and reconstruction, the microzyma will rebuild the membranous and glandular structures of the intestinal canal perfectly; convalescence will
be rapid; and the patient will enjoy better health than
before the disease was contracted.

If, however, through injudicious feeding, the application of ice or the administration of quinin, mercury, purging salts, opiates, or other destructive agents, Nature's
processes are interfered with, prematurely checked and
suppressed, then the sloughed membranes and absorbent

vessels are not reconstructed, and the intestinal tract is left in a denuded and atrophied condition.

Such a patient may arise from bed thinking he is cured; but unless he is afterward treated by natural methods, he will never make a full recovery. It will take him, perhaps, months or years to die a gradual, miserable death through malassimilation and malnutrition which frequently result in some form of wasting disease, as pernicious anemia or tuberculosis. If he does not actually die from the effects of the wrongly treated typhoid fever, he will be troubled for the rest of his life with intestinal indigestion, consti-pation, malassimilation and accompanying nervous dis-orders.

A Change for the Better

Speaking of typhoid fever, I am glad to say that for this particular form of disease the most advanced medical sci-ence has adopted the Nature Cure treatment, as practiced and taught by the pioneers of Nature Cure more than fifty years ago—that is, **straight cold water and fasting, and no drugs.**

This treatment, which medical science has found so emi-nently successful in typhoid fever, would prove equally efficacious in all other acute diseases if the allopaths would only condescend to try it. It is a strange and curious fact that, so far, they have never found it worth while to do so. Nature Cure physicians know from daily experience in actual practice that the **simple water treatment and fast-ing is sufficient to cure all other forms of acute diseases just as easily and effectively as typhoid fever.** By this is proved the **unity of treatment** in all acute diseases.

For both typhoid fever and tuberculosis, progressive medical men have now entirely abandoned the germ-killing method of treatment. They have found it abso-lutely futile to hunt for drugs and serums to kill the typhoid and tuberculosis bacilli in these, the two most destructive diseases afflicting the human family. They have been forced to admit that the simple remedies of the Nature Cure school, cold water and fasting in typhoid fever and the fresh air treatment in tuberculosis, are the only worth while methods of fighting these formidable enemies to health and life.

If they could be induced to continue their researches and experiments along these **natural** lines, they would attain infinitely more satisfactory results than through their complicated germ hunting and germ killing theories and practices.

The natural treatment of all acute diseases is fully described in Volume II of this series.

CHAPTER XII

SURGERY

THE discoverers of anesthetics are classed among the greatest benefactors of humanity because it is believed that ether, chloroform, cocain and similar nerve paralyzing agents have greatly lessened the sum of human suffering. I doubt, however, that this is true.

Anesthetics have made surgery technically easy and have done away with the pain caused directly by the incisions; but on the other hand, these marvelous effects of pain killing drugs **have encouraged indiscriminate and unnecessary operations to such an extent that at least nine-tenths of all surgical operations performed today are uncalled for.** In most instances these ill-advised mutilations are followed by lifelong weakness and suffering, which **far outweigh** the temporary pains formerly endured when **unavoidable** operations were performed without the use of anesthetics.

I do not wish to be understood as condemning unqualifiedly any and all surgical interventions in the treatment of human ailments. An operation may occasionally be absolutely necessary as a means of saving life.

Surgery is also indicated in cases of injury, such as wounds or fractured bones, in certain obstetrical complications and in other affections of a purely mechanical nature.

In all such cases anesthetics prevent much suffering which can not be avoided in any other way. But anyone who has had an opportunity to watch the prolonged misery of the victims of uncalled for operations will not doubt

122

that anesthesia has been a two edged sword which has inflicted many more wounds than it has healed.

Many physicians have recognized more or less distinctly the uselessness and harmfulness of old school medical treatment. Dissatisfied and disgusted with old fashioned drugging, they turn to surgery convinced that in it they possess an **exact scientific method** of curing ailments. They seem to think that the surest way to cure a diseased organ is to remove it with the knife—fine reasoning for school boys but scarcely worthy of men of science.

I, for one, cannot understand how an organ can be cured when, having been extirpated and preserved in alcohol, it adorns the specimen cabinet of the surgeon.

Destruction or Cure—Which Is Better?

"But," the surgeon retorts, "we do not remove organs from the body unless they have become useless", or he says, "We do not know what this or that organ is good for; therefore we might as well remove it. You will never miss it." What opinion would you form of a watch maker were he to put a spring, a wheel or a balance into a watch unnecessarily? We know that every minute part is of importance, that not a spring, wheel or balance can be removed without throwing the whole out of equilibrium. Are we to believe that the Great Artificer who constructed this wonderful mechanism called man did not know what He was about when He placed the various organs within our bodies? Are we to believe that the parts of the body are of less importance than the springs and balances of a watch?

Not long ago surgeons claimed that the thyroid gland in the neck could be removed without bad effects. They did not know what functions it performed—therefore it could not be of great importance. They found, however, that every person thus operated on died shortly after the operation. Then it was claimed that the spleen could be extirpated. Again it was found that the clever and "successful" operation was invariably followed by the death of the patient. Every now and then we read in the papers of daring and successful removals of stomachs, kidneys, parts of the brain, etc., but God pity the victims of such surgical legerdemain! Their terrible sufferings and miserable endings are never reported.

The inflamed part or organ is usually but a symptom of the disease. The irritants which cause the inflammation, growth or tumor are contained in every drop of blood. They may belong to the scrofulous, psoric, gonorrheal, syphilitic, tuberculous or pathogenic poisons, or it may be some destructive drug poison which occasions the disturbance. Suppressing morbid discharges or cutting out inflamed parts does not eliminate the causes back of the local symptoms.

Nature usually seeks the easiest possible outlet. If you block this the chances are that subsequent conditions will be worse than the first. The procedure is as futile as trying to stop running water by means of a dam. You may for a time arrest the flow but soon it will rise to the level of your obstruction, then you will be obliged to raise the dam. This will happen again and again until the rising flood will invade and damage the neighboring fields and finally break through the artificial barrier, sweeping everything before it.

Everyday experience proves that the foregoing is not mere theorizing nor slandering a noble profession. The claims of the surgeons are not borne out by actual facts. During the past seventeen years there have come under our treatment thousands of patients, both in sanitarium and home practice, whose family physicians had declared that in order to save their lives they must submit to the knife without delay. With very few exceptions these people were cured by us without the use of a poisonous drug, an antiseptic, or a knife.

Several women who years ago were confronted with removal of the ovaries are today the happy mothers of healthy children. Many of our former patients who were treated by old school physicians for acute or chronic appendicitis and were strongly urged to have the offending organ removed, are today alive and well and still in possession of their vermiform appendices. During the last seventeen years I have treated hundreds of cases of appendicitis and so far we have not lost a case and not one has been operated upon.

Other patients were threatened with operations for kidney, gall and bladder stones, fibroid and other tumors, floating kidneys, stomach troubles, intestinal and uterine disorders, not to mention the multitude of children whose tonsils and adenoids were to have been removed. All of these one time ''surgical'' cases have escaped the knife and are doing very well indeed, with bodies intact and in possession of the full quota of organs given them by Nature.

Is it not better to **cure** a diseased organ than to **remove** it? Nature Cure proves every day that the better way is at the same time the easier way.

Thousands of men and women operated upon for some local ailment which could have been cured easily by natural methods of treatment are condemned by these inexcusable mutilations to life long suffering. Many, if not actually suffering pain, have been unnecessarily unsexed and in other ways incapacitated for the normal functions and natural enjoyments of life. Cases of this kind are the most pitiable of all that come under our observation.

When we learn that a major operation has been performed upon a consultant our barometer of hope drops considerably. We know from much experience that the mutilation of the human organism has a tendency to lessen the chances of recovery. Such patients are nearly always lacking in recuperative power.

A body deprived of important parts or organs is forever unbalanced. It is like a watch with a spring or a wheel taken out. It may run, but never quite right; it is hyper-sensitive and easily thrown out of balance by any adverse influence.

The Human Body a Unit

We are realizing more and more that the human body is a homogeneous and harmonious whole, that we cannot injure one part of it without damaging other parts and often the entire organism. As previously stated, cutting in the vital organs means "cutting in the brain". It affects the functions of the nervous system most profoundly.

A physician in Vienna has written a very interesting book in which he shows that the inner membranes of the nose are in close relationship and sympathy with distant parts and organs of the body. He located in the nose one small area which corresponds to the lungs. By irritating this area with an electric needle he could provoke asthmatic attacks in patients subject to this disease. By anesthetizing the same area he could stop immediately severe attacks of asthma and of coughing. Another area in the nasal cavity corresponds to the genital organs. The doctor proved that by electric irritation applied to this area abortions could be produced, and that by anesthesia of the same area in the nose, uterine hemorrhages could be stopped.

Zone Therapy

Another late justification of my warnings against unnecessary surgical mutilations has come through the new system of zone therapy. In this also science reveals in a startling manner the connection and interdependence of the nervous system in its various parts. It shows that irritation and pains in distant parts of the body can be suspended or moderated by pressing certain spots on the fingers.

These and many other facts of experience throw a wonderful light upon the unity of the human organism. You cannot injure one part of it without affecting its entire mechanism.

The evil after effects of surgical operations do not always manifest at once. On the contrary, the surgical treatment is frequently followed by a period of seeming improvement. The troublesome local symptoms have disappeared and after effects of the mutilations have not had time to assert themselves. But sooner or later the old symptoms return in aggravated form, or a new set of complications arises. The patient is made to believe that the first operation was a perfect success and that this later crop of difficulties has nothing to do with the former, but is something entirely new. Or he is assured that the first operation did not go deep enough, that it failed to reach the seat of the trouble and must be done over again.

And so the work of mutilation goes merrily on. The disease poisons in the body set up one center of inflammation after another. These centers the surgeon promptly removes; but the real disease, the venereal, psoric or scrofulous taint, the uric or oxalic acid, the poisonous alkaloids and ptomains affecting every cell and every drop of blood in the body—these elude the surgeon's knife and create new ulcers, abscesses, inflammations, stones, etc., as fast as the old ones are extirpated.

Those who have carefully studied the previous chapters will readily comprehend these facts. They will see that acute and subacute conditions represent Nature's cleansing and healing efforts and that local suppression by knife

or drug only serves to turn Nature's corrective and purifying activities into chronic disease.

I have uttered these warnings, especially against operations on the genital organs, ever since I started to lecture
and write on this subject. Until a few years ago medical
men would have condemned them along with other Nature
Cure teachings as baseless, preposterous and malicious
attacks upon a noble profession. But lo! in the meantime
surgical science has convicted itself of past malpractice.
Surgeons now admit that cutting out the ovaries means
"cutting in the brain", and that women robbed of these
organs become the victims of nervous prostration and of
insanity.

Accidentally it was discovered that the terrible after
effects on the nervous system, mind and emotional nature
following the removal of the ovaries could be avoided if
but a tiny part of the organs, not larger than a pea, were
left. This is now admitted by every uptodate surgeon.
This reveals the immense importance of the secretions of
the ovaries and of the other ductless glands in the economy
of the body. If the secretions of a tiny part of these
organs can exert such a powerful influence upon the
human entity on all three planes of being, why not try to
restore instead of destroying them? That this is easily
possible we have proved in hundreds of such proposed
surgical cases.

The highest art of the true physician is to preserve and
to restore, not to mutilate nor destroy.

As bearing upon this discussion of surgical versus natural treatment, let us consider in detail the allopathic
conception and handling of appendicitis, following this
with the Nature Cure viewpoint and treatment.

CHAPTER XIII

APPENDICITIS

Allopathic Description and Treatment

THE disease is infective, the microorganism usually at fault being the bacillus coli. In most cases the bacillus excites the disease only in presence of some injury to the mucous membrane of the appendix. Fecal concretions or foreign bodies such as pins or grape seeds, may become the exciting causes of inflammation. Even without injury virulent bacilli may in some instances cause inflammation.

Symptoms: In an ordinary attack the initial symptoms are pain of sudden onset, at first over the whole abdomen but soon localized to the right iliac fossa; local tenderness, greatest at McBurney's point; elevation of temperature, furred tongue, constipation and vomiting. The muscles on the right side of the abdomen are rigid and frequently the right thigh is slightly drawn up. A definite swelling can usually be made out in the iliac fossa.

When perforation into the peritoneum occurs, from ulcer or from gangrene, the symptoms are those of collapse, followed by those described under general peritonitis.

Treatment (Allopathic): In all cases of appendicitis immediate operation is the best practice. Although complete recovery is the rule in ordinary cases without surgical interference, yet there is no foretelling that a perforation may not at any moment occur and cause a fatal peritonitis. Operation is of course necessary in the presence of abscess, and where there is generalized peritonitis

129

it affords the only hope of recovery though the hope is but slender.

Medical treatment finds a place only where operation is refused or in anticipation of an operation. In such cases, hot fomentations, enemata to open the bowels, morphia for the relief of pain, fluid diet (chiefly milk), and absolute rest in bed, are the chief means of treatment.

From the Nature Cure Viewpoint

The Prevalence of Appendicitis. Apropos of appendicitis the following story is told of Bill, the newsboy. He had been absent for some months from his favorite haunts and on his return was greeted by his mates with, "Hello, Bill, we hear you had appendicitis". Bill replied, "Huh, appendicitis nothing—didn't have money enough for that —it was just stomach ache!"

Like many another joke this contains more truth than fiction. The time seems near when the vulgar throng will be spoken of not as the Great Unwashed but as the Great Unoperated. Already, at national conventions of physicians, at local gatherings, and in medical journals, the proposition has been made in all seriousness that appendectomy, together with the removal of tonsils, should be performed on all infants "in order to prevent affections of these organs later in life". Why not save our progeny all future trouble by scientifically and dextrously removing their heads?

The idea prevails among the laity that appendicitis is due in most cases to the lodgment of seeds and other foreign bodies in the appendix. This, however, is merely a plausible reply to importunate questioners. As a matter of fact seeds and other foreign bodies are found in less than one percent of all cases operated upon for appendicitis.

Dr. William Osler says in "The Principles and Practice of Medicine", page 520: "Only two instances of foreign bodies in the appendix came under my observation in ten years' pathological work in Montreal; in one there were eight snipe-shot and in another five apple pits."

According to the reports of prominent surgeons, not more than fifteen percent of those operated upon for appendicitis really have this disease. The other eighty-five percent are found to be suffering with inflammations in the cecum, ascending colon or in the small intestines. Sometimes the symptoms are caused by touches of peritonitis. The majority of such ailments are diagnosed and treated as appendicitis. This magic word has attained such hypnotic power over the public mind that it sends the patients, without question or remonstrance, straight to the operating table.

Says the surgeon, "If it is appendicitis only an operation will save the patient's life". This we positively deny and have proved untrue in hundreds of cases. We have never had an operation for appendicitis performed on one of our patients and we have not lost a single case. Our own records and our reports to the Board of Health attest this fact. If our diagnosis be questioned, I answer that we have taken numerous cases which had already been treated for appendicitis by other physicians who claimed that operation was absolutely necessary.

"What of that?" may be the reply, "Why make such a fuss over the useless vermiform appendix. It is but the remains of a part of the human anatomy that has become obsolete in the course of evolutionary development."

The truth is that in the meat eating mammalia the appendix is of very small size or rudimentary. It is more fully developed in herbivorous animals, still more so in fruit eating apes and most of all in man. This flatly contradicts the statement that the appendix is the remains of a defunct and degenerated organ. Instead of deteriorating, in the course of evolution, it has become more perfectly developed.

What, then, are its uses? Dr. MacEwen, an English surgeon who claimed to have performed more operations for appendicitis than any other surgeon in England, has entirely changed front on the question of operating and now warns strongly against it. In an article on the subject he says:

"Observations of the interior of the cecum seen through defects in its walls showed that there were differences in the amount and fluidity of the secretion exuding from its mucous surface. When irritated mechanically the flow of exudate was greater and more fluid. At a variable interval after a meal—one or two hours—peristaltic effects in the colon ensued, resulting in the extrusion of its contents, and shortly after a clear, thick fluid was poured from the secreting cecal surface, and in several instances was seen to exude in considerable quantity from the appendicular orifice.

"On one occasion quite a stream of fluid poured from the appendix just before the chyme began to pass through the ileo-cecal valve. When chyme passed through this valve it did so in small quantities at a time, and there were occasional pauses in which the ileo-cecal valve seemed to close—probably by a reflex action. This fluid from the cecum and the appendix was invariably alkaline.

"Usually the flow from the ileo-cecal valve was slow, the material passing into the cecum in small quantities, which slide over the orifice of the appendix and get smeared by the exudation therefrom, as well as mixed with the exudation from the general cecal cavity.

"It seems as though there were a control over the ileo-cecal valve regulating the amount of material which passes from the small intestine into the cecum. If the valve by any means be rendered patent (open) the contents of the small intestine flow quickly into the cecum and a troublesome escape of semi-digested material ensues. When this agency is interfered with, cecal indigestion occurs, which generally ends in diarrhea of partially digested matter but which occasionally leads to masses of matter gathering in the cecum and causing constipation, with subsequent fermentative action of a kind which is apt to result in irritation of the mucous membrane and appendix.

"The appendix is regarded as a mere diverticulum of the cecum and yet its vascular and nervous supply pertains more to that of the small intestine than that of the colon.

"When it is recollected that the circular muscles of the cecum are continuous with those of the appendix and that the longitudinal cecal bands themselves end on the appendix, it will be understood how easily the nervous apparatus of the appendix may initiate the larger movements of the cecum by first inducing movements in the appendix and how inhibition of these movements may cause cecal disturbance. The same agency, by control of the vascular supply, will regulate the exudation from the appendix, and that in accordance with the impulse received from the small intestine.

"Let us look now to the character and power of this exudation emanating from the appendix and cecum.

"In the first part of the large intestine, and especially in the cecum and appendix, the lymphatic follicles and the glands of Lieberkuhn are very numerous and well developed, the latter being larger, deeper and broader than the corresponding cells in the small intestine and the goblet cells which they contain are larger. and more abundant. This all the histologists admit. So closely are those glands packed together in the cecum that the united surface presented by them is immensely larger than the ridges between the glands, which is all that is left at this place for absorption. So that the histological structure would point to the cecum and appendix being made for digestive purposes rather than for absorption.

"The succus entericus which is exuded by these cells of Lieberkuhn is of great assistance in digestion. So powerful is it that while pancreatic juice alone took six hours to dissolve fibrin and had not even attacked white of an egg in ten hours, the addition of some succus entericus to the pancreatic juice dissolved the fibrin in from three to ten minutes, and the coagulated white of an egg in from three to six minutes.

"Taking the appendix apart, though there are individual differences, one sees in most appendices that the surface is covered with glands of Lieberkuhn in an active state of secretion during health. If one takes the appendix at an average of three and a half inches and lines that space with glands of Lieberkuhn encircling the interior it is seen that a considerable amount of succus entericus may be exuded from that surface alone, more especially as it is abundantly supplied with blood.

"Therefore the secretion of the appendix, viewed alone in this sense would be a valuable aid to digestion, and the excision of that organ, except in a hopelessly diseased condition, manifestly improper."

The Danger Spot in the Intestine

Why the cecum is the danger spot in the intestinal tract is shown in the accompanying sketch. After food leaves the stomach it passes through the small intestine and enters the colon through the ileo-cecal valve. The cecum is a pouch formed by the lower end of the ascending colon, and lies below the level of the entrance of the small intestine into the colon or large intestine.

From the cecum the food residue passes upward through the ascending colon, laterally through the transverse colon, then downward and out through the descending colon, sygmoid flexure, rectum and anus. The reader will perceive that the ascending colon is the only part of the intestine in which the food residue has to move vertically upward. Therefore, by force of gravity or downward pressure, the feces tend to accumulate in the cecum and to

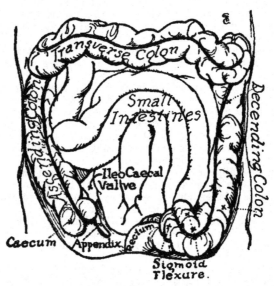

distend it. Therefore it is the dangerous spot of the intestinal tract.

If, in addition to this, there exists a tendency to sluggishness and constipation, the distention of the cecum becomes very marked; food materials accumulate and give rise to fermentation and putrefaction. These morbid processes frequently result in inflammation of the walls of the cecum, colon, adjacent small intestines and sometimes of the appendix.

At other times the fetid accumulations form encrustations. The secretions of the glandular structures in the appendix are then retained, causing congestion, inflammation and abscesses with all the accompanying symptoms of fever, rapid pulse, sharp pains in McBurney's region, etc.—in other words, the set of symptoms which are usually diagnosed as appendicitis.

The True Cause of Appendicitis

From the foregoing it becomes apparent that the great majority of appendicitis cases are caused not by foreign bodies but by chronic sluggishness of the bowels. What does the surgeon do to cure this? Snipping off the appendix does not change the faulty habits and diseased conditions which produce the intestinal indigestion and constipation.

Several years ago a member of the French Academy of Science published statistics showing that appendicitis in different countries and in different classes of society increases in exact ratio with the consumption of meat.

America heads the list in the prevalence of appendicitis and in the consumption of meat. Next in order come England, France and Germany. The disorder is much more prevalent among the well to do, meat eating classes of England, France and Germany than among the semi-vegetarian peasantry.

The principal causes of constipation and therefore of appendicitis are meat, fish and fowl, eggs, coffee and white bread. Flesh foods taken in excess result in putrefaction. This favors the development of bacteria, inflammation and diarrhea, which are followed gradually by atony and atrophy.

We have learned in Volume III of this series that an excess of nitrogenous and starchy foods, fats and sugars form disease producing substances in the human body. These pathogenic substances, together with zanthins of

coffee and tea, first stimulate but later invariably benumb
the organs of digestion. They not only make gall, kidney
and bladder stones but also form incrustations in the
bowels in the cecum and appendix. These accumulations
blockade the secretory glands and membranes, becomes a
source of constant irritation and prevent the assimilation
of food.

Why White Bread Is Constipating

The germs of grains contain two powerful ferments
called diastase and peptase. The diastase changes the
starch of the grain into sugar. The peptase changes the
gluten into proteose and peptones which serves as food
for the growing sprout in similar manner as the yolk and
white of egg serve as food for the chick. In whole grain
flour these ferments are preserved. They take the place
of yeast for the fermenting of the bread, turn the starch
into dextrine and sugar and the gluten into proteose and
peptones, thus predigesting the raw materials in the bread.
They act on the flour in the same way as do the digestive
ferments in the body.

This is the reason why whole grain meal "does not
keep" and why it requires less yeast than does white flour
for lightening. The latter in the milling process has been
deprived of the germ which contains the diastase and peptase and has also been robbed of the hulls which contain
the mineral salts and thus are the carriers of the vitamines. The small particles of hull in the whole grain meal
serve as a natural stimulant to the peristalsis of the bowels.
They loosen the starchy mass in the stomach and intestines and thus favor the penetration of the digestive
juices.

White flour bread, pastry and other products deprived
of the natural ferments and the hulls of the grain tend
to form pasty, lumpy accumulations in the intestines. I

have known horses to die from feeding on white bread. It formed solid lumps which caused intestinal obstruction and thus killed the animals. Is it any wonder human beings develop constipation and appendicitis when they try to digest foods which kill a horse?

When the ordinary constipation producing meat-white-bread-pastry-coffee diet begins to have the usual effects, drugs, laxatives and cathartics are taken to counteract the evil results. In accordance with the law of action and reaction these poisonous stimulants only hasten the chronic atrophy of the intestinal tract.

From the foregoing it becomes apparent that the best preventive of constipation and appendicitis is a well balanced vegetable diet (Vol. II) containing liberal amounts of fruits and vegetables and whole grain cereal products. The seed bearing fruits, which have been accused of causing appendicitis, are in reality the best preventives for this common ailment. This is confirmed by practical experience. Constipation and appendicitis are practically unknown among those who live on a rational vegetarian diet, but the surgeon, well paid for snipping out the appendix, has no time to waste in preaching dietetics even if he knew how.

Treatment of Acute Appendicitis

The treatment of acute appendicitis is the same as that of any other acute inflammatory feverish disease. The essentials are plenty of fresh air, absolute fasting, hydrotherapy and manipulative treatment. While fasting the patient may have as much water with dilute acid fruit juices of natural temperature as he desires.

In every instance where I have been called to attend appendicitis patients who had been under treatment by physicians of other schools, I have had to remove either hot water compresses or the ice bags. Both applications are positively harmful and destructive. I have ex-plained the action of hot water applications in Volume II. Artificial heat may temporarily relieve congestion and pain, but at the same time it keeps up the heat in the affected parts. It does not do anything to promote heat radiation and thus favors abscess formation. The ice treatment chills and freezes the parts and thus checks and suppresses the inflammatory process, leaving the affected parts in a condition of destruction or, in other words, of chronic disease.

Rational treatment lies between the two extremes of heat and ice. It is strange that none of the other schools of healing have discovered this fact. The only natural and rational way is to use for the packs, compresses and ablutions, water of the ordinary temperature as it comes from the hydrant or well. (Vol. II.)

If the patient can endure it, we apply the ordinary abdominal pack or trunk pack, with an additional wet compress over the seat of inflammation. In serious cases throat packs and leg packs may be applied in addition to the trunk pack, in order to reduce high temperature and to divert the blood from the affected parts. If the patient is so sensitive that he cannot endure the application of packs or if the inflammation runs a mild course, compresses wrung out of water fresh from the hydrant may be spread over the abdomen. Of course the compresses must be renewed day and night whenever they become hot or dry.

Neurotherapy, spinal inhibition, magnetic and mental treatment and the indicated homeopathic remedies are valuable aids in the natural treatment. Absolutely essential, however, are **complete rest, fasting, water with dilute fruit juices and hydrotherapy**. They will always be sufficient to produce a perfect cure, provided the natural remedies are applied from the start.

No food of any kind should be taken, not even milk or broth. Nature must be given a free hand. Any kind of food excites the peristalsis of the inflamed intestines, thereby preventing the healing processes. Food particles may become enclosed in the open sores and abscesses, thus causing decay, chronic irritation and "recurrent appendicitis."

After all symptoms have subsided the fasting must be continued for several days, in many cases for a week or more, in order to prevent relapses and chronic after effects. By adhering to these simple rules we have cured every case which has come under our treatment.

Fasting and cold water treatment keep the inflammatory processes below the danger point. They allow free heat radiation, prevent abscess formation and at the same time do not interfere with nature's purifying healing efforts.

What About Abscesses?

The question may be asked, "What would you do if an abscess has already formed?" Even then I would adhere to the same simple, natural treatment and trust to nature rather than to the surgeon's knife. That this is the best policy we have proved in a great many instances. Under right treatment absorption of the abscess will take place or it will break in the direction of least resistance, usually into the cecum, and discharge through the rectum or through an outlet in the abdominal walls. It is wonderful how nature in such cases, under proper treatment, seeks and finds the safest outlet.

However, abscess formation, perforation and peritonitis will not occur if the treatment is natural from the beginning. All these serious complications are the result of hot water treatment, ice packs, premature feeding or cathartics. Several cases have come under my treatment after abscess formation and perforation had taken place. The resulting peritonitis was easily controlled by the natural treatment. Most patients make good recoveries.

The Dangers of Surgical Treatment

In order to reach the seat of infection, abscess or perforation, the surgeon has to cut through many layers of tissues and then into the pus and germ filled locality. Naturally the danger of infecting the peritoneal cavity is very great. Mother Nature herself ingeniously tries to minimize the danger of infection. I have several times heard surgeons remark upon the fact that abscesses are usually surrounded by strong, fibrous walls in order to prevent rupture and to protect the organism from infection. This is an instance of Nature's wonderful provision for the protection of health and life, for emergencies and extraordinary demands upon the organism.

Much as I admire Hahnemann, I cannot agree with him that "Nature is a poor healer". As a rule, the older, the more intelligent and experienced the physician or surgeon, the more he recognizes and trusts "vis medicatrix naturae". The young man fresh from school enthusiastically cuts into everything that presents itself. His elders shake their heads and say, "Wait a while. See what Nature will do."

In my experience one of the most remarkable cases of appendicitis, complicated with general peritonitis, was that of an elderly gentleman whom I shall call Mr. X. He had been suffering from diabetes for a long time. After seeking relief by medical treatment he was converted to Christian Science and for many years he and his family were staunch believers in Mrs. Eddy's teachings. The disease, however, gained on him steadily and in his last extremity he returned to allopathic treatment.

When his physician candidly told him there was no hope, he came to us for examination and advice.

The diagnosis from the iris revealed a large itch spot in the pancreatic area. He remembered distinctly that in his youth he had suffered from a violent attack of "seven year itch" and that this had been suppressed with the usual sulphur-molasses and blue-ointment treatment. Half a year of rational living and natural treatment put him in fine condition. Then, of course, "Science had done it" and he returned to "the flesh pots of Egypt".

Later on Mr. X. visited me occasionally and told me exultingly how Christian Science was making good in every way. "Oh, doctor," he said, "if you only had Science with your Nature Cure, you would be all right. As long as I get a daily treatment from my 'healer' I can enjoy my steaks and chops and hot cakes and coffee without the slightest inconvenience." Laughingly I answered, "Look out, Mr. X., you cannot cheat Nature forever. If you do not behave you will get your spanking in spite of 'Science'." So it proved. About six months later I received a message: "Come at once. Mr. X. is dying."

Attended by a nurse I hurried to his home and found him in a very precarious condition. The trouble had originated in a very serious attack of appendicitis. This had developed into abscess and general peritonitis.

We at once applied the cold packs and spinal inhibition, together with magnetic and mental treatment. Within half an hour we had the condition under control. The terrific pains had subsided and the patient was resting easily. He said, "Doctor, for six days I have been in hell. I have suffered all sorts of pain in my life, but never anything like this. Through it all I had in attendance at one time or another six of the best Scientists in Chicago, but obtained no relief."

After the inflammation had somewhat subsided we tried to flush his bowels by enemas, but without result. We were forced to "trust to Nature". On the twenty-eighth day they moved naturally and freely. From that time on, full recovery was only a matter of careful nursing.

During the first few weeks his entire abdomen was covered with crusty looking eruptions, Nature's cleansing efforts. There has been no return of the trouble. Mr. X. is all right as long as he takes his "Science" with a liberal allowance of Nature Cure.

He told me that after his recovery from diabetes and return to a flesh diet, he suffered from constipation; that at times his bowels did not move for several days, often for a week at a time. When he mentioned this to his "healer" he was told, "Never mind, the Lord will take care of that". The Lord did take care of it until a filthy condition of the system brought about the attack of appendicitis. The healer who expected the Lord to make good for his own lack of common sense had been at one time a well known allopathic physician. Like many other people, not understanding the basic laws of health, disease and cure, he had swung from one extreme to another—from allopathic overdoing into Christian Science "nothing doing".

The Chronic After Effects of Appendicitis

It has been customary with surgeons to advise removal of the appendix even after the patient has recovered from an acute attack, in order to prevent recurrence. If appendicitis is cured in the natural way there will be no chronic after effects. Injudicious feeding, the use of drugs and surgical operations, however, may prevent perfect restoration of the affected parts and result in chronic appendicitis.

I have already explained how food materials may invade wounds and abscesses and may become enclosed in them, causing permanent irritation. If the palm of the hand has a cut we do not continually close and open it; this would interfere with the healing process. The contact of food with the raw surfaces of the inflamed cecum and appendix, in similar manner, interferes with healing.

Surgical extirpation is by no means a guarantee for the nonrecurrence of "appendicitis". I have observed in many cases that the worst attacks came after the removal of the organ. This was due to inflammation of neighboring parts, weakened by the operation.

We have learned that the appendix is a useful organ and that it performs important functions in the processes of digestion. Its extirpation, therefore, involves a serious loss to the economy of the body. We find that people thus operated upon nearly always suffer more from digestive disturbances than they did before. There is more sluggishness, constipation and gas formation. The general tone of health is not as good as formerly and resistance is lowered. Major operations invariably mean a weakening of the tissues and saturation with poisonous antiseptics. The affected parts are, therefore, less resistant to deterioration and disease.

Why Not Nature Cure First Instead of Last?

Mr. A., an Italian barber in our neighborhood, can answer this question from sad experience. His trouble started with chronic constipation and hemorrhoids. To correct the latter he was operated upon, but in consequence the rectum contracted to such an extent that another operation became necessary. Then the bowels did not move at all.

One of the most prominent surgeons in this city performed another operation, removing the appendix. After that, enemas and the most powerful drugs had no effect upon the bowels. As a last resort, other experiments failing, the eminent surgeon made an opening through the abdominal wall into the ascending colon. Through this canal, by means of a silver funnel, warm water was poured into the intestines. This brought the desired result. When the man came to us for advice he had been pouring a pint or more of warm water into the intestine, through the opening in his right side, every day for two years. While this procedure moved the bowels, the wound was beginning to show signs of necrosis and he was told by physicians that there was grave danger of cancer. This finally brought him to Nature Cure.

Under the natural regimen, within four weeks his bowels moved naturally and freely without irrigation from above. They have continued to do so ever since.

At first he did not allow the wound to close, being afraid of a recurrence of his old troubles—constipation and intestinal obstruction. He kept the channel open artificially by dailying inserting the funnel. When the bowels had acted normally for three months he allowed the wound to close. It healed perfectly and there has been no trouble since during a period of several years.

I demonstrated this case before an assemblage of students and professors in a medical college. In the course of my remarks I said: "If it was possible to make the bowels move naturally and freely by four weeks of natural diet and treatment after three years of medical and surgical experimentation, how much easier it would have been in the beginning to accomplish the cure by natural methods! How much suffering, loss of time and money might have been avoided."

CHAPTER XIV

VACCINATION

THE pernicious after effects of **vaccination** upon the system are similar to those of the various serum and antitoxin treatments.

The discovery of vaccination is usually credited to Edward Jenner, an English barber and chiropodist. The doubtful honor, however, belongs in reality to an old Circassian woman who, according to the historian Le Duc, in the year 1672 startled Constantinople with the announcement that the Virgin Mary had revealed to her an unfailing preventive against smallpox.

Her specific was inoculation with the genuine smallpox virus. But even with her (or the Virgin Mary) the idea was not an original one, because the principle of isopathy (curing a disease with its own disease products) was explicitly taught a hundred years before by Paracelsus, the great genius of the Renaissance of learning during the Middle Ages. But even he was only voicing the secret teachings of ancient folklore, sympathy healing and magic dating back to the Druids and Seers of ancient Britain and Germany.

The Circassian seeress cut a cross in the flesh of the applicant and inoculated the wound with smallpox virus. Together with this she prescribed prayer, abstinence from meat, and fasting for forty days. The fasting was undoubtedly the most efficient part of the treatment.

Since at that time smallpox was a terrible and widespread scourge, the practice of inoculation was carried all over Europe. At first the operation was performed by women and laymen; but when vaccination became popular and people showed themselves willing to pay for it, the **doctors** began to incorporate it into their regular practice.

Popular superstitions run a course very similar to that of epidemics. They have a period of inception, of virulence and of abatement, and they die as a natural result of their own falsities and exaggerations.

It soon became evident that inoculation with the virus did not prevent smallpox, but on the contrary frequently caused it; and therefore the practice gradually fell into a state of innocuous desuetude, to be revived by Edward Jenner about one hundred years later in a modified form. He substituted cowpox virus for smallpox virus.

Modern allopathy, in applying the isopathic principle, gives **large and poisonous doses** of virus, lymph, serums and antitoxins; while homeopathy, as did ancient mysticism, applies the isopathic remedies **in highly diluted and triturated doses only.** From England vaccination gradually spread over the civilized world and during the nineteenth century the smallpox disease constantly diminished in virulence and frequency until today it has become comparatively rare.

"Therefore vaccination has exterminated smallpox", say the disciples of Jenner.

Is that really so? Is vaccination actually a preventive of smallpox? This seems very doubtful, especially since the advocates of vaccination themselves do not believe it. "What," I hear them say, "we do not believe in our own theory?" Evidently you do not, my friends. If you believe that vaccination protects you against smallpox why are you afraid of "catching" it from those who are not vaccinated? If you are thoroughly protected, as you claim to be, how can you catch the disease from those who are not protected? Why do you not allow the other fellow to have his fill of smallpox and then enjoy a good laugh on him? The fact of the matter is you know full well that **you are not safe,** that you can catch the disease just as readily as can the unvaccinated.

In the years of 1870-71 smallpox was rampant in Germany. Over 1,000,000 persons had the disease and 120,000 died. Ninety-six percent of these had been vaccinated, and only four percent had not been so "protected". Most of the victims were vaccinated, once at least, **shortly before they took the disease.**

In 1888 Bismarck sent to the governments of all the German states an address in which it was admitted that **numerous eczematous diseases, even those of an epidemic nature, were directly attributable to vaccination,** and that the origin and cure of smallpox were still unsolved problems.

In this message to the various legislatures the chancellor said: "The hopes placed in the efficacy of the cowpox virus as a preventive of smallpox have proved entirely deceptive." Realizing this to be a fact, most of the German governments have modified or entirely rescinded their compulsory vaccination laws.

"But," our opponents insist, "you cannot deny that smallpox has greatly diminished since the almost universal adoption of vaccination."

Certainly the disease has diminished. But the plague, the "Black Death", cholera, the bubonic plague, yellow fever and numerous other epidemic pests which until recently occasionally decimated entire nations have also diminished and, in fact, nearly disappeared.

Not one of these epidemics was treated by vaccination. Why, then, did they abate and practically disappear? The answer is, because of the more general adoption of soap, bathtubs, all kinds of sanitary measures, such as plumbing, drainage and ventilation, and because of more hygienic modes of living.

Many of us remember how yellow fever raged in Havana during the Spanish occupancy. Within a few months after the energetic Yankees took possession and gave the filthy city a good scouring, yellow fever had entirely disappeared—without any yellow fever vaccination.

The question is now in order, why of all the dreaded plagues of the past smallpox alone survives to this day?

The answer is, **because of vaccination.** If scrofulous and syphilitic poisons were not artificially kept alive in the human blood by vaccination, smallpox by this time would be as rare as cholera and yellow fever. In this connection it must be remembered that all vaccines, serums and antitoxins are alive with morbid (bacterial) microzyma.

Thanks to the oft-repeated compulsory vaccination of every citizen, young and old, we as a nation have become saturated with smallpox virus. Is it any wonder that occasionally this latent taint breaks out in acute epidemics?

Undoubtedly the almost universal systematic contamination and degeneration of vital fluids and tissues, not alone with vaccine virus but also with many other filthy serums, antitoxins and drug poisons, accounts in a large measure for the steady increase of tuberculosis, cancer, syphilis, infantile paralysis, insanity, and a multitude of other chronic destructive diseases unknown among primitive people that have not come in contact with the blessings (?) of "syphilization", mercurialization and vaccination.

By weakening the system's reactionary powers against **one** disease, its reactionary powers against **all** diseases are weakened. In other words, creating in the body a form of chronic smallpox by means of vaccination favors the development of all kinds of chronic diseases.

Quit sowing the seed, gentlemen, and you will cease reaping the harvest. By the suppression of syphilis and by means of vaccination **you are perpetuating smallpox.**

What has **syphilis to do with smallpox?** They are very closely related and similar in appearance, symptomatology, and in their effects upon the organism. Dr. Cruwell, after having studied the subject thoroughly, says: "Every vaccination with so-called cowpox virus means syphilitic infection. Cowpox is not a disease peculiar to cattle; it is always due to syphilitic or smallpox infection from the diseased hands of human beings. Cowpox pustules have been found only on the udders of milk cows which came in contact with human hands. Cattle roaming in pasture and prairie have never been affected by cowpox, nor have domesticated steers and oxen. If this disease were a disorder peculiar to cattle both sexes would be equally affected. Jenner's cowpox was caused by the diseased hands of the syphilitic milkmaid, Sarah Nehnes."

Vaccination of healthy children and adults is often followed by a multitude of symptoms which cannot be distinguished from syphilis, viz., characteristic ulcers and eczematous eruptions, swellings of the lymphatic glands, atrophy of the mammary glands in women and in girls above the age of puberty, etc.

This explains the constantly growing demand for "bust foods" and "bust developers". A perfectly developed bust has become so rare that many hundreds of "beauty doctors" and of business concerns that make a specialty of developing the flat-bosomed realize thousands of dollars annually. One firm in this city, and a small concern at that, has made from $2,500 to $5,000 a year and has over 10,000 names on its constantly increasing list of patrons.

It is reasonable to assume that almost without exception these 10,000 women had been vaccinated from one to three times before the age of puberty. When this is realized, and the fact that vaccination dries up the mammary glands is taken into account, is it not time to pause and consider?

The figures of this one small concern represent the report of only one out of several hundred such firms doing business in all parts of the country.

Some years ago a disease similar to smallpox broke out among the sheep in certain parts of Scotland. As a pre-·ventive the sheep were vaccinated. **In the course of a few years it was noticed that a great many ewes were unable to nourish their lambs.** With the discontinuance of vaccination this phenomenon disappeared.

Do not these facts help to explain why over fifty percent of **human** mothers are now incapable of nursing their babies?

Looking Forward

At present the trend of allopathic medicine is undoubtedly toward the serum, antitoxin and vaccine treatment. Practically all medical research tends that way. Every now and then the medical journals and the daily papers announce new serums and antitoxins which are claimed to cure or create immunity to certain diseases.

Suppose the research and practice of medicine continue along these lines and are generally accepted; or, as the medical associations would have it, are forced upon the public by law. What would be the result? Before a child reached the years of adolescence it would have had injected into its blood the vaccines, serums and antitoxins of smallpox, hydrophobia, tetanus (lockjaw), cerebro-spinal meningitis, typhoid fever, diphtheria, pneumonia, scarlet fever, etc., etc.

If allopathy were to have its way, the blood of the adult would be a mixture of dozens of filthy bacterial extracts, disease taints and destructive drug poisons. The tonsils and adenoids, the appendix vermiformis and probably a few other parts of the human anatomy would be extirpated in early youth under compulsion of the health departments.

Which is more rational and sensible: the endeavor to produce immunity to disease by making the human body a swill pot for the collection of all sorts of disease taints and poisonous antiseptics and germicides, or to create **natural immunity** by building up the blood on a normal basis, purifying the body of morbid matter and poisons, correcting mechanical lesions and by cultivating the right mental attitude? Which one of these methods is more likely to be disease building—which health building?

Just imagine what human blood will be like in coming generations if this artificial contamination with all sorts of disease taints and drug poisons is to be forced upon the people.

Why Vaccination Is Responsible for Many Acute and Chronic Diseases

We have learned that every inflammatory and feverish disease is a purifying and healing effort of Nature. In accordance with this fundamental law of cure the organism tries to throw off through the sores and ulcers produced by vaccination not only the recently inoculated smallpox virus, but also all other hereditary and acquired disease taints and systemic poisons.

Allopathic physicians recognize this law and apply it in their practice. When they make use of "counter irritants" such as blisters, "Spanish flies", belladonna plasters, leeches, cupping, etc., they endeavor to remove the internal congestion and inflammation by creating artificial inflammation on the surface of the body. The Nature Cure physician accomplishes the same thing in a more natural way by wet packs and cold ablutions.

The pus-like mass exuding from the smallpox pustule

or the vaccination sore contains the virus not only of smallpox, but also of scrofula, psora, tuberculosis, syphilis, gonorrhea, anthrax, lumpy jaw and whatever else there may be of hereditary and acquired disease taints and poisons in the system of the animal or human from which the virus is secured. Such filthy exudates are inoculated into the bodies of millions of innocent victims of a "scientific" superstition.

When vaccination is followed by scrofulous or syphilitic eruptions, itchy eczemata, swellings of glandular structures, etc., in children or adults who before vaccination were free from these disorders, then people who ought to know better wonder where it all came from, "where the poor child caught it".

Fathers and mothers have been accused by the family physician of transmitting syphilis to their offspring when, as a matter of fact, the foul vaccine poison which the doctor himself had inoculated into the child was the real cause of the suspicious sores and eruptions.

An Interesting News Item

The following item appeared in several Chicago dailies on Monday, May 17, 1909, but was then promptly suppressed by those most deeply interested in upholding the vicious practice of vaccination.

"Washington, D. C., May 16.—(Special)—The bureau of animal industry made public today a report which fastens the blame for the recent outbreak of the hoof and mouth disease in Michigan, New York, Pennsylvania and Maryland on a contaminated strain of vaccine, which originally came from a foreign country. The disease was traced by inspectors of the bureau to calves that had been used for the production of virus.

"The report sets forth the belief that the epidemic of hoof and mouth disease, which it cost the federal government $300,000 to suppress, was started by these calves at Detroit after they had been used for the production of vaccine on the H. K. Mulford farms. The vaccine virus with which they were inoculated was imported from abroad (Germany) by Parke, Davis and Company, Manufacturing Chemists, and contained an infection of hoof and mouth disease. These calves, after having been used in propagating vaccine, were sent on October 16th to the Detroit stockyards to be disposed of in the market.

"On October 20th three carloads of cattle from points in Michigan reached the Detroit stockyards and some of them were put into pens that had been occupied by the vaccine calves four days previously. Some of these cattle were sold for slaughter at Detroit, while the remainder were shipped to Buffalo and some were reshipped to Danville and Watsontown, Pa., where the disease was first observed some days later. The disease spread to various places in Pennsylvania and New York and to one locality in Maryland.

"Three separate series of experiments were made. Young cattle and sheep were inoculated with the vaccine virus obtained from both firms. The hoof and mouth disease was produced in these animals by the use of vaccine of the same strain obtained from both sources, while other strains of vaccine tested gave negative results.

"The disease was also transmitted from one animal to another through several series, in two instances being transmitted by natural modes of infection.

"Light Shed on New England Outbreak"

"The investigation also indicates that the outbreaks of hoof and mouth disease in New England in 1902-03 were due to contaminated vaccine of Japanese origin imported by the Mulford Company."

Why are facts of such vital importance to the public and to our farmers suppressed after the first publication in the daily press, and who is responsible for such suppression? To this day the public is left with the impression that the cause of these epidemics is unknown.

The first point of significance in this interesting report is that the H. K. Mulford Company, of Glen Olden, Pa., used a certain smallpox vaccine virus which was contaminated with hoof and mouth disease. In May, 1908, vaccine of this strain was used for the production of vaccine virus crops from calves. The procedure is as follows: The flanks of the animals are shaved, then long slits are made in the flesh. The seed vaccine is rubbed into these wounds. The poison thus inoculated spreads through the entire organism of the animal and thoroughly contaminates blood and tissues. Then Nature endeavors to eliminate the morbid taints. The wounds in the sides of the animals become ulcerating sores. The revolting mass exuding therefrom is then prepared for the market and is used throughout the country for purposes of vaccination.

The report further explains how it was positively proved that this particular vaccine virus was contaminated with the taints of hoof and mouth disease. In consequence of this, thousands of children in all parts of the country were infected through vaccination not alone with vaccine virus but also with the cattle disease. While it is true that this virulent disease may not always prove fatal to human beings, inoculation with the virus means certain contamination with another disease taint which in the human body works insidious destruction in some other form, as scrofula, tuberculosis, eczema, etc.

Why, in the name of humanity, should we take chances of contaminating the blood of the innocent with these and other vile poisons? It has been repeatedly claimed by different investigators that cowpox is not a disease peculiar to cattle, that oxen have never shown it; that it appears only on the udders of milch cows and originates there in syphilitic infection from the hands of venereal milkers. This statement seems plausible; but whether it can be proved or not, the fact remains that cowpox as well as smallpox is a disease taint which should not be artificially propagated in the blood of human beings.

Never was humanity cursed by a blacker superstition than this, that disease can be cured and health maintained by the absorption of virulent poisons. Rational therapeutics will always **eliminate** morbid matter, not **introduce** it into the system. Without doubt, smallpox would be as extinct in civilized communities as are the plague, cholera and yellow fever, if it were not kept alive and propagated by the morbid microzyma of vaccine virus. The trouble with these disease taints, as with the inorganic poisonous drugs, is that in most cases their work of destruction in the human organism is so slow and insidious that the after effects are not always traced to their true source. The anemia, leukemia, scrofulosis, tuberculosis, eczematous eruption or ulceration of a syphilitic character are hardly ever traced by the usual methods of diagnosis to vaccination, antitoxin, serum or tuberculin treatment. Here also diagnosis from the iris of the eye is frequently of inestimable service in disclosing true cause and effect.

Another startling revelation is contained in this report. **One would expect that the calves whose blood and tissues have been so thoroughly saturated with vile disease taints would be killed and their bodies consumed by quicklime. Instead, horrifying as it may be, they were sent back to the stock yards to be sold for meat in the market!** It seems incredible that for a few paltry dollars these wealthy and respected firms who pose as protectors and preservers of public health would foist these vile carcasses upon an unsuspecting public as foodstuff. Such commerce in vaccine veal undoubtedly has been going on for years and is probably flourishing still. All we have to say to our friends, the meat eaters, is *"bon appetit!"*

While the last epidemic referred to was in progress I lectured on this subject before the "Open Forum" society in the Masonic Temple, Chicago. I read the above quoted extracts from the "Tribune" and other Chicago dailies and explained the sinister significance of these reports. After I had finished my lecture a gentleman arose from the audience and asked permission from the chairman of the meeting to tell what he knew about the subject under discussion. His remarks were reported by a stenographer in the audience and ran as follows:

"I am one of the men sent here by the government in Washington to subdue the epidemic of hoof and mouth disease in the stockyards. I am aware that the facts concerning the causes of former epidemics, as related by Dr. Lindlahr, are well known to the government officials in Washington, and there is strong evidence that the present outbreak (1914) originated in a similar way. It is also true that the facts were and are withheld from publication at the instigation of powerful influences who are interested in upholding vaccination.

"My present experience in the stockyards has also proved to me that Dr. Lindlahr is right when he says that every acute disease is a healing effort of nature and if treated right will make for cure. This is true even of hoof and mouth disease.

"As you probably know, several hundred very valuable high bred animals on exhibition in this city became infected by the disease and were condemned to be killed. On account of their great value it was decided to make an effort to save them. Animals affected by this disease die from starvation, since the tongue becomes so inflamed and swollen that they cannot take food. We placed this bunch of cattle in a high, airy loft, kept them clean and fed them through rubber tubes stuck into their throats. After the inflammation in the mouth had run its course every one of them got well."

Is this not a remarkable confirmation of Nature Cure philosophy and practice? After this test had been made and proved the easy curability of the disease, why were the farmers not informed of this wonderful discovery of a natural cure? Why was the ruthless and unnecessary destruction of thousands of valuable animals continued? The diseased animals would have done still better if instead of food nothing but water had been given. Undoubtedly anthrax and other animal diseases could be cured in the same natural manner.

After Effects of Vaccination

A few years ago I happened to attend a public clinic in a Chicago medical college. One of the subjects was a

strong, healthy looking girl about eighteen years of age.
Although in general appearance she was the picture of
health, her left hand was horribly affected. The thumb
and parts of the inner surface of the hand were disfigured
by destructive ulceration. These sores had begun to
develop about six months previous to the clinical examination.

The health record of the patient's family was excellent.
For generations past there had been no sign of scrofulous
or tuberculous diseases on either side. Father, mother
and a number of sisters and brothers were living and in
good health. The young woman herself had never in her
life suffered from a serious ailment.

All attempts of the assembled students and professors
to find a cause for this condition of the patient's hand were
futile. I approached the young woman and on looking
into her clear blue eyes discovered that the region of the
iris corresponding to the upper left arm disclosed a large
dark spot inclosed by whitish lines—in iridiagnostic terminology, a "closed lesion".

Closed lesions in the iris correspond to scar tissue in the
body. As long as a wound, ulcer or catarrhal defect is
open and active in the body it is represented in the iris
by dark, blackish shadings interwoven with white lines.
When the lesion in the body is healed and closed, this
fact is recorded in the iris by the appearance of a whitish frame around the dark shading. Thus a closed lesion
in the iris stands for the formation of new tissues or "scar
tissue" in the body.

In the case of this young woman the region in the iris
corresponding to the diseased hand exhibited the whitish
clouds of acute inflammatory activity. The scar sign in
the region of the upper arm and the peculiar ulceration
of the hand suggested to me at once the idea of vaccination.

I addressed the patient as follows: "Not long ago, say within a year or two, you have been vaccinated on the left arm, and this was followed by a large, ulcerating vaccination sore. The ulcer was cured by medicinal treatment."

Somewhat surprised, she confirmed every part of my diagnosis. She related that a year before, while coming from Europe on an ocean liner, she had been vaccinated, and that a large, ugly vaccination sore had developed which was very slow to heal and was treated for some time with "salves from the drug store".

Thereupon I gave it as my opinion to the clinic that vaccination and the suppression of the resulting ulceration were the direct cause of the tuberculous sore on the hand. My diagnosis created considerable hilarity among the allopathic students in attendance at the clinic. It seemed ridiculous to them that anything so thoroughly orthodox as vaccination could in any way be held responsible for such serious after effects, especially since the sore on the hand did not appear until six months after vaccination.

Replying to this objection, I asked why luetic sores on the body and in the throat sometimes do not appear until six months or longer after the suppression of the original lesion on the genital organs has taken place, or why cancer does not develop in an organ affected by suppressed itch (as revealed in the iris of the eye) until many years after this suppression.

To these questions orthodox medical science has, of course, no answer. The dean of the college, a liberal and discerning man, who was conducting this particular clinic, showed himself susceptible to an understanding of my side of the controversy by saying: "Dr. Lindlahr has given at least a very pertinent and plausible theory of this phenomenon, while you yourselves have given no explanation whatever. Therefore, gentlemen, please curb your hilarity and do some thinking.''

Epilepsy Caused by Vaccination

Another interesting case confirming the creation of chronic disease through vaccination is that of Mr. B., who came to us for consultation and treatment several years ago. For four years he had been suffering from a bad form of epilepsy. He had consulted with and been treated by the best physicians in Chicago, but without the slightest relief.

When I first examined his eyes I noticed in the region of the iris corresponding to the left arm a heavy, whitish streak which contained two black spots. This indicated an injury to the limb and a subacute condition.

I asked the patient whether he had at any time sustained an injury to his left arm. This he denied, but after considerable quizzing he finally answered: ''When the epileptic attacks come on I feel a pain in the left hand; this travels up the arm, and when it reaches the elbow I fall unconscious.''

Examining again the lesion in the iris, I asked, ''Has the arm been vaccinated?''

''Yes,'' he answered, ''about four years ago.''

''Did it create much of an ulceration?''

''Yes, the arm was swollen twice its size and I was confined to bed for two weeks.''

''Did the epileptic attacks commence about that time?''

''Yes, I never had any previous to that vaccination.''

Many people are suffering today from serious chronic affections of body and mind resulting from vaccination. These chronic after effects usually develop so slowly and insidiously that no one thinks of tracing them to their true cause. The diagnosis from the iris of the eye has exposed and explained many of these "obscure" cases. Allopathy, when asked about the causes of these and other serious chronic ailments, has but one answer, "Nobody knows". And it assumes that nobody **can** know.

We explain cause and effect in this case as follows:

The filthy vaccine virus injected into the arm caused blood poisoning. If the resulting ulceration had been allowed to discharge freely and fully, and if elimination had been encouraged by proper treatment instead of being hindered and suppressed by poisonous antiseptics, the blood would have purified itself and there would have been no chronic after effects. But the wounds were healed prematurely by the usual antiseptic treatment and the system was left in a poisoned condition.

The diagnosis from the eye has revealed the fact that the epileptic center is located in the cerebellum, just behind the left ear. In this connection it is significant that the **left** arm had been vaccinated.

From the description of this case it clearly follows that the treatment had to be eliminative. The toxins had to be eliminated from the arm and from the system as a whole by pure food diet and all other methods of natural treatment.

During the sixth week, in accordance with the law of crises, a sore developed on the left arm in the same location where four years before vaccination had caused the ulceration. This healing crisis verified in a remarkable manner our diagnosis of the case and also the lesions in the iris.

The discharges from the arm acted as a fontanelle and safety valve through which Nature eliminated the suppressed disease taint. After the sore had remained open for a few weeks, it healed spontaneously. Since that time Mr. B. has not had another epileptic attack. He has married and is now the happy father of several healthy children. He lives in the neighborhood of our Chicago institution and is an enthusiastic booster for Nature Cure.

According to medical science he was a "defective" who should have been sterilized for the protection of society.

In our Nature Cure practice we have met with many cases of tuberculosis, eczema, pernicious anemia, lockjaw, paralysis, etc., which were directly traceable to vaccination. Anti-vaccination societies annually report thousands of such cases, statistically recorded.

Last year (1908) in Chicago **two** deaths resulted from smallpox, while **hundreds** of serious diseases and fatalities could be traced directly to vaccination. In most cases, however, the detrimental after effects of vaccination are so insidious and obscure in their development that they are not easily traceable to their true cause—the smallpox or cowpox virus and its morbid microzyma. It remains for Iridology to bring proof positive of these hidden sequelae.

Shortly after vaccination the color of the iris darkens, especially so in the regions corresponding to the digestive and respiratory organs. This darkening of the color is noticeable also in cases where, according to common parlance, vaccination has "not taken". In fact, these persons often show in their eyes more serious vaccination defects than those in whom the regular sores developed.

What does this mean? Simply that, in strict accordance with the fundamental laws of cure, **those who develop vaccination ulcers expel through these the vaccine poison.** But children or adults who are already encumbered with scrofulous conditions and who are possessed of weak vitality are frequently not able to develop the purifying ulcerations. Consequently they retain the poisonous infection, which results in greater deterioration of the organism in general and of the digestive and respiratory tract in particular.

Worst of all, these unfortunate victims of a scientific superstition are vaccinated **again and again.** The more the filthy poison is injected into their circulation the less it "takes", to the great mystification of the medical fraternity.

Some time ago Chicago papers reported the case of a girl who had been vaccinated **ten times** "without results", and then the child was refused admission to the public schools because she was not properly vaccinated. Ten times the vaccination had not taken. How did the doctors know it had not taken? It is just possible that **internally** it had taken too much. Diagnosis from the eye would probably have revealed its harmful effects. A little child inoculated ten times with cowpox virus! Is not that sufficient to completely saturate the little body with the filthy poison?

To recapitulate: Those with whom vaccination "takes" best, retain the least of it. They succeed in expelling the virus. But those with whom, apparently, it does not "take" may be the ones most seriously affected. The darkening of the iris of the eye in the areas of the digestive and respiratory tracts fully explains why vaccination is accountable for all kinds of chronic disorders of stomach, intestines, liver, bronchi, throat and pharynx, why catarrhal affections and decay of the tonsils, pernicious anemia and tuberculosis have increased in every country where compulsory vaccination has been introduced.

Diphtheria Caused by Vaccination

Diphtheria, as we now know it, was first described by Bretonneau, a physician of Tours, France, in the year 1820, some time after the general introduction of vaccination. Many conscientious and competent investigators claim that diphtheria in its present virulent form and frequency was not known before that time, and that diphtheria has faithfully followed vaccination from one country to another, wherever the smallpox virus has polluted the blood and lowered the vitality of the people.

Whether or not we accept these radical charges in their entirety, this much is certain: diphtheria in its modern virulent form and frequency of occurrence was unknown in any country before the universal practice of vaccination.

This phenomenon is explained by the fact that **the vaccination virus,** according to evidence furnished by the diagnosis from the eye, **locates and concentrates principally in the mucous membranes of the digestive tract and of the bronchi, throat, and pharynx.** It lowers the vitality of these parts and charges them with the poisons contained in the cowpox virus. At the first opportunity Nature makes an heroic effort to throw off the scrofulous encumbrance. This opportunity may present itself when the next cold is "caught"—then the ordinary tonsilitis, pharyngitis or laryngitis may become a genuine diphtheria. **We can readily conceive how the morbid soil created by the vaccine virus may produce microzyma which will develop into diphtheria germs.**

Sometimes we are told that this or that child had diphtheria, although it had never been vaccinated. To this we answer that many times the diagnosis of diphtheria is incorrect. It is always safer for the physician to diagnose the more serious disease. If the patient recovers, the glory is so much greater. **Since the microzyma of diphtheria germs flourish in the bodies of vaccinated children and the air is polluted with them, why should not an unvaccinated child here and there succumb to the infection, especially when the blood of our children is** hereditarily contaminated with the vaccine virus back to the third and fourth generation?

It is amusing to note the confusion of the public as well as of the scientific mind on the most simple questions of hygiene. The millionaire owner of a dozen palatial quick lunch rooms in Chicago is so deeply concerned about the health of his patrons that at stated intervals, under penalty of discharge, he compels every one of his employees to submit to vaccination; yet he sees no wrong in dealing out to his customers wholesale dyspepsia and nervousness in the form of cheap sausage, white bread, pie, tea and coffee. Where one person dies from smallpox, probably thousands die from the effects of the deadly quick lunch counter.

Anterior Poliomyelitis Caused by Vaccination

About two years ago I received the following letter from New Braunfels, Texas:

"Dear Doctor: Allow me to submit to you the case of a young friend of mine. The patient is about twenty-one years of age. He was never sick in his life except with measles, and always enjoyed the best of health. A month ago on account of a supposed smallpox case in the neighborhood general vaccination was enforced. Mr. A. directly after vaccination developed blood poisoning, and this resulted in cerebrospinal meningitis. This disease left him completely paralyzed from hips down. Water and feces have to be removed artificially.

"Home doctors say to move him would mean sure death. What do you think about the case, and would you advise us to bring him to you for treatment?"

To undertake the treatment of such a case seemed a risky thing, especially when the patient had to be transported over a thousand miles. The doctors at home had pronounced the case absolutely incurable and transportation out of the question. Being entirely convinced of the efficiency of our simple, natural methods, I did not hesitate, however, to assume the responsibility and wrote to the father to that effect.

Within a week after the arrival of my letter the patient came to our sanitarium. He was completely paralyzed from the navel down. The urine had to be removed by the use of a catheter, and the bowels were emptied with great difficulty by enemas. Anterior poliomyelitis was undoubtedly caused in this case by inflammation set up by vaccine virus, though the doctors at home tried to put the blame for this terrible predicament on the fall from a horse three months previous to the onslaught of the disease. Mr. A. assured me positively that this fall did not injure him in any way. Having been a cowboy, he had had a great many falls more serious than this one. This case, being of comparatively recent origin, yielded with marvelous rapidity. Within two weeks after his arrival at the sanitarium his bladder and bowels moved freely and he began to regain the use of his legs. After nine weeks he had regained full control over his lower limbs and began to talk of going home. However, I advised him to remain longer in order to pull the roots,— that is, to eliminate the last remains of the filthy vaccine virus from his system.

Personal Experience

From the foregoing it will have become apparent that smallpox, like every other infectious disease, is **a filth disease**, that its microzyma grow in morbid soil only and that the smallpox eruptions are a sign of rapid elimination of hereditary and acquired disease taints.

A good dose of smallpox may rid the system of more

scrofulous, tuberculous and syphilitic poisons than could otherwise be gotten rid of in a lifetime. Therefore small-pox is certainly to be preferred to vaccination. The one means the **elimination of chronic disease,** the other the **making of it.**

"Cheap talk!" someone says. Not so, my friend! This is not mere talk. I was put to the test in the case of my own family and therefore speak from personal experience.

My oldest boy was born at a time when both parents were heavily encumbered with hereditary and acquired disease conditions. At birth he weighed only two and a half pounds and his chance for life seemed very slight. The eyes were of a blackish blue, especially the outer portion of the iris, and this gradually condensed into a heavy scurf rim owing to the fact that Nature's cleansing efforts in the form of skin eruptions were promptly sup-pressed with talcum powder and other home "remedies".

For the first five or six years of his life our boy was a weak, sickly child, having one after another all of the common infantile ailments. However, we soon learned to treat these by natural methods and he was **not** vacci-nated.

One day suspicious looking eruptions appeared, which soon spread all over his body. I called in two allopathic physicians to verify my own diagnosis of smallpox, which they did unqualifiedly.

We applied the **natural** treatment, which consisted of strict fasting, colon flushing and cold water applications. The child was kept day and night in wet packs—strips of linen wrung out of water of natural temperature and covered with flannel bandages—which were changed whenever they became hot and dry. The face also was kept covered with cooling compresses. In addition to this treatment I gave the indicated high potency homeo-pathic remedies.

There was hardly a spot on the boy's body that was not covered with sores. However, constant renewal of the cold packs kept the temperature below the danger point and greatly alleviated the insufferable itching peculiar to the disease.

My wife, her sister and myself by turns slept in the same room with the child without the least fear of infection, and although we had not been vaccinated since childhood we remained unaffected by the "contagious disease".

The wet packs, of course, greatly furthered the processes of elimination and the disease practically ran its course in ten days. From that time on the sores healed rapidly and nothing remained to indicate the "ravages" of the disease but a telltale mark over the left eyebrow and a few similar scars on the boy's body. These also have now entirely disappeared.

Under this natural treatment of the disease convalescence was rapid and complete, and soon after the eyes became much clearer and much lighter in color.

Since his recovery from the smallpox this boy has never had a sick day. He is now in his twenty-first year and well developed physically and mentally.

As far as I could learn there was not another case of smallpox in Chicago and vicinity at the time of the boy's illness. If the infection theory be true, from whom did he "catch" the disease and why did not one of the many persons living in the same house become infected? My answer is: This acute eliminative process was Nature's way of purifying the little body of inherited scrofulous and other disease taints.

With our younger boy we had a somewhat similar experience. When one year of age he was taken with a severe attack of cerebrospinal meningitis. Every half hour or so the little body was bent backward in the dreadful convulsions peculiar to this disease.

Again I had two allopathic physicians make a diagnosis of the case so that in future the facts might not be questioned. In both cases nothing but the natural treatment was used.

For nine days it seemed a hopeless fight to everyone who had occasion to witness it. Then both eardrums "broke" and discharged pus and blood. From that time on all symptoms began to clear up rapidly, and on the eleventh day the child first took food. Previous to that he had not received so much as a drop of milk—nothing but cold water rendered slightly acid with fruit juices. (This had also been the only "food" administered in the smallpox treatment of the little patient's brother.)

For six weeks the discharge of pus and blood from the ears continued unhindered and unchecked, but rather encouraged and promoted by natural methods of treatment and by the indicated homeopathic remedies.

As in the case of the older boy, the physical and mental improvement and development following the disease were most gratifying. While before this eliminative crisis the child had seemed somewhat slow and dull, after the recovery he was much brighter and more active physically and mentally.

Compare with this splendid recovery and subsequent improvement in general health the results that follow the orthodox drug and serum treatment of spinal meningitis. According to statistics a high percentage of the patients die and the survivors are either paralyzed or suffer from some other form of chronic after effects.

I claim that these children eliminated in a few weeks more scrofulous and psoric taints and poisons from their systems through smallpox and meningitis than would have been possible otherwise in many years, or perhaps in a lifetime.

CHAPTER XV

THE DIPHTHERIA ANTITOXIN

IN this country the antitoxin treatment for diphtheria is still in high favor, whereas in Germany where it originated many of the best medical authorities are abandoning its use on account of its **doubtful** curative results and **certain** destructive after affects.

According to the enthusiastic advocates of this treatment among the allopathic physicians in this country, the antitoxin is a ''certain cure'' for diphtheria. But how is this claim borne out by actual facts?

The Health Bulletins sent regularly to every physician in the City of Chicago by the City Health Department show a considerable number of deaths from diphtheria treated with antitoxin.

Considering the great uncertainty of medical statistics, I am not prepared to affirm whether or not the antitoxin treatment actually has reduced the mortality percentage of this disease, but we of the Nature Cure School claim and can prove that the hydropathic treatment of diphtheria insures a much lower percentage of mortality than does any other treatment.

The crucial point to be considered in this connection is: **What are the after effects of the different methods of treatment?**

This is a very important matter. I make the following claims:

(1) That the antitoxin, being itself a most powerful poison, may be and often is the direct cause of paralysis, or of death due to heart failure.

(2) That diphtheria treated with antitoxin may be and often is followed by paralysis, heart failure, or lifelong invalidism of some kind after the patient has recovered from the diphtheria itself.

(3) That these undesirable after effects of diphtheria do not occur when the disease is treated by natural methods, but that they are the result of the antitoxin treatment and of its suppressive effect upon the disease.

To prove these claims I submit the following facts: I have in my possession clippings from newspapers from various parts of the country stating death had followed the administration of the diphtheria antitoxin for prevention or "immunization", that is, where the individual had been in good health at the time the antitoxin was given.

Several cases of this kind created quite a sensation in Germany about twenty years ago. Dr. Robert Langerhans, superintendent of the Moabit Hospital in Berlin, a strong advocate of the antitoxin treatment and also of vaccination, had been one of a committee of three appointed by the municipal government of the German metropolis to investigate the efficiency of the diphtheria antitoxin. As a result of his findings he had recommended its free distribution to the poor of the City of Berlin.

Not long thereafter the doctor's cook suddenly developed sore throat and was sent to the hospital. It was thought to be a case of diphtheria, and the doctor, to protect his little son, one and one-half years old, against possible infection, administered antitoxin. Shortly afterward the child developed symptoms of blood-poisoning and died of heart-failure within twenty-four hours.

It is customary in Germany to insert a death-notice in one of the local newspapers and to invite the friends of the family to the funeral. In his announcement in the columns of the "Localanzeiger", Dr. Langerhans stated explicitly **that his little son had died after an injection of diphtheria antitoxin for immunization.**

Another similar case is that of Dr. Pistor, a prominent Berlin physician, whose little daughter contracted a slight inflammation of the throat. The child was given an injection of antitoxin and this was followed by a severe and protracted illness.

Very significant, in this connection, are certain utterances of Dr. William Osler in his "Practice of Medicine". He says on page 150:

"Of the sequelae of diphtheria, paralysis is by far the most important. This can be experimentally produced in animals by the inoculation of the toxic material produced by the bacilli. The paralysis occurs in a variable proportion of the cases, ranging from 10 to 15 and even to 20 per cent. It is strictly a sequel of the disease [Of the disease treated with antitoxin?], coming on usually in the second or third week of convalescence. . . . It may follow very mild cases; **indeed, the local lesion may be so trifling that the onset of the paralysis alone calls attention to the true nature of the disease.** . . .

"The disease is a toxic neuritis, due to the absorption of the poison. . . .

"Of the local paralysis the most common is that which affects the palate. . . . Of other local forms perhaps the most common are paralysis of the eye muscles. . . . Heart symptoms are not uncommon . . . Heart-failure and fatal syncope (death) may occur at the height of the disease or during convalescence, even as late as the sixth or seventh week after apparent recovery."

It appears to me that the mystery of these sequelae can easily be explained. It is certain that a mere sore throat, not serious enough to be diagnosed as diphtheria, cannot produce paralysis or heart-failure; but we know positively that the antitoxin can do it and does do it.

The cases that Dr. Osler refers to undoubtedly received the antitoxin treatment, because it is administered on the slightest suspicion of diphtheria, nay, even to perfectly healthy persons "for purposes of immunization".

Then is it not mostly likely that these "mysterious after effects" are caused rather by the highly poisonous anti-toxin than by the "sore throat"?

In my own practice, I am frequently consulted by chronic patients whose troubles date back to **diphtheria** "cured" by antitoxin. Among these I have met with several cases of idiocy and insanity, with many cases of partial paralysis, infantile paralysis and **nervous** disorders of a most serious nature, also with various other forms of chronic destructive diseases.

In the iris of the eye, the effect of the antitoxin on the system shows as a darkening of the color. In many instances, the formerly blue or light-brown iris assumes an ashy-gray or brownish-gray hue.

One of my secretaries had clear blue eyes up to her tenth year. About that time she had several attacks of diphtheria and a severe "second" attack of scarlet fever which were treated and "cured" under the care of an allopathic physician. She does not remember whether she was given antitoxin, but recalls that her throat was painted and her body rubbed with oil and that she had to take a great deal of medicine. Since that time her eyes have turned brown. They show plainly the reddish-brown spots of iodin in the areas of the brain, the throat, and other parts of the body.

The effect upon the iris of the eye would be very much the same whether the attacks of diphtheria had been suppressed by antitoxin or by the old-time drug treatment. A significant fact in this connection is that, while Mrs. C. was with us, following natural methods of living and under the effects of the treatments which she took regularly for several months, her eyes became much lighter and in places the original blue became visible under the brown. The nerve rings in the region of the brain, which were very marked when she first came to us, became less defined. Corresponding improvement took place in her general health and especially in the condition of her nerves.

In regard to my claim that **undesirable after effects do not occur under treatment by natural methods,** I wish again to call attention to the fact that for fifty years the Nature Cure physicians in Germany have proved that their treatment of diphtheria is **not** followed by paralysis, heart failure or the different forms of chronic, destructive diseases.

This has been confirmed by my own experience in the treatment of diphtheria and other serious acute ailments.

Now comes Dr. Tenison Deane of San Francisco, a representative in good standing of the allopathic school of medicine, and confirms my contention concerning the true cause of diphtheria, in a book entitled "The Crime of Vaccination". The author subscribes himself as follows:

"A Police Surgeon, S. F.; Asst. Surgeon, S. F. Emergency Hospital; Adjunct to Chair of Surgery, Post-Graduate School of Medicine, U. of Cal.; Assistant Skin and Venereal Clinic, S. F. Polyclinic; Prof. Surgery, Pacific Coast Regular College of Medicine; lecturer on Surgical Pathology and Bacteriology, etc."

His attainments entitle him to a respectful hearing from believers in vaccination. His strong statements should brace up the weak kneed opponents of vaccination and determine them to protect themselves and their families at any cost from the fearful hazards of this unspeakable practice. We are taught by him, as the reader must note, that the immediate effects of vaccination are as nothing compared with the latent and lasting ones.

The extracts from the book herein bring home vividly the appalling fact that health boards and vaccination doctors are systematically sowing disease of the worst forms. The author well calls vaccination "the greatest mistake ever made, the enormity of which can never be equaled nor half appreciated". In Chapter IV is the following:

History of a case: "The author will relate this case, as one that started him in his investigation and study on the subject. June 15, 1889, the author was spending his vacation on the ranch of a wealthy farmer in the northern part of the State of California, fifteen miles from the nearest town, a farm of 10,000 acres and no immediate neighbors. The farmer had a wife and seven children. The foreman, a negro, had a wife and five children. None had ever been vaccinated. Six of them were selected and vaccinated by the author:

> The farmer's wife, age 43 years.
> The farmer's daughter, age 6 years.
> The farmer's son, age 8 years.
> The farmer's son, age 25 years.
> The negro foreman, age 46 years.
> His son, age 12 years.

"All the rest were left out and were not afterwards vaccinated. On August 1, 1890, the farmer, his wife and five children went to the mountain ranch forty miles away, taking with them the foreman, his wife and five children. There had been no diphtheria in the town nor any in their neighborhood. The mountain ranch was an uninhabited virgin pine forest district with pure water, where they took up their camp.

"August 24th an epidemic of sore throat and canker sores developed among the children. Farmer's daughter, seven years old; son, nine years old, and the foreman's son, thirteen years old, developed very serious throat and constitutional symptoms and were taken to the home ranch, where a doctor was sent for. Diphtheria was the diagnosis. The farmer's wife also developed diphtheria. All the rest who had not been vaccinated cured rapidly of their sore throats. The farmer's daughter, seven years old, died. The farmer's son, nine years old, did not recuperate for one year. The farmer's wife, 44 years old, had paralysis and sequelae, which lasted over one year.

The foreman's son, thirteen years old, became very weak and did not return to normal health.

"In 1893, the farmer's son, 29 years old, died in Los Angeles, Cal., of tubercular intestinal trouble; in 1900, the foreman, at 57 years of age, died of tubercle or cancer of larynx; in 1902, the foreman's son, 25 years old, died of tuberculosis; in 1909, the farmer's wife, 63 years old, died of cancer; in 1911, the farmer's son, 30 years old, died of tubercular meningitis.

"The farmer died of old age. All the rest are living and in perfect health, nor have they ever been vaccinated. No tuberculosis has shown in any of those living, nor is there any family history of tuberculosis. All who were vaccinated in 1889 are now dead.

"In view of the foregoing, what unutterable silliness the present anti-tuberculosis crusade and the elaborate 'cancer research'. On these, millions are spent yearly, countless dumb brutes are tortured, and human beings are experimented on with every nostrum conceivable to 'modern medicine'. And all the while the state manufacture of cancer and consumption (as well as other diseases) goes briskly forward.

"It is a tragedy, repeating itself year after year, as people are forced to be vaccinated on various pretexts. School attendance, the chance to earn your bread, to go about your business—these are made dependent on getting vaccinated whenever health boards see fit to order."

Thus, one after another, the "preposterous" claims of Nature Cure philosophy are verified by "new discoveries" of scientists of the "regular" school of medicine.

A Reply to My Critics

My discussions of the germ theory of disease and of the vaccine, serum and antitoxin treatment, in a series of articles entitled "Harmonics of the Physical", published in "Life and Action", called forth a great deal of adverse criticism from physicians of the allopathic school of medicine.

Dr. E., one of these critics, refers to certain passages in my article in the October-December, 1912, number of "Life and Action", and comments upon them by quoting Drs. Osler and Andrews in favor of the antitoxin treatment in diphtheria and by giving his own opinion on the subject. He concludes his arguments as follows:

"I am a subscriber to this magazine and have also had my sister's name put on the mailing list. She has a little boy about two years old. Now, suppose she should read that article of Dr. Lindlahr's and as a result refuse to permit the use of antitoxin, and if the boy should get diphtheria, with a fatal issue as a result, I could hardly feel gratified over the fact that I had placed that reading matter at her disposal. I fully appreciate the fact that such an unhappy result might easily ensue in some one or more of the families who read 'Life and Action' and look upon its columns as a source of the truly higher light."

Perhaps Dr. E. has not read one of Dr. Osler's latest and strongest utterances, his unqualified endorsement of natural methods of healing, in the Encyclopedia Americana, quoted on page 289 of this volume.

Nature Cure in Germany

That it is possible to cure all kinds of serious acute diseases by drugless methods of healing, has been proved by Nature Cure practitioners in Germany, nearly all of whom were men who had never attended a medical school. For over half a century many thousands of them have been practicing the art of healing, in all parts of Germany. With hydrotherapy and the other natural methods they have treated successfully typhoid fever, diphtheria, smallpox, appendicitis, cerebrospinal meningitis and all other acute diseases.

It is a significant fact that, in spite of the most strenuous opposition and appeal to the lawmaking powers on the part of the regular school of medicine, the lay practitioners could not be prevented from practicing the natural methods of treatment in law and police ridden Germany.

On the contrary, during the last few generations there have been practicing in that country at all times an ever increasing number of Nature Cure practitioners, most of them laymen. This freedom of Nature Cure practice is entirely due to the success of its methods.

And this success has been demonstrated in spite of all kinds of opposition and attempted restriction. While the Nature Cure practitioner is permitted to treat those who come to him for relief, he does not have the right, as does the allopath, to cover his mistakes with six feet of earth. If one of his patients dies, a doctor of the regular school of medicine has to be called in to testify to the fact and issue the death certificate.

Thus the "lay practitioners", the "Nature Cure physicians", were and are at present constantly exposed to the strictest critical supervision by the allopaths, and if the latter can make it appear that a patient has died because the natural methods were inefficient or harmful, the lay practitioner can be prosecuted for and convicted of malpractice or manslaughter.

But in point of fact, while a number of these lay practitioners were brought before the courts, in no instance could the actual harmfulness of the methods employed by them be proven, and so many grateful patients testified in their favor that no juries could be found to convict them. The natural methods of treatment became so popular that as a matter of selfpreservation the younger generation of physicians in Germany had to "fall in line" with the Nature Cure idea in their practice.

Since Dr. E. so strongly questions the efficacy of our

methods, I may be permitted to say something about my own professional experience.

Nature Cure in America

During the last seventeen years I have treated and cured all kinds of serious acute diseases without resorting to allopathic drugs and in no instance was surgery used. In a very extensive practice I have not, in all these years, lost a single case of appendicitis, typhoid fever, smallpox, scarlet fever, etc., and only one case each of cerebrospinal meningitis, lobar pneumonia and diphtheria. These facts may be verified through the records of the Health Department of the City of Chicago.

After consideration of the foregoing statements, I leave it to my readers to judge whether the Nature Cure philosophy is inspired by blind fanaticism and based upon ignorance and inexperience, or whether it is justified in the light of scientific facts advanced by the regular school of medicine itself and as demonstrated by the wonderful success of the Nature Cure movement in Europe, which in its different forms has attained world wide recognition and adoption.

There is a popular saying, "The proof of the pudding is in the eating". The following letter explains itself:

Dear Dr. Lindlahr:—

You may remember that last winter, Mrs. White and I attended your Sunday afternoon lectures in the Schiller Building. Those lectures were an education—I might better say a revelation and an inspiration.

On the 11th of November last, our boy, aged thirteen years, was taken ill with diphtheria. I called at your office and asked your advice. You replied: "You know what to do—wet packs, no food except fruit juices, colon flushing, spinal treatment and— *no antitoxin.*"

We called an osteopathic physician, who at once sent a specimen from the boy's throat to the city laboratory, where it was pronounced diphtheria. A physician from the Board of Health came and quarantined us and inquired if we had used the antitoxin treatment. When Mrs. White replied ''No,'' he said: ''I suppose you know that the percentage of deaths of those who do not have it is very high.'' She said: ''Yes, I know, but we do not intend to use it.''

The boy had all the acute symptoms, was drowsy, with headache, and on the second day his temperature went to 105 degrees. We applied the wet body pack and by night had reduced his temperature to 100 degrees. With the aid of the osteopathic treatment, which he had each night, the boy slept well all through his illness. On the fifth day, the membrane spread from his throat to his nose, and his temperature rose again; but the wet body packs again reduced it so that it was never again over 100 degrees.

The boy was bright, his mind was clear, he was able to read, and after the first week was able to play chess with his mother. The only unfavorable symptom he had at all was an irregular pulse. He took no medicine and no food except fruit juices. We used occasionally the tepid water enema. On the tenth day he took a little lamb broth, but refused it the next day, and again asked for fruit juices. It was not until two weeks had passed that his appetite returned and he began to eat. He lost flesh, but did not lose strength in the same degree—he was able to go to the bathroom each day unaided.

On the 21st day, the osteopathic physician sent a specimen to the city laboratory which they pronounced ''positive'', and the city physician found it necessary to take as many as four or five additional specimens before he pronounced him free from the diphtheria germs. The boy was not released from quarantine until five weeks had passed.

During all this time his only attendant was his mother and the osteopathic physician who came daily. The boy has fully recovered and has suffered no bad results that often follow such diseases.

In contrast to this experience of ours, I would like to cite the case of a neighbor of ours whose little girl died of the disease under the antitoxin treatment. She recovered from the diphtheria, but her heart failed and she died suddenly. They had a regular M. D. and a trained nurse. Her mother took ill, but recovered. The father told me that their drug bill alone amounted to $75.

We want to express to you our gratitude for the knowledge and confidence that you have so freely given to us, and you are at liberty to make whatever use of this letter you desire.

Sincerely yours,

1443 Cuyler Ave., Chicago, Ill.   HINTON WHITE.

This letter and numerous similar evidences prove that my claims and assertions regarding the curability of diphtheria by natural methods are not extravagant nor untrue. In this case, as in many others, I gave directions for treatment verbally and over the telephone without having seen the patient personally.

The experience of Mr. White's neighbor is another proof of the fatal effect of the antitoxin treatment. The antitoxin "cured" the diphtheria but—the child died!

Once more I repeat: Hydropathic treatment will give equally good results in appendicitis, meningitis, scarlet fever and all other forms of acute diseases. If this be a fact, why should not my colleagues of the allopathic school of medicine give natural methods a fair trial, the more so since in Germany, even among the physicians of the allopathic school, these methods are fast superseding the use of serum and antitoxin? Is it not worth while, when thus might be avoided the "mysterious sequelae" referred to by Dr. Osler, and the many cases of chronic invalidism which he does not connect with the disease or its treatment?

CHAPTER XVI

SUPPRESSIVE SURGICAL TREATMENT OF TON-SILITIS AND ENLARGED ADENOIDS

IN many of the larger cities of our country, physicians and nurses, by order of state boards of health, are regularly visiting the public schools. They examine the children, gather statistics and give hygienic and medical advice to teachers and parents.

The idea is a good one and will be productive of much benefit, **provided** that the advisors themselves are rightly informed. Unfortunately, this is not always the case.

A large proportion of school children are nowadays afflicted with chronic tonsilitis and with inflammation or hypertrophy of the adenoid tissues, which are located in the nasal pharynx.

When these abnormal conditions are discovered by the visiting physicians or nurses, the parents are at once advised to have the offending tonsils and adenoids removed. Frequently we are consulted by parents about the advisability of having these operations performed. In the following paragraphs I shall endeavor to answer all such inquiries.

The tonsils are excretory glands. Nature has created them for the elimination of impurities from the body. Acute, subacute and chronic tonsilitis accompanied by enlargement and cheesy decay of the tonsils means that these glands have been habitually congested with pathogenic matter, **that they have had more work to do than they could properly attend to.**

These glandular structures constitute a valuable part of

181

the drainage system of the organism. If the blood is poisoned through overeating and faulty food combinations, or with scrofulous, venereal or psoric poisons, the tonsils are called upon along with other organs to eliminate these morbid taints. Is it any wonder that frequently they become inflamed and subject to decay? What, however, is to be gained by destroying them with iodin or extirpating them with the surgeon's wire snare?

Were the drains in your house too small to carry off the waste, would you seal or remove them? This, however, is orthodox philosophy of the medical schools as applied to the management of the human body.

The surgeon says: "The swollen tonsils and adenoids are closing up the nasal breathing passages; especially at night the child breathes through the mouth. This may cause all kinds of chronic ailments, deformations of the chest, changes in the facial expression, sometimes marked alteration in the mental condition and in certain cases stunting of physical and mental development.

"The removal of the tonsils will bring quick relief from all these troubles; why then delay the simple operation?"

True, "drying up" or extirpating the tonsils will give instant local relief. The voice and the breathing will become unobstructed; the Eustachian tube, which forms an air passage from the mouth to the ears, will open and the parents and the family physician will rejoice over the splendid results of the "trivial" operation. But, as usual, they take into consideration the first effects only; the secondary and lasting ones are regarded and treated as new diseases.

In case of any morbid discharge from the body, whether through hemorrhoids, open sores, ulcers or through tonsils, scrofulous glands, etc., a fontanelle has been established to which and through which systemic poisons make their exit. If such an outlet be blocked by medical or surgical treatment, the morbid matter is forced to seek another escape or else accumulate somewhere in the system.

Fortunate is the patient when such an escape can be established, because in whatever part of the system morbid excretions, suppressed by medical treatment, concentrate, there will be found the seat of chronic disease.

After the tonsils have been extirpated, the morbid matter which they would have eliminated usually finds the nearest and easiest outlet through the adenoid tissues and nasal membranes. These now take up the work of vicarious elimination and in their turn become hyperactive and inflamed.

Sometimes it happens that the adenoid tissues become affected before the tonsils. In that case, also, relief is sought through surgical treatment, and then the process is reversed; after the adenoids have been removed, the tonsils become inflamed.

When both tonsils and adenoids have been extirpated, the nasal membranes in turn become congested and swollen. Often the mucoid elimination increases to an alarming degree and frequently polypi and other growths appear; or the turbinated bones soften, swell and obstruct the nasal passages. Thus again the patient becomes a "mouth breather".

But in vain does Nature protest against local symptomatic treatment. "Science" refuses to learn from her.

When the nasal organs take up the work of vicarious elimination, the same mode of treatment is resorted to. The mucous membranes of the nose are now swabbed and sprayed with antiseptics and astringents or "burned" by cauterizers, electricity, etc. The polypi are cut out, and frequently parts of the turbinated bones as well, in order to open the air passages.

Now, surely, the patient must be cured. But, strange to say, new and still more serious troubles arise. The posterior nasal passages and the throat now become affected by chronic catarrhal conditions and there is much annoyance from phlegm and mucous discharges dropping into the throat. These catarrhal conditions frequently extend to the mucous membranes of the stomach and intestines.

When the drainage system of the nose and of the naso-pharyngeal cavities has been seriously impaired, the impurities must either travel upward into the brain or downward into the glandular structures of the neck and thence into the bronchi and the tissues of the lungs.

If the trend be upward to the brain, the patient grows nervous and irritable or becomes dull and apathetic. Frequently a child is reprimanded, even punished for laziness and inattention when it is not responsible. In many instances the morbid matter affects certain centers in the brain and causes nervous conditions, hysteria, St. Vitus' dance, epilepsy, etc. In children the impurities frequently find an outlet through the ear drums in the form of pus discharges. This frequently averts inflammation of the brain, meningitis, imbecility, insanity, or infantile paralysis.

I have frequently traced serious attacks of mastoiditis (inflammation of the mastoid cells behind the ears) directly to extirpation of the tonsils and adenoids. In such cases the surgeon trephines the skull and treats the mastoid cells with antiseptics, thereby suppressing the inflammation. I have never applied such destructive treatment and have never lost a case.

If the trend of the suppressed impurities and poisons be downward, it often results in the hypertrophy and degeneration of the lymph glands of the neck. In such cases the suppressive treatment, by drugs or knife, is again resorted to. The scrofulous poisons, suppressed and driven from the diseased glands in the neck, now find lodgment in the bronchi and lungs where they accumulate and form a luxuriant soil for the propagation of the bacilli of pneumonia and tuberculosis.

In other cases the vocal organs become seriously affected by chronic catarrhal conditions, abnormal growths and, in later stages, by tuberculosis. Many a fine voice has been ruined in this way.

Prevention and Cure

Prevention and cure of all these ailments lie not in local symptomatic treatment and suppression by drugs or knife, but in the rational and natural treatment of the body as a whole.

First of all, antitoxins, vaccines and serums must be avoided because the morbid microzyma of these filthy preparations breed scrofulous conditions and all sorts of chronic diseases. Then the diet must be regulated in accordance with the principles of natural dietetics. The little bodies must be hardened and elimination through the skin must be stimulated by air and sun baths and cold water treatment. Massage and neurotherapy must correct the spinal lesions, remove the pressure from nerves and blood vessels and increase the activity of the internal organs of elimination.

Under such general constitutional treatment, elimination will be distributed evenly, the membranes and the glandular structures of nose and mouth will be relieved and will resume their normal structure and function. Herein lies the natural, rational cure for tonsilitis, adenoid vegetations, mouth breathing and kindred diseases.

That this is not mere vagary is proved by the fact that in hundreds of cases of tonsilitis and kindred ailments treated during the last seventeen years, we have not in a single instance resorted to surgical treatment. As the regeneration of the system through natural living and treatment proceeded, the affected organs became normal.

CHAPTER XVII

WOMAN'S SUFFERING

"WOMAN'S physical suffering" is so universal among civilized races that the very phrase has become proverbial. That woman should suffer untold agonies, especially during the menstrual period, at the climacteric and in childbirth, is looked upon as unavoidable and as a matter of course.

The fact that the women of primitive races in Africa, in South America, in the Arctic circle and on our western plains are practically exempt from these chronic ailments indicates that the cause of such acute and chronic ailments must lie in artificial habits of living and in the unnatural treatment of disease common among civilized races. Many are beginning to recognize these truths. For many is dawning a new era, when knowledge will free woman from physical suffering as it has freed her from other bondage.

The various forms of female troubles usually begin to manifest at the age of puberty, when normal menstruation should commence. In many instances this flowering of the sex life is abnormal from the beginning. Frequently it is irregular, very painful, too profuse, too scanty or entirely absent. These conditions in themselves do not constitute disease but are the effects of abnormal disease conditions in the system, caused by abnormal prenatal influences, by wrong management of the infant, unnatural habits of living later in life, and by the suppressive treatment of acute and subacute diseases.

Violations of Nature's laws, which constitute the pri-

187

mary cause of disease, have been described in other parts
of this volume. Prominent among them are wrong food
combinations overrich in negative, disease producing substances which clog the system with pathogenic materials.
This leads to defective elimination through skin, intestines and kidneys. The impurities then seek an outlet
through catarrhal conditions of the tonsils, adenoids and
nasal passages. These eliminative efforts of Nature are
promptly suppressed by the extirpation of tonsils and
adenoids and by the destruction of the nasal membranes
by means of poisonous antiseptic sprays and cauterizers.

When the impurities congest the lymphatic glands in
the neck these are extirpated by the surgeon's knife.
When, as described in Chapter XI of this volume, the
pathogenic materials try to eliminate through the membranous linings of the bronchi and the digestive tract in
the form of colds, catarrhs, purgings, etc., the work of
suppression is persistently continued until the organism
in selfdefense endeavors to eliminate these systemic poisons through the membranous linings of the genital organs.
This it endeavors to accomplish through the menstrual
discharge and through leukorrhea.

Nature has established the menstrual function for the
fructifying of the ovae, but she uses it also for the purification of the organism from pathogenic matter. If these
impurities happen to be of a very irritating, poisonous
nature they may cause inflammatory and painful conditions of the genital organs.

**Leukorrhea, like all other catarrhal conditions of the
organism, is a form of vicarious elimination of systemic
poisons.** As explained in other parts of these writings,
back of all forms of catarrh is systemic poisoning. The
system is overloaded with pathogenic matter and the
organs of elimination through overwork and continued
irritation have become so clogged and inactive that they

cannot keep a clean house. Then one of two things will happen. Either Nature must find an outlet for the morbid encumbrances through the membranous linings of the internal tracts, or life will become extinct through the accumulation of impurities in the body.

What is the orthodox medical treatment of leukorrhea? Antiseptic and astringent douches and curetment. These methods not only suppress Nature's purifying efforts, but are in themselves positively destructive. The poisonous antiseptics and astringents saturate the tissues not only of the womb but also of the neighboring organs, benumb and paralyze natural function and disorganize normal structure. In other words, they embalm the tissues and in time destroy the sex function.

This is well to be considered in connection with the growing propaganda for birth control which consists largely in douching with poisonous germ killers and astringents. Such unnatural practices will result in time in permanent sterility, degeneration of tissues and tumor formation. The retention of the impurities which Nature is trying to get rid of through menstrual and leukorrheal discharges results in acute and chronic inflammations of the uterus, Fallopian tubes and ovaries. These symptoms are in turn suppressed, if possible, by the same form of local treatment.

Curetment in itself is a barbarous mutilation of the cradle of life. The surgeon dilates the neck of the womb, inserts sharp hooks in its interior and drags the womb to the mouth of the vagina. He then scrapes the internal walls of the organ with a spoonlike instrument, tearing off the tender membranes in order to force Nature to build new ones. He does not stop to consider whether, under the diseased condition of the system, they will be any better than the old ones.

The entire procedure is unnatural and barbarous. The

pulling of the womb to the entrance of the vagina may result in continued weakening and stretching of the ligaments and muscles supporting it. Frequently it causes the rupturing of adherent tissues and internal hemorrhages. The cureting itself often results in serious injury to the tender membranes of the uterus. It happens not infrequently that the spoon of the curet penetrates the walls of the uterus or badly lacerates the openings of the Fallopian tubes.

The retention of the impurities caused by cureting may set up serious subacute or chronic inflammation, ulceration and hardening of the internal tissues of the womb, and chronic metritis, only too often resulting in the formation of polypi, benignant or malignant tumors. Obstruction of the Fallopian tubes frequently follows, and this interferes with the discharge of the ovae from the ovaries into the uterus. Many women have told me that they were curetted in order to facilitate conception. What an absurdity! There is no better way to incapacitate the womb for conception than by cureting. In menstruation and in childbirth Nature opens the blood vessels of the womb from within out, through a natural process. The dilatation of the neck of the womb and the scraping away of internal membranes is done forcibly in violation of Nature's ways.

Women have come to us in the most wretched condition of health, ruined physically, mentally and spiritually through a dozen or more curetments. One sufferer had been curetted twenty-one times, hoping every time that "this would be the last one" and "bring about good health." How would this be possible, considering the normal structure and natural functions of the generative organs?

When acute and chronic inflammations, ulcers, abscesses, endurations, adhesions and tumors develop as the result of long continued suppressive treatment, what then? Surgical extirpation of the affected parts and organs is held to be the only remedy. Is this cure? **It makes a cure forever impossible.** How can that which is mutilated and extirpated be cured? The surgeon will answer, "When the organs have become useless through acute or chronic inflammation and through the development of adventitious tissues and new growth, they might just as well be removed."

Nature Cure physicians are proving in everyday practice that acute and chronic inflammations can be cured, that adhesions can be dissolved and tumors absorbed, providing they be not too large, by natural methods of living and treatment. Which is more rational and humane—to destroy, or to cure and preserve?

Shortly after I began to practice, there was brought to me for examination a woman whose ovaries were in a condition of acute inflammation due to gonorrheal infection from her husband. He believed that he had been cured of the infectious disease by allopathic suppression. In fact, he had been assured by the physician who treated him that it was perfectly safe for him to marry. Soon after marriage, however, his wife developed acute inflammation of the vagina and this extended to the ovaries. Before she came to me, arrangements had been perfected for the surgical removal of the ovaries. The operation was to take place on the following day. They had been assured that this was absolutely necessary in order to save the woman's life.

After a consultation with me she was placed under our care and treatment. At the end of the fifth month the woman was discharged as cured. Since that time she has had three children. They were brought up in harmony with the teachings of Nature Cure and are in perfect health and splendidly developed physically and mentally. The mother wrote to me a few years ago, "Doctor, thanks to Nature Cure I am the happiest woman in the world. I cannot express to you sufficiently my gratitude for saving me from the dreadful fate of an unsexed woman."

Imagine what her life would have been if the ovaries had been extirpated! The very foundation of life destroyed, deprived of the joys of motherhood, physically, mentally and emotionally defective and abnormal, destined to life-long suffering, doctoring and to premature death or possibly the insane asylum. This woman was instrumental in saving a young allopathic nurse from the same fate under practically the same circumstances. During the last eighteen years we have treated and cured, at a low estimate, more than a thousand cases of acute and chronic inflammations of the genital organs. In not a single instance were the affected organs extirpated.

Prolapsus and Displacements of the Genital Organs

The orthodox medical treatment for these abnormal conditions also consists of surgical operations, shortening of the round ligaments of the womb, cutting adhesions which hold the womb in an abnormal position, stitching of the womb to the frontal walls of the abdomen, etc. This sort of treatment is purely local, symptomatic and suppressive—not in any way curative.

The sagging of the womb and other genital organs, sometimes resulting in protrusion of the neck of the womb from the mouth of the vagina, is caused by general weakness of the system, particularly by a weakened, relaxed and prolapsed condition of the stomach and intestines. It is the sagging down of the stomach and intestines, usually loaded with old accumulations of fecal matter, which pushes down the genital organs into the bottom of the pelvis. This interferes with the free movement of the womb and crowds it into abnormal position resulting in the bending or kinking of the little organ upon itself forward or backward, and in abnormal pressure upon the bladder or the rectum. These adhesions and flexions of the womb may interfere with menstrual or leukorrheal discharges or with the entrance of the procreative germ. Such abnormal pressure on the genital organs may also result in irritation, inflammation and the formation of adhesions and tumors.

These conditions may be aggravated by subluxations, curvatures or anchylosis of the spinal vertebrae which produce pressure on the nerves passing out between the vertebrae, irritation and inflammation of the digestive and pelvic organs, resulting in weakness and atrophy and in a flabby, relaxed condition of the digestive and genital organs.

It is a fact known to every observing physician that over fifty percent of all civilized women have some kind of misplacement of the genital organs and that only a comparatively small number of these cases result in local disturbances, indicating that misplacement alone does not always create serious trouble.

It is ridiculous to assume that the small, flabby uterus of an anemic woman can obstruct the rectum and cause serious disease; but it is an excellent talking point, as effective in bringing victims to the operating table as appendicitis with its fairy tales of seeds and foreign bodies in the vermiform appendix.

Unhygienic Clothing

One of the contributing causes to woman's suffering is unhygienic clothing. Much has been said about the evil effects of the corset and of high heeled shoes. It is true that conventional ways of dressing have done as much to harm woman's health as smoking and drinking have to harm man's. Thanks to the influence of Nature Cure and physical culture movements, tight lacing has gradually been abandoned, at least until fashion may again decree the barbarous practice. But even the custom of wearing the skirts suspended from the waist line by constricting bands or belts is sufficient to cause unnatural compression of and pressure on the many organs lying within the circumference of the waist line. Such constriction always interferes more or less with the circulation of the blood, lymph and nerve currents between the upper and lower parts of the body, thereby causing congestion in the organs of the abdominal and pelvic cavities; and congestion when not properly treated is, as we have learned, the first step toward inflammation and its manifold destructive consequences.

All clothing should be worn suspended from the shoulders. Waists designed for this purpose can now be had in all up to date stores. The skirts are fastened to these waists by hooks or buttons instead of being tightly belted around the waist. A normally developed body, not weakened by the corset or waistband habit, does not require metal or bone stays to support it, notwithstanding claims to the contrary by the devotees of fashion. All artificial bracing and supporting of the body is weakening instead of strengthening.

Pessaries

Cuplike or ring shaped pessaries have been designed to support and to press upward the prolapsed womb, but these crude contrivances only serve to aggravate and to increase the weakness of the organs. Through abnormal pressure and irritation they cause acute and chronic inflammation, lasting malformations, or benign and malignant tumors.

This is so obvious that it seems incredible that men who pride themselves on their scientific knowledge will resort to the recommendation of such contrivances in order to correct conditions which are only intensified by their use.

It stands to reason that shortening of the ligaments and fastening of the womb to the abdominal wall will not overcome the causes of these abnormal conditions. They will not invigorate and strengthen the weakened abdominal organs and raise them to their normal positions, removing the abdominal pressure on the genital organs. The only way this can be done is by building up the system generally, by removing the three primary manifestations of disease, and especially by invigorating the abdominal organs through curative exercises and manipulative treatment.

While studying Nature Cure in Europe I took special courses in Thure-Brandt massage. By means of this internal manipulative treatment, adhesions, displacements, weakness of ligaments and muscles can be corrected without knife or drugs. During my first years in practice I frequently resorted to internal manipulative treatment with good results, but I found that even this was not always necessary. I learned that correction of spinal and pelvic lesions and consequent removal of pressure and irritation on the nerves, the cure of chronic constipation and malnutrition by pure food diet and hydrotherapy, the strengthening of the pelvic nerves and muscles by active and passive movements and exercises were fully sufficient to correct the local symptoms in a natural manner.

Several thousand patients cured by us in this way attest the truth of these statements; but those who failed to understand the simple reasoning of Nature Cure or who did not have the will power to withstand the arguments of friends and doctors, followed the siren call of the operating table and are sorry for it.

When the misplaced womb is torn loose by the knife, in order to be kept in the new position it must be stitched to the frontal abdominal wall. This stretches the organ and prevents its natural movements, resulting frequently in serious nerve strain and irritation. Often the womb will not stay fixed; it breaks loose and relapses into the same abnormal position. Granted that it remains fixed, woe to the woman if she become pregnant. The womb cannot assume the constantly changing positions of pregnancy, and either abortion or malformation of the fetus, together with great suffering, is the result.

The operation has done nothing to correct unnatural habits of living or to purify the system of its scrofulous, venereal and psoric taints, or of drug and food poisons. These gather in the parts weakened and irritated by the surgeon's knife, where they set up new inflammations, ulcerations, and only too often malignant tumors. As a result, one operation follows another.

We cannot cut in the genital organs without "cutting in the brain". The nervous system is a unit and, next to the brain, the genital organs represent the most complex and sensitive nerve centers. The two are intimately connected. Mutilations in the genital nerve centers invariably mean affections of the brain and of the nervous system in general. It is almost axiomatic that a woman whose uterus or ovaries have been operated on is afterwards mentally abnormal. Nervousness, irritability, and only too often nervous prostration and insanity are the sequelae of operative treatment.

In medical colleges, among students and professors, these facts are freely admitted and discussed, but the prospective patient hears a different story. "Cut loose the womb—or shorten the ligament; put it into the right position, and everything will be well." This sounds plausible and is very seductive, but everyday experiences expose the fallacy of these assurances.

Since the foregoing paragraphs were written for the first edition of this volume, the medical profession has admitted the truth of my claims and thus has convicted itself of malpractice in the past. During the last few years surgeons have not been extirpating the ovaries entirely. They now freely admit that complete excision of these organs is followed by serious nervous ailments, lowered vitality and insanity, and that these dire consequences can be averted by leaving only a tiny part "as much as the size of a pea" of the organs intact. Since the secretions of these "ductless" glands are so vitally important to the organism, why not cure the organs by natural methods instead of mutilating them?

The Climacteric or Change of Life

Under our artificial methods of living, the **climacteric,** or change of life, has become the bugbear of womanhood. It seems to be universally assumed that this period in a woman's life must be fraught with manifold sufferings and dangers. It is taken as a matter of course that during these changes in her organism a woman is assailed by serious physical, mental, and psychic ailments which may endanger her sanity and often her life.

Like rheumatism, neurasthenia, neuralgia, and hundreds of other medical terms, "change of life" is a convenient phrase to cover the doctor's ignorance. No matter what ailments befall a woman during the years from forty to fifty, be the causes ever so obscure, the diagnosis is easy. "You are in the climacteric, you are suffering from the change of life", says the doctor, and the patient, satisfied, resigns herself to the inevitable.

Frequently women come to us for consultation, and after reciting a long series of troubles conclude with the remark: "Of course, doctor, I'm in the change, and I know that lots of these things are **natural** at my time of life."

Is it true that all this suffering is natural and inevitable?

Among primitive races suffering incident to the change of life is practically unknown. The same is true in a lesser degree of the peasant population of Europe. The causes of it must, therefore, be sought in the artificial modes of living peculiar to our hyper-civilization and in the unnatural suppressive methods of treating disease.

What are the specific causes of the profound disturbances so often accompanying the changes of the climacteric?

Aside from their other physiologic functions, the menses are for women a monthly cleansing crisis through which Nature eliminates from the system considerable amounts of waste and morbid matter which under a natural regimen of life would be discharged by means of the organs of depuration, viz., the lungs, skin, kidneys and bowels.

The more natural the life and the more normal the woman's physical condition, the shorter and less annoying and painful will be the menstrual periods.

Through unnatural habits of eating, drinking, dressing, breathing, and through equally unnatural methods of medical treatment, the kidneys, skin and bowels have become inactive and benumbed. As long as vicarious monthly purification by means of the menses continues, the evil results of the torpid condition of the regular organs of depuration do not become so apparent. **The organism has learned to adapt itself to this mode of elimination.**

But when on account of the organic changes of the climacteric menstruation ceases, then the systemic poisons (pathogen) which formerly were eliminated by means of this monthly purification, accumulate in the system and become the source of all manner of trouble. All tendencies to physical, mental, or psychic disease are greatly intensified. The poisonous taints circulating in the blood over-stimulate or else depress the brain and the nervous system. As a consequence, mental and psychic disorders are of common occurrence; the more so because the waning of the sex functions is accompanied by a tendency to negativity and hypersensitiveness.

How can the ailments of the climacteric be avoided or cured?

Is it not self-evident that the easiest way to side-step the troubles incident to this critical period and to re-establish the perfect equilibrium of the organism, lies in restoring the natural activity of the organs of elimination?

This is what Nature Cure accomplishes easily and successfully with its natural methods of treatment. Air and sun baths, water treatments and massage bring new life and activity to the enervated skin. Pure food diet, neurotherapy, curative gymnastics, homeopathic or herb remedies restore the natural tonicity and functioning of the stomach, liver, kidneys, and intestines. Psycho-therapy, systematically practiced, makes every cell in the body vibrant with the higher and finer forces of the mental and spiritual planes of being.

When the natural equilibrium of the organism is thus restored, there is absolutely no occasion for the troubles of the climacteric. We have proved this in hundreds of cases. As kidneys, skin and bowels begin to function normally and freely, physical and mental conditions commence to improve, until, one after another, the dreaded symptoms disappear.

Let us compare with this common-sense, natural treatment the orthodox medical practice in such cases:

This treatment, as usual, is entirely symptomatic. The

sluggish organs of elimination are prodded by poisonous cathartics, laxatives, diaphoretics, cholagogues and tonics, all of which, after temporary stimulation, leave the organs in a more weakened, and the system in a more poisoned condition. If brain and nerves are irritated and aching, sedatives and hypnotics are given to stupefy them into insensibility. If the heart action is weak and irregular, it is whipped up by poisonous stimulants; if too fast, it is benumbed by sedatives and depressants.

Thus, instead of removing the underlying causes, every symptom is promptly suppressed. Drug poisons are added to the waste and morbid matter which are already clogging the channels of life. Under such unnatural treatment, in many instances the victims go from bad to worse. Flushes, headaches, rheumatic and neuralgic pains, melancholia, irritability, mental aberration, partial paralysis and a multitude of other symptoms appear and gradually increase in severity.

When the family physician has arrived at the end of his wits, the surgeon has his innings. He, in turn, leaves the patient in a still worse condition of chronic suffering.

These experiences are so common that the manifold troubles of the climacteric are regarded as unavoidable and as a matter of course. **Here, as in countless other instances, it is the treatment which prevents the cure. If the efficiency of common sense, natural treatment were more widely known and recognized, how much unnecessary suffering could be avoided!**

The various ailments of the female organs and their rational treatment will be fully described in Volume V of this series, "The Natural Treatment of Special Diseases".

THE EFFECTS OF SUPPRESSION OF VENEREAL DISEASE

This was the title of a chapter in the previous edition of this volume. Everything pertaining to this subject is fully explained in my booklet entitled "Who Provides the Victims of the Black Stork? Who Makes the Damaged Goods?"

CHAPTER XVIII

CANCER

IN August, 1909, I wrote the following article for the Nature Cure Magazine. Its contents confirm in so many ways the teachings of Nature Cure philosophy that I may be permitted to reproduce it in this volume.

"What We Know About Cancer"

This is the title of an able article by Burton J. Hendrick in the July number of McClure's Magazine. It is a summary of all that up to date medical science claims to know about cancer. The author has evidently made a thorough study of the subject and can be regarded as an authority in this field of inquiry.

The truth of most of his statements I knew before reading the article and could have given them expression, but they would not have been as convincing to the adherents of old schools of healing. It is for this reason that I quote so extensively from Mr. Hendrick's article. He received his training and information from the regular school of medicine and is in sympathy with its methods.

Introducing the subject of his article, he says on page 254:

"The medical profession has learned more about cancer in the last six years than in the preceding six thousand. True as this statement is, however, it must not be misconstrued. No cancer 'cure' has been discovered. Investigators have penetrated many secrets of the disease, but they have not yet restored a single human sufferer to health."

This is an unqualified admission that the regular treatment of cancer by means of drugs, surgical operations, X-Rays, radium emanations, freezing, etc., has never cured a single case of the disease. One of the characteristic symptoms of malignant tumors mentioned in every text book on pathology is that they return after extirpation. In fact every medical student is expected to state this in his examination papers as part of the definition of malignant tumors.

The same statements are made by the professor in the class room. To the patient in the consultation room, however, the facts are presented in a somewhat modified form. While no positive assurances of cures are made, the advice runs somewhat as follows: "An early operation presents the only possibility of cure; there is at least a chance that the cancer will not recur; the operation will surely tend to prolong the life of the patient, etc."

These claims, however, are not true, because the surest way to turn a benign tumor into a malignant one and to make the latter more malignant is to operate. Mr. Hendrick confirms this on page 264. He says:

"Clinical observations long ago established the fact that any irritating interference with a cancer almost always stimulates its growth. In his earliest experiments Dr. Loeb found that, by merely drawing a silk thread through a dormant or slowly developing tumor, he could transform it into a rapidly growing one. Cutting with a knife produced the same effect. This accounts for the commonly observed fact that, when extirpated cancers in human beings recur, they increase in size much more rapidly than the original growth."

Dr. Senn, the great cancer surgeon, admitted the same facts in an interview given to Chicago press representatives upon his return from his trip around the world. He was reported as saying:

"Avoid Beauty Doctors"

"Incidentally, Dr. Senn advises women who worry over their disfigurement of moles about their heads and shoulders to have those so called beauty spots removed early in life, but he tells them they should not go to beauty doctors to have the operations performed.

"He knows of hundreds of cases, he says, where cancer has resulted from the irritation of moles by an electric needle, or by constant picking it. Have a surgeon cut the mole out, is his advice, as it will hurt little and leave no scar."

To this I answered in my comments on the interview, "If the little knife of the beauty doctor causes cancer, what about the big knife of the surgeon?" Indeed, our office records show that a large percentage of malignant growths are caused directly by surgical operations on benign tumors.

Dr. Senn, however, fails to recognize a most important cause of the rapid increase in destructive chronic diseases; in reality, he has overlooked the principal factor, which is the suppression of acute diseases by poisonous drugs and surgical operations.

The more skilled the allopathic school becomes in the suppression and in the prevention of acute diseases by drugs, knife, X-ray, serums and vaccination virus, the greater will be the increase in dyspepsia, nervous prostration, insanity, locomotor ataxia, paresis, cancer, secondary and tertiary syphilis, tuberculosis and many other socalled incurable diseases. Suppression of acute diseases by drugs and knife, is the all-important factor in the creation of malignant diseases, which Dr. Senn has overlooked in his discourse on the cause of chronic destructive diseases. If he will study his experience in foreign lands in the light of these explanations, he will find that these scourges of mankind become more prevalent in direct ratio to the increase in the number of drug stores.

These theories of the origin of chronic destructive diseases find expression in all my writings. Please notice whether they are confirmed in Mr. Hendrick's statements. He says on page 255:

"One in Every Eight Women Past the Age of Thirty-five Dies of Cancer"

"It is peculiarly appropriate that the United States should take a leading part in this work. In all probability, cancer is the worst physical scourge with which we have to deal. It annually destroys half as many lives as tuberculosis; but it is an even greater menace, because, whereas the mortality from tuberculosis steadily decreases year by year, that from cancer steadily increases. The actual facts even medical men themselves hesitate to discuss. How many realize, for example, that, in England, of all women who have reached the age of thirty-five years, one in every eight dies of cancer, and one in every eleven men? Yet the latest official report of the Registrar General of England coldly declares that this is the present situation. Whether the same figures apply to the United States cannot be determined with available statistics; but as living conditions and medical practice represent about the same standards in both countries, the probability is that they do.

"Indeed, medical science would not be surprised to learn that the mortality is greater in the United States than elsewhere. We pride ourselves upon our general prosperity and enlightenment, and those seem precisely the two factors that chiefly encourage the growth of cancer. Spread out a map of the world, and mark the countries that have progressed farthest in material well-being, in education, government, sanitation (and drug stores), and other essentials of modern civilization; those are the countries that suffer from the cancer plague. In the eastern world, not Asia or Africa, but enlightened Europe; in the western, not Mexico, Honduras, or Panama, but the United States and Canada—these are the countries most grievously afflicted. No savage tribe is absolutely immune, but cancer assails most violently those peoples that have reached the highest points in civilization. And not only this, but it apparently bears heaviest upon the most sanitary and enlightened parts of these countries. In Europe the nations that suffer most are not Russia or Hungary or Italy or Spain, but Germany, France, Sweden, Norway, and, above all, England. In London, the greatest mortality is found, not in the East End, but in Hampstead, Marylebone, and Chelsea, which include the city's wealthiest parts. Similarly, in New York, the Russian Jews and Italians who so largely populate the crowded tenement sections are immune, whereas the more sanitary parts of the town are favorite breeding-places. Where diseases of known contagiousness, such as tuberculosis, typhoid fever, diphtheria, and pneumonia, most abound, cancer seems to find a less strong foothold than in other more salubrious sections; as by some mysterious and inexplorable law of compensation it finds its way mainly into the homes of the prosperous and enlightened.

"Thus cancer, like death itself, apparently loves a shining mark. It strikes, not so frequently at the vicious, the uncleanly, the miserable, but at those lives that promise most to themselves and their communities."

Dr. Senn, in an interview already referred to in this article, made the following statements:

"The negro is a negro wherever you find him. From Kaffir to Bushman and pygmy they are all Hamites.

"They are mostly a fine people physically, lean and tall, except the dwarfs. There is little tendency toward obesity; they have no apoplexy, no distended veins as we have in civilization. **Hence their freedom from cancer.**

"They are free from many other diseases that pester us also. Tuberculosis is hardly known, and only along the coast where it has been taken by the whites."

The report of his address concluded as follows:

"His investigations of the natives of Africa served to strengthen his conviction that cancer is a product of civilization, like apoplexy and scores of other exotic ailments, Dr. Senn said. He could not find nor hear of a case of cancer among the 'Hamites,' as he termed them. And from the fact that he found the disease to be an unknown one to the Esquimaux of Greenland, he was assured that climate has nothing whatever to do with it. Climate did not cause it, and climate will not cure it."

Among the primitive races in Africa, Australia and in the polar regions, acute diseases are never suppressed. Nature is allowed to eliminate through these acute reactions, unhindered and unchecked, the systemic poisons which accumulate in human bodies. In this way the morbid matter which furnishes the soil for the development of tubercle bacilli and malignant tumors is promptly eliminated. In those European countries which are lagging behind in the march of civilization, most of the doctoring among the poorer classes is done by the shepherd, the wise man or the wise woman, by means of simples, prayers and charms. Doctors and drugs are resorted to only in the gravest emergencies. Among the peasantry in Germany, I have often heard expressions such as the following: "Oh no, I would not think of curing that eruption on baby's head; it takes disease out of his body; it would be a sin to suppress it."

In the common forms of acute diseases, a physician is

seldom called. The peasants apply water treatment and home remedies—herbs, which they gather in season and preserve.

In the homes of the wealthy and refined, the doctor is called for every passing ailment. Colds, catarrhs, diarrheas, skin eruptions and every other form of acute elimination must be treated promptly and thoroughly with antiseptics, antipyretics, antitoxins, and all sorts of other "antis". Antiseptic lotions, soaps, tooth-powders, etc. are constantly applied in order to kill germs and to prevent infection.

On the other hand, wrong habits of living, food poisoning, alcohol, nicotine, vaccine and antitoxins systematically poison the human organism, and when nature endeavors, by means of acute reactions, to free the system of morbid accumulations, she is thwarted by suppressive treatment. These practices repeated from generation to generation must lead finally to deterioration of blood and tissues and to the development of hereditary taints. That is why "cancer loves a shining mark". Hendrick continues on page 256:

"If all the lap dogs of Fifth Avenue and our other fashionable quarters were examined, a considerable proportion would be found to be afflicted with one or more malignant tumors."

It is, indeed, a significant fact that dogs are more often afflicted by malignant tumors than are other animals. They partake of man's unnatural food. The lap dogs of Fifth Avenue and other fashionable quarters especially are pampered with sweetmeats and highly seasoned tidbits from the tables of the rich and are doctored as carefully by the veterinary surgeon as their mistresses are by high-priced specialists.

Judging from the following quotation, page 257, the author seems to think that nature "just for spite" creates

cancer in order to undo the work of medical science. He
fails to see that medical science "spites" nature and reaps
what it sows.

"These considerations bring us face to face with a most startling
circumstance: that nature seems to be subtly attempting to undo
much of the work of modern medical science. We save yearly by
diphtheria antitoxin the lives of thousands of babies and children,
only that they may grow up to become victims of cancer. We rescue
many thousands of young men and women from tuberculosis, so
that they may reap, as their whirlwind, an even more dreadful
malady."

The author explains at great length that cancer is not
contagious; that it can be transmitted only by means of
transplantation of the cancer cells themselves into the
flesh of healthy individuals and that even then it "takes"
only in a small percentage of cases.

In the cancer laboratories, the experiments are made
entirely on mice and rats, because these animals are cheap
and plentiful. Speaking of the attempts to transplant
cancerous growths from one animal to others he says,
page 264:

"In the early attempts there were only a small proportion of
'takes.' Thus, the first experimenters failed because they used only
one or two, or, at most, a dozen animals. But one of the important
facts learned is that, in the first transplantations, only a few animals, even of the same species, are susceptible to these grafts.
Sometimes only one mouse in a hundred can be inoculated. At the
Imperial Cancer Institute in London, a primary tumor has been
transplanted nearly four hundred times without being made to
grow on a single mouse.

"In two years the Buffalo Laboratory inoculated 1,600 mice with
the Jensen strain of tumor, and, of these, 1,250 proved absolutely
resistant. The remaining 350 animals, in which cancers developed,
were kept under the closest observation."

These interesting observations confirm my claim that
in order to develop cancer or any other chronic destructive
disease a certain diathesis or diseased condition of the
body is needed. In order to develop tuberculosis or cancer
something more is necessary than the tubercle bacillus or
the cancer cell; there must be that in the system on which

these parasites (or rather their microzyma) live and thrive. If the cancer cell of its own accord could create cancer every animal inoculated with it would develop the fatal disease. The cancerous growth in itself is only a symptom of the disease; the real disease is the constitutional taint (the morbid matter which develops normal microzyma into cancer cells) which stimulates and feeds the malignant growth; therefore a real cure can consist only in eliminating from the system the poisons which irritate the cells and stimulate them into unlimited multiplication.

Extirpation by drugs, knife or freezing only removes the local manifestations of a constitutional taint or miasm. Malignant tumors grow in ''bad blood'' only; their favorite breeding places are to be found in scrofulous and psoric constitutions, especially where hereditary conditions are aggravated by food and drug poisoning or where spinal lesions irritate the nerves and the tissues which these nerves supply. What, then, can be gained permanently by destroying the local growth, when the disease soil from which it springs, or the spinal irritation, still remains? Our claim that cancer is a constitutional disease is again confirmed by the admission that cancer is hereditary. Even death, Nature's most radical operation, does not cure cancer; it returns in the offspring.

I quote as follows:

''The Question of Heredity in Cancer''

''Results recently obtained in experimental breeding, however, indicate that cancer is hereditary—at least in mice. Recent experiments at the Harvard Medical School, conducted by Dr. E. E. Tyzzer, tend to substantiate this impression.

''Dr. Tyzzer found a female mouse with a large growing tumor and mated her with a normal healthy mouse. In a short time this couple had one hundred descendants, all of which were kept under close observation. It takes about five months for a mouse to reach maturity—reach the period, that is, when it becomes susceptible to cancer. Mortality among the young animals is high, and of this brood, one hundred strong, thirty-five died of common mice infections before attaining mature age. Of the sixty-five that reached the cancerous period, twenty developed tumors, of which they ultimately died. One in every three, in other words, fell victim to the mother's disease. According to Dr. Bashford, of the British Cancer Institute, one out of every twenty-five hundred mice naturally develops cancer. Unquestionably the disease is far more common than this; but the frightful mortality among Dr. Tyzzer's one hundred mice can be explained only on the grounds of heredity. That the descendants of this cancerous parent inherited the disease outright, that the cancer cell or possibly a cancer parasite was directly transmitted from mother to offspring, does not necessarily follow. The tuberculous children of tuberculous parents inherit, not the disease, but a constitution especially adaptable to it (what is really transmitted are the cancer microzyma), and so these cancerous mice probably derive from their parent an increased susceptibility.''

The foregoing statements show that advanced medical science concedes the heredity of cancer, not by direct transmisison of the cancer cells but by disposition, diathesis, or, as we should express it, by hereditary taints. If the parent organism is tainted with poisonous miasms it is to be expected that the seminal cell originating therefrom will be similarly affected. The fetus being only a multiplication of the parent cell, abnormal and diseased constituents of this cell (diseased microzyma) reproduce themselves as do the normal constituents. Weeds often multiply more rapidly than do useful plants.

Hahnemann, the father of homeopathy, recognized the hereditary transmission of disease taints and proclaimed it in his theory of psora. He taught that the ordinary itch eruptions (scabies) are accompanied by the elimination of internal scrofulous taints, which in turn, are a survival of the ancient leprosy. He asserted that systematic suppression of the external lepra continued throughout the ages, gradually transformed this external skin disease into the internal psora, which manifests occasionally on the surface in the acute forms of itch, lice, crab-lice, hives, itchy eczemata, etc., and internally, as tuberculosis, cancer, sarcoma, asthma and other chronic destructive diseases.

The following quotations from Hahnemann's book, ''The

Nature of Chronic Diseases'', will make interesting reading in connection with our present subject.

For a hundred years, Hahnemann's theory of psora has been scouted and ridiculed by the allopathic schools, and even among homeopaths but few have accepted this theory. Now we are confronted by the remarkable fact that, at this late day, the diagnosis from the eye confirms the observations and speculations of the great genius of homeopathy.

After the suppression of itch eruptions, lice or crab-lice, there appear, in certain parts of the iris, spots ranging in color from light brown to dark red. These ''itch spots'' indicate the localities in the body in which the suppressed disease taints have concentrated.

These suppressions represent not only the psoric taints which Nature was trying to eliminate through the eruptions and parasites, but also the poisons contained in the bodies of the parasites and the drug poisons which were used to kill them. It has been proved that the bodies of the parasites contain a poisonous taint called by homeopaths, psorinum. When the minute animals burrowing in and under the skin are killed by drug treatment, the morbid taints in their bodies are absorbed by the human organism and added to the psoric taints which Nature was trying to eliminate. Thus, after suppression, the organism is cumbered with three poisons instead of one; first, the hereditary and acquired scrofulous and psoric taints which the tissues of the body were throwing off into the blood stream and which the blood stream was feeding to the parasites on the surface; second, the morbid taints contained in the bodies of the parasites and, third, the drug poisons used as suppressants.

These facts explain why the itch spots in the eye frequently indicate serious chronic, destructive diseases in the corresponding parts of the body; why in asthma and tuberculosis we often find itch spots in the lungs; why cancer of the liver is indicated by itch spots in the liver area, etc. That itch or psora is actually at the bottom of the cancerous diathesis is attested by the fact that all cancer patients whom we have treated and cured have, with two exceptions, broken out with itchy, burning eruptions at one time or another during the natural treatment. The bodies of most of these patients were inflamed with fiery eruptions from head to foot for days and often for weeks.

We allow these healing crises to run their course unhindered and unchecked; we rather encourage them by air and sun baths, cold water treatment and homeopathic remedies. When the parasites have consumed the poisonous taints on which they feed, they depart as they came, no one knows whence nor whither. Béchamp's microzyma now explain the mystery. For the removal of lice we prescribe only water and comb; even antiseptic soaps must be avoided lest they kill the parasites burrowing in the skin and flesh.

Speaking of cancer heredity, Hendrick says on page 264:

"Families in which cancer seems abnormally prevalent are familiar facts of everyday life. Several of these apparently cancerous families, the most notable being the Bonapartes, having figured in history. Napoleon himself died of cancer of the stomach, as did his father, his brother Lucien, and his sisters Caroline and Pauline. Among human beings, however, cancer is so common that any large family is almost certain to have its victims. On the other hand, the fact that when cancer is common in a family it almost always takes the same shape in all sufferers—the cancerous Bonapartes, for example, all dying of cancer of the stomach—supports the popular idea that heredity is an important factor."

It is reported by the biographers of Napoleon that at different times in his life he suffered with the itch, and undoubtedly it was suppressed in due form; this and the subsequent development of cancer by the great Corsican furnish historical confirmation of the theory of psora.

"Does Nature Ever Cure Cancer?"

"Medical science has now established one fundamental fact: that, in practically all bacterial infections, the employment of drugs, as direct curatives, is virtually useless. No factor, extrinsic to the body itself, ever cured a human being of typhoid fever, diphtheria, tuberculosis, or any other bacterial disease."

This is good Nature Cure doctrine. Much suffering could be prevented if the medical profession would always keep these truths in mind and act accordingly. Unfortunately, however, for humanity, medical practice on the whole continues along the old lines—antiseptics, antipyretics, serums, antitoxins and surgical extirpations are employed as much as ever before.

In a foot note to the previously quoted paragraph, our author swerves from the straight path of Nature Cure reasoning back into allopathic doctrine. He says:

"The only apparent exceptions to this rule are the successful use of quinin in malaria and mercury in syphilis. These diseases, however, are caused, not by (vegetable) bacteria, but by animal parasites." (?)

In other articles I have shown that quinin and mercury are by no means exceptions to the rule that poisonous drugs do not cure diseases. I have demonstrated that they merely suppress Nature's acute healing and cleansing efforts and change them into chronic destructive forms of disease. I have proved that mercury is the most terrible of all suppressants; that it is responsible for the existence of secondary and tertiary syphilis and for the majority of all cases of locomotor ataxia, paralysis agitans and paresis.

Page 265:

"The really curative agency is this great physical power called immunity. This may be defined as the resistance manifested by the normal body to any extrinsic forces that seek to destroy it. The animal organism is not passive in the face of these attacks; when assailed, it rouses itself and brings against the invader powerful though hitherto quiescent forces."

This also is good Nature Cure doctrine. By the very name which we have chosen for our school of healing we have indicated that Nature, not the doctor, cures. All that we can do is to remove obstructions, to correct mechanical lesions, to build up the blood on a natural basis, and to promote elimination. The actual regeneration of diseased tissues is accomplished by the ''physician within''. Here we touch elbows with the metaphysician; the difference is that the latter expects the Lord to do it all, while we believe in giving Him a helping hand. Thus Nature Cure travels the common sense middle road between the allopathic extreme of suppression and the other extreme of metaphysical nihilism.

The fundamental law of cure—''Every acute disease is the result of a healing and cleansing effort of nature''—affirms the fact that the really curative agency is the great Life Force. What the old school of medicine calls disease, we call Nature's healing effort.

Page 265:

''For every minute body that assails it from without, it produces an anti-body within; for every toxin evolved by the invading bacteria, it produces its antitoxin. Though these forces in some shape always exist within us, it is only when the specific disease appears that they manifest themselves in useful form. Thus, when the diphtheria toxin assails us, the body in turn manufactures its diphtheria antitoxin to destroy it. If the patient recovers, these antitoxins remain in the blood indefinitely—which explains why, when once we have rid ourselves of a specific contagious disease, we seldom contract it again.''

This expresses the allopathic conception of the bacterial origin of diseases. From the Nature Cure viewpoint the microzyma, omnipresent in living protoplasm, develop in the morbid soil of the diphtheria sore throat into diphtheria germs and these feed on and decompose the morbid matter, which is probably the product of vaccine virus. Naturally, as the food supply decreases the diphtheria germs decrease also. It is this which explains the gradual subsidence of the inflammatory process, not the germ devouring leucocytes, nor the mysterious, never yet identified obsonins or antitoxins.

Fevers, inflammations, skin eruptions and mucous discharges consume and eliminate the morbid matter in which bacteria grow and thrive. We have an example of this in yeast fermentation. Yeast germs will grow in a sugar solution only; when they have split up all the sugar into alcohol and carbonic acid, fermentation ceases because the germs have nothing to feed on; but they are not dead by any means. Transplanted into another sugar solution they will thrive lustily.

Man's powerful poisonous antiseptics, antipyretics and antitoxins do not allow fevers and inflammations to consume the morbid matter in the system; they interrupt the processes of oxydation (combustion) and elimination before nature has had a chance to perform her work of housecleaning and repair; in other words, while nature merely regulates the work of housecleaning, poisonous antiseptics, germicides and antitoxins stop it entirely.

The cure of bacterial diseases, therefore, is due to the fact that the disease soil in which germs and bacteria thrive and multiply has been removed from the system. In other words, bacteria are not the unmitigated evil they are pictured to be; like everything else in nature, they serve a useful purpose. They are scavengers which consume and remove waste and morbid matter. It would be just as sensible to kill the "white wings", working with brooms and shovels in our streets, as to kill these busy microbes in our bodies. So long as we are foolish enough to burden our system with all sorts of morbid matter to such an extent that our organs of elimination cannot take care of it, nature must provide some other radical forms of housecleaning, such as fevers, inflammations, catarrhal conditions, bacterial diseases, etc.—otherwise we would perish in our own impurities.

We do not have to kill these useful little scavengers; their activity ceases and they become innocuous, when they have consumed the morbid matter on which they live. They cannot thrive in pure blood and normal tissues, any more than yeast germs can grow in a fluid devoid of sugar.

Upon What Does Natural Immunity Depend?

Natural immunity depends upon the following factors:

First: Upon perfect nutrition and drainage, and resulting from these.

Second: Upon the normal composition and purity of the vital fluids and tissues.

Third: Upon adequate nerve supply to the cells and organs

Fourth: Upon the vigor and harmony of the vibratory activities on all three planes of being.

Page 266:

"These records soon disclosed a momentous fact. While most of the cancers kept increasing in size until the animal died, a few clearly stopped growing, and others began to retrogress, in many cases diminishing to the vanishing point. An inspection of the animals more graphically emphasized the same fact. In some the cancer grew as large as a hazelnut or an almond, and then slowly began to grow smaller. When they disappeared, they left absolutely no trace, not even a scar, and there was no recurrence. The skin and hair above the spot where this malignant tumor had been became white, glossy, and indistinguishable from the remaining surface. In the course of two years' observation it developed that about twenty per cent of all mouse cancers ultimately disappeared. In a few cases these were fairly large; in most instances they were quite small, perhaps an eighth of an inch in diameter. In other words, the smaller the tumor, the greater chance it had to become absorbed.

"Cancer, in Principle, Is Not an Incurable Disease"

"What did this mean? Simply this: that cancer was a curable disease; the destructive cells did not necessarily mean death. Clearly nature herself knew how to rid the animal body of this malignant growth. The presence of the cancer cell started into life certain forces that arose in all their might and threw off the incubus. These simple experiments for all time took human cancer out of the class of incurable diseases. Precisely how nature accomplishes this work is not known now, and may indeed never be known; the method may be too complex for the human mind to grasp: but, in principle, the disease can be mastered.''

This mystery also is readily explained by the work of the minute scavengers, the microzyma. When the cancer soil is consumed they cease producing cancer cells.

When, during the last few years, I asserted that we could cure cancer by natural methods of treatment, my claims were scouted and ridiculed. Many a poor sufferer has missed his chance of recovery because he believed that his only possible salvation lay in a surgical operation. Now comes advanced medical science and positively confirms my claim that cancer is curable, and in many instances, even selfcurable.

If the constructive forces in Nature can cure cancer spontaneously, how much more effective and speedy will be their work of cleansing and repair aided by our natural methods of treatment. If cases of spontaneous cures are more closely investigated it will be found that they are preceded by itch eruptions or some other form of vigorous elimination. Not long ago I heard of a man who was cured of consumption by a good dose of smallpox. The smallpox in this case acted as a healing crisis.

Page 268:

''Dogs Can Be Cured of Cancer''

''Though we cannot cure cancer in human beings, we can cure it in dogs. It was at the Loomis Laboratory, through experiments conducted by Dr. S. P. Beebe and Dr. George W. Crile, of Cleveland, that its curability was demonstrated.

''At these experiments nine dogs in succession were cured of malignant growths and restored to normal health. The experimenters accomplished this result simply by transfusing into the diseased animals the blood of other dogs that were demonstrated to be immune to this type of cancer. They inoculated a considerable number of dogs; in some the tumor developed and in others it failed to do so. The latter were therefore regarded as resistant to the disease. After the growth had gained marked headway and the patients manifested nearly all the symptoms of cancer in its last stages, practically all the blood in their bodies was drained off. In its place was transfused the blood of animals which had proved resistant to inoculation. In nine out of ten cases the sick dogs got well; their tumors entirely disappeared, their condition became normal, and their own blood could then be used to effect similar cures. These experiments seem to indicate that, while the immune properties in cancer are not found in the serum when it is separated from the blood, they may be found when the whole body of the blood is used. Another explanation is that the blood of the diseased animal contains nourishment especially adaptable to the cancer cell, and that when this was withdrawn, the cancer cell was virtually deprived of its food. On the other hand, the blood of the second animal furnished no nourishment to the cancer, as evidenced by the fact that, after the inoculation of the growth, it failed to develop. When this blood, therefore, was transfused into the body of the diseased dog, it supplied wholesome nourishment to his normal tissues, but absolutely none to the cancer cells, which consequently atrophied and disappeared.

"For dogs afflicted with this particular tumor, science has thus discovered that great medical desideratum—an actual cure for cancer. In the course of the writer's visit to the Buffalo Laboratory, a large, fine, valuable English bulldog was brought in fearfully afflicted with this disease; the treatment was at once begun, and in a few weeks he will unquestionably be sent back entirely well.''

The foregoing proves conclusively our assertion that cancer is not a local ailment but a constitutional blood disease. I have always claimed that the root of cancer is in every drop of blood in the body and that therefore local extirpation by any means whatsoever is worse than useless.

Common sense should teach us that the only possible cure for these deep-seated disorders can consist in nothing less than a thorough purification, regeneration and vitalization of the organism as a whole, and **such indeed is the case.**

Nature Cure Has Solved the Problem

Referring to the cure of cancer in dogs by the transfusion of blood of healthy animals into the bodies of diseased ones, Mr. Hendrick continues:

"With human beings the reproduction of the conditions of the experiment is absolutely impossible. For practical purposes it would be impossible to accomplish this, and the experiments, therefore, outside of their practical importance in restoring suffering dogs to health, are interesting chiefly for the new light which they shed upon the general problem, and for the additional demonstration that cancer, in itself, is not incurable.''

However, we of the Nature Cure school say that it is not necessary to pump the diseased blood out of the organism. In the natural methods of living and of treatment we possess the means of **purifying and regenerating that blood while it is in the body.** That this is possible we have proved in a number of cancer cases.

It is obvious, however, that the earlier the disease is treated by the natural methods, that is, before the breaking down process has far advanced, the easier and quicker will be the cure.

I maintain that external cancers in the first stages of development, that is, before they have grown to large proportions, belong to the easily curable forms of disease. Cures become more difficult when the tumors affect internal vital parts and organs, but even then we have been successful in many cases.

This article has already far outgrown the limits originally assigned to it, but I cannot refrain from illustrating my deductions by at least one typical case taken from our clinical records.

About six years ago there came to us a Polish woman whose head, on the right side, was covered by an enormous cancerous growth. She gave to us the following history of her case:

At first she had a large wen on the right side of her head. This was removed by a beauty doctor. The wound healed, but soon after opened and formed an ugly sore. This was treated surgically in a north side hospital. After a while the wound opened again and became more virulent than before. Skin grafting was now resorted to in order to cover the large exposure of raw flesh, yet the wound refused to stay cured, and two more operations were performed in the same hospital. Powerful antiseptics were used to cauterize the sores, and they were burned with hot irons. This was done so thoroughly that a piece of the bone became charred and worked out during our course of treatment; it resembled a piece of charcoal. After the fourth operation, when the entire side of the head was covered by a cancerous mass, she was dismissed as incurable. She then came under our treatment and after five months the sores had entirely disappeared and the wounds, including the hole in the skull, were covered with new, sound skin.

During the treatment, the patient passed through the usual crises in the forms of catarrhs, coughs, diarrheas, itchy skin eruptions, etc. After the wounds on the head had healed perfectly, she began to use meat and coffee. Within a few weeks the scars reopened and began to bleed. She then confessed she had transgressed our rules. After returning to the natural regimen and treatment, the wounds closed again. Later on she repeated the same experiment with the same results. Since then there has never been a recurrence of her trouble and today she is in perfect health. She has never had occasion to employ doctors since she was with us. In the meantime she has married, and now has three healthy children.

Since this article was written for the Nature Cure Magazine in 1909, certain discoveries by Dr. H. C. Ross of London, England, have confirmed my claims that cancer is not at all of local and accidental origin, but that it is constitutional, and that it may be caused by the gradual accumulation in the system of certain toxins (morbid microzyma) which develop in decaying animal matter.

One day, while experimenting in his laboratory, Dr. Ross brought living cells into contact with a certain anilin dye on the slide of a microscope, and noticed that they began at once to multiply by cell division (proliferation).

Dr. Ross realized that he had made an important discovery and continued his experiments under the microscope in order to find out what other substances would cause cell proliferation. He found that certain xanthins and albuminoids derived from decaying animal matter were the most effective for this purpose and induced more rapid cell proliferation than any other substances he was able to procure.

Dr. Ross obtained these "alkaloids of putrefaction", as he called them, from blood which had been allowed to putrefy in a warm place. He found that albuminoids derived from decaying **vegetable** substances did not have the same effect.

His discoveries led him to believe that the "alkaloids of putrefaction" produced in a cut or wound by the decaying of dead blood and tissue cells are the cause of the rapid multiplication of the neighboring live cells, which gradually fills the wound with new tissues.

Thus, for the first time in the history of medicine, a rational explanation of Nature's methods for repairing injured tissues has been advanced.

Dr. Ross applied his theory still farther to the causation of benign and malignant growths, reasoning that the "alkaloids of putrefaction" produced in or attracted to a certain part of the body by some local irritation are the cause of the rapid, abnormal multiplication of cells in tumor formations.

In benign tumors the abnormal proliferation of cells takes place slowly, and they do not tend to immediate and rapid decay and deterioration.

In malignant tumors the "wild" cells, created in immense numbers (from microzyma feeding on psoric taints and systemic poisons), decay almost as rapidly as they are produced because the abnormal growths are devoid of normal organization. They have no established, regular blood and nerve supply, nor are they provided with adequate venous and lymphatic drainage. They are, therefore, cut off from the orderly life of the organism and doomed to rapid deterioration.

The processes of decay of these tumor materials liberate large quantities of "alkaloids of putrefaction", and these in turn stimulate the normal, healthy cells with which they come in contact to rapid, abnormal multiplication. (The alkaloids of putrefaction change the microzyma of normal cells into the morbid microzyma of cancer cells.)

The malignant growth, therefore, feeds on its own products of decay, aside from the systemic poisons and morbid materials already contained in the blood and tissues of the body.

These morbid products permeate the entire system. They are carried by the circulation of the blood into all parts of the body. This explains why cancer is a constitutional disease, why it is, as I stated it, "rooted in every drop of blood".

It also explains why cancer, or rather the disposition to its development (diathesis), is hereditary.

If the original cancerous growth is removed by surgical intervention, X-rays, the electric needle, cauterization, or any other form of local treatment, the poisonous materials (alkaloids of putrefaction) in the blood will set up other foci of abnormal, "wild" proliferation. Medical science has applied the term "metastasis" to such spreading and reappearing of malignant tumors after extirpation.

Dr. Ross' findings throw an interesting light on the relationship between cancer and meat eating. Is it not self evident that in a digestive tract filled most of the time with large masses of partially digested and decaying animal food enormous quantities of "alkaloids of putrefaction" are created? These are absorbed into the circulation, attracted to any point where exists some form of local irritation, and then stimulate the cells in that locality to abnormal proliferation.

"But," it will be said, "meat-eating alone does not account for cancer, because vegetarians also succumb to the disease."

It is true that very rarely vegetarians are afflicted with cancer; but it must be remembered that vegetarians may be affected hereditarily with psoric and scrofulous taints, that a high protein vegetarian diet may be disease producing as well as a meat diet, and that a natural diet **without treatment** may not be sufficient to eliminate the cancer soil. Alkaloids of putrefaction are constantly produced in every animal and human body. They form in the excretions of living cells and in the decaying protoplasm of dead cells, and if the organs of elimination do not function properly, these morbid materials will accumulate in the system and produce morbid microzyma.

Will Radium Cure Cancer?

Newspapers and magazines almost daily bring articles, news items and discussions about the interesting element, radium. The propaganda is so persistent and orderly that one cannot help suspecting the artistic hand of the press agent. Factions are forming in the medical profession for and against the use of the metal in the treatment of cancer and other diseases. Schweninger, a prominent European physician, says the radium treatment is a gigantic swindle. Others claim to have produced, within forty-eight hours, most marvelous cures of cancer by means of the radium rays. The surgeons declare there may be some good in the radium treatment, but that, after all, the safest way lies in the early removal of tumors by the knife.

The extravagant claims of the radium advocates are

bound to arouse new hope in many thousands of people who suffer from the dread cancer malady, and undoubtedly multitudes will try the new remedy, only to be disappointed in the end.

It seems cruel to kill the hopes of those who have pinned their faith to the miracle-working power of radium; but it is not right to give positive assurance of cures when this method of treatment is still in the period of dangerous experimentation and when it is a well known fact that malignant tumors tend to recur after local extirpation within a period of two years. For this latter reason alone, it will require several years to prove the efficacy of radium treatment. Furthermore, it is not right to lead inquiry into doubtful and dangerous paths, when the only rational and effective way has already been discovered and positively demonstrated.

About ten years ago, similar positive and extravagant claims were made for the Roentgen-rays. Institutions for X-ray treatment sprung up all over the country. What has been the result? It is now a well established fact that the X-rays, instead of curing cancer, create it. Already evidence is accumulating which indicates that the radium emanations are just as dangerous as the X-rays.

These agents, on account of immense vibratory velocity and power, are altogether too strong and too destructive for the tissues of the human body. Their work is slow and insidious, but nevertheless certain. The pernicious effects of the X-rays do not manifest until a few years after exposure. I have over thirty newspaper clippings gathered during the last ten years which report the development of cancer-like growths after exposure to X-rays. One of the first victims was an assistant to Thomas A. Edison. After repeated exposure to the rays, in the course of scientific experimentation, the flesh of his body decayed and fell off in pieces until death ended his terrible suffering. Thousands of others have suffered the same fate, but I have failed to hear of a single, well authenticated case of cancer cured by the Roentgen-rays.

Several cases have come under my observation where the application of these rays for some insignificant local lesion was followed by the development of cancer-like decay of the flesh, and finally death—in one instance, suicide.

The radium rays are more powerful than the X-rays, and while they may destroy the abnormal cells of the cancerous growth, they have also a weakening and destructive effect upon the normal cells of the surrounding tissues and nearby organs. But these destructive after effects may not manifest for many months or for several years after exposure. Authentic reports of such cases are already on record.

The following quotations taken from an article in the December, 1913 issue of "The New Age", entitled "New Rare Elements of Great Cost", vividly describe the immense power of the X-ray emanations and report the death of several scientists as a result of exposure to the radium rays:

"New Rare Elements of Great Cost"

"What will radium do? That is the question that is still puzzling science, for the metal has strangely contradictory properties. It has been found valuable in the treatment of cancer by Dr. Abbé, who claims to have made many cures with it. The Paris Radium Institute announces a large percentage of cures out of many cases of surface cancer. All kinds of cutaneous affections have been treated successfully, and chronic rheumatism and tuberculosis have yielded to the treatment.

"There is a strong anti-radium party in the medical profession which points out that Dr. John H. Edwards, president of the British Electro-therapeutic Society, suffered from a cancerous growth due to constant exposure to radium. His left arm had to be amputated. Another, Clarence Dally, had to have his fingers amputated, then his arm, and he finally died from the same cause. There have been other deaths, too, laid to the effect of radium, notably those of Wolfram G. Furths, of Chicago; Dr. Louis Weigel, of Rochester, and

M. Radignet, of Paris. The debate over radium's curative power is still on, full force.

"Of all its strange properties, perhaps the oddest, and without precedent as far as science knows, is that a fragment of radium is always six degrees Fahrenheit hotter than its surrounding medium. This seems in direct defiance to one of the most important of physical laws, the law of the conservation of energy. Radium gives out heat incessantly and yet remains superheated. William Ramsey declares that a given bulk of radium would melt its own weight in ice every hour and keep on doing so for a thousand years.

"Radium is the only substance with the property of self-electrification. The energy contained within a tiny particle of it is amazing. Sir William Ramsey has estimated that the energy in a ton of radium, could it be utilized, would be sufficient to propel a ship of 15,999 tons with engines of 15,000 horsepower at a speed of fifteen knots an hour continuously for thirty years. To do that now requires a million and a half tons of coal.

"These are but a few of its powers. Daily others are discovered, but even so radium is yet an unsolved riddle."

The foregoing statements certainly indicate the necessity of caution in the application of the radium rays and emanations.

However, the principal point at issue in this controversy is: Why should we experiment with these dangerous and doubtful agents when we are already in possession of a safe and certain method for curing benign and malignant tumors in their incipient and even somewhat advanced stages of development? This does not refer to surgical extirpation, because this is just as futile to cure cancer as are all other purely local methods of treatment. The simple reason for this is, as has been explained previously, that cancer is not a local ailment, but a manifestation of constitutional disease.

CHAPTER XIX

WHAT ABOUT THE "CHRONIC"?

It Takes So Long

"YES, Nature Cure is all right, but it takes so long."
Now and then we hear this or a similar remark.
Our answer is: "No, it does not take long. It is the
swiftest cure in existence."

This wrong idea has grown out of the fact that, as a
rule, **we have to deal with none but the most advanced
cases** of so called incurable diseases. The afflicted turn
to the Nature Cure physician only after all other methods
of treatment have been tried and found of no avail.

As long as there remains a particle of faith in the medicine bottle, the knife or the metaphysical formula of the
mind-healer, people prefer these "easy" methods which
require no effort on their part, rather than the Nature
Cure treatment which necessitates personal exertion, selfcontrol, the changing or giving up of cherished habits.
This is what most of us evade as long as we can. "Exercise, the cold blitz-guss, no meat, no coffee? Not for me!
I'd rather die!"

Afraid of Cold Water

The most dreaded "terror on the threshold" seems to
be cold water. Undoubtedly it has kept away thousands
from Nature Cure and thereby from the only possible cure
for their chronic ailments. If we could achieve equally
good results without our "heroic" methods of treatment,
the roads leading to our institutions would be crowded
with anxious ones clamoring for admission.

After all, this foolish fear is entirely groundless. Cold water is no more to be dreaded than the "bogey man". It is one of our fundamental principles of treatment never to do anything that is painful to the patient. We always "temper the wind to the shorn lamb"—the coldness of the water and the force of the manipulations to the sensitiveness and endurance of the subject. Beginning with mild, alternately warm and cool sprays, which are pleasant and agreeable to everyone, we gradually increase the force and lower the temperature until the patient is so inured to cold water that the "blitz-guss" becomes a delightful and pleasurable sensation, a positive luxury.

It is amusing to watch the gradual change in the attitude of our patients toward the cold water treatment. In some instances we have had to spend hours in earnest persuasion before we could induce a particularly sensitive person to try the first mild spray. A few weeks later, if, perchance, something interfered with the continuation of the cold water treatment, the patient would vigorously protest against taking the other treatment without it.

There is certainly no finer tonic than cold water, no more exhilarating sensation than that produced by the skillful application of alternating douches and the "blitz".

The real cause of this cold water scare, we believe, is to be found in the boasting of the "veterans". When, with chest distended and chin in air, they brag to newcomers or to their friends about their heroism and the calmness with which they allow the cold water hose to be turned on them, the listener shudders and exclaims: "This cold water may be all right for you, but it would never do for me."

No doubt it is this bravado of the initiated which keeps many a novice from the first plunge into the mysteries of Nature Cure. If these timid ones only knew what they miss!

Business Versus Cures

From a business point of view it would, perhaps, be better for us to leave off the cold water altogether. It would certainly be much less trouble; but the rugged honesty of Father Kneipp, the champion of the cold water treatment branch of Nature Cure, has descended upon his followers and compels them to tell the whole truth and nothing but the truth, **to make use of everything that is likely to be of benefit to the patient and to effect a real and lasting cure.**

Our friends, the osteopaths, chiropractors and naprapaths, have only a pitying smile for our arduous labors. They ask, "Why fool with cold water and drive patients away, when pleasant manipulations bring the business?" If we query in return, "Do your pleasant manipulations cure obstinate chronic ailments?" they answer: "We do not expect to cure them. The effort involves too much labor and spoils the reputation of our work. Not one in a hundred chronics has the patience and perseverance to be cured. Besides, if a patient comes too long to the office for treatment he drives others away."

Some of the most "successful" osteopaths, chiropractors and naprapaths in this city make it a rule not to treat a patient longer than six weeks or two months.

In a number of cases this may be sufficient to produce marked primary improvement, but it is not enough to launch the patient into a healing crisis and, therefore, does not produce a **real** cure because it does not remove the underlying causes of the disease. Furthermore, if a healing crisis be produced under manipulative treatment the physician, if he does not understand the law of crisis, may suppress the healing crisis by more manipulative treatment. (See page 421, Loban.) If after a while the latent chronic condition again manifests in external symptoms, the patient returns for another course of treatment. He was "cured" so quickly before he feels sure of the same result again.

In justice to the osteopaths, chiropractors and naprapaths, it must be said that we are not referring to those chronic diseases which are directly caused by lesions of the spine or other bony structures. If such lesions be the sole cause of the trouble, their correction by manipulative treatment may produce a cure within a few weeks.

But notwithstanding the teachings of orthodox osteopathy, the majority of chronic ailments have their origin in other causes. In most cases the existing spinal lesions are themselves the result of other primary disease conditions which must be overcome before the spinal lesions will **remain corrected.**

The mode of treatment depends upon the object that is to be accomplished. If it is to make the patient "feel better" with the least possible expenditure of time, money, personal effort and self control on his part and the least amount of exertion on the part of the physician or "healer", then spinal manipulations or metaphysical formulas may be in order. But if the object is to cure actually and permanently a deep seated chronic disease, **all** methods of natural treatment, intelligently combined and adapted to the individual case, are required in order to accomplish satisfactory results.

Pull the Roots

Cutting off their tops does not kill weeds. The first sign of improvement in the treatment of a chronic disease does not mean a cure.

Diagnosis from the iris of the eye, borne out by every day practical experience, discloses the fact that symptomatic manifestations of disease are due to underlying constitutional causes; that the chronic symptoms are

Nature's feeble and ineffectual efforts to eliminate from the system scrofulous, psoric or syphilitic taints and the disease products resulting from food and drug poisoning, or to overcome the destructive effects of surgical mutilations.

An abatement of symptoms is, therefore, not always the sign of a real and permanent cure. The latter depends entirely on the elimination of the hereditary and acquired constitutional taints and poisons.

When, under the influence of natural living and methods of treatment, the body of the chronic becomes sufficiently purified and strengthened, a period of marked improvement may set in. All disease symptoms gradually abate, the patient gains in strength both physically and mentally and feels as though there was nothing the matter with him any more.

But the eyes tell a different story. They show that the underlying constitutional taints have not been fully eliminated—the weeds have not been pulled up by the roots. **This can be accomplished only by healing crises,** by Nature's cleansing and healing activities in the form of inflammatory and feverish processes. **Anything short of this is merely preliminary improvement,** ''training for the fight'' **but not a cure.**

When you order a suit of clothes from your tailor you do not take it away from him half finished; if you do you will not have a satisfactory garment.

No more should you interfere with your cure after the first signs of improvement. Continue until you have thoroughly eliminated from your system the hidden constitutional taints and the drug poisons which are the cause of your troubles. After that you can paddle your own canoe; right living and right thinking will then be sufficient to maintain perfect health and strength, physically, mentally and morally.

Is the Chronic to Be Left to His Fate Because Allopathy Says He Is Incurable?

Frequently we have been severely criticized by our friends, our coworkers or our patients for accepting seemingly hopeless chronic cases. They exclaim: "You know this man has locomotor ataxia and that woman is an epileptic; you certainly do not expect to cure them!" or "Doctor, don't you think it injures the institution to have that dreadful looking person around? He is nothing but skin and bones and surely cannot live much longer."

Sometimes open criticism and covert insinuation intimate that our reasons for taking "incurables" are mercenary.

If we should dismiss today those of our patients who, from the orthodox and popular point of view, are considered incurable, there would not remain ten out of a hundred. Yet our total failures are few and far between. Many such seemingly hopeless cases have come for treatment month after month, in several instances for a year or more, apparently without any marked advance; yet today they are in the best of health.

Yes, it is hard work and frequently thankless work to deal with these cases. It would be much easier, much more remunerative and would bring more glory if we should confine ourselves to the treatment of acute diseases, for it is there that Nature Cure works its most impressive miracles. On the other hand, to achieve the seemingly impossible, to prove what Nature Cure can accomplish in the most stubborn chronic cases, sustains our courage and is its own compensation.

The word "chronic" in the vocabulary of the old school of medicine is synonymous with "incurable". This is not strange, for since the medical and surgical symptomatic

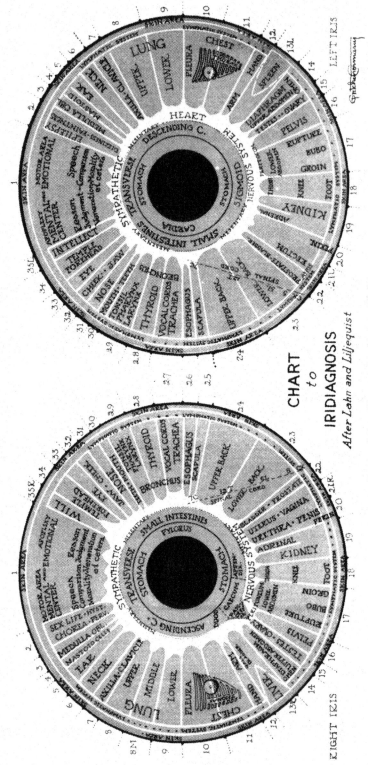

CHART
to
IRIDIAGNOSIS

After Lahn and Liljequist

Revised by Henry Lindlahr, M. D.

treatment of acute diseases creates the chronic conditions, it certainly cannot be expected to cure them.

If by continued suppression Nature's cleansing and healing efforts have been perverted into chronic disease conditions, the following directions are given in the "regular" works on medical practice:

"When this disease reaches the chronic stage, it is no longer curable. The patient may be advised to change climate or occupation. As for medication, the symptoms are treated as they arise."

We know that the symptoms are Nature's healing efforts; when these are promptly treated, that is, suppressed, it is not surprising that the chronic does not recover. In fact **it is the treatment which makes and keeps him a chronic.**

Why Nature Cure Achieves Results

Nature Cure achieves results in the treatment of chronic diseases because its theories and practices are entirely opposite to those just described. However, when the Nature Cure physician claims that he can cure cancer, consumption, epilepsy, paralysis, Bright's disease, diabetes or certain mental derangements, the allopath expresses only derision and contempt. He will not even condescend to examine any evidence in support of our claims.

Since, then, Nature Cure offers to the so called incurable the only hope and the only possible means of regaining health, why not give him a chance? Many times apparently hopeless cases have responded most readily to our treatment, while more promising ones offered the most stubborn resistance. Even with the best possible methods of diagnosis it is hard to determine just how far the destruction of vital organs has progressed or how deeply they have been impregnated with drug poisons.

Therefore it is often an impossibility to predict with

certainty just what the outcome will be. This can be determined only by a fair trial. In the past we have treated many a case that, according to the rules and precedents of orthodox science, should be dead and buried long ago; yet these individuals are today alive and in the best of health.

Every now and then incidents like the following renew our enthusiasm and our confidence in Nature Cure: Recently three cases were sent by three former patients who had been under treatment several years ago. These three had been among the worst cases ever treated in our institution. When they came to us, one was supposed to be dying with cancer, the second was in the advanced stages of tertiary syphilis and the third had survived several operations for the removal of the appendix and the ovaries. At the time the latter took up our treatment she had been advised to undergo another operation for the removal of the uterus.

These "incurables" had been exceedingly trying. More than once the one or the other had quit, discouraged, only to return, knowing that after all Nature Cure was their only hope. After they left us we lost track of them and often wondered how they were getting on. All three were reported by the newcomers as being in good health. What if it did take months or even years to produce the desired results? What would have been the fate of these three patients if it had not been for "slow" Nature Cure?

Discouraged patients frequently ask: "Why do others recover so quickly when I show such slow improvement? This cure seems to be all right for some diseases but evidently it does not fit my case."

This is defective reasoning. True Nature Cure fits every case because it includes everything good in natural healing methods. **In stubborn cases Nature Cure is not to blame for the slow and unsatisfactory results; the difficulty lies** in the character and advanced stage of the disease—in failure to turn to natural methods soon enough.

In the following chapters I shall briefly outline the natural methods of diagnosis, prognosis and treatment of chronic diseases.

CHAPTER XX

DIAGNOSIS AND PROGNOSIS

Diagnosis from the Nature Cure Viewpoint

THE allopathic school of medicine lays more stress upon correct diagnosis than upon treatment. This is the natural result of looking upon all chronic disease as incurable. Many times have I seen the presiding professor in a clinic spend an hour or more in analyzing minutely the anatomical, physiological and psychological aspects of a case.

To my question—"What is the cause of the trouble?" he would answer—"Nobody knows."

"What can we do for him?"

"Nothing. The case is incurable. Give him a placebo (make-believe)."

Our professor on Diseases of the Eye, Ear and Nose was doing post-graduate work in Vienna. From time to time he reported to our class his experiences in this great center of medical science. In one of these letters he wrote as follows: "This is certainly the greatest place in the world for doctors, but I doubt whether it is for patients. All that the doctors seem to be interested in is to see their diagnoses verified on the postmortem table. Treatment is of secondary importance." Contrast this with the attitude of the Nature Cure school toward diagnosis and treatment of chronic diseases.

Though we make more thorough examinations and give a more minutely accurate diagnosis and prognosis of disease in all its forms than does any other school of medical science, from our viewpoint diagnosis is of relatively small importance in the treatment and cure of any particular disease. To us, curing is far more vital than diagnosing.

Here our orthodox colleagues interpose: "This shows your Nature Cure to be empirical and not at all scientific. How can you cure if you do not first determine what is the disease?"

To this we answer: "The unity of disease is a fact in Nature. All disorders can be traced back to three primary manifestations, namely: (1) Lowered vitality; (2) Abnormal composition of blood and lymph; (3) Accumulation of waste materials, morbid matter and poisons."

It then follows that whoever succeeds in correcting these three underlying causes, thereby removes whatever disease originates from them.

Very simple, is it not? What is more, it is absolutely incontrovertible logic. To show that we are wrong it is necessary to disprove the Nature Cure postulate of the unity of disease and cure, as explained in Chapter VI.

To illustrate: Suppose a stranger should come to me and say, "Doctor, I am suffering from some serious chronic disease. Can you cure me without the customary examination?"

I should say to him without hesitation, "If that is your wish, I shall gladly do so. And furthermore, I am confident of excellent results, if in the nature of the case improvement be possible."

In accordance with the primary law of disease, I would first instruct the patient how to avoid all waste of vitality in his habits of thinking, feeling, eating, drinking, bathing, breathing, working, resting, and in his sex life.

I should then instruct him how to regulate his meals and combine his foods in such a way as to take in a minimum of disease producing and a maximum of blood build-

ing and purifying food elements. By blood building and
purifying food elements I refer to the juicy fruits and
fresh, leafy vegetables.

I would apply all methods of natural treatment which
tend to make the skin, bowels and kidneys more active
and alive. I would use good, old fashioned massage to
"squeeze" the morbid matter out of the tissues into the
venous and lymphatic circulation and to stimulate the
inflow of red arterial blood with its freight of oxygen and
other elements of nutrition.

Next in order would be Swedish movements and the
best suited manipulative treatment based on our principles of neurotherapy tending to correct spinal and other
mechanical lesions in bony structures, muscles, ligaments
and connective tissues.

I would teach him how to distinguish discordant and
destructive from harmonious and constructive thinking
and feeling, and how to help himself by positive, optimistic affirmations and suggestions.

In response to these teachings and treatments the patient's condition would gradually improve and he would
steadily advance toward the enjoyment of perfect health.
The only conditions which might prevent this happy consummation would be (1) vitality so lowered as to make
response to treatment an impossibility; (2) destruction of
vital organs beyond the possibility of repair; or (3) mechanical obstructions such as congenital malformation,
large tumors, large stones, etc., which might have to be
removed by surgical operation.

These statements are made not to discourage thorough
examination, diagnosis and prognosis, but to show the
wonderful possibilities and the simplicity of Nature Cure
philosophy and practice. While the foregoing claims are
in absolute conformity with Nature's laws, corroborated
by long experience and conclusive tests, it is quite true

that thorough examination gives the physician a much better understanding of abnormal conditions with which he must contend, and thereby greatly facilitates efficient treatment.

Moreover, the patient is entitled to a correct diagnosis of his case and to a rational and reliable prognosis. Such explanation, in conformity with the findings in the case, confirms the faith of the patient in the physician and secures his hearty cooperation in bringing about the desired results.

Nature Cure Diagnosis

In our methods of examination and treatment we combine all that has proved true and efficient in all systems, from the oldest to the most advanced, whether "orthodox" or "irregular", provided it conforms to the fundamental laws of cure. This is what makes Nature Cure philosophy and practice the only true eclectic system of treating human ailments.

On pages 240-241 will be found reproductions of a few sheets from our "Diagnosis Report" booklet. After thorough examination the findings are typewritten on these sheets and bound together to form a booklet. One copy is presented to the patient, another to the physician who commits the case to our care and the third remains in our files.

It will be seen that in these reports we give both the scientific standard and the patient's standard of blood, urine, sputum, etc. The patient's standard is estimated according to sex, age, height, weight, etc. The next column contains a report of the patient's own specimen which he may compare with the scientific standard and with his own standard.

On the back pages of the booklet are given full explanations of the scientific names and terms employed in these

PHYSICAL

Head and Neck:

Circulatory System:

Blood Pressure (Systolic):

Respiratory System:

Digestive System:

Urinary

Perspira

Lympha

Reflexor

Extremi

Height:

Weight

Special

Remark

IRIDIAGNOSIS

We do not claim that the Diagnosis from the Iris of the Eye reveals all abnormalities in the body, but we can affirm that Nature's records in the iris furnish a great deal of valuable information as to abnormal processes and especially as to the underlying causes of acute and chronic disease. These records in the iris reveal the inherent vitality and "tone" of the system, the presence of hereditary disease taints and of drug poisons, the nature and location of morbid encumbrances and the progress of all diseases through the hereditary acute, chronic catarrhal, and final destructive catarrhal stages.

This method of diagnosis is of special importance because it reveals many obscure causes of disease, which cannot be discovered in any other way.

COLOR: Normally light blue in the Indo-Caucasian race and its sub-races; and light brown in all preceding races. Gradual darkening of the color is associated with increasing morbid encumbrances of the system and lowered vitality. Gradual clearing up of darker color and disappearance of abnormal pigments, indicates purification of the system and progress towards normal.

DENSITY: Degree of density corresponds to degree of vitality and tissue tone.

The following and other abnormal processes are favorably influenced by the proper kind of spinal manipulation in the indicated areas.

Headaches, Insomnia, Eye Disorders, Catarrhal Deafness, Etc.

Dizziness, Catarrh of Nose & Throat.

Goiter, Tonsilitis, Etc.

Heart Trouble, Lung Disorders.

Stomach and Liver Troubles.

LINDLAHR HEALTH RESORT   LINDLAHR COLLEGE of NATURE CURE   LINDLAHR SANITARIUM

URINE ANALYSIS

microscopical tests determine by the kidneys from the blood, ry, but also indicate whether the work of the various organs and tory findings invariably suggest cient in the diet.

our figures in the "normal" of by the authorities of the regular dards of normality of the medical ditions of the "average healthy"

then the average condition of s, drug poisoning, and proximit the normal, that is, below the would obtain if habits of living are how natural and rational. This the laboratory findings from ing to the Nature Cure standard.

Solids in Urine.

olids be too low for your weight defective kidney-elimination is ve.

f solids points to an excessive ally overburden not only the

Acidity of Urine.

andpoint, the normal acidity been demonstrated that individ f a neutral reaction.

s about mainly by an excess of es in the foods. If allowed to fually undermine the entire o

Indican.

en points to auto-intoxication the intestines. Indican may m. Being an abnormal waste do with the preparation and t nce of the other findings fro physicians.

Lindlahr Nature Cure Institutes

HENRY LINDLAHR, M. D., PRESIDENT

MAIN OFFICE
525 SOUTH ASHLAND BOULEVARD
CHICAGO, ILLINOIS

Examination
Reports

(Copyright 1916 by The Lindlahr Nature Cure Institutes)

Name

Address

PRESERVE THESE REPORTS FOR FUTURE REFERENCE

DIAGNOSIS FROM T[ ]

RIGHT EYE

Color:

Density:

Scurf Rim:

Psora:

Symp. Wreath:

Nerve Rings:

Lymphatics:

Drug Signs:

Acute Signs:

Subacute Signs:

Chronic Signs:

Closed Lesions:

LABORATORY REPORTS

B. BLOOD COUNT	Normal	Specimen	Specimen	Specimen
Leukocytes	7,500			
Erythrocytes	5,000,000			
Ratio—White to Red	1 to 666			
Hemoglobin	100 %			
Color Index	1			
Pathological Cells	None			
Differential Count	—			
C. SPUTUM EXAMINATION	Normal	Specimen	Specimen	Specimen
	None			

LABORATORY REPORTS

Age: Height: Ft.   In.   Weight: Lbs.   Kgs.

A. URINE ANALYSIS	Normal Per KG.	Patient's Normal	Specimen	Specimen	Spec
Appearance	Clear Straw	Clear Straw			
Volume	22.5				
Density	1015	1015			
Solids	.786				
Reaction	Neutral	Neutral			
Acidity	0°	0°			
Sulphates	.02				
Chlorides	.06				
Phosphates	.10				
Urea	.225				
Ammonia	0				
Sugar	0				
Acetone	0				
Albumin	0				
Indican	0				
Blood	0				
Bile	0				
Special					

BASIC DIAGNOSIS

Physical—Digestive Organ-System:

Moral—Reproductive Organ-System:

Mental—Respiratory Organ-System:

REMARKS:

Similar causes produce different effects upon different individuals.

SPINAL ANALYSIS

Regions	OSTEOPATHY. Lesions	NEUROPATHY. V. M. R. Palp.	CHIROPRACTIC. Majors	NAPRAPATHY. Ligatights	SPONDYLOTHERAPY. Ref. Hyp.
Cervical					
Thoracic					
Lumbar					
Sacrum					
Coccyx					
Innominata					
Ribs					
Sternum					
Clavicles					
Special					
Remarks					

HISTORY SHEET

Date: Number:

Name: Nativity:

Address: Telephone:

Age: Sex: Civil State: Occupation:
Children:

Family History:

Personal History:

Sleep: Appetite: Periods:

SEE REVERSE SIDE

reports. In this way the various reports have some meaning to the layman, whereas the ordinary report on blood, urine, etc. from a chemical laboratory has little or no meaning to the patient, unless fully explained, and even then it is usually soon forgotten. Our unique examination report is not only fully comprehensible to the layman, but it is also of great value in ascertaining improvement or deterioration when subsequent examinations are made.

But while our physical and laboratory examinations are made in accordance with the most advanced methods of the regular school of medicine, our interpretation is often at wide variance with the established theories of the old school of medicine. Some of these differences are pointed out in the explanations on the back pages of the examination sheets.

The diagnosis from the iris of the eye is of great interest and importance, not only because it gives accurate information about causes of disease which cannot be diagnosed in any other way, but also because these wonderful records confirm the fundamental principles of Nature Cure philosophy and practice. This fact must be strongly impressed upon the mind of the reader so that it may not be lost sight of in studying the interesting revelations of the signs in the iris.

We have heretofore made the statement, and it is here repeated, **that we do not claim to be able to read in the iris all the details of disease and of specific pathological conditions. I do claim emphatically, however, that this science contains so much of paramount importance in the diagnosis and rational treatment of disease that the conscientious physician and even the intelligent layman cannot afford to ignore nor discredit it.**

As will be seen by reference to our examination reports, we do not by any means depend upon this method of examination and diagnosis alone. But by combining iridiagnosis with all other approved methods of examination we find that one elucidates and confirms the others.

In our diagnosis work the patient proceeds from one physician to another, each one making his own particular tests as regards eyes, spine, vital organs, etc. without any reference to the results of the other examinations. The patient is pleasantly surprised to notice that the eye diagnostician finds and describes the same "lesions" in the eyes which the spinal therapist discovers in the spine and nerve centers, and which the medical examiner finds through his physical examination. If their reports are correct they will be confirmed by the findings in the laboratory as well. This explains why we very rarely fail in giving a reliable diagnosis and prognosis of a case which has undergone thorough systematic examination by our combined methods.

CHAPTER XXI

THE TREATMENT OF CHRONIC DISEASES

THE old school of medical science defines **acute diseases** as those which run a brief and more or less violent course, and **chronic diseases** as those which run a protracted course and have a tendency to recur.

Nature Cure attaches a broader and more significant meaning to these terms. This has become apparent from my discussion of the causes, the progressive development and the purpose of acute diseases in the preceding pages.

From the Nature Cure viewpoint, the chronic condition is the latent, constitutional disease encumbrance, whereas acute disease represents Nature's efforts to rectify abnormal conditions, to overcome and eliminate hereditary or acquired morbid taints and systemic poisons and to reestablish normal structure and functions.

To use an illustration: In a case of permanent or recurrent itchy psoriasis, the old school physician would look upon the itchy skin eruption as the "chronic disease", while we see in the external eczema an attempt of the healing forces of Nature to remove from the system the inner, latent hereditary or acquired psora, which constitutes the real chronic disease.

It stands to reason that the exterior eruptions should not be suppressed by any means whatever, but that the only true and really effective method of treatment consists in eliminating from the organism the inner, latent psoric taint. After this is accomplished the external "skin disease" will disappear of its own accord.

As another illustration of the radical difference in our

244

respective points of view, let us take hemorrhoids (piles). The allopathic doctor considers the local hemorrhoidal enlargement in itself the chronic disease, while the Nature Cure physician looks upon hemorrhoids as one of Nature's efforts to rid the system of certain morbid encumbrances and poisons which have accumulated as a result of sluggish circulation, chronic constipation, defective elimination through kidneys, lungs and skin, and from many other causes.

These constitutional abnormalities, which are the real chronic disease, have to be treated and corrected. After this has been done, the hemorrhoidal enlargements and discharges will take care of themselves.

It is, therefore, absolutely irrational, and frequently followed by the most serious consequences, to extirpate the piles or to suppress the hemorrhoidal discharges, and thereby to drive these concentrated poison extracts back into the system.

In a number of cases we have traced paralysis, insanity, tuberculosis, cancer and other forms of chronic destructive diseases to the forcible suppression of hemorrhoids.

Chronic disease, from the viewpoint of Nature Cure philosophy, means that the organism has become permeated with morbid matter and poisons to such an extent that it is no longer able to throw off these encumbrances by vigorous, "acute" eliminative effort. The chronic condition, therefore, represents the slow, cold type of disease, characterized by feeble, ineffectual efforts to eliminate the latent morbid taints and impediments from the system. These efforts may take the form of open sores, skin eruptions, catarrhal discharges, chronic diarrhea, etc., etc.

If acute diseases are treated in harmony with Nature's laws, they will leave the body in a purer, healthier condition. But if the treatment is wrong, if under the old school methods fever and inflammation (Nature's methods of elimination) are checked and suppressed with poisonous drugs, serums and antitoxins, or if, instead of purifying and invigorating cells and tissues, the affected parts and organs are extirpated with the surgeon's knife, Nature is not allowed to get rid of the disease matter and the poisonous taints and morbid encumbrances remain in the organism.

In this way originate the worst forms of chronic diseases which now afflict civilized races.

The truth of this assertion is proved by the fact that the most destructive chronic diseases are not found among any of the primitive peoples of the earth, as the negroes in Africa and Australia and the Esquimaux of the arctic regions. They are not found among people who do not use drugs. The different forms of venereal disease, cancer, tuberculosis, many forms of paralysis and paresis, etc., are unknown in those countries whose inhabitants live in harmony with Nature. The reason is that these people have not learned to suppress Nature's acute purifying and healing efforts by poisonous drugs and surgical operations.

The Cell

Let us now study the actual condition of the cells, tissues and organs of the body in chronic disease.

We know that the human body is made up of millions of minute cells of living protoplasm, and that the life of the protoplasm and especially of the germ plasm is inherent in the microzyma. Though these cells are so small that they have to be magnified under the microscope several hundred times before we can see them, they are individual living beings which grow, eat, drink and throw off waste matter, just like the large conglomerate cell which we call "man".

Each one of these little cells has its own business to

attend to, whether it be digestion, assimilation, elimination or the performance of any other of the thousand and one functions and activities which make up the metabolism of the human organism.

If these little beings are well individually, the man is well. If they are starved or ailing, the entire man is similarly affected. We know now that the health of the cell depends upon the well being of its microzyma. The whole depends upon the parts. In the human body as well as in a nation or a city, the welfare of the entire community depends upon the well being of its individual members.

If governing bodies would realize and apply these truths and pay more attention to the provision of wholesome surroundings and proper conditions of living for their subjects, to an adequate supply of pure food and a normal combination of work and rest, instead of concentrating their best efforts upon restrictive and punitive measures (allopathic treatment), there would be few social problems to solve.

It is our duty to provide the most favorable conditions of living for the little cells that make up the individual human organism. If we do that, **there will be no occasion for disease.** "Natural immunity" will be the result.

Herein lies the vital difference between the attitude of Nature Cure and that of the allopathic school toward disease. The latter spends all its efforts in fighting the disease symptoms, while the former confines itself to creating health conditions in the habits and surroundings of the patient from the standpoint that the disease symptoms will then take care of themselves, that they will disappear because of non-support. It is the application of the injunction "Resist not evil but overcome evil with good" to the treatment of physical disease.

Under the influence of wrong habits of living and the suppressive treatment of diseases, all forms of waste and

morbid matter (the feces of the cells), together with food,
drink and drug poisons, accumulate in the system, injure
the cells and obstruct the minute spaces (interstices)
between them. These morbid encumbrances impinge upon
and clog the blood vessels, the nerve channels and the
other tissues of the body. This is bound to interfere with
the normal functions of the organism and in time leads to
deterioration and organic destruction.

In this connection we wish to call attention to a difference in viewpoint between the school of Osteopathy and
the Nature Cure school. Osteopaths and Chiropractors
attribute disease almost entirely to ''impingement'' (abnormal pressure) upon nerves and blood vessels due to
dislocations and subluxations of the vertebrae of the spine
and of other bony structures. **They do not take into consideration the impingement upon and obstruction of nerve
channels and blood vessels all through the system caused
by local or general encumbrances of the organism with
waste matter, morbid products and poisons that have accumulated in cells and tissues.**

The Life of the Cell

Every individual cell must be supplied with food and
with oxygen. These it receives from the red arterial blood.
The cells must also be provided with an outlet for their
waste products. This is furnished by the lymphatic and
venous circulations which constitute the drainage system
of the body. If drainage is defective, the effect upon the
organism is similar to the effect produced when drains are
obstructed and sewage is forced back into a building.

Furthermore, every cell must be in unobstructed communication with the nerve currents of the organism. Most
important of all, it must be in touch with the sympathetic
nervous system through which it receives the life force

which vivifies and controls all involuntary functions of the cells and organs in the body.

Each individual cell must be supplied with two sets of nerve connections, one to convey its sensations and needs to "headquarters", the nerve centers in brain and spinal cord; the other to carry impulses from the cranial, spinal and sympathetic centers to the cell, governing and directing its activities.

For instance, if the cell be hungry, thirsty, cold or in pain, it telegraphs these sensations to headquarters in the brain or spinal cord, and from there directions necessary to comply with the needs of the cell are sent forth in the form of nerve impulses to the centers controlling the circulation, the food and heat supply, the means of protection, etc., etc.

This circuit of communication from the cell over the afferent nerves to the nerve centers in the brain or spinal cord, and from these centers over the efferent nerves back to the cell or to other cells is called "the reflex arc".

Let us use an illustration: Suppose the fingers come in close contact with a hot iron. The cells in the finger tips experience a sensation of burning pain. At once this sensation is telegraphed over the afferent nerves to the nerve centers in the brain or spinal cord. In response to this call of distress the command comes back over the efferent nerve filaments: "Withdraw the fingers!" At the same time the impulse to withdraw the fingers is sent over the motor nerves to the muscles which control the movements of the hand.

If the means of communication between the different parts of the organism are obstructed or cut off entirely, the individual cell is bound to deteriorate and to die, just as a person lost in a barren wilderness and cut off from his fellow men must perish.

In warfare it is a well known fact that if one of the contending armies succeeds in cutting off the food supply or the telegraphic communication of the other army with its headquarters, the activities of the enemy are seriously handicapped. So the waste materials in the system, the disease taints, narcotic and alcoholic poisons, etc., obstruct the nerve passages and thus interfere with the functions of the cell by cutting off its means of communication.

What has been said will serve to elucidate and emphasize the necessity of perfect cleanliness, inside as well as outside of the body. It justifies the dictum of Kuhne, one of the pioneers of Nature Cure, "Health is cleanliness." Anything that in any way interferes with or obstructs the circulation of vital fluids and nerve currents in the system is bound to create abnormal conditions and functions which constitute disease.

When the morbid encumbrances and obstructions in the organism have reached the point where they seriously interfere with the nourishment, drainage and nerve supply of the cells, the latter cannot perform their activities properly, nor can they rid themselves of the impediment. They may be compared to individuals who are forced to live in unwholesome surroundings and who cannot do their best work under these unfavorable conditions.

In this way originates chronic disease, which means that the cells have become incapable of arousing themselves to acute eliminative effort in the form of inflammatory febrile reactions.

In my lectures I sometimes liken the cell thus encumbered with morbid matter and poisons to a man buried in a mine under the débris of a "cave in" in such a manner that it is impossible for him to free himself of the earth and timbers which are pinning him down. In such a predicament the man is unable to help himself. His fellow-workers or his friends must come to his aid and remove the obstructing masses so that he may be able to free himself.

This is a good illustration of the condition of the cells of the body in chronic disease. They also have become unable to help themselves and need assistance until they can once more arouse themselves to self-help by means of acute eliminative effort.

What can we do to help them? **We must endeavor, in the first place, to furnish the cells with the right nourishment.** We must abstain from everything that may be injurious to the body in food and drink so as to relieve the cells of all unnecessary work.

Whatever one may think of vegetarianism as a continuous mode of living, a little consideration will make it plain that a rational vegetarian diet is the "sine qua non" in the cure of chronic diseases. It builds up the blood on a normal basis, excludes all food and drink poisons and thereby gives the organism an opportunity to throw off the old accumulations of waste and morbid materials.

In chronic disease, every drop of blood and every cell of the organism is affected. In order to produce a cure, the old tissues must be broken down and removed and new tissues built up. The more thorough the change in diet, the greater and more rapid will be the changes for the better in cells and tissues, especially if only pure and eliminating foods are used.

For these reasons it is advisable to omit meat from the dietary. All animal flesh contains the morbid excretions and other waste products of the animal organism, and this means additional work for the cells already over burdened with systemic poisons.

Then we must work for elimination. Cold water applied to the surface of the body is the most powerful stimulant to the circulation. It pulls and pushes the blood through the system. One actually feels the blood rushing through the arteries and veins with greater force.

The cold water treatment makes the skin more alive and active, stirs up and accelerates the circulation throughout the system and thus promotes the elimination of systemic poisons through the skin.

This stimulating effect of cold water upon the organism has been proved by counting the number of red blood corpuscles in a drop of blood before and after the application of the cold "blitz-guss". In some instances they were found to have doubled in number. This does not mean that in an instant twice as many red blood corpuscles had come into existence; but it does mean that before the cold "guss" one-half of them were dozing lazily in the corners. The cold water stirred them up, forced them into the circulation, made them travel and attend to business.

Another powerful means to promote elimination is **thorough, systematic massage.** The deep kneading, twisting, rolling and stroking actually squeezes the stagnant morbid matter and the waste products out of the tissues into the circulation, to be carried off through the venous drainage. This allows the red blood with its nourishment and fresh supply of oxygen to flood the cells and organs.

Massage is very effective as a means of regulating the blood supply in the system. In every chronic disease there is obstruction or congestion in some part of the organism, causing high blood pressure in the interior of the body and insufficient blood supply to surface and extremities. Massage distributes the blood quickly and evenly.

Of great importance is neurotherapy. Impingement on nerves and blood vessels should be corrected by expert manipulation. As a matter of fact, hardly a person can be found today whose spine is not abnormal in one way or another, just as there is not a single perfectly normal human iris.

Neurotherapy removes abnormal pressure upon nerves and blood vessels and establishes a free and abundant flow of nerve and blood currents.

Air and light baths, by stimulating the skin in a natural manner to increased activity, also contribute to the attainment of the various good results just described.

Next comes **physical exercise.** Corrective and curative gymnastics **combined with deep breathing** promote the combustion (oxidation) of morbid materials and in this way facilitate their elimination from the system.

Life itself is dependent upon breathing. The Life Force enters the body with every breath we draw. Show me a man with well developed, full breathing lungs and I will show you a man with good vitality.

Last but not least among the natural methods of treating the cell in chronic disease we mention **the right mental and emotional attitude.** Fear, anxiety and all kindred emotions congeal the nerve matter and thereby shut off the supply of nerve force. The cells and tissues actually starve and freeze. On the other hand, the emotions of hope, confidence and cheerfulness relax and open blood vessels and nerve channels and allow the free and unobstructed inflow and circulation of fluids and of vital energy.

The different methods of natural treatment and their practical application in chronic diseases are fully described in the treatment section of Volume II of this series.

When, through natural methods of living and of treatment, the morbid encumbrances have been removed sufficiently to provide and maintain normal blood supply, better venous and lymphatic drainage and the unobstructed flow of the nerve currents, when lesions of the bony structures have been corrected by skillful adjustment and when, through the right mental attitude, a free and abundant inflow of Life Force has been established, then the cells and tissues of the body become once again able to arouse themselves to an acute eliminative effort and the organism is ready for a healing crisis.

To recapitulate—the objects to be obtained by the natural treatment of chronic diseases are:

(1) to economize vitality;

(2) to promote assimilation;

(3) to promote the elimination of waste and morbid matter;

(4) to correct mechanical lesions;

(5) to adjust and to harmonize mental and emotional conditions.

In the following chapters the laws and principles underlying healing crises and their periodicity will be fully described.

CHAPTER XXII

CRISES

CRISIS in the ordinary sense of the word means change, either for better or for worse. In medical parlance the term "crisis" has been defined as "a decisive change in the disease, resulting either in recovery or in death".

We of the Nature Cure school distinguish between "healing crises" and "disease crises", according to the character and the tendency of the acute reaction. If an acute disease is brought about through the accumulation of morbid matter to such an extent that the health or the life of the organism is endangered, in other words, if the disease conditions are forcing the crisis, we speak of disease crisis. But if acute reactions take place in the system because conditions have become more normal, because the healing forces have gained the ascendancy and forced the acute inflammatory processes, we refer to them as healing crises.

Healing crises are simply different forms of elimination by means of which Nature endeavors to remove the latent chronic disease encumbrance from the system. The most common forms of these acute purifications are acute catarrhal colds and hemorrhoidal discharges, boils, ulcers, abscesses, open sores, skin eruptions, diarrheas, hemorrhages, abnormal perspiration and all sorts of inflammatory processes.

Healing crises and disease crises may seem very much alike. Patients often tell me: "I have had this before. I call it an ordinary boil (or cold, or fever)."

That may be true. The former disease crisis and the

255

present healing crisis may be similar in their outward manifestations. **But they are taking place under entirely different conditions.**

When the organism is loaded to the danger point with morbid matter it may arouse itself in self-defense to an acute eliminative effort in the shape of cold, catarrh, fever, inflammation, skin eruption, etc. In these instances, the disease conditions bring about the crisis and the organism is on the defensive. These are disease crises.

Such unequal struggles between the healing forces and pathogenic conditions sometimes end favorably and sometimes fatally.

On the other hand, healing crises develop because the healing forces are in the ascendancy and take the offensive. They are brought about through natural methods of living and of treatment, and always result in improved conditions.

A simple allegory may assist in making clear the difference between a healing crisis and a disease crisis:

For years a prize fighter holds the championship because he keeps himself in perfect physical condition and before every contest spends many weeks in careful training. When he faces his opponent in the ring, he has eliminated from his organism as much waste matter and superfluous flesh and fat as possible by a strictly regulated diet and a great deal of vigorous exercise. As a consequence, he comes off victorious in every contest and easily maintains his superiority.

These victories in his career, like healing crises in the organism, are the result of training and preparation. The prize fighter in the one case and Vital Force in the other are on the offensive from the beginning of the struggle and have the advantage from start to finish.

Rendered over confident by long continued success, our champion gradually permits himself to drift into a weakened physical condition. He omits his regular training and indulges in all kinds of dissipation.

One day, full of self conceit and underestimating the strength of his challenger, he enters the ring without adequate preparation and is ingloriously defeated by a man who, under different circumstances, would not be a match for him.

So, in the case of a patient in a disease crisis, fatal termination may be due to the excessive accumulation of waste and morbid matter in the system, to lowered vitality and to lack of preparation. Victory or defeat in acute reactions, as well as in the "ring", depends upon right living and preparatory training.

In the healing crisis, vitality is the stronger and gains the victory in the struggle; in the disease crisis disease conditions have gained the ascendancy and bring about the defeat of the healing forces.

Under conditions favorable to human life, a body endowed with healthy blood and tissues and good vitality cannot be affected by acute disease. Such an organism is practically immune to all forms of inflammatory febrile reactions. These always indicate that there is something in the system which Nature is trying to correct or to get rid of, namely, pathogenic matter.

Healing Crises

In the catechism of Nature Cure I have defined healing crises as follows: A healing crisis is an acute reaction resulting from the ascendancy of Nature's healing forces over disease conditions. Its tendency is toward recovery, and it is, therefore, in conformity with Nature's constructive principle.

The possibility of producing healing crises and thereby curing chronic ailments depends upon the following conditions:

(1) The patient must possess sufficient vital energy and power of reaction to respond to the natural treatment and to a change of habits.

(2) The destruction and disorganization of vital fluids and organs must not have advanced too far.

Some patients become frightened at the idea of crises. They exclaim: "I came here to get well, not to grow worse."

However, there is no occasion for alarm. Healing crises occur in mild form only because under the influence of natural living and treatment, Nature has the advantage in the fight. The healing forces of the organism have gained the ascendancy over the disease conditions.

In fact, **Nature never undertakes a healing crisis until the system has been prepared for it,** until the organism is sufficiently purified and strengthened to conduct the acute reaction to a favorable termination.

Furthermore, it is well to remember that crises cannot be avoided, because it is through fevers and inflammatory processes that Nature effects the cure,—that she decomposes pathogen into simpler compounds suitable for elimination.

On the other hand, if a patient is possessed of good vitality, is not too heavily encumbered with pathogenic materials classified in Column VI of Diagram on page 347, and if the organs of elimination are in good working order, the purification and adjustment of the organism may proceed gradually without the occurrence of marked acute reactions or crises. When the morbid encumbrances consist largely of highly complex ptomains, leukomains and alkaloids which resist neutralization by alkaline mineral elements, then Nature has to resort to bacterial activity and inflammatory processes in order to reduce these pathogenic materials to simpler compounds (see Column V) suitable for elimination through the natural channels.

Healing Crises, When Properly Conducted, Are Never Fatal to Life

When well assisted by right, natural methods of living and of treatment, healing crises are never dangerous or fatal to life. The only danger lies in suppressing these acute reactions by drugs, knife, ice or other means.

If acute reactions are suppressed, the constructive healing crisis may be changed into a destructive disease crisis. Therefore we earnestly warn our patients never to interfere in any way with a healing crisis lest the chronic condition become worse than before.

When Nature, with all the force inherent in the human organism, has finally worked up to the point of a healing crisis, another defeat by a new suppression may be beyond her powers of endurance and recuperation. Fatal collapse may then be the result.

Therefore, take heed! If you are not willing to endure healing crises, do not undertake the treatment. Nothing good in life comes to us unless we pay the price. He who is too cowardly to conquer in a healing crisis may forfeit his life in a disease crisis.

Drugs Versus Healing Crises

Our explanations of the natural laws of cure and of natural therapeutics are often greeted by old school physicians and students with remarks like the following:

"You speak as if you had the monopoly of eliminative treatment and of the production of crises. With our laxatives, cathartics, diuretics, diaphoretics and tonics, we are accomplishing the same thing. What is more effectual for stimulating a sluggish liver and cleansing the intestinal tract than calomel followed by a dose of salts? What will produce more profuse perspiration than pilocarpin; or what is a better stimulus to the kidneys than squills or buchu? Can we not by means of stimulants and depressants regulate heart action to a nicety?

"We accomplish all this in a clean, scientific manner, without resorting to unpleasant dieting and to the applications of douches, packs and manual treatments. Isn't it more dignified and professional to write a Latin prescription? How much better the impression on the laity than soaking and rubbing!"

Let us see if these statements be true, whether laxation, urination or perspiration produced by poisonous drugs is identical in character and in effect with the elimination produced by healing crises brought on through natural living and natural methods of treatment.

Mercury, in the form of calomel, is one of the best-known cholagogues. It is the favorite laxative and cathartic of allopathy. The prevailing idea is that calomel acts on the liver and the intestines; but **in reality these organs act on the drug.**

All laxatives and cathartics are poisons; if it were not so, they would not produce their peculiar, drastic effects. Because they are poisons, Nature tries to eliminate them from the system as quickly and as thoroughly as possible. In order to do this, the excretory glands and membranes of the liver and the digestive tract greatly increase the amount of their secretions and thereby produce a forced evacuation of the intestinal canal.

Thus the system, in the effort to eliminate the mercurial poison, expels also the other contents of the intestines. This may affect a temporary cleansing of the intestinal tract, **but it does not and cannot cleanse the individual cells throughout the body of their impurities.**

Second and Permanent Effects of Artificial Purging

"Action and reaction are equal and opposite." In accordance with the law of action and reaction, the temporary irritation and over-stimulation of the sensitive membranes of the digestive organs are followed by corresponding weakness and exhaustion, and if this procedure be repeated it becomes habitual. As atrophy progresses the dose of the purgative must be increased in order to accomplish the desired result and this, in its turn, hastens the degenerative changes in the system.

Such enforced artificial purging may flush the drains and sewers but does not cleanse the inner chambers of the house. The cells in the interior tissues remain encumbered with morbid matter. **A genuine and truly effective house-cleaning must start in the cells and must be brought about through the initiative of the vital energies in the organism, through healing crises and not through stimulation by means of poisonous irritants.**

When, under a natural regimen of living and of treatment, the system has been sufficiently purified, adjusted and vivified the cells themselves begin the work of elimination.

This is what takes place: the morbid matter and poisons thrown off by the cells and tissues are carried by means of the venous circulation to the organs of elimination, the bowels, kidneys, lungs and skin, and to the mucous membranes lining the interior tracts, such as the nasal passages, the throat and bronchi, the digestive and genito-urinary organs, etc.

These organs of elimination become overcrowded with the rush of morbid matter and the accompanying congestion and irritation cause the acute inflammatory processes and feverish symptoms characterizing the various forms of colds, catarrhs, skin eruptions, diarrheas, boils and other acute forms of elimination which we call healing crises. In other words, **what the old school of medicine calls the disease, we look upon as the cure.**

Acute elimination brought about in this manner is, as

previously explained, Nature's method of housecleaning. It is a true healing crisis, **the result of purification and increased activity from within the cell, produced by natural means.**

Here interposes Friend Allopath: "You claim that you bring about your acute reactions by natural means only, and that these are never injurious to the organism. What difference does it make if the circulation is stimulated and elimination increased by a cold water spray or by digitalis? The cold water stimulation produces a reaction just as digitalis does and the one must therefore be as injurious as the other."

To this I reply: The stimulating effect on heart and circulation produced by digitalis is the first action of a highly poisonous drug; the second lasting effect is weakening and depressing. On the other hand, the first action of a cold water spray is depressive; it sends the blood into the interior of the body and leaves the surface bloodless. The sensory nerves at once report this sensation of cold to headquarters in the brain, and immediately the command is telegraphed to the vasomotor centers which control the circulation, "Send blood to the surface!" As a result, the blood is carried to the surface and the skin becomes warm and rosy with the glow of life. In this case the **stimulation** is the **second and lasting** effect of the water treatment, from which there is no further reaction unless the patient be in a very weakened condition. Then the treatment must be modified accordingly.

Similarly, the stimulation produced by exercise, massage, neurotherapy, or the exposure of the nude body to light and air, is natural stimulation produced by harmless, natural means. It is entirely due to the fact that conditions in the system have been made more normal, as explained in other chapters.

Drugs, stimulants and tonics, while they do produce an

artificial, temporary stimulation, do not change the underlying abnormal conditions in the organism. Likewise, the
flushing of the colon with water, the use of laxative herb
teas and decoctions, or forced sweating by means of Tur-
kish or Russian baths, though not as dangerous as inorganic minerals and poisonous drugs, cannot be classed
among the natural means of cure. These agents, which by
many persons are looked upon as natural treatment, irritate the organs of elimination to forced, abnormal activity
without at the same time arousing the cells in the interior
of the body to natural elimination.

Dr. H. Lahmann, one of the foremost scientists of the
Nature Cure movement, made a series of interesting experiments. From certain patients he gathered the natural
perspiration produced by ordinary exercise in the sunshine. These excretions of the skin were evaporated and
analyzed and were found to contain powerful toxins.

When, however, profuse sweating was produced in the
same patients by high temperature of the hot air box or the
electric light cabinet, their perspiration, when evaporated
and analyzed, was found to contain only small amounts of
toxins. Thus Dr. Lahmann proved that

(1) sweating, and the elimination of disease matter are
    two different processes;

(2) artificially induced sweating does not eliminate dis-
    ease matter;

(3) the organism cannot be forced by irritants and stimu-
    lants and artificial means, but eliminates morbid mat-
    ter only in its own natural manner and when it is in
    proper condition to do so.

In a lesser degree this applies also to fasting. Under
certain conditions it becomes a necessity but it may easily
be abused and overdone. This subject is treated at length
in Chapter XXVII.

That the medical profession does not understand the

principle of natural elimination is proved by the fact that in cases where the system works up to some form of natural elimination in the way of purging, catarrhal discharges, skin eruptions, etc., they forthwith suppress these purifying processes by poisonous drugs or other agents.

Do We Never Fail?

Certainly we fail, but our failures are usually due to the fact that the sick, as a rule, do not consider Nature Cure except as a last resort. The methods and requirements of Nature Cure appear at first so unusual and exacting that most persons seek to evade them as long as they have the least faith in the miracle working power of the poison bottle, a metaphysical healer or the surgeon's knife. When health, wealth and hope are entirely exhausted, then the chronic sufferer grasps at Nature Cure as a drowning man clutches at a straw. But even though ninety percent of the cases which come to us are of the apparently incurable type, our total failures are few and far between.

If there is sufficient vitality in the body to react to natural treatment and if the destruction of vital parts and organs has not advanced too far, a cure is possible. Often the seemingly hopeless cases yield the most readily.

Our success is due to the fact that we do not rely on any one method of treatment, but combine in our work everything that is practical and beneficial in all different systems of natural healing.

The Law of Crises

Everywhere in nature and in the world of men we find the Law of Crises in evidence. This proves it to be a universal law, ruling all cosmic relations and activities.

Wars and revolutions are the healing crises in the life of nations—of social and political life.

Heresies and reformations are the crises of religion.

In strikes, riots and panics we recognize the crises of commercial life.

Staid old Mother Earth herself has in the hoary past repeatedly changed the configuration of her continents and oceans by great cataclysms or geological crises.

When the sultry summer air has become pregnant with poisonous vapors and miasms, atmospheric crises, such as rainstorms and electric storms, cool and purify the air and charge it anew with life giving ozone.

In like manner will healing crises purify the disease laden bodies of men.

Emanuel Swedenborg gives us a wonderful description of the law of crises in its relationship to the regeneration of the soul. I quote from the chapter in which he describes the working of this law, entitled, "Regeneration is Effected by Combats in Temptation".

"They who have not been instructed concerning the regeneration of man think that man can be regenerated without temptation. But it is to be known that no one is regenerated without temptation; and that many temptations succeed, one after another. The reason is that regeneration is effected for an end, in order that the life of the old man may die, and the new life which is heavenly be insinuated. It is evident, therefore, that there must be a conflict" (healing crisis); "for the life of the old man resists and determines not to be extinguished; and the life of the new man can only enter where the life of the old is extinct.

"Whoever thinks from an enlightened rationale, may see and perceive from this that a man cannot be regenerated without combat, that is, without spiritual temptations; and further, that he is not regenerated by one temptation, but by many. For there are very many kinds of evil which formed the delight of his former life, that is, of the old life. These evils cannot all be subdued at once and together; for they cleave tenaciously, since they have been inrooted in the parents for many ages back'' (the scrofula of the soul) ''and are therefore innate in man, and are confirmed by actual evils from himself from infancy. All these evils are diametrically opposite to the celestial good'' (perfect health) ''that is to be insinuated and which is to constitute the New Life.''

Thus the inspired Seer of the North draws a vivid picture of what we call healing crises in their relation to moral regeneration.

We cannot help recognizing the close agreement of physical and spiritual crises. This, again, demonstrates the continuity and exact correspondence of Natural Law on the different planes of being.

We of the Nature Cure school know that this great Law of Crises dominates the cure of chronic disease. Every case is another verification of it; in fact, every decided advance on the road to perfect health is marked by acute reactions.

The cure invariably proceeds through the darkness and chaos of healing crises to the light and beauty of perfect health, periods of marked improvement alternating with acute eliminative activity (the ''spiritual temptations and combats'' of Swedenborg) until perfect regeneration has taken place.

CHAPTER XXIII

PERIODICITY

IN many forms of acute disease, crises develop with marked regularity and well defined periodicity. This phenomenon has been observed and described by many physicians. It is not so well known, however, that under the treatment of **chronic** diseases by natural methods crises develop in accordance with certain laws of periodicity.

This periodicity is governed by the septimal law, or the law of sevens, which seems to be the basic law governing the vibratory activities of this planetary universe.

The law of sevens dominates the life of individuals and of nations and of everything that lives and has periods of birth, growth, fruitage and decline.

The law of sevens governs the days of the week, the phases of the moon, the menstrual periods of the woman. Every observing physician is aware of its influence on feverish, nervous and psychic diseases.

Over two thousand years ago Pythagoras and Hippocrates distinctly recognized and proclaimed the laws of crises and of periodicity in their bearings on the cure of chronic diseases. They taught that alternating, well defined periods of improvement and of crises were determined and governed by the law of periodicity or the law of numbers (the septimal law).

The following quotations are taken from the Encyclopedia Britannica, Vol. XV, p. 800:

''But this artistic completeness was closely connected with 'the third cardinal virtue' of Hippocratic medicine—the clear recognition of disease as being equally with life a process governed by what we should now call natural laws, which could be known by observation and which indicated the spontaneous and normal direction of recovery, by following which alone could the physician succeed. . . .

"Another Hippocratic doctrine, the influence of which is not even yet exhausted, is that of the healing power of nature. Not that Hippocrates taught, as he was afterwards reproached with teaching, that nature is sufficient for the cure of diseases; for he held strongly the efficacy of art. But he recognized, at least in acute diseases, a natural process which the humours went through—being first of all **crude**, then passing through **coction** or digestion, and finally being expelled by resolution or **crisis** through one of the natural channels of the body. The duty of the physician was to foresee these changes, 'to assist or not to hinder them,' so that 'the sick man might conquer the disease with the help of the physician.' The times at which crises were to be expected were naturally looked for with anxiety; and it was a cardinal point in the Hippocratic system to foretell them with precision. Hippocrates, influenced as is thought by the Pythagorean doctrine of numbers, taught that they were to be expected on days fixed by certain numerical rules, in some cases on odd, in others on even numbers— the celebrated doctrine of 'critical days'. It follows from what has been said that **prognosis**, or the art of foretelling the course and event of the disease, was a strong point with the Hippocratic physicians. In this perhaps they have never been excelled. Diagnosis, or recognition of the disease, must have been necessarily imperfect, when no scientific nosology, or system of disease, existed, and the knowledge of anatomy was quite inadequate to allow of a precise determination of the seat of disease; but symptoms were no doubt observed and interpreted skillfully. The pulse is not spoken of in any of the works now attributed to Hippocrates himself, though it is mentioned in other works of the collection.

"In the treatment of disease, the Hippocratic school attached great importance to diet, the variations necessary in different diseases being minutely defined. . . . In chronic cases diet, exercises and natural methods were chiefly relied upon."

The author of this article in the Britannica does not see that it is the modern, orthodox "scientific nosology, or system of disease", which obscures the simplicity and precision of the Hippocratic philosophy of disease and cure.

These wonderful truths, with other wisdom of the ancients, were lost in the spiritual darkness of the middle ages. Modern medicine looks upon these claims and teachings of the Hippocratic school as "superstition, without foundation in fact". However, the great sages of antiquity, drawing upon a source of ancient wisdom deeply hidden from the selfsatisfied scribes and wise men of the schools, after all proclaimed the truth.

Every case of chronic disease properly treated by natural methods proves the reality and stability of the law of crises. It is, therefore, a standing wonder and surprise to one who knows, that this all important and selfevident law is practically unknown to the disciples of the regular schools.

The Septenary Law in Nature and in the Life of Man

To Dr. J. R. Buchanan belongs the credit of having written a very interesting little book on the Law of Periodicity. While he has traced its workings in many domains of life and action, he was not aware of some of its plainest manifestations in Nature as well as in the life of man. He evidently did not recognize that our planetary universe is built on this law of sevens; that the atoms of matter and all forces and energies in Nature obey the rule of the septenary.

He also apparently failed to discern one of the plainest manifestations of the law, namely, its rule in the constructive changes (healing crises) occurring in chronic diseases under the salutary influence of natural living and treatment.

As far back as human traditions and records reach, the septenary law was known and revered as one of the basic principles in Nature. Madame Blavatsky in ''The Secret Doctrine'' devotes over two hundred pages to this interesting subject. On page 638 of Volume II she says:

''All the ancient cosmologies—the oldest cosmographies of the two most ancient people of the fifth root-race, the Hindu Aryans and the Egyptians, together with the early Chinese races, the remnants of the fourth or Atlantean race—based the whole of their mysteries on the number ten; the higher triangle standing for the invisible and metaphysical world, the lower three and four, or the septenate, for the physical realm.

"It is not the Jewish Bible that brought the number seven into prominence. Hesiod used the words, 'the seventh is the sacred day', before the Sabbath of Moses was ever heard of. The use of number seven was never confined to any one nation. This is well testified by the seven vases in the Temple of the Sun, near the ruins of Babian in Upper Egypt; the seven fires burning continually for ages before the altars of Mithra; the seven holy fanes of the Arabians; the seven peninsulas, the seven islands, seven seas, mountains and rivers of India; and of the Zohar; the Jewish Sephiroth of the seven splendours; the seven Gothic deities; the seven worlds of the Chaldeans and their seven spirits; the seven constellations mentioned by Hesiod and Homer; and all the interminable sevens which the Orientalists find in every manuscript they discover."

And on page 658 of the same volume:

"There is a harmony of numbers in all nature; in the force of gravity, in the planetary movements, in the laws of heat, light, electricity, and chemical affinity, in the forms of animals and plants, in the perceptions of the mind.

"The direction, indeed, of modern natural and physical science is towards a generalization which shall express the fundamental laws of all by one simple numerical ratio.

"We would refer to Professor Whewell's 'Philosophy of the Inductive Sciences' and to Mr. Hay's researches into the laws of harmonious coloring and form. From these it appears that the number seven is distinguished in the laws regulating the harmonious perception of forms, colors and sounds, and probably of taste also, if we could analyze our sensations of this kind with mathematical accuracy.

"So much so, indeed, that more than one physician has stood aghast at the septenary periodical return of the cycles in the rise and fall of various complaints, and naturalists have felt themselves at an utter loss to explain this law.

"The birth, growth, maturity, vital functions, healthy

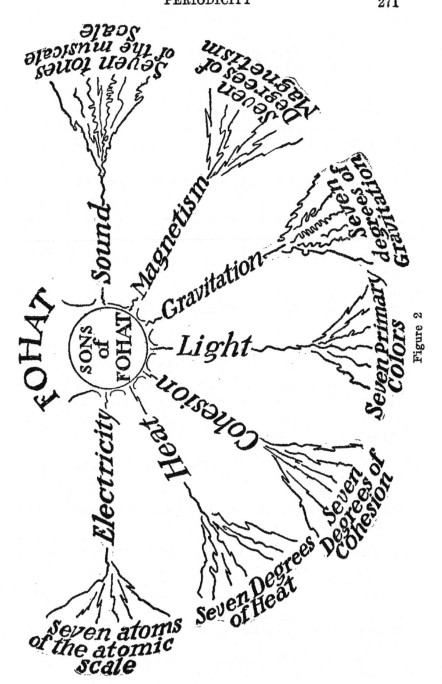

Figure 2

revolutions of change, diseases, decay and death, of insects, reptiles, fishes, birds, mammals, and even of man, are more or less controlled by a law of completion in weeks (or periods of seven days)."

Fohat, in the Buddhistic allegory, stands for the source of all life and power in this universe, for that which we call God. Fohat sends forth seven sons, or rays. Each one of these in turn has seven sons, making forty-nine in all. Fohat, the primary cause, becomes apparent to our sensory organs in the seven primary manifestations known in our modern scientific vernacular as motion, sound, heat, light, cohesion, electricity and magnetism. These primary manifestations each gives rise to seven degrees of vibratory activity, viz., in sound, to seven primary tones; in light, to seven primary colors, etc. Later on we shall find that the cycles in human life are made up of forty-nine years. (See Fig. 2.)

Here we have the occult number seven times seven, which, as scientific research proves, becomes more and more apparent in the physical structure and the vibratory activities of our planetary universe. Hellenbach, the well known scientist, confirms the esoteric doctrine of Buddhism when he says:

"It has been established that, from the standpoint of phenomenal law, upon which all our knowledge rests, the vibrations of sound and light increase regularly, that they divide themselves into seven columns, and that the successive numbers in each column are closely allied, i.e., that they exhibit a close relationship which not only is expressed in the figures themselves, but also is practically confirmed in chemistry as in music, in the latter of which the ear confirms the verdict of the figures. The fact that this periodicity and variety is governed by the number seven is undeniable, and it far surpasses the limits of mere chance, and must be assumed to have an adequate cause, which cause must be discovered.

"We thus see that chemical variety, so far as we can

grasp its inner nature, depends upon numerical relations, and we have further found in this variety a ruling law for which we can assign no cause; we find a law of periodicity governed by the number seven.''

Periodicity of the Atom

As described elsewhere (Chapter XXVIII), the atoms of matter are made up of negative particles of electricity moving with infinite velocity and creating whirls in the ether, which verifies the teachings of Pythagoras, according to which all matter is made up of three factors, substance, motion and number. In the light of modern science, substance is the primordial ether; motion, the negative electrical charges in the ether; and numbers, the number of electrons vibrating in the atom.

Modern science, furthermore, has discovered that the weight of the atom depends upon the number of electrons it contains, and the character of the element of which the atom is the smallest particle depends upon the number of electrons in the atom and their modes of vibration. Science has succeeded in ascertaining approximately the number of electrons in hydrogen, the lightest of all elements. We are told that an atom of this element contains about eight hundred electrons. This is one of the achievements of modern science which fills us with wonder at the Godlike possibilities of the human mind when it works on a basis of natural law.

As before stated, the number of electrons in the atoms increases in direct ratio with their increasing atomic weight, or vice versa, which is determined by the weight of the hydrogen atom as a unit. In other words, what the pound is as a commercial measure of weight, the weight of the hydrogen atom is in relation to the weight of atoms.

A trained musician can produce by his voice or on a musical instrument a sol tone or any other tone in the musical scale, because when given the pitch, he knows exactly the musical quality of the note. So the trained chemist knows by the location of the atom in the ascending atomic scales its qualities and characteristics.

The Russian chemist, Mendeleeff, was the first one to complete a table of the atoms arranged in groups of seven according to their increasing atomic weights. At the time he constructed this table, many of the atoms of matter known to science at the present time were not discovered, but by means of the periodic arrangement of the atoms scientists were able to foretell what qualities these atoms would possess if they were discovered.

For instance, when Mendeleeff constructed his table the element fitting into the pigeonhole now occupied by helium had not been discovered. Later this element was discovered by the spectrum in the sun and therefore named helium, after Helios, the Greek word for sun or the sun god. Still later the element was discovered on earth. It is found in small quantities in the air which we inhale.

When this element was actually discovered by science, it was found to have all the properties and characteristics assigned to it by science in accordance with its location in the septenary groups of the atoms. In similar manner many other elements not known fifty years ago have been discovered since that time and have been found to fit exactly into the pigeonholes reserved for them in the periodic tables of Newlands and Mendeleeff.

Thus modern science demonstrates that our planetary universe is built on the laws of music and thereby justifies the ancient esoteric conception of the "music of the spheres" which expresses itself in the order and beauty of Nature. All Nature save man plays in tune and produces harmony. By virtue of his sovereign will and power of free choice and volition, man may play in discord, either through ignorance or through willful violation of the law, thus himself creating all that he looks upon as evil.

The seven primary colors of the spectrum are another manifestation of the septenary law or the law of periodicity. As science progresses in its research it becomes more and more apparent that the ether, gravitation, light, sound, heat, electricity, magnetism and all other forms of

Red	*Do*	*Na*-23
Orange	*Re*	*Mg*-24
Yellow	*Mi*	*Al*-27
Green	*Fa*	*Si*-28
Blue	*Sol*	*P*-31
Indigo	*La*	*S*-32
Violet	*Si*	*Cl*-35
Red	*Do*	*K*-39
Orange	*Re*	*Ca*-40
Yellow	*Mi*	*Sc*-44
Green	*Fa*	*Ti*-48
Blue	*Sol*	*V*-51
Indigo	*La*	*Cr*-52
Violet	*Si*	*Mn*-55

forces and energies manifest in groups or degrees of sevens. The following diagram gives an illustration of the principle in its application to the groups of the atoms, to the tones of the musical scale and to the grouping of the primary colors.

The corresponding units in the lower and higher scales form octaves, as, for instance, the Do tones in the musical scales, or the red shades in the color scales. They are the same as to vibratory quality but differ as to pitch or shade.

The same is true of the atoms of matter when arranged in accordance with their increasing atomic weights. Thus sodium, the first atom in one septenary row, corresponds to or forms an octave with potassium, the first atom in the next row. They resemble one another in physical and chemical qualities in a manner similar to the resemblance exhibited by the units in the octaves of sounds and colors.

In giving the atomic weights of the atoms I have omitted the fractions as unessential for the purpose of this illustration.

Crises, or "Friday" Periods

In accordance with the law of periodicity, the SIXTH period in any seven periods is marked by reactions, changes, revolutions or crises. It is, therefore, looked upon by popular superstition as an unlucky period. Friday, the sixth day of the week, is regarded as an unlucky day—Friday is "hangman's day"; according to tradition the Master, Jesus, was crucified on Friday.

Counting from the first sixth or Friday period in any given number of hours, days, weeks, months, years or groups of years, as the case may be, every succeeding seventh period is characterized by crises.

This explains why 13 is considered an unlucky number. It represents the second critical or Friday period.

However, there is really no cause for this superstitious fear of Friday and the number 13. It is due to a lack of understanding of Nature's laws. By intelligent cooperation with these laws we may turn the critical periods in our lives into "healing crises" and beneficial changes.

We should not fear the crisis periods of the larger life and the changes in our outward circumstances which they may bring any more than we should fear crises in the physical body.

A thorough understanding of the nature and purpose

of healing crises in acute and chronic diseases has taught
me the nature and purpose of evil in general. It has made
me understand more clearly the meaning of "Resist not
Evil" and of the saying: "We are punished **by** our sins,
not **for** our sins." It has shown me that evil is not a
punishment or a curse, but a necessary complement of
good; that it is corrective and educational in its purposes;
that it remains with us only so long as we need its salutary lessons.

The evil of physical disease is not due to accident or
to the arbitrary rulings of a capricious Providence, nor
is it always "error of mortal mind". From the Nature
Cure philosophy and its practical application we have
learned that, barring accidents and conditions or surroundings unfavorable to human life, it is caused in every
instance by violations of the physical laws of our being.
So the social, political and industrial evil of the larger
life is brought about by violations of the law in the
respective domains of life and action.

So long as transgressions of the physical laws of our
being result in hereditary and acquired disease encumbrances, we must expect reactions which may become
either disease crises or healing crises. Likewise, so long
as ignorance, selfishness and selfindulgence continue to
create evil in other domains of life, we must expect there
also the occurrence of crises, of reaction and revolution.
When knowledge, selfcontrol and altruism become the
sole motives of action, "evil" and the crises it necessitates will automatically disappear.

Therefore **we should not be afraid of changes and crises
periods but cooperate with them clear eyed and strong
willed.** Then they will result in improvement and further
growth.

Life is growth, and growth is change. The only death
is stagnation. The loss of friends, home or fortune may

seem for the time being an overwhelming calamity; but
if met in the right spirit, such losses will prove stepping
stones to greater opportunity and higher achievement.

Many of our patients formerly looked upon their diseased conditions as great misfortune and undeserved
punishment; but since it brought them in contact with
Nature Cure philosophy and showed them the necessity
of complying with the laws of their being, they now look
upon the former "evil" as the greatest blessing in their
lives, because it taught them how to become the masters
of fate instead of remaining the playthings of Nature's
destructive forces.

Why should we fear even the greatest of all crises,
physical death, when it, too, is but the gateway to larger
life, greater opportunities and more beautiful surroundings? Why should we mourn and grieve over the death
of friends and relatives when they have only emigrated
to another, better country?

Suppose we ourselves were to enter upon the great
journey today or tomorrow, shouldn't we be glad to meet
some of our friends on the other side and to be welcomed,
advised and guided by them in the new surroundings?

Therefore we should not fear or endeavor to avoid the
crises in any domain of life and action, but meet them and
cooperate with them fearlessly and intelligently. They
then will always make for greater opportunity and higher
accomplishment.

The Law of Sevens Applied to Individual Life

We find that our primary division of time into weeks
consisting of seven days is in accord with the septenary
law. In like manner the years in a lifetime arrange themselves into groups of sevens, seven times seven years forming a cycle which corresponds to the forty nine sons of
Fohat. When we apply to the seven periods in the cycle

of life the names of the days of the week, the panorama of life unfolds itself as follows:

The first, or Sunday period, includes the first seven years of life. This is the birthday period characterized by the weakness and helplessness of the newborn and its entire dependence upon parents or guardians.

The second, or Monday period, includes the years from eight to fourteen. This is the age of childhood, still characterized by weakness and dependence. Esoteric science teaches that the end of the first period marks the development of reason, willpower and selfcontrol in a sufficient degree to impose upon the individual the obligation of personal responsibility. In other words, with the completion of the seventh year the child becomes to a certain degree morally responsible. The age of childhood is best adapted for the acquisition of the simpler forms of useful knowledge.

The third, or Tuesday period, reaches from the fifteenth year to the twenty first. This is the period of youth, or adolescence, and should also be spent under the guidance and protection of parents or guardians. It is still a period of immaturity and should be utilized for the further acquisition of knowledge and for active preparation for the business of life. Nearly all civilized countries take cognizance of the completion of the third period by fixing the legal age at twenty one. Civil law thus recognizes the fact that at the completion of the third cycle the individual is qualified to take care of himself, to paddle his own canoe on the stream of life.

The fourth period (Wednesday), extending from the twenty second to the twenty eighth year, is characterized by the beginning of an independent struggle for existence. During this time of life the normal individual endeavors to establish himself firmly in some line of work, business or profession.

During the fifth (Thursday) period of life, which extends from the twenty ninth to the thirty fifth year, the individual should succeed in establishing himself firmly enough to be able to found and support a family and thus to fulfill one of the primary purposes of existence, the reproduction of the species. This period is therefore called the age of maturity and fruitage.

Nature, however, does not intend us to continue indefinitely in the security of a well established routine of life and therefore during the sixth or Friday period provides for reactions, changes, or "crises" from the thirty sixth to the forty second year. With the achievement of primary objectives comes unrest and the striving for the satisfaction of new ambitions and for the attainment of higher ideals. Success in a financial way on a small scale leads to larger undertakings and more risky speculations. The attainment of financial independence gives rise to political ambitions, to the desire for distinction in other fields of endeavor or to the awakening of altruistic and philanthropic impulses.

The sixth or Friday period is, therefore, characterized by sudden upheavals and changes in business affairs and home surroundings and the taking up of new lines of endeavor. This period of life is also frequently characterized by changes in the physical conditions, by the development of disease crises as the result of wrong living and wrong treatment of minor ailments in the past. These changes and reactions in the affairs of life naturally involve unrest, uncertainty, losses, deprivations and the necessity for fresh starts, reconstruction on a new basis and all the anxiety and concentrated effort which this requires. This sixth period of the cycle is therefore considered unlucky, but if we understand the law of periodicity and the true significance of the sixth or Friday period, we look upon the reactions and changes which it brings about not as ''unlucky'', unfortunate or destructive, but as experiences necessary for the further development of our latent faculties, capacities and powers, as necessary exercise for the strengthening of our physical, intellectual and moral fibre. If Nature allowed us to continue indefinitely in the snug security of old accustomed surroundings and circumstances, we would stagnate and fossilize.

Better to burn out the flame of life in a few years of brief but intensely interesting and useful activity than to drag along through a century of humdrum, selfcentered stagnation. This optimistic conception of the nature and purpose of seeming misfortunes, trials and tribulations of life has become to me a matter of positive conviction since I have had occasion to verify it in many thousands of cases.

During the seventh period the effects of the sixth or crisis period continue and adjust themselves. It is a period of reconstruction, of recuperation and rest, and thus the best preparation for a new cycle of sevens which begins with the fiftieth year.

In this connection it is interesting to note that the Mosaic law recognized the law of periodicity and fixed upon **Sunday as the first** day or ''birthday'' of the week, and upon **Saturday** (the Sabbath) **as the last or ''rest''** day in which to prepare for another period of seven days.

Orthodox science now admits that the normal length of human life should be about one hundred and fifty years. This would constitute three cycles of forty nine years each, the first corresponding to youth, the second to maturity and the third to fruition.

The Law of Sevens in Febrile Diseases

If we apply the law of periodicity to the course of acute febrile or inflammatory diseases we find that the **sixth** day from the beginning of the first well defined symptom marks the first ''Friday period'' or the first crisis of the disease, and that every seventh day thereafter is also distinguished by aggravations and changes either for better or for worse.

The Law of Sevens in Chronic Diseases

Applied to the cure of chronic diseases under the influence of natural methods of living and of treatment, the law of crisis and periodicity manifests as follows:

When a chronic patient, whose chances of cure are good, is placed under proper (natural) conditions of living and of treatment he will, as a rule, experience five weeks of marked improvement.

The sixth week, if conditions are favorable, usually marks the beginning of acute reactions or healing crises.

This means that the healing forces of the organism have grown strong enough to begin the work of acute elimination.

By all sorts of acute reactions, such as skin eruptions, diarrheas, feverish, inflammatory and catarrhal conditions, boils, abscesses, muco-purulent discharges, etc., Nature now endeavors to remove the latent, chronic disease taints from the system.

The allopathic school of medicine looks upon these acute reactions as the disease; we of the Nature Cure school recognize them as milestones on the road to cure.

The entire structure of allopathy is built upon a misconception of the true nature of disease. At this fundamental point the ways of the old school and the Nature Cure school part, never to meet again.

Many allopathic physicians who read the foregoing statements will indignantly deny their truthfulness. They will claim that the old school of medicine also regards acute reactions as manifestations of Nature's eliminative activity and that it endeavors to promote the same by all possible means.

We are aware that in many instances the teachings of the allopathic school acknowledge, theoretically at least, the eliminative character of acute diseases. But how does practice agree with theory?

Skin eruptions and boils are "cured" (into the body) with metallic ointments; coughs, mucous discharges and diarrheas are arrested by opiates and astringents; fevers and inflammations are subdued by quinin, coal tar products or the ice bag; headaches and pains of all kinds are stopped by morphin, cocain, phenacetin, salicylates, etc.; excited nerves and restless brain are paralyzed and stupefied with bromids and chloral; syphilitic ulcers and gonorrheal discharges are checked by cauterization, drying powders or strong antiseptic injections; scrofulous glands and goiters are "absorbed" by iodin; diseased tonsils or the inflamed appendix are extirpated with the surgeon's knife;—and so on, ad infinitum.

Are such suppressive tactics calculated to induce and promote elimination?

The character of healing crises and the time of their occurrence in any given case can often be accurately predicted by means of the **diagnosis from the iris of the eye** (Vol. VI),—from Nature's records in the iris.

But **the best of all methods of diagnosis is the cure itself, because weak spots and morbid taints in the organism are revealed through the healing crises.**

The Same Old Aches and Pains

Frequently we hear from a patient in the throes of crises: "These are the same old aches and pains that I had before. It is exactly the same trouble I have been suffering with for many years. This is not a crisis!—I have caught a cold, or I have eaten something which does not agree with me."

The patient has forgotten what we taught regarding the law of crises. He loses sight of the fact that healing crises are nothing more nor less than a coming-up-again of old disease conditions, **an acute manifestation of ailments which had become chronic through neglect or suppression.**

Of course they are "the same old aches and pains". Nature Cure does not create new diseases. Crises mean the stirring up and eliminating of hereditary and acquired taints and poisons. Under the right methods of treatment any previous disease condition suppressed by drugs or knife or by mental effort may recur as a healing crisis.

They are the same old aches and pains which so often gave trouble in the past, **but they are now running their course under different conditions** because the patient is now living in harmony with Nature's laws.

Under the natural regimen Nature is encouraged and assisted in her cleansing and healing efforts. She is allowed in her own wise way to "tear down the old and build up the new".

The old schools of healing proclaim Mother Nature a "poor healer". But we of the Nature Cure school believe that the wisdom which created this wonderful, complex mechanism which we call the human body knows also how to preserve and to repair it. Every healing crisis passed under natural conditions assisted by natural methods of treatment leaves the body purified and strengthened and nearer to perfect health.

Our critics and opponents frequently ask how we know that our methods are "natural" and "in harmony with Nature's laws".

To this we reply: **The timely appearance of healing crises, their orderly development and favorable termination constitute the best criterion of the correctness and naturalness of the methods of treatment employed.** The prompt arrival and beneficial results of acute reactions are a certain indication that the healing forces of the organism are in the ascendancy and that the treatment is in conformity with the natural laws of cure and with the **constructive** principle in Nature.

Another question we frequently hear is: "Do healing crises develop in every chronic disease under natural treatment?" Our answer is: If the condition of the patient is not favorable to a cure, that is, if the vitality be too low and the destruction of vital parts too far advanced, the healing crises may be proportionately delayed or may not occur at all. In such cases the disease symptoms will increase in severity and complexity and become more destructive instead of more constructive until the final fatal crisis. The end may come quickly or the patient may decline gradually toward the fatal termination.

Again, patients ask us: "Through how many crises shall I have to pass?" We tell them—just as many as you need; no more, no less. So long as there is anything wrong in the system, crises will come and go; but each crisis, if successfully passed, is another milestone on the road to perfect health.

It is intensely interesting to observe in how orderly and intelligent a manner Nature proceeds in her work of healing and repair. One problem after another is taken up and adjusted.

First of all the digestive organs are put into better condition because further progress depends upon proper assimilation and elimination. The bowels must act freely and naturally before any permanent improvement can take place. A treatment which fails to accomplish this first premilinary improvement will surely fail to produce more important results.

In this connection it is a significant fact that nearly all

our patients, when they come under our care, are suffering from stubborn constipation in spite of (or on account of) lifelong drugging. Neither medicines nor operations had given them anything but temporary relief, and the trouble had grown worse instead of better.

If the old school methods of treatment were not successful in relieving simple constipation, what can they be expected to cure, since it is evident that the overcoming of constipation is the primary necessity for any other improvement?

A system of treatment which cannot accomplish this, cannot accomplish anything. Is it strange, therefore, that a school of medicine which, with all its vaunted knowledge and wisdom, has not succeeded in curing simple constipation, flatly denies that natural methods can cure cancer, epilepsy, locomotor ataxia and other so called incurable diseases?

Our Greatest Difficulty

The greatest difficulty in our work lies in conducting our patients safely through the stormy crisis periods. The first, preliminary improvement is often so marked that the patient believes himself already cured. He will say: "Doctor, I am feeling fine! There is nothing the matter with me any more! I cannot understand why I shouldn't go home and continue the natural regimen there!"

This feeling of mental elation and physical well being is usually the sign that the first general improvement has progressed far enough to prepare the system for a healing crisis. Therefore my answer to the overconfident patient may be something like this: "Remember what I told you. The first improvement is not the cure, it is only the preparation for the real fight. Look out! In a few days you may whistle another tune."

And sure enough, usually within a few days after such

a conversation the patient is down in the slough of despond. His digestive organs are in a wretched condition. He is nauseated, his tongue is coated, he is suffering from headache or from any one of a multitude of other symptoms, according to his individual condition. In fact, many of the old aches and pains which he thought already cured may come again with renewed force.

Healing crises, representing radical changes in the system, are always accompanied by physical and mental weakness, because every bit of vitality is drawn upon in these reconstructive processes. The entire organism is shaken to its very foundation—deepseated chronic disease taints are being stirred up throughout the system.

The eliminative processes of the healing crises are often accompanied by great mental depression and a feeling of strong revulsion from the natural regimen and everything connected with it.

The patient may think that, after all, Nature Cure is not for him, that he is growing worse instead of better. In proportion to the severity of the changes going on within him, he may become disheartened and despondent. Often he exhibits all the mental and emotional symptoms of homesickness.

In these critical days it requires all our powers of persuasion to keep the depressed and discouraged patient from giving up the fight and "taking something" to relieve his distress. He insists that "something" must be done for him and cannot understand how he will ever get out of his "awful condition" without some good strong medicine.

If our patients were not continually and thoroughly instructed regarding the laws of crises and of periodicity and if we did not strongly advise and encourage them to persevere with the treatment, few of them would hold out during these critical periods.

This explains why so many people fail to be cured and it also explains why natural living and selftreatment often do not meet with the desired results if carried on without the instruction and guidance of a competent, experienced Nature Cure physician.

So long as the improvement continues everything is lovely and hope soars high. But when the inevitable crises arrive the sufferer believes that after all he made a mistake in taking up the natural regimen, especially when friends and relatives do their best to destroy his confidence in the natural methods of cure by ridicule and dire prophecies of failure.

Frightened and discouraged, the patient may return to the "flesh-pots of Egypt" and to the good old pills and potions and ever afterwards will tell his friends that "he tried Nature Cure and the vegetarian diet, but it was no good."

Mother Nature remains a "book sealed with seven seals" to those who mistrust, despise and counteract her, who rely on man made wisdom and the ever changing theories and dogmas of the schools.

But on the other hand, every crisis conducted to a successful termination in accordance with Nature's laws becomes an inspiration to him who follows her guidance and assists her with intelligent effort and loving care.

CHAPTER XXIV

THE TRUE SCOPE OF MEDICINE

ONE able to read the signs of the times cannot help observing the powerful influence which Nature Cure philosophy is already exerting upon the trend of modern medical science. In Germany the younger generation of physicians has been forced by public demand to adopt the natural methods of treatment, and the German government has introduced them in the medical departments of its army and navy.

In English speaking countries the foremost members of the medical profession are beginning to talk straight Nature Cure doctrine, to condemn the use of drugs and to endorse unqualifiedly the Nature Cure methods of treatment. As an illustration I quote from an article by Dr. William Osler in the Encyclopedia Americana, Vol, X, under the title of "Medicine":

Dr. Osler on "Medicine"

"**The new school does not feel itself under obligation to give any medicines whatever,** while a generation ago not only could few physicians have held their practice unless they did, but few would have thought it safe or scientific. Of course, there are still many cases where the patient or the patient's friends must be humored by administering medicine or alleged medicine where it is not really needed, and indeed often where **the buoyancy of mind which is the real curative agent,** can only be created by making him wait hopefully for the expected action of medicine; and some physicians still cannot unlearn their old training.

But the change is great. **The modern treatment of disease relies very greatly on the old so called 'natural' methods, diet and exercise, bathing and massage,**—in other words, giving the natural forces the fullest scope by easy and thorough nutrition, increased flow of blood, and removal of obstructions to the excretory systems or the circulation in the tissues.

"One notable example is typhoid fever. At the outset of the nineteenth century it was treated with 'remedies' of the extremest violence,—bleeding and blistering, vomiting and purging, and the administration of antimony and mercury, and plenty of other heroic remedies. Now the patient is bathed and nursed and carefully tended, but rarely given medicine. This is the result partly of the remarkable experiments of the Paris and Vienna schools in the action of drugs, which have shaken the stoutest faiths; and partly of the constant and reproachful object-lesson of homeopathy. No regular physician would ever admit that the homeopathic preparations, 'infinitesimals', could do any good as direct curative agents; and yet it was perfectly certain that homeopaths lost no more of their patients than others. **There was but one conclusion to draw,—that most drugs had no effect whatever on the diseases for which they were administered.**"

Dr. Osler is one of the greatest medical authorities on drugs now living. He was formerly professor of materia medica at the Johns Hopkins University of Baltimore, U. S., and now holds a professorship at Oxford University, England. His books on medical practice are in use in probably every university and medical school in English speaking countries. His views on drugs and their real value as expressed in this article should be an eye opener to those good people who believe that we of the Nature Cure school are altogether too radical, extreme, and somewhat "cranky".

However, what **Dr. Osler says regarding the "New School" is true only of a few advanced members of the medical profession.**

On the rank and file the idea of drugless healing has about the same effect as a red rag on a mad bull. There are very few physicians in general practice today who would not lose their bread and butter if they attempted to practice drugless healing on their patients. Both the profession and the public needs a good deal more education along Nature Cure lines before rational methods can become general.

In the second sentence of his article **Dr. Osler admits the efficacy of mental therapeutics and therapeutic faith as a curative agent** and ascribes the helpful effects of medicine to their stimulating influence upon the patient's mind rather than to any beneficial action of the drugs themselves.

With regard to the origin of the modern treatment of typhoid fever, however, the learned doctor is either misinformed or purposely misrepresents the facts. The credit for the introduction of hydropathic treatment of typhoid fever does not belong to the "remarkable experiments of the Paris and Vienna schools". These schools and the entire medical profession fought this treatment with might and main.

For thirty years Priessnitz, Bilz, Kuhne, Father Kneipp and many other pioneers of Nature Cure were persecuted and prosecuted, they were dragged into the courts and tried on the charges of malpractice and manslaughter for using their sane and natural methods.

Not until Dr. Brandt of Berlin wrote an essay on the good results obtained by the hydropathic treatment of typhoid fever and it had in that way received orthodox baptism and sanction, was it adopted by advanced physicians all over the world.

Through Nature Cure treatment of typhoid fever, the mortality of this disease has been reduced from over 50 per cent under the old drug treatment to less than 5 per cent.

But the average medical practitioner has not yet learned from the Nature Cure school that **the same simple fasting and cold water treatment used so effectively in the cure of typhoid fever, is just as effective in the treatment of every other form of acute disease** as, for instance, scarlet fever, diphtheria, smallpox, cerebro-spinal meningitis, appendicitis, etc. **Therefore, we hold that there is no necessity for the employment of poisonous drugs, serums and antitoxins for these purposes.**

Referring to the last two statements in Dr. Osler's article, homeopaths have as a matter of fact lost fewer patients than have allopaths. The effect of homeopathic medicine, moreover, is not altogether negative, as Dr. Osler implies. The discovery of the minute microzyma as the basis of the human organism on the one hand, and of the unlimited divisibility of matter on the other, explains the rationality of the infinitesimal dose. Health and disease are resident in the microzyma; therefore the homeopath treats this primary unit of life, and the size of the dose is apportioned to the size of the patient.

When Dr. Osler says that most drugs have no effect whatsoever, he makes a serious misstatement. While they may not contribute to the cure of the disease for which they are given, they are often very harmful in themselves.

Almost every virulent poison known to man is found in allopathic prescriptions. It is now definitely established by the **diagnosis from the iris of the eye** that these poisons have a tendency to accumulate in the system, to concentrate in certain parts and organs for which they have a special affinity, and there to cause continual irritation and actual destruction of tissues. The greater part of all chronic diseases are created or complicated by the suppression of acute diseases by means of drug poisons and through the destructive effects of drugs themselves.

Dr. Schwenninger, the medical adviser of Prince Bismarck, and later of Richard Wagner, the great composer, has published a book entitled "The Doctor". This work is the most scathing arraignment and condemnation of modern medical practice, especially of poisonous drugs and of surgery. Dr. Treves, the body physician of the late King Edward of England, is no less outspoken than Drs. Osler and Schwenninger in denunciation of the practice of drugging.

Only a few men who, like these, have achieved financial and scientific independence in the medical profession can afford to speak so frankly. The great majority of physicians, even though they know better, continue in the old ruts so as to be considered ethical and orthodox and in order to hold their practice. **It is not the medical profession that has brought about this reform in the treatment of typhoid fever and other diseases. They have been forced into the adoption of the more advanced natural methods through the pressure of the Nature Cure movement in Europe and America.**

Dr. Osler's statements, made with careful deliberation in a contribution to the Encyclopedia Americana, are certainly a frank declaration as to the ineffectiveness of drug treatment and an unqualified endorsement of natural methods of healing.

But it seems to me that Dr. Osler "pours out the baby with the bath". That is, I am inclined to think that his opinion regarding the ineffectiveness of drugs is entirely too radical. **There is a legitimate scope for medicinal remedies in so far as they build up the blood on a natural basis and serve as tissue foods.**

Many people who have lost their faith in old school methods of treatment have swung to the other extreme. In fact, Dr. Osler himself stands accused of being a "medical nihilist".

Many of those who have adopted natural methods of living and of treating disease have acquired an actual horror of the word "medicine". However, this extreme attitude is not justified.

It also appears that some of the readers of my writings are under the impression that we of the Nature Cure school absolutely condemn the use of all medicines. This, however, is not the case.

The Position of Nature Cure Regarding Medicinal Remedies

We do condemn the use of drugs **in so far as they are poisonous and destructive, and in so far as they suppress acute diseases or healing crises,** which are Nature's cleansing and healing efforts; but, on the other hand, we realize that there is a wide field for the helpful application of medicinal remedies in so far as they act as foods to the tissues of the body and as neutralizers and eliminators of waste and morbid materials.

In every form of chronic disease there exists in the system an excess of certain morbid materials and a deficiency of certain mineral constituents, "organic" salts. which are essential to the normal functions of the body.

Thus, in all anemic diseases the blood is lacking in iron, which picks up the oxygen in the air cells of the lungs and carries it into the tissues, and in sodium, which combines with the carbon dioxide (coal gas) that is constantly being liberated in the system and conveys it to the organs of depuration, especially the lungs and the skin. In point of fact, oxygen starvation is due in a much greater degree to the deficiency of sodium and the consequent accumulation of carbon dioxide in the system (carbonic acid asphyxiation) than to the lack of iron in the blood, as assumed by the old school of medicine.

Foods or medicinal remedies which supply this deficiency of iron and sodium in the organism tend to overcome the anemic conditions.

The great range of uric acid diseases, such as rheumatism, calculi, arterio-sclerosis, certain forms of diabetes and albuminuria, are due on the one hand to the excessive consumption of acid producing foods, and on the other hand to a deficiency in the blood of certain alkaline mineral elements, especially sodium, magnesium, lithium and potassium, whose office it is to neutralize the acids which are created and liberated in the processes of starch and protein digestion.

In another chapter I have explained the origin and progressive development of uric acid diseases (see page 350). The volume on "Natural Dietetics" contains additional proof that practically all diseases are caused by or are complicated with acid conditions in the system.

Any foods or medicines which provide the system with sufficient quantities of the acid binding, alkaline mineral salts prove good medicine for all forms of acid diseases. Lime, potassium, phosphorus and silicon are needed to impart textile strength and stamina to the bony and fleshy tissues of the body.

The mineral constituents necessary to the vital economy of the organism should, however, be supplied in the **live, organized** form. This will be explained more fully in subsequent pages.

From what I have said it becomes apparent that it is impossible to draw a sharp line of distinction between foods and medicines. All foods which serve the above named purposes are ''good medicines'', and all non-poisonous herb extracts and homeopathic remedies that have the same effect upon the system are, for the same reason, good ''foods''.

The **medical** treatment prescribed by the Nature Cure school consists largely in the proper selection and combination of food materials. This must be so. It stands to reason that Nature has provided with in the ranges of the **natural** foods all the elements which man needs in the way of food and medicine.

But it is quite possible that, through continued abuse, the digestive apparatus has become so weak and abnormal that it cannot function properly, that it cannot absorb and assimilate from natural foods a sufficient quantity of the elements which the organism needs. In such cases it may be very helpful and, indeed, imperative to prescribe the **organic** mineral salts in the forms of fruit, herb and vegetable juices, extracts or decoctions. Among the best food remedies are extracts of leafy vegetables such as lettuce, spinach, Scotch kale, cabbage, Swiss chard, etc. These vegetables are richer than any other foods in the salts of positive mineral elements. The extract may be prepared from one or more of these vegetables according to the supply on hand or the tolerance of the digestive organs and the taste and preference of the patient. They should be ground to a pulp in a vegetable grinder, then pressed out in a small fruit press which can be secured in any department store. One or two teacups per day will be sufficient to supply the needs of the system for mineral salts. This extract should be prepared fresh every day.

The ''Tissue Remedies'' first prepared by Schuessler, one of the pioneers in the Nature Cure movement, are refined triturations of the positive mineral elements needed by the human organism. However, they remain in the inorganic mineral state and therefore cannot supplant the organic mineral salt combinations prepared in the best possible form in Nature's own laboratory in the fruits, vegetables, cereals and dairy products.

The Difference Between Organic and Live, Organized Matter

Professor Béchamp, the discoverer of the microzyma, has pointed out distinctly the difference between **organic** and **live, organized** substances. He taught that what chemists call "organic" matter consists of various combinations of carbon with other elements of matter, while "live, organized" substances are those which contain live microzyma. He says on page 44 of "The Blood," "The distinguishing of **organic matter reduced to the condition of definite proximate principles** (that is to say, **of the organic matter** of the chemists, which is not living) from **natural organic matters,** such as they exist in animals and plants; that is to say, of the organic matter of physiologists and of anatomists, which is reputed living or as having lived. The proximate principles are naturally unalterable, do not ferment even when they are left in contact with a limited quantity of ordinary air, in water at a physiological temperature. On the other hand, **natural organic matters,** under the like conditions or absolutely protected from atmospheric germs, invariably alter and ferment."

This distinction made by the great scientist between the "organic" and "live, organized" substances to me is as interesting and important as the discovery of the microzyma. It confirms what I have frequently claimed, that Nature's live foods and medicines in vegetable and animal matter cannot be imitated and substituted by the chemist in the laboratory. The organic matter of the chemist is not alive with microzyma whose ferments produce all the great changes in the normal metabolic processes of the living body. **In order to produce live, organized foods and medicines the chemist should have the power of creating microzyma.**

While I admit that the so called organic compounds are less destructive than inorganic minerals like mercury, arsenic, etc., in the crude, earthy form, it is also true that the carbohydrate and protein compounds produced by the chemist in the laboratory cannot take the place of Nature's live foods and medicines in vegetable, animal and human protoplasm. It is for this reason that the Schuessler "Tissue Foods" never take the place of the products of Nature's own laboratory, because they are not even **organic** substances.

The claims of Professor Béchamp are proved by the fact that organic or proximate food substances (both are identical in nature) cannot sustain life. It has been proved by scientists of the Nature Cure school, long ago, that animals fed on chemically pure starch, white sugar or other organic or proximate food elements die sooner than animals who receive no food but water. The obvious explanation now is that organic compounds do not contain the microzyma whose ferments are necessary to "digest" the food materials.

Medicinal Remedies

This brings us face to face with another revelation as regards the chemistry and physiology of digestion. Formerly it was assumed that all the ferments which digest the foods are produced by the body. It now appears that to a large extent the ferments which digest the foods are produced by the microzyma in the foods themselves, provided, of course, that the foods are of the live, organized varieties.

The homeopathic medicaments, as will be explained at length in another chapter, produce their good results because they work in harmony with the laws of Nature.

We never hesitate, therefore, to prescribe for our patients homeopathic medicines, herb juices and extracts, which assist in the elimination of morbid matter from the system and in building up blood and lymph on a normal basis; that is, remedies which supply the organism with the mineral elements in which it is deficient, in the **live, organized,** easily assimilable form. Herein lies the legitimate scope of medicine.

All medicinal remedies which build up the system on a normal, natural basis and increase its fighting power against disease without in any way inflicting injury upon the organism are endorsed by the adherents of the Nature Cure methods of treatment.

But we reject all drugs or medicines which tend to hinder, check or suppress Nature's cleansing and regenerating processes. We never prescribe anything in the least degree poisonous. We avoid all anodynes, hypnotics, sedatives, antipyretics, laxatives, cathartics and like harmful agents. Judicious fasting, cold water applications, manipulative treatment, and, if necessary, warm water injections in case of constipation, will do everything that is claimed for poisonous drugs.

Inorganic Minerals and Mineral Poisons

For many years past physicians of the various schools of medicine, diet experts and food chemists have been divided on the question as to whether mineral substances which **in the live form** enter into the composition of the human body may safely be used in foods and medicines in the **inorganic** form.

The medical profession holds almost unanimously that this is permissible and "good practice", so that nearly every allopathic medical prescription contains some such inorganic substance or, worse, one or more virulent mineral poisons, as mercury, arsenic, phosphorus, etc.

So far the discussion about the usefulness or harmfulness of inorganic minerals as foods and medicines has been largely theoretical and controversial. Neither party had positive proofs for its contentions.

But Nature's records in the iris of the eye settle the question forever. One of the fundamental principles of the science of diagnosis from the iris of the eye is that nothing shows in the iris by abnormal signs or discolorations except that which is abnormal in the body or injurious to it. When substances which are uncongenial or poisonous to the system accumulate in any part or organ of the body in sufficient quantities, their presence is indicated by certain signs and abnormal colors in the corresponding areas of the iris.

In this way Nature makes known by her records in the iris which substances are injurious to the body and which are harmless.

Certain mineral elements, such as iron, sodium, potassium, lime, magnesium, phosphorus, sulphur, etc., which are among the important constituents of the human body, may be taken in the **live** form in fruits and vegetables or in herb extracts in large amounts, in fact far beyond the actual needs of the body, but **they will not show in the iris of the eye** because they are easily eliminated from the system.

If, however, the same minerals be taken in the **inorganic** form in considerable quantities, the iris will exhibit certain well defined signs and discolorations in the areas corresponding to those parts of the body in which the mineral substances have accumulated.

Obviously, Nature does not intend that these mineral elements should enter the organism in **the inorganic form,** and therefore the organs of depuration are not designed to neutralize and eliminate them. Thus, for instance, any amount of iron may be taken in vegetable or herb extracts but will not show in the iris. Whatever is taken in excess of the needs of the body will be promptly eliminated.

If, however, similar quantities of iron be taken for the same length of time in the inorganic mineral form, the iron will accumulate in the tissues of stomach and bowels and begin to show in the iris in the form of a rust brown discoloration in the corresponding areas of the digestive organs, directly around the pupil.

In similar manner, sodium, which is one of the most important mineral elements in the human body, if taken in the **inorganic** form such as sodium bicarbonate or sodium salicylate, will show in a heavy, white ring near the outer edge of the iris. Sulphur will show in the form of yellowish discolorations in the area of stomach and bowels. Iodin in the inorganic form, prepared from ash of sea weeds, shows in the iris in well defined bright red spots. Phosphorus appears in whitish-yellow streaks and clouds in the areas corresponding to the organs in which it has accumulated.

An interesting exception to this rule is our common table salt (NaCl, sodium chlorid), which is an inorganic mineral combination. So far, iridologists have not discovered any sign in the iris indicating that this mineral substance accumulates abnormally in the body. It may be that this salt is more easily eliminated from the system, since it is normally present in large amounts in the blood serum. It is also possible that the salt is split up into sodium and chlorid and that these units enter into new chemical combinations.

This might explain why salt is the only inorganic mineral substance which is extensively used as food by humanity in general. Advocates of the liberal use of

table salt usually argue that animals guided by their
natural instinct do not hesitate to habitually visit "salt
licks". Animals will do this when the vegetation on
which they subsist is deficient in mineral salts as the
result of deficiency of the minerals in the soil.

It must be remembered that animals, as well as human
beings, may acquire bad habits. Horses will founder on
oats when they have free access to grass and hay. In
Montana at one time we kept in confinement a splendid
elk. He would eat more chewing tobacco in a day than
could have been consumed by a dozen cowboys.

Though undoubtedly a limited amount of inorganic
sodium chlorid can be utilized by the body, I do not
encourage the excessive use of salt, either in cooking
food or at the table. Taken in considerable quantities,
it is very injurious to the tissues of the body. The boil-
ing of foods precipitates the salts of sodium, magnesium,
potassium, etc. This is the reason why "cooked foods"
crave more salt than raw food. The various aspects of
the table salt problem have been fully discussed in an
article in the Nature Cure Cook Book, entitled "To Salt
or Not to Salt".

Before the days of canned vegetables and fruits, scorbut
or scurvy was a common disease among mariners and
others who had to subsist for long periods of time on
salted meats and were deprived of vegetables. The disease
manifested as a breaking down of the gums and other
tissues of the body, accompanied by bleeding and much
soreness. As soon as these people partook of fresh fruits
and vegetables, the scurvy disappeared. The minerals
which occur in organized combinations in these foods
furnished the building stones which imparted textile
strength to the tissues and stopped the disintegration of
the fleshy structures.

The Nature Cure regimen aims to provide sodium

chlorid as well as the other mineral elements and salts required by the body in **organized form** in foods and medicines.

When the use of inorganic minerals is discontinued and the proper methods of eliminative treatment are applied, these mineral substances are gradually dislodged and carried out of the system. Simultaneously with their elimination disappear their signs in the iris and the disease symptoms which their presence had created in the organism.

In this connection it is a significant fact that those minerals which are congenial to the system, that is, those which in their **organized** form enter into the composition of the body, are much more easily eliminated, if they have been taken in the **inorganic** form, than those substances which are naturally foreign and poisonous to the human organism, such as mercury, arsenic, bromids, the different coal tar preparations, etc.

This is proved by the fact that the signs of the minerals which are normal constituents of the human body disappear from the iris of the eye much sooner than the signs of those minerals which are foreign and naturally poisonous to the system.

The difficulty we experience in eliminating mineral poisons from the body would seem to indicate that Nature never intended them to be used as foods or medicines. The intestines, kidneys, skin, mucous membranes, and other organs of depuration are evidently not constructed or prepared to cope with inorganic, poisonous substances and to eliminate them completely. Accordingly, these poisons show a tendency to accumulate in certain parts or organs of the body for which they have a special affinity or, where the resistance is lowered, there to act as destructive irritants.

The diseases which we find most difficult to cure, even

by the most radical application of natural methods, are cases of drug poisoning. Substances which are foreign to the human organism, especially the inorganic mineral poisons, positively destroy tissues and organs and are much harder to eliminate from the system than the encumbrances of morbid materials and waste matter produced in the body by wrong habits of living. The obvious reason for this is that our organs of eliminations are intended and constructed to excrete only such waste products as are formed in the organism in the processes of metabolism.

Tuberculosis or cancer may be caused in a scrofulous or psoric constitution by overloading the system with meat, coffee, alcohol or tobacco; but as soon as these bad habits are discontinued, and the organs of elimination treated by natural methods, the encumbrances will be eliminated and the much dreaded symptoms will subside and disappear, often with surprising rapidity.

On the other hand, mercury, arsenic, quinin, strychnin, iodin, etc., accumulate in the brain, spinal cord, and the cells and tissues of the vital organs, causing actual destruction and disintegration. The tissues thus affected are not easily rebuilt and it is exceedingly difficult to stir up the destructive mineral poisons and to eliminate them from the system.

Therefore it is an indisputable fact that many of the most stubborn, so called "incurable" diseases are drug diseases.

The Importance of Natural Diet

While certain medicinal remedies in organized form may be very useful in supplying **quickly** a deficiency of mineral elements in the system, we should aim to keep our bodies in a normal, healthy condition by proper food selection and combination. A brief description of the scientific basis of "natural dietetics" will be found in the chapter on Diet.

Undoubtedly Nature has supplied in overabundance all the elements which the human organism needs in natural foods, otherwise she would be a very poor organizer and provider.

We should learn to select and combine food materials in such a manner as to supply all the needs of the body in the best possible way and thus insure perfect health and strength without the use of medicines.

Which is more in harmony with the basic laws of morality and with wise common sense,—to leave people in total ignorance of the principles of natural dietetics, thus allowing them to drift into all sorts of diseases through food and drink poisoning and then to "cure" them with artificial chemical preparations; or, to teach them how to eat and drink in such a way as to establish perfect, natural immunity to disease? Which depends upon vicarious salvation? Which constitutes rational self-help in conformity with personal responsibility?

Why should we attempt to cure anemia with inorganic iron, hyperacidity of the stomach with baking soda, swollen glands with iodin, the itch with sulphur, rachitic conditions in infants with lime water, etc., etc., when these mineral elements are contained in abundance and in live, organized form in fruits, vegetables and herbs?

Unfortunately, however, a great many individuals, through wrong habits of living and of treating their ailments, have weakened their digestive organs to such a degree that they are incapable of properly assimilating their food and require, at least temporarily, natural stimulative treatment and a supply of the indispensable organic mineral salts through medicinal food preparations.

In such cases the mineral elements must be provided in

the most easily assimilable form in vegetable extracts which should be prepared fresh every day.

What has been said is sufficient, I believe, to justify the attitude of the Nature Cure school toward medicines in general. It explains why we condemn the use of inorganic minerals and poisonous substances, while we find a wide and useful field for medicinal remedies in the form of blood and tissue foods.

CHAPTER XXV

HOMEOPATHY

WHEN we recommend the use of homeopathic remedies the "medical nihilist" protests: "Don't talk homeopathy to me! I didn't come to you for drugs; I have had enough of them."

When we explain that these remedies are so highly refined that they cannot possibly do any harm, he becomes still more indignant. "I don't need any of your mental therapeutics in homeopathic form!" he exclaims. "I, too, believe in the power of mind over matter but I have no faith in your sugar of milk pellets. They are poor substitutes for the real article. That kind of sugar-coated suggestion might work with some people, but not with me!"

When I first entered upon the study of medicine, I, too, could not believe in the curative power of homeopathic doses; but experience caused me to change my mind. The well selected remedy administered at the right time often works wonders.

True homeopathic medicines in high potency doses are so highly refined and rarefied that they cannot possibly produce harmful results or suppress Nature's cleansing and healing efforts; on the contrary, if employed according to the law of homeopathy—"Like cures like"—they assist in producing acute reactions or "healing crises", thus aiding Nature in the work of purification and repair.

In order to make clear the minuteness of the high potency dose I will briefly explain the process of tritura-

307

tion. To begin with, the more dilute and refined the dose, the higher the potency.

The first potency is prepared by mixing one part of the drug with nine parts of milk sugar. Milk sugar is used because it is a constituent of the human organism and therefore neutral. The mixture is macerated in a mortar for about twenty minutes. The product constitutes the first trituration or potency of the drug.

To one tenth of the first potency is added nine parts of milk sugar and the mixture treated as in the first trituration. The product constitutes the second trituration or potency.

To one tenth part of the second potency is added nine parts of milk sugar as before, constituting the third potency. This process may be repeated to the hundred thousandths or much higher potencies. The true Hahnemannian homeopath would consider the fiftieth potency as a low one,—still it represents a dilution of the drug written with fifty naughts. In the higher potencies alcohol may be substituted for the milk sugar.

Homeopathy works with the laws of cure, not against them. "Similia similibus curantur" translated into practice means that a drug capable of producing a certain set of disease symptoms **in a healthy body** when given in large, physiological doses, will relieve or "cure" a similar set of symptoms **in the diseased organism** if the drug be given in small, homeopathic doses.

For instance, belladonna given in large, poisonous doses to a healthy person will cause a peculiar headache with sharp, stabbing pains in forehead and temples, high fever, violent delirium, dilation of the pupils, dryness and rawness of the throat, scarlet redness of the skin, and extreme sensitiveness to light, jars and noise.

It will be observed that this is a fair picture of a typical case of scarlet fever. A homeopathic physician when

called to a scarlet fever patient exhibiting in a marked
degree three or more of the above described symptoms,
would prescribe a trituration of belladonna, say 6-X. In
numberless cases fever has subsided and its symptoms
rapidly disappeared under such treatment.

The reader may say: ''I do not see any difference between this and the allopathic suppression of disease by
drugs.''

There is a great difference. The allopathic physician
may use the same remedy, belladonna, in the same case,
but he will give from ten to twenty drops of **tincture of**
belladonna, repeated every three or four hours. These
doses are from twenty to forty thousand times stronger
than the homeopathic 3-X or 6-X.

Herein lies the difference. The allopathic dose allays
the fever symptoms by paralyzing the organism as a whole
and the different vital organs and their functions in particular. This is frankly admitted in every allopathic
materia medica. But by such dosing Nature is forcibly
interrupted in her efforts of cleansing and healing; **the
acute reaction is suppressed but not cured.** If fever be
a healing effort of Nature, it may be controlled and
modified, but must not be suppressed. A minute dose of
homeopathic belladonna, acting on the innermost cells of
the organism and their microzyma, which the coarse allopathic doses would paralyze, stimulates these cells to effort
in the right direction. It brings about conditions similar
to those produced by healing crises and thus assists Nature's purifying effort; it is cooperation instead of counter-
operation.

After this brief discussion of the practical application
of homeopathy, let us now ascertain in how far its laws
and theories agree with and corroborate the laws and
principles of Nature Cure philosophy.

Hahnemann discovered the law of ''similia similibus

curantur" accidentally while investigating the effects of quinin on the human organism. Ever since then it has been applied successfully by him and his followers in treating human ailments.

However, this law has been used empirically. Neither in the "Organon" nor in any other writings or teachings of Hahnemann and the homeopathic school can be found a clear and concise explanation of **why** "like cures like". The proof offered has been negative rather than positive.

Therefore the allopath says: "You tell me that 'like cures like' and that you can prove it at the sickbed; but unless you can give me good and valid reasons why it should be so I cannot and will not believe that it is your 'similar' which cures the patient. How do I know it is your 'potency'? The patient might recover just as well without it."

With the aid of the three laws of cure, I shall endeavor to give the reasons and furnish the proofs for my contentions. The laws alluded to are: **The Law of Cure, the Law of Dual Effect and the Law of Crises.**

"Similia similibus curantur" is only another way of stating the fundamental law of Nature Cure: Every acute disease is the result of a cleansing and healing effort of Nature.

If a certain set of disease symptoms is the result of a healing effort of Nature, and if I give a remedy which produces the same or similar symptoms in the system, am I not aiding Nature in her attempt to overcome the abnormal condition?

In such a case, the indicated homeopathic remedy will not suppress the acute reaction, but will help it along, thus accelerating and hastening the curative process.

In the last analysis, disease resides in the cell. The well being of the organism as a whole is dependent upon the health of the individual cells of which it is composed.

This has been explained more fully in connection with the action of stimulants.

In order to cure the man we must free the cell of its encumbrances. Elimination must begin in the cell, not in the organs of depuration. Laxatives and cathartics, by irritating the digestive tract, may cause a forced evacuation of the contents of the intestinal canal but they do not eliminate the poisons which clog cells and tissues.

The eliminating organs do not make waste products; they are elaborated in the tissues of the body. Stimulating the activity of the kidneys or the skin with drugs does not neutralize and oxidize the morbid materials in cells and tissues.

In stubborn chronic diseases, when the cells are too weak to throw off the latent encumbrances of their own accord, a well chosen homeopathic remedy is often of great service in arousing them to acute reaction.

For instance, if the system is heavily encumbered with scrofulous taints and if its vitality is lowered to such an extent that the individual cell cannot of itself throw off the morbid encumbrances by means of a vigorous, acute effort, **sulphur,** if administered in doses sufficiently triturated and refined to affect the minute cells composing the organism and the still more minute microzyma of the cells, will start "disease vibrations" similar to those of acute scrofulosis and thus give the needed impetus to acute eliminative activity on the part of the individual cell.

The acute reaction once started may develop into vigorous forms of scrofulous elimination such as skin eruptions, glandular swellings, abscesses, catarrhal discharges, etc.

Are High Potency Doses Effective?

The question now arises: How large or how small must be the dose in order to affect the minute cell or the still smaller microzyma?

In the administration of medicines, the size of the dose
is adjusted to the size of the patient. If half a grain of
a certain drug is the normal dose for an adult, the proper
dose of the same drug for an infant, say one year old, is
one twelfth of a grain. How small, in proportion, then,
should be the dose given to a cell a billion times as small
as an infant! Can we conceive how infinitely small must
be the dose to fit the microzyma?

The dose given to an adult would paralyze or perhaps
kill an infant. In like manner the minute cell or microzyma would be benumbed and paralyzed by the drug suited
to the infant's organism.

But this is how allopathy effects its fictitious cures. It
suppresses inflammatory processes by paralyzing the cells
and organs and their vital activities.

Homeopathy adapts the smallness of the dose to the
smallness of the microorganism which is to be treated.
Herein lies the reasonableness of the high potency dose.

The cell resembles man not only in physical and physiological aspects, but also in regard to the moral law.

Elimination must commence in the cell and by virtue of
the cell's personal effort. Its work cannot be done vicari-
ously by drugs or the knife. Large allopathic doses of
medicine may be given with the idea of doing the work for
the cell by violently stimulating or else benumbing the
organism as a whole or certain ones of the vital organs;
but this is demoralizing and destructive to the cell. The
powerful doses calculated to affect the body and its organs
as a whole make superfluous or paralyze the individual
efforts of the cell, and thus intensify the chronic disease
conditions in cells and tissues.

Alms giving, prison sentences, and capital punishment
have a similar "allopathic" effect upon man, the individual cell of the social body. Instead of providing for
him the proper environment and the opportunity for nat-

ural development and for working out his own salvation, society takes this opportunity away from him and weakens or makes impossible his personal efforts.

The Efficacy of Small Doses

The late revelations of chemistry, Roentgen rays, X-rays, radioactivity of metals, etc., throw an interesting light upon the seemingly infinite divisibility of matter. A small particle of a given substance may for many years throw off a continuous shower of corpuscles without perceptibly diminishing its volume.

For illustration we may take the odoriferous musk. A few grains of this substance will fill a room with its penetrating aroma for years. When we smell musk or any other perfume, minute particles of it "bombard" the end filaments of the nerves of smell in the nose. Therefore the musk must be casting off such minute particles continually without apparent loss of substance.

With the aid of this recent knowledge of the true nature of matter, of the minuteness and complexity of the atom, we can now understand how the highly triturated and refined homeopathic remedy may still retain the "dynamic force" of the element, as Hahnemann expressed it, and how a remedy so "attenuated" may still be capable of exerting an influence upon the minute cell or the still more minute microzyma. Since chemistry and physiology have acquainted us with the finer forces of Nature, demonstrating that they are mightier than the things we can apprehend by weight and measure, the claims of homeopathy do not appear so absurd as they did a generation ago.

Undoubtedly, the good effect produced by a well-chosen remedy is heightened and strengthened by the mental and magnetic influence of the prescriber. The positive faith of the physician in the efficacy of the remedy, his sympathy and his indomitable will to assist the sufferer affect both the physical substance of the remedy and the mind of the patient.

The varying mental and magnetic qualities of prescribers have undoubtedly much to do with the varying degree of efficaciousness of the same remedy when administered by different physicians.

The true Hahnemannian homeopathist, who believes in his remedies as in his God, will concentrate his intellectual and spiritual forces on a certain remedy in order to accomplish certain well defined results. The bottle is not allowed to become empty. Whenever the "graft" runs low, it is replenished with distilled water, alcohol, milksugar, or another neutral vehicle. Every time he takes the medicine bottle into his hands these potent thought forms are projected into it: "You are the element sulphur (or whatever it may be). You produce in the human body a certain set of symptoms. You will produce these symptoms in the body of this patient."

If there be any virtue at all in magnetic, mental and psychic healing, the homeopathic remedy must be an effecttive agency for transmitting these healing forces from prescriber to patient.

Transmission of these higher and finer forces, whether directly, telepathically, or by means of some physical agent, such as magnetized water, a charm or simile, etc. is the modus operandi in all the different forms of ancient and modern magic, "white" or "black". It is the active principle in mental healing, Christian Science, sympathy healing, voodooism, witchcraft, etc.

We may assume that the infinitely minute and sensitive microzyma are even more easily affected by the higher and finer forces and vibrations than the comparatively large and complex cell.

Homeopathy and the Law of Dual Effect

I have formulated the Law of Action and Reaction in its application to the treatment of diseases as follows: "**Every agent affecting the human organism has two effects: a first, temporary one and a second, lasting one. The second effect is directly opposite to the first.**"

Allopathy, in giving large, physiological doses, **takes into consideration only the first effect of the drug,** and thereby accomplishes in the long run results directly opposite to those which it desires to bring about. It produces the very conditions which it tries to cure. As an example, note the permanent effects of laxatives, stimulants, and sedatives upon the system. This has been explained more fully in Chapter XXX.

On the other hand, the homeopathic physician may use the same remedies as the allopath, provided they produce symptoms similar to those of the disease, but he administers the various drugs in such minute doses that their first effect is noticed only as a slight "homeopathic aggravation", while their second and lasting effect is relied on to relieve and cure the disease.

In other words, **homeopathy** produces as the first effect a condition "like the disease", **and counts on the second and lasting effect of the drug to bring about the opposite, or health, condition.**

If, in accordance with the law of dual effect as applied to drugs, the **first,** temporary effect of the homeopathic remedy is **equal to the disease,** it is self evident that the **second,** lasting effect of the remedy must be **equal to the cure.**

This law has been proved by homeopathy for over a hundred years. An experienced homeopathic prescriber would no more doubt it than he would doubt the law of gravitation.

Homeopathy and the Law of Crises

If the remedy be well chosen in accordance with the law of "similia similibus curantur", the first homeopathic aggravation, which corresponds to the crisis of Nature Cure, will be followed by speedy readjustment. Nature has her way, the disorder runs its course, and the return to normal conditions is quicker and more perfect than if the homeopathic remedy had not been employed or if Nature's healing processes had been forcibly interrupted and suppressed by large, poisonous allopathic doses. Homeopathy assists Nature in removing the old encumbrances, whereas allopathy changes the acute, inflammatory healing effort into chronic, destructive disease.

The Economics of Homeopathy

The law of "like cures like" is also of great practical importance from another point of view, that of economics.

The best engineer is he who accomplishes the maximum result with the minimum expenditure of force and with the least friction. The same is true of the physician and his remedies.

We have learned that drugs given in coarse allopathic doses attack and affect the organism as a whole. If, for instance, there is a catarrhal affection of the mucous membranes of the respiratory tract accompanied by fever, the allopath will give quinin in large doses to change this condition. He may accomplish his aim; but if so, he does it by paralyzing the heart, the respiratory centers, the red blood corpuscles and the excreting cells of the mucous membranes. The body as a whole and certain parts in particular are saturated with the drug poison and correspondingly weakened. As allopathy itself states it: "Quinin reduces fever by depressing the metabolism" (the vital functions).

Homeopathic materia medica teaches that bryonia has a special affinity for the mucous membranes of the respiratory tract and that its symptomatic effects correspond closely to those described in the preceding paragraph.

If, in accordance with the law of "similia similibus curantur", a homeopathic dose of bryonia be given to a patient exhibiting these symptoms, the remedy, as has been demonstrated, will assist Nature in her work of cure. In doing this it will not attack and affect the entire organism, but only those mucous tissues for which it has a special affinity and which, as in the case of this patient, are the most seriously affected.

In other words, **the large allopathic dose paralyzes the whole organism** in order to produce its fictitious cure. The **small homeopathic dose**, on the other hand, **goes right to the spot where it is needed,** and by mild and harmless stimulation of the affected parts assists and supports the cells in their acute eliminative efforts.

Homeopathic medication, therefore, is not only curative in its effects but also conservative and in the highest degree economic.

Homeopathy a Complement of Nature Cure

Having proved the accuracy of Hahnemann's law of "similia similibus curantur" and having occasion daily to observe its practical results in the treatment of acute and chronic diseases, we should not be justified in omitting homeopathy from our system of treatment. The triturated homeopathic doses of certain drugs may be of great service in bringing about the acute reactions which we so earnestly desire, especially in the treatment of chronic diseases of long standing.

I am aware of the fact that in severe and obstinate conditions homeopathy is often apparently of no avail. But when the system has been purified and strengthened by our natural methods—a rational vegetarian diet, hydrotherapy, neurotherapy, massage, corrective exercise, air and sun baths, normal suggestion, etc.—the homeopathic remedies will work with much greater promptitude and effectiveness.

It is the combination of all the various healing factors which constitutes the perfect system of treatment.

No disease condition, even when apparently hopeless, can be pronounced incurable unless all these different healing factors, properly combined and applied, have been given a thorough trial. It is no charlatanic boast, but the simple truth, when we affirm that the various natural methods of treatment, as we of the Nature Cure school apply them, can and do cure so called incurable diseases, such as tuberculosis, cancer, locomotor ataxia, epilepsy, eczema, neurasthenia, insanity, and the worst forms of chronic dyspepsia and constipation—always providing that the patient possesses sufficient vitality to react to the treatment and that the destruction of vital parts and organs has not advanced too far. Hence our claim that while there are incurable patients, there are no incurable diseases.

CHAPTER XXVI

NATURAL DIETETICS

THE chemical composition of blood and lymph depends upon the chemical composition of food and drink and upon the normal or abnormal condition of the digestive organs.

The purer food and drink, the less it contains of morbid matter and poison producing materials and the more it contains of the elements necessary for the proper execution of the manifold functions of the organism, for the building and repair of tissues and for the neutralization and elimination of waste and systemic poisons, the more normal and the more natural will be the diet.

The system of dietetics of the Nature Cure school is based upon the composition of MILK, which is the only perfect natural food combination in existence.

In its composition milk corresponds very closely to red, arterial blood and contains all the elements which the new born and growing organism needs in exactly the right proportions, providing, of course, that the human or animal body which produces the milk is in good health and lives on pure and normal foods.

Therefore, if any food combination or diet is to be normal or natural it must approach in its chemical composition the chemical composition of milk or of red, arterial blood. This furnishes a strictly scientific basis for an exact science of dietetics and proves true not only in the chemical aspect of the diet problem but also in every other aspect and in its practical application.

The orthodox school of medicine pays little or no attention to rational food regulation. In fact, it knows nothing about it, because the subject of natural dietetics is as yet not taught in medical schools.

As a result, the dietary advice given by the majority of old school practitioners is something as follows: "Eat what agrees with you: plenty of good, nourishing food. There is nothing in dietetic fads. What is one man's meat is another man's poison, etc., etc."

However, if we study dietetics from a strictly scientific point of view we cannot help finding that certain foods— among these especially the highly valued fleshfoods, eggs, pulses and cereals—create in the system large quantities of morbid, poisonous substances; while fruits and vegetables which are rich in the organic salts, tend to neutralize and to eliminate from the system the waste materials and poisons created in the processes of protein and starch digestion.

The accumulations of waste and systemic poisons are the cause of the majority of diseases arising within the human organism. Therefore it is imperative that the neutralizing and eliminating food elements be provided in sufficient quantities.

Around this revolves the entire problem of natural dietetics. While the old school of medicine looks upon starches, sugars, fats and proteids as the only elements of nutrition worthy of consideration, **Nature Cure aims to reduce these foods in the natural dietary and to increase the purifying and eliminating fruits and vegetables.**

In this volume we cannot go into the details of the diet question. They have been treated in Volume III. I will mention here in a general way that **in the treatment of chronic diseases,** with few exceptions, **I favor a strict vegetarian diet** for the reason that most chronic diseases are created, as before stated, by the accumulation of the feces of the cells in the system.

Every piece of animal flesh is saturated with the excrement of the cells in the form of uric and many other kinds of acids, alkaloids of putrefaction, xanthins, ptomains, etc. The organism of the meat eater must dispose not only of its own impurities produced in the processes of digestion and of cell metabolism, but also of the morbid substances that are already contained in the animal flesh.

Since the cure of chronic diseases consists largely in purifying the body of morbid materials, it stands to reason that a chronic must cease taking these in his food and drink. To do otherwise would be like sweeping the dirt out of a house through the back door and throwing it in again through the front door.

Whether one approves of strict vegetarianism as a continuous mode of living or not it will be admitted that the change from a meat diet to a non meat diet must be of great benefit in the treatment of chronic diseases.

The cure of chronic conditions depends upon radical changes in the cells and tissues of the body, as explained in a former chapter. The old, abnormal, faulty diet will continue to build the same abnormal and disease encumbered tissues. The more thorough and radical the change in diet toward normality and purity, the sooner the cells and tissues of the body will change toward the normal and thus bring about a complete regeneration of the organism.

Anything short of this may be palliative treatment, but is not worthy the name of "cure".

The various systems for dietetic treatment for chronic diseases are outlined in Volume II.

CHAPTER XXVII

FASTING

NEXT in importance to building up the blood on a natural basis is the elimination of waste, morbid matter and poisons from the system. This depends to a large extent upon the right (natural) diet; but it must be promoted by the various methods of eliminative treatment: fasting, hydrotherapy, massage, physical exercise, air and sun baths, and, in the way of medicinal treatment, by homeopathic remedies.

Foremost among the methods of purification stands **fasting,** which of late years has become quite popular and is regarded by many people as a panacea for all human ailments. However, it is a two-edged sword. According to circumstances it may do a great deal of good or a great deal of harm.

Kuhne, the German pioneer of Nature Cure, claimed that "disease is a unit", that it consists in the accumulation of waste and morbid matter in the system. Since his time many "naturists" claim that fasting offers the best and quickest means for eliminating systemic poisons and other encumbrances.

To "fast it out" seems simple and plausible but it does not always prove to be successful in practice. Fasting enthusiasts overlook the fact that **in many cases lowered vitality and weakened powers of resistance precede and make possible the accumulation of morbid matter in the organism.**

If the encumbrances consist merely of superfluous flesh and fat or of accumulated waste materials, fasting may be sufficient to break up the accumulations and to eliminate the impurities that are clogging blood and tissues.

If, however, the disease has its origin in other causes or if it be due to a weakened, negative constitution and lowered powers of resistance, fasting may aggravate the abnormal conditions instead of improving them.

We hear frequently of long fasts extending over many weeks, recklessly undertaken without the prescription and guidance of a competent dietetic adviser, without proper preparation of the system and the right subsequent treatment. Many a good constitution has thus been permanently injured and wrecked.

When Fasting Is Indicated

Persons of sanguine, vital temperament, with the animal qualities strongly developed, enslaved by bad habits and evil passions, will be greatly benefited by occasional short fasts. In such cases, the experience aside from promoting morbid elimination affords a fine drill in self discipline, strengthening of self control and conquest of the lower appetites.

Vigorous, fleshy people, positive physically and mentally, especially those who do not take sufficient physical exercise, should take frequent fasts of one, two or three days' duration for the reduction of superfluous flesh and fat and for the elimination of systemic waste and other morbid materials. Such people should never eat more than two meals a day and many get along best on one meal.

However, different temperaments and constitutions require different treatment and management.

People of a nervous, emotional temperament, especially those who are below normal in weight and physically and mentally "negative", may be seriously and permanently injured by fasting. They should never fast **except in acute**

diseases and during eliminative healing crises, when Nature calls for the fast as a means of cure.

People of this type are usually thin, with weak and flabby muscles. Their vital activities are at a low ebb and their magnetic envelopes (aura) are wasted and attenuated like their physical bodies. The red aura, which is created by the action of the purely animal functions and forces, is more or less deficient or entirely lacking. Such people have the tendency to become abnormally sensitive to conditions in the magnetic field (the astral plane).

Next to the hypnotic or mediumistic process, there is nothing that induces abnormal psychism as readily as fasting. During a prolonged fast the purely animal functions of digestion, assimilation, etc. are almost completely at a standstill. This depression of the physical functions arouses and increases the psychic functions and may produce intense emotionalism and abnormal activity of the senses of the spiritual material body, the individual thus becoming abnormally clairvoyant, clairaudient and otherwise sensitive to conditions on the spiritual planes of life.

This explains the spiritual exaltation, visions of "heavenly" scenes and beings or the fights with demons which are frequently, indeed uniformly reported by hermits, ascetics, saints, yogi, fakirs and dervishes.

Fasting facilitates hypnotic control of the sensitive by positive intelligences either on the physical or on the spiritual plane of being. In the one case we speak of hypnotism, in the other of mediumship, obsession or possession. These conditions are usually diagnosed by the medical practitioner as nervousness, nervous prostration, hysteria, paranoia, delusional insanity, double personality, mania, etc. The various forms of abnormal psychism are fully described in "Nature Cure Eugenics".

The destructive effects of fasting are intensified by solitude, grief, worry, introspection, religious exaltation or any other form of depressive or destructive mental and emotional activity.

Spirit "controls" often **force** their subjects to abstain from food thus rendering them still more negative and submissive. Psychic patients when controlled or obsessed will frequently not eat unless they are forced or fed like an infant. When asked why they do not eat, these patients reply, "I mustn't. They will not let me." When we say, "Who?" the answer is, "These people. Don't you see them?" pointing to a void and becoming impatient when told that no one is there. The allopathic school says "delusion"; we call it abnormal clairvoyance.

In other instances the control tells the subject that his food and drink are poisoned or unclean. To the obsessed victim these suggestions are absolute reality.

To place persons of the negative, sensitive type on prolonged fasts and thus to expose them to the dangers just described is little short of criminal. Such patients need an abundance of the positive dairy products and vegetable foods in order to build up and strengthen their physical bodies and their magnetic envelopes which form the dividing and protecting wall between the terrestrial and astral planes.

A negative vegetarian diet, consisting principally of nuts, cereals and pulses but deficient in animal foods (the dairy products, eggs, honey) and in the vegetables growing in or near the ground, **may result in conditions similar to those which accompany prolonged fasting.**

Animal foods are elaborated under the influence of a higher life element than that controlling the vegetable kingdom and foods derived from the animal kingdom are necessary to develop and stimulate the positive qualities in man.

In the case of the psychic who is already deficient in the physical (animal) and over developed in the spiritual qualities, it is especially necessary in order to restore and maintain lost equilibrium to build up in him the animal qualities.

Fasting in Chronic Diseases

At all times some of our patients may be found fasting, but they do not begin until the right physiological and psychological moment has arrived—until the fast is indicated. When the organism, or rather the individual cell, is ready to begin the work of elimination, then assimilation should cease for the time being because it interferes with the excretory processes going on in the system.

To fast before the system is ready for it, means mineral salts starvation and defective elimination.

Given a vigorous, positive constitution, encumbered with too much flesh and with a tendency to chronic constipation, rheumatism, gout, apoplexy and other diseases due to food poisoning, a fast may be indicated from the beginning. But it is different with persons of the weak, negative type.

Ordinarily the organism resembles a huge sponge which absorbs the elements of nutrition from the digestive tract. During a fast the process is reversed, the sponge is being squeezed and gives off the impurities contained in it.

However, this is a purely mechanical process of flushing and deals only with the mechanical aspect of disease—with the presence of waste matter in the system. It does not take into consideration the chemical aspect of disease.

We have learned that most of the morbid matter in the system has its origin in the acid end products of protein and starch metabolism.

In rheumatism and gout the colloid and earthy deposits collect in the joints and muscular tissues; in arteriosclerosis, in the arteries and veins; in paralysis, epilepsy and kindred diseases, in brain and nerve tissues.

The accumulation of these waste products is due, in turn, to a deficiency in the system of the alkaline, acid binding and acid eliminating mineral elements. In point of fact, almost every form of disease is characterized by a lack of these organic mineral salts in blood and tissues.

Stones, gravel (calculi), etc. grow only in blood surcharged with acid elements and they must be dissolved and eliminated by rendering the blood alkaline. This is accomplished by the absorption of alkaline salts contained most abundantly in the juicy fruits, leafy and juicy vegetables, the hulls of cereals and in milk.

How are these all important solvents and eliminators to be supplied to the organism by total abstinence from food?

Prolonged fasting undoubtedly lowers the patient's vitality and powers of resistance. But **natural** elimination of waste products and systemic poisons (a healing crisis) depends upon **increased** vitality and activity of the organism and the individual cells that compose it.

For these reasons we find in most cases that proper adjustment of the diet, both as to quality and quantity, together with the various forms of natural treatment, must precede fasting. The great majority of chronic patients have become chronics because their skin, kidneys, intestines and other organs of elimination are in a sluggish condition. As a result the system is overloaded with morbid matter which must be promptly eliminated to prevent reabsorption. Even normal organs, unless properly prepared, eliminate waste with difficulty. This may explain why patients frequently suffer severely without any demonstrable lesion in the iris.

The atrophic condition of the organs of depuration makes prompt elimination impossible and there are not enough alkaline mineral elements to neutralize the destructive acids. Therefore the impurities remain and accumulate in the system and may cause serious **aggravations and complications.**

Therefore before fasting is enforced it is wiser first to build up the blood on a normal basis by natural diet and to put the organs of elimination in good working order by natural methods of treatment. This is, indeed, the **only rational** procedure and will always be followed by the best results.

When under the influence of a rational diet the blood has regained a more normal composition; when mechanical obstructions to the free flow of blood and nerve currents have been removed by manipulative treatment; when skin, kidneys, bowels, nerves and nerve centers, in fact every cell in the body has been vitalized into vigorous activity by the various methods of natural treatment— then the cells themselves begin to eliminate their morbid encumbrances. The waste materials are carried in the blood stream to the organs of elimination and incite them to acute reactions or healing crises in the form of diarrheas, catarrhal discharges, fevers, inflammations, skin eruptions, boils, abscesses, etc.

Now the sponge is being squeezed and cleansed of its impurities in a natural manner. The mucous membranes of stomach and bowels are called upon to assist in the work of house cleaning; hence the coated tongue, lack of appetite, digestive disturbances, nausea, biliousness, sour stomach, fermentation, flatulency, and occasionally vomiting and purging.

These digestive disturbances are always accompanied by mental depression, "the blues", homesickness, irritability, fear, hopelessness, etc.

With the advent of these cleansing and healing crises the physiological and psychological moment for fasting has arrived. All the processes of assimilation are at a standstill. The entire organism is eliminating.

We have learned that these healing crises usually arrive during the sixth week of natural treatment.

To take food now would mean to force assimilation and thereby to stop elimination and perchance to interfere with or check a beneficial healing crisis.

Therefore we regard it as absolutely essential for the patient to stop eating as soon as any form of acute elimination makes its appearance and we do not give any food except acid fruit juices diluted with water until all signs of acute eliminative activity have subsided, whether this requires a few days, a few weeks or a few months.

Some time ago we treated a severe case of typhoid malaria. No food except water mixed with a little orange or lemon juice passed the lips of the patient for seven weeks. When all disease symptoms had disappeared we allowed a few days for the rebuilding of the intestinal mucous membranes. Thereafter food was administered with the usual precautions. The patient gained rapidly and within six weeks weighed more than before the fever.

A thorough discussion of the technique of fasting as well as regimen for fasting and for breaking the fast, suited to various constitutions and types of diseases, will be found in Volume II.

Fear of Fasting Unfounded

The majority of those who undergo their first long fast are most pleasantly surprised to find that the terrors of ''starvation'' exist only in people's minds. It has happened that people stranded on barren islands or lost in desert places or entombed in mines, even where they had water, have died apparently from starvation in the course of a week or two. It is now fully proved by thousands who have fasted for long periods ranging from forty to ninety days that death in such cases is not due to actual starvation. The real cause must be fear and apprehension—proving again that the things we fear we materialize.

We cannot reiterate too often that fear is a perversion of the great law of faith. **It is faith in evil.** By submitting to fear we give evil power over us. The most necessary requirement therefore for a successful fast is the profound conviction that it cannot harm us in any way but that on the contrary it will prove of great benefit, physically, mentally and morally, because it not only will purify the body but will strengthen will power and self control.

Self control the master key to higher attainment. There is no other practice that has so desirable an effect upon the highest and finest qualities of the soul as fasting under the right conditions. It subdues the lower animal cravings, appetites and passions. It proves to us that we can master even the most primitive instinct of animal and human nature. To attain such control is the very purpose of being. Self mastery is the key to all higher development, mentally, morally and spiritually. It is the only key to mastership. This is the gist of the teachings of all the saviors of mankind and of the wise men of all the ages. It is the sum and substance of science, philosophy and religion.

Nature Cure philosophy of natural living in strict accord with Nature's laws is for this reason the only true and safe foundation for all higher development. While he who has not mastered completely his physical habits of living may claim high mental and spiritual development, these great attainments will not save him from physical and consequent mental and moral shipwreck if he persists in violating Nature's laws on the physical plane. **Time and again I have seen people of high attainments who had become spiritual giants and a source of inspiration to thousands of hungering souls suffer mental and moral shipwreck before their work was finished, thus cutting short the most**

brilliant careers and consigning to oblivion great constructive movements which might have blessed humanity
for ages to come. All because they attempted to master
spiritual and psychical conditions before they had learned
to conquer the physical.

The most brilliant woman I have ever known, a woman
whose writings were epoch making in the realms of science
and philosophy, had many a friendly tilt with me over my
"radical ideas". She contended that a little meat and
coffee did not hurt anybody but were necessary in order
to maintain a positive condition of body and mind, and that
allopathic drugs had their good as well as bad effects.

The result of her "positive" diet and of the poisonous
heart tonics which she was in the habit of taking in order
to suppress symptoms of uric acid poisoning, brought
about a total collapse at a time of life when her work had
just attained its highest degree of usefulness to humanity.
Through pathogenic clogging and the benumbing effects
of long continued drug poisoning her system failed to
react to further stimulation and she passed away after a
few days' coma. There was no reason why, under natural
living and treatment, her life should not have been doubled
in years.

Strict compliance with the natural laws of living means
much more than the curing of physical pains or frazzled
nerves. It is the foundation for all higher development on
the mental, moral and spiritual planes. He who has not
learned to control his physical habits will never attain
mastership on the intellectual, moral or spiritual planes of
being. Those who have attained perfect control on the
physical plane find the way clear and easy to higher attainment. It is a fact we see continually verified in every day
experience that most people find it more easy to exert
necessary self control in moral matters than in their common, every day habits of life.

CHAPTER XXVIII

WHAT IS POSITIVE, WHAT IS NEGATIVE?

EVERYWHERE in the literature of today and in the social vernacular we meet with the expressions "positive" and "negative". Science speaks of positive and negative substances, forces and energies. We hear of positive and negative personalities and traits of character. Nature Cure philosophy claims that all disease—physical, mental, moral, spiritual and psychical—is originally negative, and that health on all planes of being is positive. Let us see, then, whether we can define what constitutes positivity and negativity.

As regards substances, science divides the atoms of matter and their corresponding elements into positive and negative, according to their electromagnetic qualities. In lectures I have frequently been asked the question: "How do you know whether a substance is positive or negative?" It is a relative proposition, very much as with heat and cold. Nobody can fix the dividing line where cold ceases and heat begins. The scales of heat and cold on the various kinds of thermometers are based on arbitrary starting points and standards. So, also, is the positivity and negativity of atoms a relative proposition.

For instance, if we arrange the elements of matter found in animal and human bodies and in the foods which they require in such a manner that the negative elements, carbon, oxygen, hydrogen, nitrogen, phosphorus, sulphur, fluorin, chlorin, and iodin are placed to the left of hydrogen, and the positive elements, iron, lime, sodium, potassium, manganese, magnesium and lithium, on the right of hydrogen, then we find that hydrogen is positive to the negative elements on its left but negative to the positive alkaline mineral elements on the right.

For, while hydrogen is the positive and dominating element in negative substances like acids, ptomains, alkaloids, xanthins, etc. it has to relinquish its dominating position at the approach of a positive alkaline mineral element. The latter will take its place and change the negative acid or xanthin into a new substance, a neutral salt. Both kinds of elements display varying degrees of positivity and negativity among themselves.

However, there are certain tests by which positive and negative polarity can be determined. The positive pole of a magnet attracts negative elements and repels the positive. In similar manner can the polarity of substances be determined by electrolysis. Positive substances will gravitate towards the negative pole, and vice versa.

The law of polarity is one of the fundamental laws, if not **the** fundamental law, of Nature. On it are based the constitution and vital activities of this universe. According to this basic law of Nature **every entity seeks vibratory correspondence or union in or with another like entity of opposite polarity.**

In harmony with this law, electromagnetically positive atoms are attracted to and seek vibratory union with negative atoms, and vice versa. This attraction which manifests in the mineral kingdom as electromagnetic affinity, appears in the vegetable kingdom in the rudiments of sex life. Separation of the sexes becomes physically complete in the animal kingdom. On the human plane, sex influence manifests in and modifies the mental, ethical, moral and spiritual qualities as well as the purely physical characteristics. Thus the law of polarity or the law of sex runs all through Nature, from the affinities and repulsions of atoms to the subtle sympathies and antipathies, affinities or "Wahlverwandtschaften" of the most highly developed and cultured human beings.

What Are Electricity and Magnetism?

This question could be answered by saying, "Everything is electricity". One modern scientist never tires of saying, "There is nothing but electrons"—and electrons are negative particles or charges of electricity.

A few thousand years ago Pythagoras and many other wise men and mystics of antiquity claimed that "all matter is made up of three elements, substance (the one primordial substance), motion and numbers". Now, advanced modern science seems to verify the teachings of the ancient wise men.

The discovery and the study of the X-rays, of radium and radioactivity has revealed the fact that the atoms of all the different kinds of matter are made up of negative charges or particles of electricity, called electrons or corpuscles, which revolve around one another without ever touching as the planets in the starry heavens swing around their central suns. These electrical whirls or vortices tear through the ether (primordial substance) like the centripetal force of the eddy tears through the water.

Furthermore, it has been found that the number of the particles of negative electricity (electrons) vibrating in the atom determine the physical qualities of the atom or element. In other words, whether an atom or element impresses our sensory organs with the physical properties of iron, carbon, hydrogen, oxygen or of any one of the other elements of matter depends upon the number of electrons in the atom and their modes of vibration.

It has been found that the number of electrons or corpuscles in the atom determine its atomic weight. Science, in its wonderful achievement, has gone so far as to count, approximately, the number of electrons in the atoms—at least in the lighter ones.

The electrons, or negative charges of electricity in the atom, are accompanied or surrounded by spheres of positive electricity.

Thus we find the teachings of the ancient wise men and mystics verified by the discoveries of modern science. The "primordial substance" of Pythagoras is the ether in various stages of refinement. "Motion" is the oscillation or vibration of the electrons in the atom, and "numbers" is the number of electrons or corpuscles which make up the atom of matter.

Science teaches that the electromagnetically negative atom has more (negative) corpuscles than are necessary to balance its positive electricity, and that the electromagnetically positive atom has fewer negative corpuscles than are needed to balance its positive sphere of electricity. It is this deficiency or superfluity of negative corpuscles which constitutes positive and negative magnetism or polarity, which causes the desire of the negative atom to equalize its polarity by union with a positive atom. This is what constitutes the chemical affinity or valency—combining power—of the various atoms or elements of matter. The greater the surplus of negative corpuscles in an atom, the greater will be its desire or chemical affinity for atoms having a deficiency of negative electrons or which are, in other words, surcharged with positive electricity.

Therefore, according to the predominance of the positive or negative qualities in force, matter or entity, we speak of them as positive or negative. We learn from the foregoing that the law of polarity is fundamental in Nature. On the activities which it provokes and regulates is built the entire structure of the universe. The cessation of these activities for the fraction of a second would cause the universe to disappear into nothingness in a flash.

Polarity of Substance

From the foregoing it becomes apparent that a substance is positive or negative according to the electromagnetic quality of the elements of which it is composed. Thus we speak of wheat as being a negative food because it contains very large amounts of negative food elements in the forms of starch, dextrin, sugar, fat and protein, while it ranks exceedingly low in positive mineral elements (Vols. II and III, tables of food analysis and "Dietetics in a Nutshell.")

On the other hand we speak of spinach as being a positive food because it contains only negligible amounts of starch, protein and sugar, but large amounts of positive mineral elements.

Polarity and the Life Elements

However, the positivity or negativity of substances as well as of forces and energies is influenced by another factor of equal importance. This second factor is the life element which dominates the substance, force or energy in question. In every higher sphere matter is made to vibrate to higher velocities and is moulded into compounds of greater refinement and of increasing complexity. The higher the degree of complexity, refinement and vibratory activity of a compound or substance, the greater its potential energy.

Four distinct life elements or ranges of vibratory activity control the four great kingdoms of Nature. The lowest plane is under the domination of the electromagnetic life element; the next higher, or vegetable kingdom, is controlled by the vitochemical life element; the still higher animal kingdom is animated by the spiritual or animal life element, and the highest, or human plane, by the soul life element.

On the lowest plane the electromagnetic life element binds together the elements into the simple inorganic compounds of the mineral plane. The vibrations of this plane are the slowest and its substances are the coarsest in our planetary universe.

In the vegetable kingdom the vitochemical life element by the aid of sun energy builds up the elements and compounds of air, water and minerals into the refined and complex living molecules of organic vegetable matter.

While the compounds of the mineral kingdom are crystalloid in structure, the substances of the vegetable kingdom are colloid or amorphous (without form) in structure. It is well to remember this distinction in order to be able to judge whether foods or medicines belong to the mineral or the vegetable kingdom. For instance, water belongs to the mineral kingdom as proved by the fact that it crystallizes in the form of snow and ice.

However, here a vital distinction becomes necessary. Most chemists look upon carbon compounds as organic and alive and as belonging to the vegetable kingdom. Prof. Béchamp, the discoverer of microzyma, has shattered this scientific error also. He pointed out that carbon compounds are not alive and do not belong to the vegetable kingdom as long as they are not the product of living microzyma. This constituted the difference between ordinary calcareous rocks unable to produce fermentation and the calcareous rock of the ''chalk of Sens'' capable of producing fermentation. The term ''organic'' for carbon compounds belonging to the mineral kingdom is therefore inappropriate. The term should be applied only to substances that are alive, have organs and are capable of using organs. All such things are alive by virtue of their microzyma. In these discussions I have not deviated from common usage in the employment of the term ''organic'' but truly living beings I have called **organized** or **alive** in distinction from the lifeless carbon compounds of the mineral kingdom. As, for instance, white sugar may be called by chemists "organic" but it is no longer alive, while the **natural** product of the maple, cane and beet, is **live** food in the true sense of the word. The dead product of the refineries is crystalloid in form, while live, unrefined sugar is amorphous.

The spiritual life element governing the animal kingdom seizes upon the living matter of the vegetable plane and refines, organizes and vivifies it to still higher potencies of vital force and creative energy.

The life principle governing the animal kingdom has been called the spiritual life element because it manifests in the phenomena of consciousness, animal intelligence and volition.

The life element dominating the human kingdom has been called the soul life element because it manifests in the human entity as self consciousness which differs from animal consciousness in that it is capable of reasoning and philosophizing upon its own nature, origin and destiny, of which the animal is incapable. The intellectual and volitional capacity of the animal is limited and circumscribed by heredity and instinct.

Materialistic science would make us believe that animal instinct is altogether the product of adventitious influences, of the struggle for nutrition in an hostile environment, of the struggle for reproduction, etc. This, however, is unthinkable on the face of it. If that were true, then the various individuals of the same species or family of animals would not display that marvelous uniformity and identity of structure and of instinctive impulse. There would be as many different shades and degrees of physical, intellectual and volitional qualities and tendencies as there are individuals according to the varying conditions of hostile environment, of struggle for nutrition, reproduction, etc.

We find, however, that marvelous as is the instinctive recognition and application of social, mathematical and geometrical principles revealed in the doings of the bee and the ant, their intellectual and social activities are the same today as they were thousands of years ago. They must be fixed and regulated by something more stable than the struggle for existence, for nutrition and reproduction in an hostile environment, and this something is the spiritual life element which manifests in animal intelligence and instinct.

On the other hand we find that human intelligence is not hampered by heredity and instinct but is capable of infinite development and expansion until it has assimilated all there is to be learned and experienced in the sidereal universe. We cannot imagine limitations of the possibilities of growth and expansion of the human mind and soul anywhere this side of the Godhead itself.

To recapitulate: The four great kingdoms of earth life are animated and governed by four distinct life elements which are equivalent to progressively higher, more refined and more potent ranges of vibratory activity. Increase of vibratory activity means increase of potential and kinetic or working energy. The building of atoms into molecules involves the absorption of the energy which builds, into that which it is building; therefore every additional atom in the molecule means additional inherent potential energy.

Every higher kingdom of Nature in addition to its own life elements is animated by the qualities of the life elements governing the lower kingdom. Thus the vegetable kingdom in addition to the vitochemical life element is animated by the electromagnetic life element of the mineral kingdom, etc.

While as yet on this earth plane we have become acquainted with only four kingdoms of Nature and their

corresponding life elements, I do not believe these constitute the entire range of vibratory planes or of life and
action. In accordance with the septimal law we may
expect three higher kingdoms of Nature or of life and
action in this planetary universe. Possibly these are the
astral, spiritual and celestial spheres of life—or whatever
the names by which they may be designated.

The ascending life elements, or progressive manifestations of vital force, resemble the power of steam at different degrees of tension. Steam at ten pounds of pressure
may be sufficient to run a churn or grindstone but it would
not be powerful enough to run a harvester or a traction
engine. Steam at one hundred pounds' pressure can perform a much greater amount and variety of work than
steam at fifty pounds' pressure. In similar manner, each
higher expression of vital force exhibits more powerful
potential and kinetic energy and produces substances of
greater refinement and complexity than a lower one. The
greater the tension of steam, the greater its capacity for
work; the higher the vibratory tension of the life element,
the more potent, complex and refined its manifestations
and products.

This is illustrated in the formation of ice. The "cold"
which solidifies the molecules of water is absorbed and
becomes latent in the icy crystals which it builds. When
the particles of ice disintegrate under the influence of
"heat", cold is liberated. In similar manner the "heat"
which gives warmth and comfort to our homes is sun
warmth which was absorbed in the formation of vegetable cells in the growing plants and trees of primeval
jungles and forests. Coal, though classed among the minerals, possesses infinitely greater heat producing qualities
than other minerals because originally its elements were
elaborated under the vibratory influence of the vitochemical or vegetable life element. The latter element ranges

much higher in the scale of vibratory activities than does the electromagnetic life element which elaborates and controls the simple compounds and crystals of the mineral kingdom.

The animal cell being synthesized under the operation of the spiritual or animal life element, is alive with still higher potencies of vital force than those in the vegetable cell. It is for this reason that animal food substances contain something that is not present in vegetable protoplasm, namely, the animal life element or animal magnetism. This aspect of the food question is overlooked by our friends, the simon pure vegetarians or advocates of raw food diet who exclude from their dietary even the dairy products.

However, in order to receive the benefits of the animal life element or animal magentism in our diet, we do not need to consume animal flesh with its systemic poisons and alkaloids of putrefaction. This subtle but potent life principle which is absent in the products of the vegetable kingdom is presented to us in the most refined form, unimpaired by cooking, in the dairy products because Nature has refined milk, eggs and honey and charged them with the highest potencies of animal magnetism to serve as food for the newborn animal and human.

It is interesting to note that the "newly" discovered vitamines of orthodox medical science are identical with the life elements of Nature Cure philosophy. In fact the word "vitamine" is a literal translation of "life element". I predict that one of the next great "new" discoveries of medical science will be the fact that the positive mineral elements are the carriers of the life elements in the lower kingdoms of Nature. The life elements in the mineral and vegetable kingdoms are vital force transformed into electromagnetic and vitochemical or physiochemical energies. Positive mineral elements are good conductors; negative elements are poor conductors for these electro magnetic energies. We cannot conduct electricity over ropes made of starchy or protein matter: this requires wires made of metals. Science now admits that nervous energy in a form of electromagnetic energy. This explains the great importance of the mineral elements as carriers and conductors of the vital or nervous energies in animal and human bodies.

Sexual Polarity

As already explained, the principles of positivity and negativity affect sexual, mental, emotional and psychical activities as well as the qualities of so called inanimate substances, forces, and energies. In sex life, the positive male qualities manifest as creative power, initiative, self reliance, aggressiveness and love of material and intellectual domination. The corresponding faults are coarseness, self indulgence, obstinacy and intellectual vanity.

The predominating negative qualities of the female sex nature are intuitional, emotional, passive, conservative, and pacific. The corresponding faults are excessive emotionalism, deceitfulness and personal vanity.

The mental and emotional activities under the headings of positive and negative, arrange themselves somewhat as follows:

Mental and Emotional Polarity

Positive	Negative
Will power	Indecision
Self-control	Vacillation
Self-reliance	Self-indulgence
Courage	Diffidence
Aggressiveness	Laziness
Initiative	Fear
Confidence	Worry
Faith	Anxiety
Cheerfulness	Apprehension

Positive	Negative
Creativeness	Hatred
Happiness	Jealousy
Love	Selfishness
Helpfulness	Depression
Altruism	Melancholy
	Self-pity

Psychical Polarity

Considered from the psychical viewpoint, positivity means predominance of reason, will power and self-control over the emotions, appetites and passions—independence and poise of character. These positive qualities are the best safeguards against psychical negativity or subjectivity which may lead to hypnotic subjection, mediumship, obsession and possession and their various manifestations of abnormal psychism. These are fully described in "Nature Cure Eugenics", the third volume in this series.

CHAPTER XXIX

HEALTH IS POSITIVE, DISEASE NEGATIVE

IN order to prove the truth of this proposition we must study the workings of the law of polarity in the lower kingdoms, insofar as these are concerned in the production of wholesome foods and medicines and of harmful substances and destructive poisons. Chemical science so far has discovered in animal and human bodies and likewise in the foods which feed and sustain them, seventeen elements in appreciable quantities. These seventeen elements must be present in animal and human bodies and consequently in their food supplies in well balanced and sufficient quantities to fill all their requirements and thus to insure healthy tissue and normal function.

If some of these elements are present in overabundance and if others are deficient or entirely lacking in food and drink, then the chemical balance of the organism and its functions will be disturbed and abnormal function or disease will, sooner or later, be the inevitable result.

Let us now study more closely the chemical processes which determine health or disease. Practically all diseases arising in animal and human bodies, always barring accidents and surroundings uncongenial to life and health, are caused ultimately by the deleterious or destructive action of certain acids, ptomains, alkaloids, xanthins or other pathogenic substances and toxins. These disease producing chemical substances to which we refer collectively as pathogen are made up of hydrogen in combination with negative elements. If food and drink consist almost entirely of these negative, pathogen

344

producing elements, then in time abnormal or diseased conditions must develop.

The foods most highly valued by the medical profession and the laity for their "nourishing" qualities, namely proteins, dextrins, starches, fats and sugars are, when chemically pure, made up of hydrogen in combination with negative, acid forming elements. These are carbon, oxygen, hydrogen, nitrogen, phosphorus and sulphur. Hydrogen is the basic element in all acids. Oxygen is found in practically all acids, ptomains, xanthins and colloids. These two basic elements are reinforced in pathogenic (disease producing) substances by more or less of carbon, nitrogen, phosphorus, sulphur, chlorin, fluorin, iodin and other negative elements found in foods, medicines and tonics. Carbon, hydrogen and nitrogen are the basic elements in all toxic substances in the body.

This explains why the customary American meat-white-bread-potato-pie-and-coffee diet, unbalanced by organic mineral salt foods, must in time produce abnormal conditions in the tissues and functions of the human body. In Chapter VI of the "Nature Cure Cook Book and A B C of Natural Dietetics" I have quoted a selection of disease producing acids, ptomains, xanthins, colloids and toxins. It will be seen that not one of these contains a single positive element. Nor have I been able to find one in any other of these negative, pathogenic substances.

Naturally the question arises, how can we prevent the formation of these negative, disease producing substances? The answer to this is now self evident; namely, by providing in foods and medicines sufficient amounts of positive, alkaline, mineral elements in the live, organic form. If this is taken into consideration and properly attended to then the positive mineral elements will, through chemical affinity, unite with the negative atoms and molecules and thus produce chemically balanced combinations which are not injurious but rather beneficial in the vital economy of the body.

Physiological science now admits that all cell waste is chemically acid and that it must be neutralized by alkaline elements as quickly as it is formed in order to prevent the accumulation of morbid waste products. Thus the salts eliminated through the kidneys and skin are neutralized acids. When through the excessive intake of negative

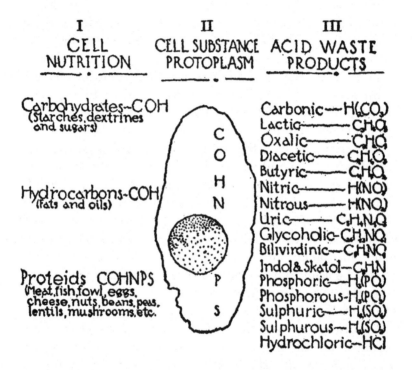

foods and the subsequent excessive production and neutralization of acids, more salts are formed than can be eliminated by the organs of depuration, then these salts also form morbid deposits and become pathogenic substances in rheumatic joints, in calculi, "hardened" arteries and obstructed capillaries. The "new discoveries" of orthodox science confirm my claim that originally all disease is negative or acid. They also verify the fundamental principles of natural dietetics.

The diagram on page 346 illustrates the chemical changes involved in cell nutrition and in the neutralization and elimination of cell waste.

Column I. The three principal classes of cell foods are:

IV	V	VI
POSITIVE ALKALINE MINERAL ELEMENTS	NEUTRALIZED WASTE PRODUCTS	PTOMAINS and LUKOMAINS
	Sodium carbonate—$NaH(CO_3)$	Cadaverin—$C_5H_{14}N_2$
Iron———Fe	Urea————$CO(NH_2)_2$	Cholin—$C_5H_{13}NO_2$
	Calcium oxalate—$Ca(C_2HO_4)$	Amylamin—$C_5H_{13}N$
	Potassium acetate—$K(C_2H_3O_2)$	Gadinin—$C_7H_{17}NO_2$
Lime———Ca	Magnesium butyrate—$Mg(C_4H_7O_2)$	Betain $C_5H_{11}NO_2$
	Sodium nitrate—$Na(NO_3)$	Hydrocollidin—$C_{10}H_{15}N$
Sodium———Na	Sodium nitrite———$Na(NO_2)$	Putrescin—$C_4H_{12}N_2$
	Sodium urate—$Na(C_5H_3N_4O_3)$	Neurin—$C_5H_{13}NO$
Potassium———K	Iron glycoholate—$Fe(C_{26}H_{42}NO_5)$	Mydatoxin—$C_6H_{13}NO_2$
	Iron bilivirdinate—$Fe(C_{16}H_{18}NO_4)$	Guanidin—CH_5N_3
Lithium———Li	Indican salt———$K(C_8H_6NSO_4)$	Gerontin—$C_7H_{17}N_2$
	Sodium phosphate—$Na_2H(PO_4)$	Paraxanthin—$C_7H_8N_4O_2$
Magnesium—Mg	Sodium phosphite—$Na_2H(PO_3)$	Xanthin—$C_5H_4N_4O_2$
	Calcium sulphate———$Ca_2(SO_4)$	Xanthocreatin—$C_5H_{10}N_4O$
Manganese—Mn	Calcium sulphite—$Ca_2(SO_3)$	Reducin—$C_5H_{10}N_4O_2$
	Sodium chloride———$NaCl$	

1. Carbohydrates—starches, dextrins and sugars. These food substances, when chemically pure, contain carbon, oxygen and hydrogen.

2. Hydro-carbons—fats and oils, when chemically pure, contain carbon, oxygen and hydrogen.

3. Proteids—when chemically pure, contain carbon, oxygen, hydrogen, nitrogen, phosphorus and sulphur.

Column II. Shows the schematic outline of a cell with its nucleus. The cell substance or protoplasm, when chemically pure, contains the elements carbon, oxygen, hydrogen, nitrogen, phosphorus and sulphur. These correspond to the elements contained in the cell foods in Column I.

Column III. Contains some of the most common forms of cell waste. The cell protoplasm and its food materials are broken down in the metabolic processes of cell life, of digestion, nutrition and elimination into their component atoms and molecules. These enter into new combinations, for no atom or group of atoms will remain alone and isolated if it has a chance to combine with other chemical units; the same as a normal human being will not remain alone and separated from association with his fellow beings if he can prevent it. **Since acids are made up of hydrogen plus electromagnetically negative elements, and since pure protoplasm consists of hydrogen plus four or five other negative acid forming elements, it follows that all cell waste must be of an acid nature, or must consist of other negative pathogenic materials such as ptomains, leukomains, etc.**

The acid cell waste products given in Column III are convertible into neutral salts, by combination with positive alkaline mineral elements, shown in Column IV. These alkaline elements neutralize acids by replacing the hydrogen atoms, thus changing the harmful acids into neutral salts.

A number of these salts, the products of acid neutralization by alkaline elements, are given in Column V. For instance, carbonic acid is changed into sodium carbonate. Urea is one of the normal end products of proteid and carbohydrate metabolism. Sulphuric and sulphurous acids are changed by combination with calcium into calcium sulphate or sulphide, etc.

Column VI. Contains morbid products of abnormal cell and food metabolism which are constituents of what we designate as pathogen.

These substances when they accumulate in the system in excessive quantities may cause (in the form of leucocytes and colloid matter) capillary obstruction, followed by inflammation and exudation of the pathogenic materials into the neighboring tissues, resulting in putrefactive changes as described in the chapters dealing with inflammation. These morbid processes favor the development of normal as well as abnormal microzyma into bacteria. The bacteria feed on and decompose the pathogenic materials (leucocytes and colloids) into simple compounds, suitable for neutralization by alkaline elements and for elimination through the natural channels. When the pathogenic materials have been decomposed the bacteria are either eliminated from the system or the microzyma consume the protoplasm of their own bacteria, leaving nothing but the microzyma themselves. These under favorable conditions, that is, in a congenial morbid soil in their own or other bodies, may again develop into scavengers, or bacteria, as science calls them. That this process under certain circumstances actually takes place is admitted by orthodox science. They give the name "spores" to what Bechámp called microzyma.

The foregoing explains why healing crises become necessary when the pathogenic encumbrances in the body of a "chronic" contain excessive amounts of morbid substances classified in Column VI.

The following quotation is taken from the "Principles of Bacteriology" by A. C. Abbott, M. D., a standard work used in many medical colleges, page 54:

"`. . . .` but as soon as these conditions (the life requirements of the cell) become altered by the exhaustion of nourishment, the presence of detrimental substances, unfavorable temperatures, etc., there appears in their life cycle the stage to which we have referred as **spore-formation.** This is the process by which the organisms are enabled to enter a state in which they resist deleterious influences to a much higher degree than is possible for them when in the growing or vegetative condition.

"In the spore, resting, or permanent state, as it is variously called, no evidence of life whatever is given by the spores; though as soon as the conditions which favor their germination have been renewed these spores develop again into the same kind of cells as those from which they originated, and the appearances observed in the vegetative or growing stage of their history are repeated.

"Multiplication of spores, **as such,** does not occur; they possess the power of developing into individual rods of the same nature as those from which they were formed, **but not of giving rise to a direct reproduction of spores.**

"When the conditions which favor spore-formation are present, the protoplasm of the vegetative cells is seen to undergo a change. It loses its normal homogeneous appearance and becomes marked by granular, refractive points of irregular size and shape. These eventually coalesce, leaving the remainder of the cell clear and transparent. When this coalescence of highly refractive particles is complete the spore is perfected. In appearance the spore is oval or round, and very highly refractive—glistening. It is easily differentiated from the remainder of the cell, which now consists only of a cell-membrane and a clear, transparent space which surrounds the spore. Eventually both the cell-membrane and its fluid contents disappear, leaving the oval spore free; it then gives the impression of being surrounded by a dark, sharply defined border. When thus perfectly developed, the spore may be regarded as analogous to the seeds of higher plants. Like the seed, it evinces no evidence of life until placed under conditions favorable to germination, when there develops from it a cell identical in all respects with that from which it originated. Its tenacity of life, as in the case of seeds, is almost unlimited. It may be kept in a dry state, and this has actually been done, for years, without losing the power of germination. . . ."

The spores or microzyma herein described are of exceptionally large size. The microzyma of other cells or bacteria may be so minute that they escape observation through the microscope.

Acid Diseases

The human body is made up of acid and alkaline constituents: in order to have normal conditions and functions of tissues and organs both must be present in the right proportions. If either the acid or the alkaline elements are present in excessive or insufficient quantities, then abnormal conditions and functions; that is **Disease,** will be the result.

Acidity and alkalinity undoubtedly play an important part in the generation of electricity and magnetism in the human organism. Every electric cell and battery contains acid and alkaline elements; and the human body is a dynamo made up of innumerable minute electric cells and batteries in the forms of living, protoplasmic cells and organs.

It has been claimed that what we call "vital force" is **Electricity** and **Magnetism** and that these forms of energy are manufactured in the human body. This, however, is but a partial statement of the truth. It is true that vital force manifests in the body as electricity and magnetism, but life or vital force itself is not generated in the system.

Life is a primary force. It is the source of all activity animating the universe. From this primary force other, secondary forces are derived, such as electricity, magnetism, mental, emotional and nervous energy.

These secondary, derived forces and energies cannot be changed back into vital force in the human organism. Nothing can give life but LIFE itself.

When the physical body is dead, as we call it, the life which left it is active in the spiritual body. It is independent of the physical organism just as electricity is independent of the incandescent bulb in which it manifests as light.

After this digression we shall return to our study of the cause and development of acid diseases. Nearly every disease originating in the human body is due to or accompanied by the excessive formation of different kinds of acids or other pathogenic substances in the system. These are formed during the processes of protein and starch digestion and in the waste products of cells and tissues.

Of these various waste products uric acid probably causes the most trouble in the organism. The majority of diseases arising within the human body are due to its erratic behavior. Together with oxalic acid and oxylates it is responsible for arteriosclerosis, arthritic rheumatism and the formation of calculi. Their presence in excessive quantities aggravates all other forms of disease.

Dr. Haig of London has done excellent work in the investigation of uric acid poisoning, but he becomes onesided when he makes it the scapegoat for all disease conditions originating in the organism. In his philosophy of disease he fails to take into consideration the effects of other acids and systemic poisons. For instance, he does not mention the fact that carbonic acid is produced in the system somewhat similarly to the formation of coal gas in the furnace; and that its accumulation prevents the entrance of oxygen into the cells and tissues, thus causing asphyxiation or oxygen starvation, which manifests in the symptoms of anemia and tuberculosis.

Neither does Dr. Haig explain the effects of other destructive byproducts formed during the digestion of starches and proteins. Sulphurous acid and sulphuric acid (vitriol) as well as phosphorus and phosphoric acids **actually burn up the tissues of the body.** They destroy the cellulose membranes which form the protecting skins or envelopes of the cells, dissolve the protoplasm and allow the latter to escape into the circulation. This, together with pathogen obstruction, accounts for the symptoms of Bright's disease—the breaking down of the cells and the presence of albumen (cell protoplasm) in blood and urine, the clogging of the circulation, the consequent stagnation and the accumulation of blood serum (dropsy) and the final breaking down of the tissues (necrosis) resulting in open sores and ulcers.

Excess of phosphorus and the acids derived from it overstimulate the brain and the nervous system, causing nervousness, irritability, hysteria and the different forms of mania.

An example of this is the "distemper" of a horse when given too much oats and not enough grass or hay. The excess of phosphorus and phosphoric acids formed from the protein materials of the grain, if not neutralized by the alkaline minerals contained in grasses, hay or straw, will overstimulate and irritate the nervous system of the animal and cause it to become nervous, irritable and vicious. These symptoms disappear when the ration of oats is decreased and when more fresh grass or hay is fed in place of the grain. Hard working horses develop distemper when their food contains over five percent total protein. What about inactive humans consuming much larger proportions of protein and starchy foods?

Similar effects to those products upon the horse by an excess of grains are caused in the human organism, especially in the sensitive nervous system of the child, by a surplus of proteid foods, of meat, eggs, grains and pulses.

Still, when patients suffering from overstimulation of the brain and nervous system consult the doctor, his advice in almost every instance is: "Your nerves are weak and overwrought. You need plenty of good, nourishing food (broths, meat and eggs), a good tonic and rest." The remedies prescribed by the doctor are the very things which caused the trouble in the first place.

As stated before, uric acid is undoubtedly one of the most common causes of disease and therefore deserves especial attention. Through the study of its peculiar behavior under different circumstances and influences the cause, nature and development of all acid diseases will become clearer.

Like urea, uric acid is one of the end products of proteid digestion. It is formed in much smaller quantities than urea, in proportion of about one to fifty, but the latter being more soluble is more easily eliminated from the system.

The principal ingredient in the formation of uric acid is **nitrogen,** one of the six elements which enter into all proteid or albuminous food materials, also called nitrogenous foods. Uric acid, as one of the byproducts of metabolism, is therefore always present in the blood and in moderate quantities serves useful purposes in the economy of the human and animal organism as do the other waste materials. It becomes a source of irritation and cause of disease only when it is present in the circulation or in the tissues in excessive amounts.

How Uric Acid Is Precipitated

The potentially alkaline blood takes up uric acid, dissolves it and holds it in solution in the circulation until it is neutralized, its salts carried to the organs of depuration and eliminated in perspiration and urine. If, however, through the excessive use of nitrogenous foods or through defective elimination, **the amount of uric acid and other waste products in the system is increased beyond a certain limit,** the blood loses its power to dissolve and neutralize these substances and they form a sticky, gluelike "colloid" substance which occludes or blocks up the minute blood vessels (capillaries) so that the blood cannot pass readily from the arterial system into the venous circulation.

This interference with the free passing of the blood increases in proportion to the distance from the heart, because the farther from the heart the less force behind the circulation. Therefore we find that slowing up of the blood currents, whether due to uric acid occlusion or to any other cause, is more pronounced in the surface of the body and in the extremities than in the interior parts and organs.

This occlusion of the surface circulation can be easily observed and even estimated by a simple test. Press the tip of the forefinger of one hand firmly on the back of the other and then release it. A white spot will be formed where the blood has receded from the surface because of the pressure. Now observe how quickly or how slowly the blood returns into this white patch.

Dr. Haig states that if the reflux of the blood take place within two or three seconds the circulation is normal and not obstructed by uric acid. If, however, the blood does not return for four or more seconds it is a sign that the capillary circulation is obstructed by colloid occlusion. In this connection I would call attention to the fact that the accumulation of carbonic acid in the cells and tissues and the resulting oxygen starvation may produce similar interference with the circulation and result in the same symptoms (including the slow reflux of blood after pressure) as those which Dr. Haig ascribes to the action of uric acid alone.

When this obstruction of the circulation by uric or carbonic acid or other pathogenic substances prevails throughout the body, the blood pressure is too high in the arterial blood vessels and in the interior organs, such as heart, lungs, brain, etc., and too low in the surface, the extremities and in the venous circulation. This gives rise to the much dreaded high blood pressure.

The return flow of the blood to the heart through the veins is sluggish and stagnant because the force from behind, that is, the arterial blood pressure, is obstructed by pathogen which clogs the minute capillaries that form the connection or bridge between the arterial and the venous systems.

Because of this interference with the normal circulation and distribution of the blood, uric acid produces many annoying and deleterious effects. It irritates the nerves, the mucous membranes and other tissues of the body, thus giving rise to headaches, rheumatic pains in joints and muscles, congestion of blood in the head, flushes, dizziness, depression, fainting and even epilepsy.

Other results of uric acid irritation are inflammatory and catarrhal conditions of the bronchi, lungs, stomach, intestines, genito-urinary organs; also rapid pulse, palpitation of the heart, angina pectoris, etc.

These colloid substances occlude the minute ducts and capillaries in liver, kidneys and other organs, interfering with their normal functions and causing the retention of morbid matter in the system.

All these troublesome and destructive effects of uric acid poisoning may be greatly augmented by excessive accumulation of sulphuric, phosphoric and other acids and by the formation of ptomains, leukomains and poisonous alkaloids incidental to the metabolism of protein substances.

The entire group of symptoms caused by the excess of uric acid or pathogen in the system and the resulting occlusion of the capillary blood vessels by colloid substances is called **collemia.**

If in such a condition of collemia the amount of uric acid in the circulation is still further increased by the taking of uric acid producing food and drink and the saturation point of the blood is reached, that is, if the blood becomes overcharged with acid materials, a curious phenomenon may be observed: **the collemic symptoms suddenly disappear** as if by magic, giving way to a feeling of physical and mental buoyancy and strength.

This wonderful change has been wrought because the blood has lost its capacity for dissolving uric acid and holding it in solution and the acid has been precipitated, thrown out of the circulation and deposited in the tissues of the body.

After a period of rest, that is, when no uric acid and xanthin producing foods have been taken for some time, say over night, the blood regains its alkalinity and its capacity for dissolving and carrying uric acid and begins to reabsorb it from the tissues. As a consequence the blood again becomes saturated with uric acid and the collemic symptoms reappear.

This explains why the hilariousness and exaltation of spirits at the banquet is followed by "Katzenjammer" in the morning. It also explains why many people do not feel "fit for their day's work" unless they take a stimulant of some kind, "a hair of the dog that bit them", on arising. Their blood is filled with pathogen to the point of saturation and the extra amount of xanthins contained in the meat, coffee or alcohol causes uric acid precipitation, giving temporary stimulation and relief.

Every time this precipitation of uric acid from the circulation is repeated some of the morbid materials remain and accumulate in different parts and organs. If these irritating substances become lodged in the joints and muscles, arthritic or muscular rheumatism is the result. If acids, xanthins and oxalates of lime form earthy deposits along the walls of arteries and veins, these vessels harden and become inelastic and their diameter is diminished. This obstructs the free circulation of the blood and causes malnutrition of the brain and other vital organs. Furthermore, the blood vessels become brittle and

*This chapter appeared in the Nature Cure Magazine before the publication of Powell's "Fundamentals and Requirements of Health."

break easily and there is danger of hemorrhages. This explains the origin and development of arteriosclerosis (hardening of the arteries), high blood pressure and apoplexy.

Apoplexy may also be caused by other acids and drug poisons which soften, corrode and destroy (gummata) the walls of the blood vessels in the brain.

In individuals of certain constitutions accumulations of uric acid, xanthins, oxalates of lime and various other earthy substances form stones, gravel or sandy deposits in the kidneys, the gall bladder and in other parts and organs.

Thus Haig distinguishes two distinct stages of uric acid diseases: the **collemic** stage, marked by an excess of uric acid or pathogen in the circulation and resulting in occlusion of the capillary blood vessels and in local irritation; and the **arthritic stage**, marked by permanent deposits of uric acid and other earthy substances in the tissues of the body.

During the prevalence of the collemic symptoms, that is, when the circulation is saturated with uric acid, the urine is also highly acid. When precipitation of the acid materials from the blood into the tissues has taken place the amount of acid in the urine decreases materially.

I have repeatedly stated that xanthins have the same effect upon the system as uric acid. Caffein and theobromin, the narcotic principals of coffee and tea, are xanthins and so is the nicotin contained in tobacco. Peas, beans, lentils, mushrooms and peanuts, besides being very rich in uric acid producing proteids, carry also large percentages of xanthins which are chemically almost identical with uric acid and have a similar effect upon the organism and its functions.

From what has been said it becomes clear why the meat eater craves alcohol and xanthins in the form of coffee, tea, etc. When by the taking of flesh foods the blood has become saturated with uric acid and the annoying symptoms of collemia make their appearance in the forms of lassitude, headache, and nervous depression, then alcohol and the xanthins contained in coffee, tea and tobacco will cause the precipitation of the acids from the circulation into the tissues of the body and thus temporarily relieve the collemic symptoms and create a feeling of well being and stimulation.

Gradually, however, the blood regains its alkalinity and its acid dissolving power and enough of the acid deposits are reabsorbed by the circulation to cause a return of the symptoms of collemia. Then arises a craving for more alcohol, coffee, tea, nicotin, or xanthin producing foods in order to again obtain temporary relief and stimulation, and so on, ad infinitum.

The person addicted to the use of stimulants is never himself. His mental, moral and emotional equilibrium is always unbalanced. His brain is muddled with poisons and he lacks the self-control, clear vision and steady hand necessary for the achievement of success in any line of endeavor.

We can now understand why one stimulant creates a craving for another, why it is almost impossible to give up one stimulant without giving up all others as well.

From the foregoing it will have become clear that **the stimulating effect of alcohol and of many so-called tonics depends upon their power to clear the circulation temporarily of uric acid or pathogen.** Those who have read this chapter carefully will know why this effect is deceptive and temporary and why it is followed by a return of the collemic symptoms in aggravated form, and how these are gradually changed into chronic pathogenic conditions.

Not understanding the deceptive effects of artificial stimulation and acid precipitation, your friends will say to you, "Why shouldn't I take a cup of coffee (a toddy or a cigar, as the case may be) when I know it does me good?"

In order to give a better idea of the various phases of uric acid poisoning, I have used the following illustration in some of my lectures:

A man may carry a burden of fifty pounds on his shoulders without difficulty or serious discomfort. Let this correspond to the normal solving power and carrying capacity of the blood for uric acid. Suppose you add gradually to the burden on the man's back until its weight has reached 150 pounds. He may still be able to carry the burden, but as the weight increases he will begin to show signs of distress. This increase of weight and the attendant discomfort correspond to the increase of uric acid in the blood and the accompanying symptoms of collemia.

If you increase the burden on the man's shoulders still further, beyond his individual carrying capacity, a point will be reached when he can no longer support its weight and he will throw it off entirely. This climax corresponds to the saturation point of the blood when the limit of its acid carrying capacity is exceeded and its acid contents are precipitated into the tissues.

The Treatment of Acid Diseases

The treatment of acid diseases is the same as of all other diseases that are due to violation of Nature's laws, namely, purification of blood and tissues from within, and building up of the vital fluids (blood and lymph) on a natural basis through normal habits of eating, dressing, bathing, breathing, working, resting and thinking as outlined in this and other volumes of this series.

In severe cases which have reached the chronic stage, the treatment must be supplemented by more aggressive methods of strict diet, hydrotherapy, curative gymnastics, massage, neurotherapy and homeopathic medication.

The only permanent preventive for acid diseases is not to take in excessive amounts of pathogen making food and drink.

If we substitute the terms pathogen and pathogenic for Dr. Haig's "uric acid," we have a still better picture and a clearer understanding of the condition prevailing in a human body saturated with colloid or mucoid matter in the form of uric acid and other waste and morbid materials which accumulate in the system as the result of an excessive intake of negative food materials (proteids, starches and fats) and of normal cell and tissue waste. The accumulation of these morbid byproducts of digestion and of the metabolic changes in the system is further increased through defective elimination.

The mucoid detritus clogs the capillaries and forms morbid deposits in the system, especially in those parts and organs whose vitality and resistance are already lowered.

Nature attempts to rid the system of these pathogenic encumbrances through the mucous membranes of the internal tracts and cavities, thus giving rise to all kinds of catarrhal troubles, but orthodox medical science with its suppressive treatment of catarrhal conditions forces the disease matter again into the system.

If through the chilling of the skin or for any other reason an excessive amount of this mucoid matter is concentrated into a weakened organ the tiny capillaries become clogged so that the blood cannot pass through. This distends the capillaries, the pressure from behind forces the mucoid matter and leucocytes from the blood vessels into the neighboring tissues, thus developing inflammation and fever wherever the mucoid obstruction occurs.

The statements made in the preceding pages concerning the disease producing effects of high acidity on the system have been repeatedly verified in our institutional practice and through special laboratory experiments conducted by Dr. Jean du Plessis, a member of our staff.

Before proceeding to explain the nature of these experiments, let us consider briefly the role performed by acids, alkalines and salts in the human body.

During the chemical changes which occur in the cells of the body and in the food while it is being digested or metabolized, acid compounds are formed in considerable quantities. The more the foods contain of negative elements, the greater the production of acids, ptomains, xanthins, etc. However, from the following it will become evident that the system is strongly fortified against the accumulation of these negative pathogenic substances. The blood and lymph contain from two-tenths to three-tenths percent of potential alkalies; hence all acids tend to be neutralized into salts immediately upon their formation. These chemical reactions take place in conformity with the following laws:

When an acid combines with a base (one or more alkaline elements) the positive alkaline element neutralizes the acid and changes it into a salt. These salts are easily eliminated through the kidneys and skin.

Should the potential alkalinity of the blood be insufficient to neutralize all the acids and other pathogenic substances, then kidneys and skin eliminate the acid products as such in order to maintain a slight predominance of the basic (alkaline) elements over the acids and other negative substances in the blood stream. The amount of acid found in the urine during the twenty-four hours, therefore, furnishes a reliable clue as to the amount of acid which the system is unable to neutralize. The amount of salts in the urine, on the other hand, indicates the amount of acids which the system has succeeded in neutralizing.

Physicians, students and nurses employed in our institutions have submitted at different times to dietetic experiments in order to practically demonstrate the foregoing statements. When their urine showed a low state of acidity as the result of a vegetarian low protein diet they were given three consecutive meals rich in negative, acid forming proteins, starches and fats, such as eggs, legumes, bread, potatoes, butter, etc., with no additions of fruit and leafy vegetables. In every instance the acidity of the urine increased considerably during the next twenty-four hours.

The ordinary mixed diet or a vegetarian diet like the above, persisted in for a considerable length of time, inevitably results in hyperacidity and this causes irritation and in time destruction of cells and tissues. Nerve cells being especially sensitive, are more readily affected than other cells. This is the reason why hyperacidity causes nervousness, neurasthenia, neuritis and neuralgia. In this relation some very important work has been done by Dr. Crile of Cleveland, Ohio. The following illustration represents the results of some of his experiments:

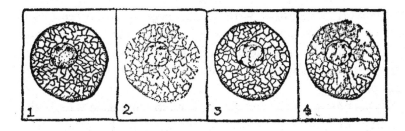

No. 1. Cell of a normal, healthy rabbit. Note clear outline.

No. 2. Cell of rabbit after the ingestion of small doses of dilute hydrochloric acid. Note pale, indistinct outlines due to destructive irritation by acid.

No. 3. Cell of rabbit having taken same amount of hydrochloric acid as No. 2, followed by an equivalent amount of sodium bicarbonate (baking soda). Compare No. 1 with No. 3 and note improvement due to neutralizing action of sodium bicarbonate ($NaHCO_3$).

No. 4. Cell of rabbit having undergone same test as No. 3, but instead of being killed right away was kept alive and awake for thirty hours. No. 4 is as bad as No. 2, showing the temporary effect of inorganic baking soda.

This proves our contention that the positive, alkaline mineral elements in order to be congenial to cell life must be taken in the live, organized form in the protoplasm of fruits, vegetables, and dairy products.

The individuals before mentioned, under the same environment, were again given the same kind and the same amounts of food as previously described, but this time fresh fruits and green vegetables were added to the high protein diet; thereby the acidity was reduced more than one-half during the next twenty-four hours.

After having been told of the neutralizing action of the positive mineral elements found in fruits and vegetables, our patients frequently answer: "If I take plenty of fruits and vegetables with meat, eggs, white bread and pastry the starches and proteids surely cannot hurt me, because the alkaline elements in the fruits and vegetables will neutralize the acids produced by the flesh foods, eggs and pastry."

Experiments, however, prove that in each case where the acidity was thus neutralized, invariably the amount of solid, waste products was raised dangerously high. Vigorous, healthy eliminating organs may be able to cope with this extra work for some time. Sooner or later, however, they are bound to give way under the strain and will then fail to eliminate even the regular daily amount. The urine, in such cases, shows a percentage of solids less than normal, indicating the retention of these waste products in the system.

The autopsy of a well known Chicago physician and surgeon who died in middle life when he should have been at his best as far as professional efficiency is concerned, showed deposits of urates and carbonate of sodium in the heart muscles.

We see this further verified in the composition of stones, gravel and earthy deposits in various parts of the body. For instance, kidney and bladder stones are composed of the following constituents, mentioned in the order of their frequency:

(1) uric acid and urates of sodium, potassium and calcium;

(2) phosphates of sodium and calcium;

(3) oxids of calcium;

(4) carbonates of calcium;

(5) xanthins, cystin, indican, etc.

Nos. 1, 2 and 5 result from excessive protein food.

Nos. 3 and 4, from excess of starches, sugars and fats.

This means that these calculi are made up largely of salts which are neutralized acids.

The only safe rule, therefore, as regards diet, is to limit the consumption of starches, proteins and fats—the pathogen or mucous forming elements—to the proportions and amounts which science and experience has taught us to be the normal.

Acidity During Healing Crises

Another phenomenon of frequent occurrence during healing crises also confirms our teachings concerning the nature of acid diseases. During the first five weeks of natural living and treatment the acidity is greatly reduced. As a rule, from the beginning of the sixth week on, acute eliminative crises develop in the forms of purgings, skin eruptions, boils, acute catarrhal discharges, inflammations, fevers, hemorrhoids, hemorrhages, etc.

With the onset of these acute reactions we usually find a considerable increase in the acidity of the urine. Frequently it rises to 110° and even as high as 150°. Since these patients for many weeks past have lived on a low protein diet, in other words have not consumed acid forming materials, there is but one explanation for the sudden rise in acidity and other waste products in the urine. That is, they must have come from the pathogenic deposits in the tissues of the body.

This sudden increase of waste products in the urine and other excretions of the body during healing crises also confirms our claim that these acute reactions are indeed purifying, healing efforts of Nature.

The Cause and Cure of High Blood Pressure

It is a matter of frequent occurrence that patients come to us whose urine registers 100° to 150° acidity. Such abnormally high acidity is usually accompanied by high blood pressure. As explained in the previous pages, there is a direct relationship between the two. Hyperacidity means excessive amounts of colloid or mucoid matter in the circulation. These obstruct the capillary circulation, especially in the surface. This in turn makes the blood surge back into the internal large blood vessels of the heart, lungs and brain.

During the last few years high blood pressure has become the bugbear of the medical profession and of life insurance companies. Many years ago in my lectures and in the first issues of the Nature Cure Magazine I called attention to the prevalence of colloid obstruction and its causes, and also explained the natural treatment. Life insurance companies are losing many millions of dollars of new business annually because they reject people on account of high blood pressure. Thereby they admit that their eminent medical advisers are unable to cope with this simple problem.

Under natural living and treatment hyperacidity and high blood pressure decrease with wonderful rapidity. Many patients have come to us because examiners of life insurance companies had rejected them on account of arteriosclerosis, high blood pressure and heart disease. This, together with fear of apoplexy, induced them to give natural methods a fair trial. We have taken many such patients who registered a blood pressure of 250° or more and reduced it to normal or near normal within three to nine months time. They were then able to secure life insurance without further difficulty.

One of the stock arguments most frequently met with in talking natural dietetics to our friends and patients is the following:

"There must be something wrong with your vegetarian theory, because I know men and women seventy or eighty years old who have lived on the ordinary meat diet and have used tea and coffee, tobacco and whisky all their lives."

The obvious answer to this is that these fortunate ones were born with excellent constitutions and good vitality. Their organs of elimination happened to be strong enough to throw off the food and drink poisons so that they did not endanger life and health. But it so happens that few of us are endowed with such excellent constitutions and active organs of depuration; therefore we cannot indulge in reckless habits of living without suffering the penalty. Because my neighbor can drink a quart of whisky every day and consume a dozen cigars without showing any **immediate** ill effects, it is not to be assumed that I can do likewise with impunity.

Another common argument met with is that of the Christian or Mental Scientist: "Why should I pay attention to rules of diet, since Nature in her great wisdom transmutes foods in the system into substances most needed and best adapted to the body?"

Anyone who has read carefully the preceding pages will see that this is not scientific reasoning, but superficial sophistry. Surely Nature will do the best she can to maintain the integrity of the human organism to the very limit of her resources. Nature Cure philosophy teaches and emphasizes this over and over again. But there is a limit to Nature's ability to neutralize injurious and toxic substances. One thing is sure, she does not change her immutable laws of chemical affinity to please the fancies of Mental or Christian Scientists.

Arguments of Mental Scientists

If the reasoning of these "Scientists" be true it should hold good in the animal creation which is truly under the guidance and control of Mother Nature. It is now positively proved that the terrible beri-beri disease results from the prevalence of unpolished rice or white flour products in the diet. Pigeons or other test animals fed for a few months on white flour or polished rice develop symptoms of the disease and die unless they are given in time small quantities of the hulls of the grain or polishings of rice which contain the positive mineral elements (and together with these the vitamines, life elements) which neutralize the poisonous acids and ptomains responsible for the development of beri-beri, scorbut, rachitic diseases, etc.

A striking example of the disease producing effect of a one sided starchy diet occurred a few years ago when the Kronprinz Frederick, a German raider, surrendered to the United States authorities at Newport News because ninety percent of the crew were ill with a disease resembling beri-beri. The explanation was that during the many months of chasing and being chased on the high seas, they were unable to make port anywhere and had been thereby limited to a daily dietary of potatoes, rice, cereals, meat, coffee, and cakes and bread made from white flour.

After medical treatment had utterly failed to bring about any improvement in the condition of the men, a dietary of fruits and vegetables brought speedy recovery.

As long as forty years ago scientists of the Nature Cure school proved by actual experimentation that animals fed on nothing but white sugar or pure starch (organic but not live food) died sooner than those who received no food at all.

If Christian Scientists by concentration on metaphysical formulae can change the results of such experiments on animals or human beings, then I shall gladly admit the truth of their theories.

CHAPTER XXX

CONSERVATION OF VITALITY

IN Chapter V I named as the first of the primary manifestations of disease, **lowered vitality**.

What can we do to increase vitality? Old school physicians and the public in general seem to think that this can be done by consuming large quantities of "nourishing" food and drink and by the use of stimulants and tonics.

Everlastingly weak, sickly humanity cries out in despair: "Oh, doctor, if you could only prescribe for me some nourishing food or tonic to give me more strength, then I would be all right!" Through all the ages alchemists, doctors and scientists have been searching in vain for the wonderful elixir which will rejuvenate the body, cure all human ills and prolong human life indefinitely.

Ever since I began to study the problems of health, disease and cure I have been convinced that we would be able to cure all disease instantaneously if we could increase the activity of vital energy sufficiently. **All disease is caused by something that interferes with, diminishes or disturbs the normal inflow and distribution of vital energy throughout the system.**

Acute disease represents a temporary increase in activity of the vital force in order to overcome obstructions in the system caused by pathogenic conditions. Chronic disease is permanent obstruction to the activity of vital energy. In chronic disease the cells and tissues of the body are so heavily encumbered with waste, morbid matter and poisons that they cannot rouse themselves to acute healing efforts in the form of acute disease or healing crises. In other words, acute disease is the battle between the healing forces and the diseased condition. Cure means the victory of the vital energies over pathogenic obstruction.

Vitality, physical and mental energy, power of resistance and capacity for the enjoyment of life are various forms and manifestations of vital energy, and these are transmutations of vital force. The problem, then, before us in the healing of disease as well as in maintaining the highest possible efficiency and capacity for the enjoyment of life, is to increase the inflow and distribution of life force, which means "life more abundant".

This glorious consummation has been and always will be doomed to failure as long as the medical profession and the laity look for the source of vital energy in "nourishing foods, strengthening tonics and stimulants". These substances cannot give life because they are secondary manifestations of life. Secondary derived energies cannot be transmuted back into life force—the primary source of all force. If this were possible we could, indeed, prolong life indefinitely.

The relationship of the life force and its derivatives, vitality, strength and recuperative power, to foods, medicines, drugs and stimulants has been described as follows in the Nature Cure Cook Book and A. B. C. of Natural Dietetics:

This life force which flows into us from the one great source of all life in this universe—from that which we call God, Nature, Creative Force or Universal Intelligence —is the primary source of all energy, from which all other forms and kinds of energy are derived.

It is as independent of the body and of food and drink as the electric current is independent of the glass bulb and the carbon thread through which it manifests as heat and light. The breaking of the glass bulb, though it extinguishes the light, does not in any way diminish the amount of electricity back of it.

In a similar manner, if the physical body should "fall dead", as we call it, the vital energy would keep on acting with undiminished force through the spiritual material body, which is the exact duplicate of the physical body but whose material atoms and molecules are infinitely more refined and vibrate at infinitely greater velocities than do those of the latter.

This is not merely a matter of faith and of speculative reasoning, but a demonstrated fact of natural science.

When St. Paul said (I Cor. 15:44) "If there is a natural body there is also a spiritual body" he stated an actual fact in Nature.

Indeed, it would be impossible to conceive of the survival of the individual after death without a material body which serves as the vehicle of consciousness, memory and of the reasoning faculties and as an instrument for physical functions. Without a body it would be impossible for the soul to manifest itself to other souls or to communicate with them.

Therefore, if survival of the individual after death be a fact in Nature, and if the achievement of immortality be a possibility, a spiritual material body is a necessity.

Someone may say, "If the life force is independent of the physical body and of food and drink, why do we have to eat and drink to keep alive?"

The answer is: Food and drink are necessary to keep the organism in the right condition, so that vital force can manifest and operate through it to the best advantage. To this end food is needed to build up and to repair the tissues of the body. It also serves to a certain extent as fuel material, which is transmuted into animal heat and vital energy.

Furthermore, just as coal has to come in touch with fire before it can be transmuted into heat, so the life force is needed to "burn up" or to "explode" the fuel materials. When "life" has departed even large amounts of sugars, fats, proteins, tonics and stimulants are not able to produce one spark of vital energy in the body.

On the contrary, digestion and assimilation of food and drink and elimination of waste materials require the expenditure of considerable amounts of vital energy. Therefore all food taken in excess of the actual needs of the body wastes vital force instead of giving it.

If these facts were more generally known and appreciated people would not habitually overeat under the mistaken idea that their vitality increases in proportion to the amount of food they consume; neither would they believe that they can derive strength from poisonous stimulants and tonics. They would not be so much afraid of fasting. They would better understand the necessity of fasting in acute diseases and healing crises and would avail themselves more frequently of this most effective means of purification. They would no longer believe themselves in danger of dying if they were to miss a few meals.

Briefly stated, all that food and drink can do is to keep the body in normal, healthy condition. On this depends the flow of life force into the body and its free distribution by way of the nervous system to the various organs and to every individual cell.

Anything and everything in natural methods of living and of treatment that will help to build up the blood on a normal basis, that will purify the system of waste and morbid matter, that will correct mechanical lesions and harmonize mental and emotional conditions will insure a greater supply of life force and its derivatives, strength, vitality, resisting and recuperative power. In other words, the more normal, healthy and perfect the organism, the more copious will be the inflow of vital energy.

Never before in any writings dealing with dietetics or food chemistry has there been revealed the true relationship between the life force and food, medicines, tonics and stimulants.

All the different schools, systems and cults of healing deal only in a partial way with the problem of vital force. Some confine their efforts to dietetic measures, others to the administration of drugs and to surgical treatment. The hydropath stimulates the flow of vital fluids and nerve currents through hot and cold water applications. Manipulative schools of healing endeavor to facilitate the distribution of vital energy through the system by correcting mechanical lesions in the bony structures, ligaments, muscles and connective tissues. Mental scientists, Christian scientists and spiritual healers confine their efforts to establishing the right mental and spiritual attitudes. All these and other systems of treating human ailments deal only with **one or several phases of the problem.**

The only system so far devised that endeavors to combine and apply all that is good in natural healing methods is Natural Therapeutics. It draws the line only at the employment of destructive methods such as the use of poisonous drugs, promiscuous, uncalled for surgical operations, hypnotism and mental therapeutics based on erroneous and misleading premises.

Ignorance of the simple truths before explained leads to the most serious mistakes. Physicians and people in general do not stop to think that excessive eating and drinking tend to **rob** the body of vitality **instead of supplying** it.

The Romans had a proverb: "Plenus venter non studet libenter"—"a full stomach does not like to study". The most wholesome food if taken in excess will clog the system with waste matter just as too much coal will dampen and extinguish the fire in the furnace.

Furthermore, the morbid materials and systemic poisons produced by impure, unsuitable or improperly combined foods clog the cells and tissues of the body, cause unnecessary friction and obstruct the inflow and the operations of the vital energies, just as dust in a watch clogs and impedes the movements of its mechanism.

The greatest artist living cannot draw harmonious sounds from the strings of the finest Stradivarius if the body of the violin be filled with dust and rubbish. Likewise, the life force cannot act perfectly in a body filled with morbid encumbrances.

The human organism is capable of liberating and manifesting daily a limited quantity of vital force, just as a certain amount of capital in the bank will yield a specified sum of interest in a given time. If more than the available interest be withdrawn the capital in the bank will be decreased and gradually exhausted.

Similarly, if we spend more than our daily allowance of vital force, "nervous bankruptcy", that is nervous prostration or neurasthenia, will be the result.

It is the duty of the physician to regulate the expenditure of vital force according to the income. He must stop all leaks and guard against wastefulness.

Stimulation by Paralysis

This heading may seem paradoxical but it is borne out by fact. Stimulants are poison to the system. Few people realize that their exhilarating and apparently tonic effects are produced by the paralysis of an important part of the nervous system.

As we have learned, **wholesome food and drink** in themselves do not contain and therefore **cannot convey life force to the human body. Much less can this be accomplished by stimulants.**

The human body has many points of correspondence with a watch. Each has a motor or driving mechanism and an inhibitory or restraining apparatus.

If it were not for the inhibiting balances, the wound watchspring would run off and spend its force in a few moments. The expenditure of the latent force in the wound spring must be regulated by the inhibitory and balancing mechanism of the timepiece.

Similarly, the nervous system in the animal and human organism consists of two main divisions: the "motor" or driving and the "inhibitory" or restraining mechanism.

The driving power is furnished by the sympathetic nerves and the motor nerves. They convey the vital energies and nerve impulses to the cells and organs of the body, thus initiating and regulating their activities.

We have found that the human body is capable of liberating in a given time, say in twenty four hours, only a certain limited amount of vital energy, just as the wound spring of a watch is capable of liberating in a given time only a certain amount of kinetic energy.

As in the watch the force of the spring is controlled by the regulating balances (the anchor), so **in the body the expenditure of vital energy must be regulated** in such a manner that it is evenly distributed over the entire running time. **This is accomplished by the inhibitory nervous system.**

Every motor nerve must be balanced by an inhibitory nerve. The one furnishes driving force, the other applies the brake. For instance, the heart muscle is supplied with motor force through the spinal nerves from the upper dorsal region, while the pneumogastric nerve retards the action of the heart and in that way acts as a brake.

Another brake is supplied by the waste products of metabolism in the system, the uric acid, carbonic acid, oxalic acid, etc. and the many forms of xanthins, alkaloids and ptomains which make pathogen. As these accumulate in the organism during the hours of wakeful activity they gradually clog the capillary circulation, benumb brain and nerves, and thus produce a feeling of exhaustion and weariness and a craving for rest and sleep.

In this way, by means of the inhibitory nervous system and the accumulating fatigue products in the body, Nature forces the organism to rest and to recuperate when the available supply of vital force runs low. The lower the level of vital force, the more powerful will become the inhibitory influences.

Furthermore, **stimulants benumb and paralyze temporarily the inhibitory nervous system.** In other words they "lift the brakes" from the motor nervous system and allow the driving powers to run wild when Nature wanted them to slow up or stop.

To illustrate: A man has been working hard all day. Toward night his available supply of vitality has run low, his system is filled with uric acid, carbonic acid and other benumbing fatigue products and he feels tired and sleepy. At this juncture he receives word that he must sit up all night with a sick relative. In order to brace himself for the extraordinary demand upon his vitality, our friend takes a cup of strong coffee or a drink of whisky or whatever his favorite stimulant may be.

The effect is marvelous. The tired feeling disappears and he feels as though he could remain awake all night without effort.

What has produced this apparent renewal and increase of vital energy? Has the stimulant added to his system one iota of vitality? This cannot be, because stimulants do not contain anything that could impart vital force to the organism. What, then, has produced the seemingly strengthening effect?

The caffein, alcohol or whatever the stimulating poison may have been has precipitated the fatigue products from the blood and deposited them in the tissues and organs of the body. Furthermore, the stimulant has benumbed the inhibitory nerves, it has lifted the brakes from the driving part of the organism so that the wheels are running wild.

But this means we draw upon the reserve supplies of vital energy which Nature wants to save for extraordinary demands upon the system in times of illness or extreme exertion. Therefore this procedure is contrary to Nature's intent. Nature tried to force the tired body to rest and sleep so that it could store up a new supply of vital force.

Under the paralyzing influence of the stimulant upon the inhibitory nerves the organism now draws upon the reserve stores of nerve fats and vital energies for the necessary strength to accomplish the extra night work.

At the same time, remaining awake and active during the night prevents the storing up of a reserve supply of vital energy **for the next day's work,** which means that the latter also has to be done at the expense of the reserve supply of life force.

Only during sleep do we replenish our reserve stores of vitality. The expenditure of vital energy ceases, but its liberation in the system continues.

Therefore sleep is "the sweet restorer". Nothing can take its place. No amount of food and drink, no tonics or stimulants can make up for the loss of sleep. Continued complete deprivation of sleep is bound to end in a short time in physical and mental exhaustion, in insanity and death.

That the body during sleep acts as a storage battery for vital energy is proved by the fact that **in deep, sound sleep the aura disappears entirely from around the body.**

The aura is to the organism what the exhaust steam is to the engine. It is formed by the electromagnetic fluids which have performed their work in the body and then escape from it, giving the appearance of a many colored halo.

With the first awakening of conscious mental activity after sleep the aura appears, indicating that the expenditure of vital energy has recommenced. The return of the aura is more fully described in the chapter entitled "Magnetic Treatment."

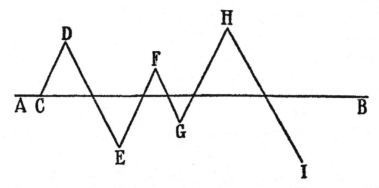

The Effects of Stimulants upon the Physical Organism

In the preceding diagram we have an illustration of the true effect of stimulants upon the system. The horizontal line A-B represents the normal level of available vital energy in a certain body for a given time, say for twenty four hours. At point C a stimulant is taken. This paralyzes the inhibitory nerves and temporarily precipitates the fatigue products from the blood.

As we have seen, this allows an increased, unnatural expenditure of vital energy which raises the latter to point D. But when the effect of the stimulant has been spent the vital energy drops from the artificially attained high point back not only to the normal level, but below it to point E.

The increased expenditure of vital energy was made possible at the expense of the reserve supply of vitality; therefore the depression following it is in proportion to the preceding stimulation.

This is in accordance with the law, "Action and reaction are equal, but opposite".

The falling of the vital energy **below the normal** to point E is accompanied by a feeling of exhaustion and depression which creates a desire to repeat the pleasurable experience of an abundant supply of vitality and thus leads to a repetition of the artificial stimulation. As a result of this the expenditure of vitality is again raised above the normal to point F, only to fall again below the normal, to G, etc., etc.

In this way the person who resorts to stimulants to keep up his strength or to increase it, is never normal, never "on the level", never at his best. He is either over-stimulated or abnormally depressed. His efforts are bound to be fitful and his work uneven in quality. Furthermore, it is only a matter of time until he exhausts his reserve supply of vital energy and then suffers nervous bank-ruptcy in the form of nervous prostration, neurasthenia or insanity.

Such a person is acting like the spendthrift whose capital in the bank allows him to expend ten dollars a day, but who instead draws several times the amount of his legitimate daily income. There can be but one outcome— in due time the cashier will inform him that his account is overdrawn.

The same principles hold true with regard to stimulants given at the sickbed.

One of the arguments I constantly hear from students and physicians of the old school of medicine is: "Some of your methods may be all right, but what would you do at the sickbed of a patient who is so weak and low that he may die at any moment? Would you just let him die? Would you not give him something to keep him alive?"

I certainly would if I could. But I do not believe that poisons can give life. If there is enough vitality in that dying body to react to the poisonous stimulant, then that same amount of vitality will keep the heart beating and the respiration going a little longer at the slower pace. Nature regulates the heart beat and the other functions according to the amount and availability of vital force. If the heart beats slow it is because Nature is trying to economize vitality.

In the inevitable depression following the artificial "whipping up" of the vital energies, many times the flame is snuffed out entirely when otherwise it might have continued to burn at the slower rate for some time longer.

However, I do not deny the advisability of administering stimulants in cases of shock. When a shock has caused the stopping of the wheels of life, another shock by a stimulant may set them in motion again.

The Effects of Stimulants upon the Mind

The mental and emotional exhilaration accompanying the indulgence in alcohol or other poisonous stimulants is produced in a manner similar to the apparent increase of physical strength under the influence of these agents. **Here, also, the temporary stimulation and seeming increase of power are effected by paralysis of the governing and restraining faculties of mind and soul:** of reason, modesty, reserve, caution, reverence, etc.

The moral, mental and emotional capacities and powers of the human entity are governed by the same principle of dual action that controls physical activity. We have on the one hand the motor or driving impulses and on the other hand the restraining and inhibiting influences.

In these higher realms appetite, passion, imagination and desire correspond to the motor nervous system in the physical organism and the power of the will and reasoning faculties represent the inhibitory nervous system.

The exhilarating and stimulating influence of alcohol and narcotics such as opiates, "hashish", etc. upon the animal spirits and the emotional and imaginative faculties is caused by the benumbing and paralyzing effect of these stimulants upon the powers of **will, reason** and **self control,** which are the brakes on the lower appetites, passions and desires.

However, what is gained in emotionalism and imagination is lost in judgment and logic.

Alcohol, nicotin, caffein, theo-bromin, luppulin (the bitter principle of hops), opium, cocain, morphin, etc., when given in certain doses, all affect the human organism in a similar manner.

In small quantities they seemingly stimulate and animate; in larger amounts they depress and stupefy. **In reality, they are paralyzers from the beginning and in every instance** and their apparent, temporary tonic effect is deceptive. They benumb and paralyze not only the physical organism but also the higher and highest mental and moral qualities, capacities and powers.

These higher and finer qualities are located in the front part of the brain. In the evolution of the species from lower to higher, the brain gradually developed and enlarged in a forward direction. Thus we find in the lowest order of fishes that all they possess of brain matter is a small protuberance at the upper extremity of the spinal cord. As the species and families rose in the scale of evolution, the brain developed proportionately from behind forward and became differentiated into three distinct divisions—**the medulla oblongata, the cerebellum, and the cerebrum.**

The medulla oblongata, situated at the base of the brain where it joins the spinal cord, contains those brain centers which control the purely vegetative, vital functions, the circulation of the blood, respiration, regulation of animal heat, etc.

The cerebellum, in front of and above the medulla, is the seat of the centers for the coordination of muscular activities and for maintaining the equilibrium of the body.

The frontal brain, or cerebrum, contains the centers for the sensory organs, also the motor centers which supply the driving impulses for the muscular activities of the body and in the occipital and frontal lobes the centers for the higher qualities of mind and soul, which constitute the governing and restraining faculties on which depend the powers of self control.

Thus we see that the development of the brain has been in a forward direction, from the upper extremity of the spinal cord to the frontal lobes of the cerebrum, from the low, vegetative qualities of the animal and the savage to the complex and refined activities of the highly civilized and trained mind.

It is an interesting and most significant fact that **paralysis of brain centers caused by alcohol and other stimulants, or by hypnotics and narcotics, proceeds reversely to the order of their development during the processes of evolution.**

The first to succumb are the brain centers in the frontal lobes of the cerebrum which control the latest developed and most refined human attributes. These are **modesty, caution, reserve, reverence, altruism.** Then follow in the order given, **memory, reason, logic, intelligence, will power, self control,** the **control of muscular coordination** and **equilibrium** and, finally, **consciousness** and the vital activities of **heart action** and **respiration.**

When the conscious activities of the soul have been put to sleep paralysis extends to the subconscious activities of Life or Vital Force. Respiration and heart action become weak and labored and may finally cease entirely.

In order to verify this let us study the effects of **alcohol,** the best known and most used of stimulants. Many people believe that alcohol increases not only physical strength but mental energy also. Medical science considers it a valuable tonic in all cases of physical and mental depression. It is often administered after surgical operations and in accidents with the idea of prolonging life. I have frequently found the whisky or brandy bottle at the bedside of infants and on it the directions of the attending physician.

Watch the effect of this tonic on a group of convivial spirits at a banquet. Full honor is done to the art of the chef and the wine flows freely. The flow of animal spirits increases proportionately—conviviality, wit and humor rise by leaps and bounds. But the apparent joy and happiness are in reality nothing but the play of the lower animal impulses unrestrained by the higher powers of mind and soul.

The words of the after dinner speaker, who when sober is a sedate and earnest gentleman, flow with unusual ease. The close and unprejudiced observer notices, however, that what the speaker has gained in eloquence, loquacity and exuberance of style and expression, he has lost in logic, clearness and good sense.

As King Alcohol tightens his grasp on the merry company, the toasters and speakers lose more and more their control over speech and actions. What was at first mischievous abandon and merry jest gradually degenerates into loquaciousness, coarseness and querulous brawls. Here and there one of the maudlin crowd drops off in the stupor of drunkenness.

If the liquor be strong enough and the debauch continued long enough it may end in complete paralysis of the vital functions or in death.

Hypnotism and Obsession

Again we find the seeming paradox of "stimulation by paralysis" exemplified in the phenomena of hypnotism and obsession. **The abnormally exaggerated sensation, feeling and imagination of the subject under hypnotic control are made possible because the higher, critical and restraining faculties and powers of will, reason and self control are temporarily or permanently benumbed and**

paralyzed by the stronger will of the hypnotist or of the obsessing intelligence.

There is a most interesting resemblance between the effects of stimulants, narcotics or hypnotic control and blind, unreasoning faith. **The latter also benumbs and paralyzes judgment and reason.** It gives full sway to the powers of imagination and thus may produce seemingly miraculous results.

This explains the modus operandi of faith cures as well as the fitful strength of the intoxicated and the insane, or the beautiful dreams and "delusions of grandeur" of the drug fiend.

The close resemblance and relationship between hypnotic control and faith became vividly apparent to me while witnessing the performance of a professional hypnotist. His subject on the stage was a young woman who under his control performed extraordinary feats of strength and resistance. Several strong men together could not lift or move her in any way.

What was the reason? In the ordinary, waking condition her judgment and common sense would tell her: "I cannot resist the combined strength of these men. Of course they can lift me and pull me here and there." As a result of this doubting state of mind she would not have the strength to resist.

However, the control of the hypnotist had paralyzed her reasoning faculties and therewith her capacity for judging, doubting and "not believing". Her subconscious mind accepted without the shadow of a doubt the suggestion of the hypnotist that she did possess the strength to resist the combined efforts of the men and as a result she actually manifested the necessary powers of resistance.

It is an established fact that the impressions (records) made upon the subconscious mind under certain conditions, as for instance under hypnotic influence, absolutely control the activities of the physical body.

Does not this throw an interesting light on the power of absolute faith, on the saying: "Everything is possible to him who believeth"? Blind, unreasoning faith benumbs and paralyzes judgment and reason in similar manner as do hypnotic control or stimulants, and in that way gives free and full sway to the powers of imagination and auto-suggestion for good or ill, for "white magic" or "black magic" according to the purpose for which faith is exerted.

It also becomes apparent that such blind, unreasoning faith cannot be constructive in its influence upon the higher mental, moral and spiritual faculties. **These can be developed only by the conscious and voluntary exercise of will, reason and self control.**

The limited space of this volume allows me to touch but briefly upon these vital physiological subjects. They will be treated more fully in Vol. IV of this series, entitled "Nature Cure Eugenics, or Man-Building on the Physical, Mental and Moral Planes of Being".

From the foregoing it will have become evident that we cannot increase vital force in the body through any artificial means or methods from without, by food, drink or stimulant. What we can and should do, however, is to put the organism into the best possible condition for the liberation and manifestation of life force or vital energy.

The more normal the chemical composition of the blood and the more free the tissues from clogging impurities, poisons and mechanical obstructions such as lesions of the spinal column, the more abundant will be the available supply of vital energy, and the freer its liberation.

Therefore perfect, buoyant health which ensures the greatest possible efficiency and enjoyment of life, can be attained and maintained only by strict adherence to natural ways of living and, when necessary, by the natural treatment of disease.

CHAPTER XXXI

ONANISM OR MASTURBATION

Undoubtedly one of the most serious leaks of vital force is created through onanism or masturbation. This destructive habit is frightfully common among those who can least afford it, namely young people and children who need their vital energies for the upbuilding of their physical organism and for the development of their mental, imaginative and creative faculties, capacities and powers. There is a close relationship between genius and virility. Positivity on all planes of being depends largely upon sexual virility. Therefore the wasteful expenditure of sex fluid and sex life stunts growth and development in all directions. It lowers resistance to physical disease and creates negative conditions on the mental, moral and spiritual planes of being which may lead to serious mental and psychical disorders.

The main reason why this body and soul destroying habit is so common among those of tender age is because the subject, like that of venereal diseases, is too much avoided in discussions and instruction in the school, church and home. The topic is taboo especially among those who pride themselves on their education and refinement.

In view of the untold harm done by this foolish avoidance and concealment of a vital problem, religious instructors, teachers, parents and physicians should learn how to deal properly with this delicate but vital phase of child life. Therefore the free discussion of the subject should be encouraged among those most deeply concerned and in health culture literature.

First let us examine some of the causes of this disease,

for disease it truly is of body, mind and soul. The true causes of it are not well enough understood. The seed of this weakening indulgence is frequently sown during the prenatal period. Abnormally strong sexuality in one or both parents may be transmitted hereditarily. **Especially so if intercourse takes place during pregnancy.** This is one of the worst crimes that can be committed against the pregnant mother and the unborn. In the animal world the female is never sexually active during the period of gestation; but in this respect as in many others man has sunk below the standard of the animal.

It is a sad commentary on our system of education, scholastic as well as religious, that our young people are not instructed before and after marriage in these all important laws of nature. To do this should be the duty of the minister who unites them in marriage or of the family physician. We all know how the slightest prenatal characteristics are repeated in the offspring; how the unborn infant is apt to be "marked" by transitory impressions, especially by sudden fright and other strong emotions. Is it any wonder that the most powerful of human emotions should leave its impress upon the growing sex centers in the brain and nervous system of the child, causing abnormal and precocious development?

Truly in such cases perversion is born and bred in the flesh and bone before the child sees the light of day. The mother cannot be blamed for this "slaughter of the innocents", for she has not been instructed on the subject. Even when intuitively abhorrent to her, being dependent, she thinks she must submit in order to maintain her hold upon the man, and many a life is thus cursed from its very beginning. The fault lies primarily with those of the medical profession who teach our young men that the free indulgence of sexual passion is not only legitimate but necessary to manly vigor.

This dictum of pseudo science is almost universally concurred in by spiritual guardians and other teachers. No more pernicious falsehood was ever promulgated from the abyss of Hades. If our young men were taught that greater happiness is attained by the exchange of tender affection than by the indulgence of the coarser animal appetites and that the creative forces thus preserved develop and strengthen their finest capacities of body, mind and soul they would be wise as well as chivalrous in protecting mother and child and in conserving their own moral integrity.

Many a man whom we have thus advised has become a lifelong friend in consequence. In no other way is it possible to call forth the deepest gratitude and unfailing esteem of a true woman.

Young men should be made aware that in this regard as well as in other habits desire grows in exact ratio to indulgence, and that through such indulgence he who should be the master becomes the abject slave. This is true of overeating, drinking, gambling and drugging as well as of the habits under discussion.

This places the responsibility not so much with the "defective" child as with the ignorant or inconsiderate parents.

Before leaving this delicate but highly important subject I wish to call attention to one phase of it which I occasionally meet in my professional work. Now and then a woman confides to me that the real cause of her physical, nervous and mental ailments lies in excessive intercourse; that this produces loathing and revulsion which she dares not reveal to her husband, being afraid that she might disappoint and offend him.

On several occasions I have taken it upon myself, without the knowledge of the patient, to have a confidential talk with the husband and to apprise him of the situation.

In every instance the man expressed great surprise and regret for having in his ignorance caused such suffering and anguish of mind. His reply would be somewhat as follows: "I was under the impression that her desire was as strong as mine and often thought it necessary to her. I will cheerfully exercise self control for her sake as well as my own." In several instances understanding and confidence established in this way between husband and wife have transformed a very unhappy relationship into perfect and affectionate harmony.

What a commentary upon a system which permits people to enter upon a relationship of such vital importance in total ignorance of its fundamental laws!

What a curious revelation of the workings of the human mind and heart in love and marriage! Ignorance as well as excessive delicacy and hypersensitiveness prevent many well-intentioned people from establishing a thorough understanding concerning this intimate relationship. This leads to much unnecessary suffering, unhappiness and anguish of spirit which might easily be avoided by a freer and more sympathetic exchange of conjugal confidence.

Among the animals copulation does not take place except for reproduction. While I am not prepared to take the extreme stand that this should be the ironclad rule in the human family, still continence is certainly to be desired, and self mastery will enhance true conjugal affection and love instead of diminishing or destroying it. Few men are aware of the fact that the normally constituted woman craves affection and kindly consideration rather than sexual indulgence.

Many men, afraid of real or imaginary weakness, remain single because they have a false idea of the sexual demands of woman. A free and confidential understanding in regard to these matters between those who contemplate matrimony would frequently prevent marital unhappiness.

Stimulating Influence of Meat Eating

Next in importance to prenatal influence comes the diet after weaning and during early childhood and adolescence. Most of the poisonous acids and alkaloids contained in the flesh of dead animals are powerful stimulants. I have frequently noticed that people who have long abstained from meat on first partaking of it again experience symptoms resembling those of intoxication.

We have learned elsewhere in this volume that these stimulating principles of meat are similar to alcohol, caffein, thein and nicotine and that meat eating invariably fosters an appetite and craving for these other stimulants.

The legumes or pulses, peas, beans and lentils, are close seconds to meat in pathogen producing qualities. Eggs also contain considerable ready made uric acid and a great deal of phosphorous and sulphur which form many nerve stimulating acids, alkaloids and ptomains. For these reasons meat, pulses and eggs are always danger foods to the child.

The most serious aspect of this question lies in the stimulative influence of these food poisons on the sex centers in the brain and nervous system. It is a well known fact, verified by close observation, that flesh foods stimulate the sexual passions to a marked degree. This tendency is greatly increased by the use of coffee, tea, and alcoholic stimulants in the form of wines, liquors and medicines. If the sensitive nervous organism of a child is overwrought by these powerful irritants there can be but one result, precocious sexual awakening.

Next to prenatal influence and stimulating food and drink, ignorance is the main cause of sexual perversion. If religious instructors, teachers and parents do not early enough give the child the necessary information concerning the sex functions and their legitimate use and abuse, the child may learn concerning these things from unscrupulous and vicious servants and playmates in a way not at all conducive to health and morality. This subject, instead of being something to be shunned as unclean by refined and sensitive people, is most sacred and worthy of confidential discussion between parent and child. What more beautiful and inspiring picture can we think of than a loving and sympathetic parent introducing to the child mind the marvels of creative life and its modes of manifestation in the vegetable, animal and human kingdom? The workings of the procreative principle may be thus traced through the ascending kingdoms of nature with the utmost delicacy and with no offense to the sensibilities of teacher or child.

Effects of Masturbation

Next in order we must consider the weakening and destructive effects of masturbation. I have become thoroughly convinced through much experience in dealing with such cases that the destructive effects of onanism are in many instances more of a mental and psychical than of a physical nature. Too weak to resist the almost uncontrollable desire, the victim of the disease struggles vainly in loneliness and silence with no one to confide in and no one to go to for advice and encouragement. The vague allusions to the terrible consequences of the habit which he hears and reads about here and there, the terrifying literature of quack doctors and unscrupulous medical publicists who prey upon the fears of these unfortunates, fill their minds and souls with remorse, dread of the future and expectancy of impotency and early decline.

As is always the case, fear materializes that which it fears. Fear is faith in evil, and faith has creative power for evil as well as for good. Deep down in his soul the victim of morbid imagination sees himself weak, diseased, impotent, prematurely old and in an early grave, and ''as he thinketh in his heart so is he''.

Much experience in an extensive practice along these lines has taught me that the physical effects of the habit can be overcome easily by natural methods of living and treatment as soon as the patient ceases to violate the most sacred laws of his being. Sympathetic advice and the right kind of suggestive treatment will greatly aid him in doing this.

His self confidence must be aroused, his faith renewed and his will power strengthened. I find this as a rule more difficult than the regeneration of the physical organism. He must be made to realize that his consciousness is part of the universal intelligence, that his will is an expression of divine creative force, that these are superior to the weakness and the animal desires and propensities of the lower self.

The best way to awaken and to strengthen this constructive faith is to practice the formulas given in the last chapter of this volume on pages 495 to 499. This auto-suggestive treatment may be practiced at any time during the day when there is an opportunity for concentration, even though it be for only a few minutes. The best time in the twenty-four hours for practicing this mental magic is just before dropping to sleep. If this is done faithfully and persistently, with fervent desire of the spirit and uncompromising determination of the soul, the patient cannot possibly fail in his resolve. This mental attitude was what Jesus had in mind when he said, "What things soever ye desire, when ye pray, **believe** that ye receive them and **ye shall have them**". Simple as these methods may seem, there is no better way to strengthen the weakened will, or to overcome bad habits and establish better ones.

How to Regenerate the Physical Body

The natural ways of living and of treatment are the simplest and most efficient remedies for overcoming physical and nervous debility. A well balanced vegetarian diet will nourish the body abundantly, while it does not overstimulate the sex centers in the brain and spinal cord as is done by meats and eggs, coffee, tea, alcoholic liquors and tobacco. Nothing on earth stimulates a sluggish circulation and tones up a debilitated nervous system like a brisk cold rub in the mornng and a cold sitz bath in the evening. The morning cold rub (Vol. II) should be followed by deep breathing and other exercises while nude. If an open airbath cannot be provided the exercises should be taken before an open window. Deep breathing not only provides a generous supply of oxygen but takes in the breath of life itself.

Corrective gymnastics, especially internal massage and the exercises while lying on the back (Vol. II) will strengthen and vivify the flabby muscles and debilitated nerves of the abdominal and genital organs.

Overeating and the use of meat, eggs, coffee, tea, alcoholic liquors and tobacco should be strictly avoided. Faithful adherence to this natural regimen will overcome indigestion, malnutrition, constipation and sluggish circulation, which usually accompany sexual weakness and nervous debility and help to produce them.

Doctors almost universally treat involuntary emissions too lightly. They say that such discharges are an indication that the sex organs are generating an excess of sex fluids, and that these might just as well be got rid of through nocturnal emissions. Some doctors and many habitual masturbators apply similar sophistry to the practice of onanism. Such opinions, however, are based upon grave error. It is a fact that, as a rule, the sexually strongest individuals are not subject to involuntary emissions, while those so afflicted are most often weakly, sickly and of the nervous, debilitated type.

The true explanation is the following: Any excess of sex

fluids is normally absorbed into the system through the lymphatic structures of the inguinal glands, and serves to stimulate and invigorate all the vital functions and the creative capacity of mind and soul. But if these glands are engorged with pathogenic materials the sex fluids are not absorbed into the system; they stagnate in the sex organs and cause abnormal sexual stimulation, neurotic dreams, unnatural craving for intercourse or masturbation, or, as an alternative, involuntary emissions. Such pathogenic obstruction in the absorbent glandular structures we overcome by natural diet and treatment, particularly by manipulative treatment of the lymphatic glands themselves, for the purpose of relieving them of pathogenic engorgement. In hundreds of the most stubborn cases we have proved the wonderful efficacy of these natural methods in combination with constructive mental, moral and psychical influences.

In order to correct actual impotence, doubt and nervous impatience must be overcome. Perfect confidence and serenity must be established. The treatment should be undertaken not in a spirit of doubt and anxiety, but in the "I-do-not-care-whether-I-succeed-or-not" attitude of mind, exactly the same attitude with which one must meet insomnia or the performance of difficult tasks in any line of effort; as, for instance, passing a difficult examination or giving a public performance. While in all effort there must be strong resolve to succeed and the concentration of mind necessary to do so, this must be accompanied by the "care-less" attitude of mind.

A Word of Warning

It is the duty of all parents to warn their growing children of the pitfalls and vices which lie in their path and threaten their welfare. Too often this duty is shirked or postponed until boys and girls learn from impure sources what they should have learned quietly and without undue emphasis from their fathers and mothers. Fathers have not fulfilled their duty to their sons until they have counseled them along the following lines:

There are two roads before the young man starting out in life and leaving his boyhood days behind him. One is the Good Road, the other the Bad Road. To follow the first is uplifting, inspiring, wholesome, healthful, character building, and will lead to the making of a true man. To follow the second is degrading, low, miserable, destructive, and leads to the deepest mire of depravity.

The young man who leans to the good will be guided by his own conscience as to what is right or wrong and will not easily be led astray, but the one whose conscience is not thus active, readily becomes a victim to folly and a misguided life and dearly does he pay for it in time.

The one deep pitfall, the one great crime facing a young man in his teens, is self abuse. It is the crime of crimes as regards personal health and manhood. The young man who practices it is committing slow suicide, nothing short of self murder. The victim who indulges in this low vice has this advantage, that he can commit his acts in secret and for a long time without being suspected, but oh! with what terrible results!

The luster of his eyes, once bright, becomes dim and faded, the healthy freshness of youth disappears from his face and it becomes pale, sad, sickly and full of pimples. His breath grows putrid, his eyes sunken, his cheeks hollow. He loses interest in his work, becomes neglectful and slovenly, is dissatisfied, grows dreamy where he should be alert; his health breaks down, he grows irritable and fretful, shuns company, especially the other sex, seeking to be alone that he may indulge his solitary vice.

Month by month he sinks deeper into the mire until he has no willpower of his own and no desire to stop this horrible practice which is sapping his very life blood. Like a drunkard he becomes debauched and depraved. His mind weakens, he grows more and more listless, unsteady and unreliable; his growth is stunted; he lacks courage and self-respect, is timid, shy and cowardly. The very essence of life is drained from his system, till he becomes utterly unfit for business and is lost forever to the nobleness of true manhood.

Broken in health, he becomes alarmed. At last he realizes his true condition. A thousand horrors rise before his vision. Through sleepless nights he is haunted with remorse. His nerves give way, insanity stares him in the face; the asylum looms up before him, a living tomb.

Countless thousands thus destroy forever their chances for success in life and are swept into untimely graves, who otherwise might have become leaders, noble characters, fathers of happy families, nation builders, great artists or writers. Only he who lives the true and unstained life can perceive and understand the beauty of life and nature and the grandeur of the universe.

My boy, if you have ever fallen a victim to self abuse, stop it. Stop it now, STOP IT FOREVER. HEED THE WARNING! Do not blight your future life with this damnable curse. Do not exchange your health, your happiness, your manhood for a ruined life, a horrible nightmare which words fail to picture. Instead, seek that which is good, noble and uplifting. You are the one that must act, you are the one to choose; you have come to the parting of the ways. Upon you depends the future.

Cultivate courage, cheerfulness, nobleness of character, and contentment and happiness will be the natural result. In fact this is the only way to secure them. Aim to be of some use to humanity. Let good deeds crown your life. According to the great law of compensation, as you give, so will you receive; no more, no less. Read good books; study the fine arts and become familiar with the **great** geniuses of the world. Cultivate the finer qualities of mind and heart. Love to do the right; be kind and just in all your dealings.

And once more, HEED THE WARNING, AND DO NOT BE AFRAID TO ASK QUESTIONS.

CHAPTER XXXII

SPINAL MANIPULATION AND ADJUSTMENT

By Jean du Plessis, M. D.

History

In many European countries "bone-setters" have, in a crude way, been treating strains and sprains of the spinal column since time immemorial. These bone-setters usually belong to the peasantry and the art has been transmitted in the same families from father to son for many generations.

Incidentally, these simple people observed that their treatment relieved not only sprained, tired and painful backs — the result primarily aimed at — but frequently exerted a favorable influence upon disease processes in remote organs and parts. This empirical discovery has gradually led to a wider application of this method of treatment.

The various modern systems of spinal manipulation, namely, osteopathy, chiropractic, naprapathy, neuropathy, spondylotherapy and our own neurotherapy, are all of distinctly American origin.

During the last quarter of a century millions of Americans through personal experience have become staunch adherents to one or more of these systems of treatment. This fact has been instrumental in directing the attention of numerous sincere and scientific investigators to the spinal column with its associated structures as a mechanism through which to apply therapeutic measures.

It therefore behooves every health seeker to acquaint

himself with the theories and claims of these various systems of manipulative treatment.

Osteopathy

The autobiography of Dr. A. T. Still contains the following interesting statement:

"In the year 1874 I proclaimed that a disturbed artery marked the beginning to an hour and a minute when disease began to sow its seeds of destruction in the human body. That in no case could it be done without a broken or suspended current of arterial blood, which by Nature was intended to supply and nourish all nerves, ligaments, muscles, skin, bones and the artery itself. * * * * The rule of the artery must be absolute, universal and unobstructed or disease will be the result. I proclaimed then and there that all nerves depend wholly on the arterial system for their qualities such as sensation, nutrition and motion, even though by the law of reciprocity they furnish force, nutrition and motion to the artery itself."

It may be argued that as early as 1805 the Ling System of Swedish Movement was founded on the same principle, namely, "permanent health through perfect circulation". The evidence at hand, however, strongly suggests that the founder of osteopathy arrived at his conclusions independently.

The further claims of Dr. Still as to the cause and cure of disease are briefly as follows: Partial displacements of any of the various bones of the body exert pressure on neighboring **blood vessels,** thereby interfering with the circulation to the corresponding organs. These displacements, called "bony lesions", are best "reduced" by manipulations called osteopathic "moves".

Chiropractic

In 1895, Dr. D. D. Palmer put forth the following claims as to the cause and cure of diseases: Sprains of the spine result in partial displacement of one or more of the vertebrae which go to make up the spinal column thus exerting pressure on the neighboring **nerves**. This shuts off the vitality of the organs supplied by the affected nerves, hence disease results. These displacements, called "vertebral subluxations", are best "adjusted" by means of manipulations in the form of chiropractic "thrusts".

As soon as osteopathy and chiropractic were properly established, the more broad-minded exponents of both systems began mutual investigation and amalgamation. As a result, we find that only seven years after the birth of chiropractic, osteopathic literature began to mention vertebral subluxations as pressing on **nerves**, thereby causing disease. On the other hand, advanced chiropractors soon began to realize the importance of relaxing tense muscles prior to delivering their thrusts. They also began to pay attention to the bony lesions other than those occurring in the spine. Many of the chiropractic principles and much of its technique of today has been gleaned from osteopathy, while the reverse statement holds equally true.

Naprapathy

The "connective tissue doctrine of disease" was first proclaimed by Dr. Oakley Smith in 1907. It may be briefly stated as follows: A vertebrae does not become misplaced without being fractured or completely dislocated. What is called a bony lesion by the osteopath and a subluxation by the chiropractor, is in reality a "ligatight", that is a shrunken condition of the connective tissue forming the various ligaments that bind the vertebrae together.

Ligatights are best "corrected" by means of naprapathic "directos". These differ from chiropractic thrusts in that they aim not at adjusting subluxated vertebrae but at stretching definite strands of shrunken connective tissue. Ligatights occur not only in the spine but also **in**

Dr. Smith has evolved a charting system for recording the thorax and pelvis, in fact, wherever connective tissue is found in the body.

the various types of ligatights found upon spinal analysis, as well as the directos to be employed for their correction.

Spondylotherapy

This method of treatment, introduced by Dr. Albert Abrams, consists of stimulating one or more of the spinal nerve centers by means of concussion (light hammering), deep pressure or electricity. The aim in view is to originate nerve reflexes that will relieve or modify the disease process in the part of the body to be treated.

Dr. Abrams also lays stress on the fact that inflammatory processes almost invariably give rise to more or less localized tender spots in the region of the spine with which the nerves of the inflamed parts are associated. It can readily be demonstrated that these tender spots are either the forerunners or the symptoms of spinal lesions.

Neuropathy

This system of manipulative treatment was originated in 1899 by Drs. John Arnold and Harry Walter of Philadelphia. Their claims may be briefly stated as follows: Morbid matter, poisons and irritants of various kinds, acting upon the vasomotor nerves which control the blood vessels, produce abnormal changes in circulation which, if perpetuated, finally lead to disease manifestations.

The nerve impulses coming from diseased parts travel to the spinal cord and, like all other nerve impulses, are transmitted along those branches of the spinal nerves which supply the structures (muscles, blood vessels, etc.) along each side of the spine. Here these impulses bring about abnormal circulatory changes similar to those found in the diseased organs or parts.

Since nerve impulses are transmitted from diseased organs to the spine, it is evident that they can be made to travel also in the reverse direction. Neuropathic treatment, therefore, consists of manipulations and thermal applications which aim at correcting the abnormal circulatory changes as found in the spine, thereby correcting corresponding abnormal processes in the organs or parts supplied by the nerves coming from that region of the spine.

These men also emphasized the fact that the circulation within the blood vessels, being propelled by the heart, needs less attention during disease than the circulation of the fluids in the spaces between the cells and through the lymph vessels and glands. Neuropathy, therefore, also lays great stress on applying manipulation and thermal applications to the lymphatic system.

Dr. A. P. Davis of Los Angeles was the first to attach the name ''neuropathy'' to a system of manual and mechanical treatment which, however, is not based on the above principles.

Neurotherapy

While the exponents of the above systems of spinal manipulation differ widely in their theories as to the cause of disease and the means of removing such cause, their methods of treatment furnish considerable evidence of satisfactory results. This seems to suggest that there must be some real value in each system and that a great deal of the difference between these apparently opposed methods of treatment lies in the claims of their exponents. It will be shown presently that, in their final analysis, the osteopathic spinal lesion, the chiropractic subluxation and the naprapathic ligatight represent one and the same thing.

Natural Therapeutics is broad enough to embrace all

methods of treatment, no matter what their source, provided they harmonize with the fundamental laws of cure.

Gradually, therefore, after having gathered the **constructive** elements from **all** the various methods of manipulation, after considerable spinal dissection and, above all, after close observation of the results obtained in hundreds of obstinate acute and chronic cases, we of the school of Natural Therapeutics have evolved our own system of spinal manipulation and have named it **neurotherapy.**

Before proceeding with the discussion of neurotherapy, let us pause for a brief survey of the spine and its associated structures so that we may grasp more readily that which is to follow.

Anatomy of the Spine

The spinal column or backbone is made up of a series of separate bony segments called vertebrae. These are placed one on top of another thus forming a strong supporting pillar or column. Throughout the length of this runs a hollow cylindrical canal which lodges and protects the spinal cord.

Between the vertebrae of human beings are found pads of tough, resilient fibrocartilage (gristle) which form the main bonds of union and serve as shock absorbers.

To the vertebrae are attached strong bands of tough fibrous tissue called ligaments which serve to restrict the motions of the spine. These motions are regulated by the spinal muscles which are responsible for actively holding the vertebrae in alignment.

Between the adjacent vertebrae on either side are found oval openings called intervertebral foramina, which communicate with the spinal canal and each of which contains the following structures:*

*The profession is indebted to Dr. Harold Swanberg for the light he has thrown on this important part of the anatomy.

(a) The spinal nerve, composed of fibres which bring inquiries (impulses) from the various parts of the body to the cord, as well as fibres which convey instructions from the cord to the outlying organs and parts. The spinal cord, therefore, is the switchboard, as it were, of the nervous system controlled by the brain.

(b) A few small arteries which carry nourishment to the corresponding segment of the spinal cord.

(c) A few small veins and lymph vessels which drain waste products away from the corresponding segment of the cord. The nerve cells in each segment of the cord, therefore, are supplied on both sides by arteries and drained by veins and lymphatics.

(d) A small amount of fibrous connective tissue which surrounds all these structures and forms a cobweb-like arrangement the meshes of which are filled with:

(e) Semifluid compressible fat tissue which is the most abundant substance present and fills all space not occupied by the other structures.

The Mechanics of the Skeleton

A careful study of the mechanics of the skeletons of all backboned animals reveals the significant fact that the spine comprises the central sustaining shaft which supports all the rest of the framework. For instance, the skull is attached to it in front, the ribs and forelimbs to the sides, the hip bones, hindlimbs and tail in the rear.

Broadly speaking, the various parts of the skeleton are mere offshoots from this central pivot, the spine. In the field of biology this is perhaps best illustrated in the gradual development of the complete skeleton of a frog from the "lineshaft" of a tadpole.

Another important fact is that all backboned animals walk on all-fours. The suspension of the spine in a horizontal direction makes possible a perfect interlocking of the articular processes of the vertebrae.

The human spine, however, has to perform its function in the erect position. This not only prevents the proper interlocking of the vertebrae but also brings the weight of the head and chest outside the center line of the body, thus necessitating the development of the normal curves of the spine maintained by powerful supportive muscles along the back.

In the erect position, the weight of the body, sustained by the spinal column, rests upon the pelvic circle or platform. This in turn is supported from underneath by the two thigh bones. Since these fit into sockets which are placed well toward the **front,** the body weight resting upon the **rear** of this platform actually falls far behind these two points of support, the thigh bones.

From an engineer's standpoint, therefore, the biped man indulges in a constant struggle to maintain the erect position thereby rendering his weight-bearing column more susceptible to strains and sprains of all kinds.

Spinal Lesions and Their Causes

The term "lesion" in its broadest sense signifies any departure from the normal. Spinal lesions may be defined as those deviations from the normal of the bones (subluxations), ligaments (ligatights) or muscles of the spine, which lead to or result from disease in corresponding organs and parts.

Since the spine is the weight-bearing shaft which supports the entire framework all external force, no matter where or how applied, is transmitted to this central axis.

From the time the infant falls out of its cradle, through the "rough-and-tumble" life of childhood, all the way through youth and maturity to old age, the human spine is constantly subjected to falls, jars, blows, twists, over-exertion, fatigue, etc. These mishaps, however, the individual promptly dismisses from his mind; hence he rarely sees the relation between a past accident and his present ailment.

The above mentioned strains and sprains, unless severe enough to produce an actual dislocation, result in a wrenched or overstrained condition of the ligaments of the injured joint. Since the body manifests a constant tendency to return to normal, this strain is frequently repaired during sleep when all muscles are relaxed and the spine is in a recumbent position with no weight to support. In more severe cases, however, the proliferation and subsequent shrinking of the connective tissue of the injured ligaments decreases the motility of the affected intervertebral joint or series of such joints.

The function of a stiffened region of the spine is readily compensated for by an increased motility of the spinal joints above and below it. Being thus allowed to remain inactive, it becomes fixed to a varying degree. This process is greatly facilitated by the presence of an excessive amount of waste products in the system.

A process of stiffening tends to follow also sprains of such joints as the ankle, the wrist, the knee, etc. However, since it is hardly possible for these joints to shift their function, the slight adhesions which form here are readily broken up.

In view of all the foregoing facts, is it any wonder that osteopaths, chiropractors and naprapaths would have us believe that as long as human beings are unfortunate enough to possess spinal columns these will persist in getting out of order?

It should be remembered, however, that the spine is immune against all such injuries as previously enumerated unless they are **severe** enough or **prolonged** enough to overcome the resistance of the supporting muscles and ligaments. In other words, the degree of force required to produce a lesion is determined by the degree of strength of the spine.

Injuries, therefore, constitute merely the exciting cause of lesions. The predisposing factor is a weak spine, which in turn is the result of insufficient exercise, malnutrition, faulty posture in standing, sitting or lying and other debilitating factors.

Another important cause of spinal lesion, from the standpoint of Natural Therapeutics, is the following: Nerve impulses coming to the spinal cord from inflammatory processes, are promptly reflected to the supporting structures of the region of the spine. Here these abnormal impulses subsequently bring about sufficient irritation to produce lesions such as will be described presently.

Since abuse of function causes disease even in an individual with a perfectly normal spine, it is evident that many spinal lesions are the effects and not the primary causes of disease. These secondary lesions in turn tend to perpetuate the original disturbance, thereby establishing a vicious circle.

The Nature and Effects of Lesions

Osteopaths, chiropractors and naprapaths all put forth different claims as to what spinal lesions actually are and just how they produce the harmful effects for which they are held responsible. Spinal dissection confirms some of these claims and contradicts others. Out of consideration for our nonprofessional readers we must of necessity omit excessive technical detail. Suffice it to say that a lesion is **invariably** associated with an increase in and a shrunken condition of the connective tissue comprising the ligaments of the affected joint. Most noticeable is a decrease in the thickness and the resiliency of the intervertebral disk—either in part or as a whole.* In major lesions dissection reveals, in addition to the above, a slight shifting of the adjacent articular processes upon each other.

Either a bony or a ligamentous lesion alters both the size and the shape of the adjacent intervertebral foramen. This tends to interfere with the functions of the structures passing through it. Within each foramen the spinal nerve is comparatively well protected. It occupies on an average only one fifth of the total area, is situated in the largest part of the foramen, is free from all bony contact and is imbedded in semifluid compressible fat tissue. The functions of the blood and lymph vessels, however, are more readily disturbed by changes in the size and shape of the foramen.

As the nerves and vessels leave the foramen, the fat surrounding them gradually decreases while the connective tissue increases in amount, until finally they are entirely clothed in fibrous connective tissue. Shrinkage of this connective tissue, brought about as previously described, is bound to have an untoward effect, if not on the nerves and vessels within the foramen then surely on their branches immediately outside the foramen. Irritation to the nerve, according to a law in neurology, first increases and later decreases the intensity of the nerve impulses conveyed to the corresponding organs or parts, thus giving rise first to acute and later to chronic disturbances.

The motility of a joint in which a lesion occurs is invariably decreased. This is due partly to the shrunken connective tissue already described and partly to tension or infiltration of the muscles governing that joint. The

---

*As a result of wrong living it is usual for the disks to become compressed and less resilient with advancing years. Finally the adjacent vertebrae may become entirely ankylosed.

degree of normal activity in any joint determines the amount of blood supply to that joint **and to its adjacent structures.** Restricted motion of an intervertebral joint, therefore, will impair the nutrition of the corresponding segment of the spinal cord. This will naturally pervert the functions of the nerve cells from which originate the nerve fibres coming through the affected foramen.

Interference with the nerve supply to any part of the body predisposes that part to the secondary causes of disease, thereby leading first to functional and later to organic derangement.

Other Structural Lesions

It should be born in mind that lesions occurring in other joints of the body give rise to disturbances also. This is especially true of the joints uniting the hip bones and the ribs to the spine.

The so called "innominate" lesions are far more frequent than is generally suspected. During pregnancy all the joints of the pelvis become more supple. Even after pregnancy these joints frequently remain in a relaxed condition due to improper food and irrational living before, during and after this important period.

Again, in order to compensate for rigidity in the "small of the back", the joints between the hip bones and the spine almost invariably become abnormally relaxed. As already explained, the erect position places the pelvis at a mechanical disadvantage, thereby subjecting these joints to a considerable strain. Should they be weakened from any cause, then falls, twists, false steps, over exertion, etc. frequently result in lesions which give rise to sciatica, urinary and menstrual disturbances and other pelvic disorders.

Lesions at the junction between the ribs and the vertebrae, between the coccyx and the sacrum and in other joints of the frame work are of great importance also. Lack of space, however, excludes the discussion of their causes, nature and effects.

The Detection of Lesions

In diagnosing any given abnormal manifestation, a careful analysis of the corresponding region of the spine furnishes indispensable information as to the rôle played by structural lesions in causing or perpetuating the trouble in question. The most elaborate examination, therefore, is incomplete without a painstaking analysis of the spine and those parts of the framework attached to it.

The most important steps in this procedure consist in noting peculiarities of gait and posture, the absence or presence of the normal spinal curves, the relative tone of the spinal tissues, the absence or presence of tender spots along the spine, the alignment of the vertebrae, ribs and hip-bones; but, above all, **the degree of motility** of each joint of the spine and its attached structures.

The above procedure necessitates the viewing of the bodily mechanism through the eyes of an engineer. It also requires a sense of touch sufficiently keen to detect the least variation in the density and the motility of the various parts of the spine and framework; it literally means "seeing" with the finger tips.

Every vertebrae apparently out of line does not necessarily indicate the presence of a lesion. It may merely signify a deformed spinous process.

On the other hand, where inspection and palpation of the spine suggest no apparent abnormalities, tests for motility frequently reveal obscure lesions in the form of more or less fixed joints. This impaired mobility is usually compensated for by increased pliability of the joints above and below it.

Briefly stated, a spinal lesion manifests, among other characteristics, varying degrees of tenderness and muscular rigidity during its acute stage and tension in the joint during its chronic stage. In all puzzling cases an X-ray examination is of great assistance.

The space allotted to this article necessarily crowds out the discussion of chiropractic nerve tracing and other detail procedures, which will become apparent upon glancing at the following chart.

Structural Analysis—Neurotherapy

Structural analysis constitutes only one of several procedures to be employed in arriving at a definite diagnosis. It must be supplemented by physical examination, iridiagnosis, urine, gastric and fecal analysis, blood count, sputum examination, basic diagnosis and every other method of examination that will throw light on the past and present condition of the patient.

Not until after the findings from all these sources have been compared and correlated can there be established a diagnosis that will reveal not only the nature of the abnormal process but also its underlying causes, both primary and secondary.

The Correction of Lesions

Acute lesions require rest of the injured part, careful inhibition over the tender areas and, in severe cases, cold packs. Graded massage and passive movements are to be given at an early date. Thrusts and directos during this period are not only uncalled for but prove positively detrimental.

Chronic lesions, as above stated, constitute joints that have become stiffened to a varying degree. Treatment, therefore, should aim at reestablishing normal motility. We caution against the manipulation of tubercular joints in the spine or elsewhere and also against indiscriminate attempts at the breaking up of long standing ankyloses.

Although the application of neurotherapy differs with each individual case, the procedure in general consists of the following steps. These are not necessarily administered in this sequence nor are they all employed at the same time.

(a) The muscles governing the affected joints are deeply kneaded if infiltrated, and stretched if contracted.

(b) The spine as a whole is put on a good general stretch in every direction. The ligaments of the stiffened joints naturally are the first to feel this force because those of the normal joints are slack.

(c) To the tensed joints are applied such osteopathic moves as tend to reestablish normal motility in every direction. These enhance the metabolism of the joints and the neighboring structures including the spinal cord.

(d) To the bony lesions, careful chiropractic thrusts are given. These tend to readjust the shifted particular processes by stretching those bands of shrunken connective tissue which are responsible for maintaining the bony lesion.

(e) The ligamentous lesions are corrected by means of naprapathic directos. These aim at stretching the definite strands of shrunken connective tissue in the ligaments of the affected joints.

(f) Spondylotherapy concussion is given whenever indicated.

(g) At the end of each treatment the flabby areas of the spine are stimulated and the overactive areas and tender spots are carefully inhibited by neuropathic manipulations.

This last procedure is of the utmost importance because

". . . in addition to correcting structural lesions, every osteopathic spinal twist, stretch or pressure, every chiropractic thrust, every naprapathic directo, will and does originate nerve reflexes."* These reflexes exert either a beneficial or a detrimental influence on some other abnormality from which the patient may be suffering at the time.

In recent years chiropractors have been teaching that during and after the removal of a lesion the disease process caused by that lesion gradually reverses itself. It begins to pass from the abnormal back to the normal. The symptoms which manifest themselves as a result are spoken of as "retracing" symptoms. These are looked upon by the medical profession as "aggravations" if they occur in the diseased part itself. Should they appear elsewhere they are dealt with as "complications". Naprapaths have been referring to such symptoms as "repair changes".

The school of Nature Cure for more than half a century has recognized these apparently alarming symptoms as **attempts at reconstruction** or healing crises. These crises tend to develop during each and every disease process, whatever its cause, no matter whether it is being treated correctly or wrongly or not at all. For further information regarding the law of crises, the reader is referred to Chapter XXII.

For the purpose of restoring the normal curves of the spine, **active movements** (curative gymnastics) are devised. These aim at developing those groups of muscles which are responsible for maintaining the normal spinal curves, thereby keeping the weight of the head and chest within the center-line of the body.

Other active and stretching movements are devised for promoting suppleness and for strengthening the spine as

*Quoted from an article by the writer in the Practice Builder Magazine of July, 1916.

a whole. These exercises are specific for each case and are not prescribed until the more severe lesions have been corrected.

Physical culturists in general devote entirely too much time and effort to those exercises which bring into play mainly the upper and lower extremities. If they realized that man is as young as his spine is limber and strong, they would pay more attention to developing the spine and to limbering up each of its joints. By so doing they will derive twice the benefit in one-half the time and will prevent the harmful effects resulting from indiscriminate exercises which do not take into consideration the normal spinal curves or the presence of lesions.

The Relation of Neurotherapy to Other Methods of Healing

According to the teaching of Doctors Still, Palmer and Smith, the human organism is self-regulating—health is automatic. Disease is merely a process during which health is laboring under difficulties—it is **health handicapped**. Since the body is also a self-repairing organism, treatment calls for nothing more nor less than the removal of handicaps. Spinal lesions and their correction, therefore, constitute all there is to the cause and cure of disease.

In this relation note the following quotation from the naprapathic propaganda literature: ''If a puddle of water on the floor is produced by a small leak in the roof, find, treat and cure the leak. . . . The naprapath, instead of treating the organic or functional disturbance (the puddle), finds, treats and cures the diseased ligament (the leak).''

If a puddle of water is on your floor as the result of a leak in your roof, would you leave the puddle to spoil your floor and merely patch up the leak, leaving your roof in such a condition that it is liable to spring other leaks? That is what the naprapath, chiropractor or osteopath does when he merely adjusts the spine.

Would you not carefully wipe up the puddle, repair the leak and so reinforce your whole roof that it will be able to withstand future rain storms? That is what Natural Therapeutics does when it promotes the elimination of morbid matter from the system (the wiping up), readjusts the spine (the repairing), and makes it lesion-proof by means of corrective exercises (the reinforcing).

It is encouraging to note that osteopaths in general have already detected the inadequacy of their slogan, "Find the lesion and remove it." The fact, however, that they are gradually adopting also the allopathic maxim, "Find the germ and kill it," proves that they are not as yet familiar with the fundamental laws of cure. As evidence of this, osteopaths are today advocating the use of germicides, antitoxins, serums and vaccines. In addition, they practice major surgery and allow advertisements of patent medicines in their journals.

Let it be understood that in order to manifest perfect health the body cells demand not only an unimpaired nerve supply, but also the proper amount and kind of nourishment, as well as the prompt elimination of their waste products.

Given an unimpaired nerve supply **under natural surroundings,** health would be automatic.

It is essential to "adjust" not only a patient's spine but also his food supply, his mental attitude, his environment and his habits of living in general.

CHAPTER XXXIII

NEUROTHERAPY

Osteopathy, chiropractic, naprapathy, neurotherapy and spondylotherapy are various systems of manipulative treatment which have been devised mainly to correct spinal and other bony lesions, shrinkage and contracture of muscles, ligaments and other connective tissues.

Dr. du Plessis has explained in the previous chapter in detail the philosophy and practice of these various systems. I shall only throw upon them a few sidelights from the viewpoint of Natural Therapeutics.

Important as these methods are in the treatment of acute and chronic diseases, by themselves they are not all-sufficient because they deal only with the mechanical causes of disease, not with the chemical, thermal, nor with the mental and psychical. The most efficient spinal treatment cannot make good for the **bad effects of an unbalanced diet** which contains an excessive amount of poison producing materials and is deficient in the all important mineral elements or organic salts. Just as surely as mental therapeutics and a natural diet cannot correct bony lesions produced by external violence, just so surely is it impossible to cure monomania or obsession, or to supply iron, lime, sodium, etc., to the system by correcting spinal lesions.

The trouble with the manipulative schools and their graduates is that they adhere too closely to the mechanical theory and treatment of disease; that they reject practically all natural methods of treatment aside from manipulative, and that so far as the osteopathic school is

417

concerned its practitioners show a strong tendency to fall back upon the old school methods of drugging and of surgical treatment. This is due to the fact that in many types of diseases manipulative treatment by itself has proved insufficient to produce satisfactory results.

In order to do justice to our patients and not neglect our responsibilities toward them **we must use in the treatment of disease all that is good in all the natural methods of healing.** In serious chronic cases any single one of these methods, whether it be pure food diet, hydrotherapy, massage, spinal treatment, mental therapeutics or homeopathy, is not by itself sufficient to achieve satisfactory results or to produce them fast enough.

To use an illustration: Suppose a wagon full of freight requires the combined strength of six horses to move it and suppose that number of horses is available. Would it not be foolish to try to move the load with one, two, three, four, or even five horses? Would not common sense suggest the saving of time and effort by putting all six horses to work at once?

In Natural Therapeutics every one of the various methods of treatment is supplemented and assisted by all the others.

The manipulative schools of healing maintain that practically all disease is caused by mechanical abnormalities of the spinal column or of muscles, ligaments and other connective tissues, due to injury or impingement. The philosophy of Natural Therapeutics, on the other hand, points out that a large percentage of such spinal and other mechanical lesions are secondary manifestations of disease, not primary causes; that acute or subacute inflammatory conditions in the interior of the body may cause nervous irritation and thereby contraction of muscles and ligaments and, as a result of these, luxations of vertebrae or of other bony structures.

The naprapathic theory of disease postulates that it is the shrinkage and contraction of the connective tissues, which serve as a support and protection for the nerve matter contained in the nerve trunks and filaments, that causes interference with the normal nerve supply of cells and tissues and thereby abnormal function and disease.

The philosophy of Natural Therapeutics points to the fact that this shrinkage and contraction of the connective tissues surrounding and permeating the nerve trunks and filaments is caused by certain acids and other pathogenic materials which are produced by faulty diet and defective elimination, and that the same causes produce accumulation of waste and morbid matter in the tissues of the body which, all through the system, interfere just as effectually with nutrition, drainage and innervation of the cells and tissues as do spinal lesions and ligatights.

While the other systems of manipulative treatment confine themselves almost entirely to the correction of bony and other connective tissue lesions, to "pressing the button" as it is called, neurotherapy besides this, aims at other very important results.

In disease the tissues are either in an abnormally tense and contracted or in a weak, relaxed condition. The functional activities are either hyper-active as in acute inflammation, or sluggish and inactive as in chronic atonic and atrophic conditions. These extremes can be powerfully influenced and equalized by manipulative inhibition, relaxation or stimulation.

During an acute attack of gastritis, for instance, the neurotherapist would exert strong inhibition on the nerves which supply the stomach. This is accomplished by deep and persistant pressure on the nerves where they emerge from the spinal openings (foramina). This diminishes the rush of blood and nerve currents to the inflamed organ, and thereby eases but does not suppress the inflammatory process and the attending congestion and pain.

In case of extreme tension in any part of the system, relaxation of the shrunken tissues can be brought about by gentle but persistent stretching of the nerves and adjacent muscles and ligaments, in a manner similar to that of the naprapathic directos.

When the vital organs and their functions are weak and inactive or when nerves, muscles, ligaments and other connective tissues are in a relaxed, atonic or atrophic condition, certain stimulating movements applied to the nerves where they emerge from the spinal column will energize the vital functions all through the system. Many patients imagine that such manipulative treatment is superficial. To them it is just "rubbing" and seems all alike. They do not realize that manipulative stimulation applied to the nerves near the surface of the body travels all along their branches and filaments like electricity along a complicated system of copper wires, and thus reaches the innermost cells and organs of the body, making them more alive and active. This internal stimulation of vital activities is attained also by good massage through energizing the nerve endings all over the surface of the body.

Some of my readers may entertain the idea that the chiropractic, naprapathic and osteopathic schools have practically the same conception of acute diseases and healing crises as the school of Natural Therapeutics. This, however, is not the case. On the contrary, osteopaths, naprapaths and chiropractors on the whole adhere to the allopathic idea of acute disease as being in itself harmful and dangerous to health and life, something which therefore ought to be checked as quickly as possible.

If anyone should doubt this, the following extracts from

an article in the April-May, 1913, number of the International Chiropractic Journal, entitled "Fevers", by Dr. Joy M. Loban, will convince him to the contrary. Similar criticisms of the Nature Cure conception of acute disease and healing crises have of late appeared in osteopathic journals.

"The latest current, I have said, is the Nature Cure current. It offers a seductive course in which to steer. Let us test it with our compass and take for our test the question of fever, contrasting the Nature Cure theory and the Chiropractic theory and measuring them with the facts.

"The Chiropractic theory, which I affirm, is briefly this: The primary cause of every fever is vertebral subluxation impinging nerves so as to disturb the heat-regulating mechanism of the body. The subluxation operates chiefly (in fever) by controlling the caliber of blood-vessels and thus the amount of blood in a given part of the body at a given time. For an explanation of the heat-regulating mechanism of the body see any standard Physiology. Butler, on Diagnostics, contains a brief description. Fever is a process, instituted through the co-operation of primary cause (subluxation) and secondary cause (poison, germ, etc.) which is destructive to the body and tends to destroy life unless checked. It is a malign process which Nature strives to prevent and to correct when once in operation.

"The Nature Cure theory, which I deny, is in brief: Fever is a process resulting from a house-cleaning effort on the part of Nature, who seeks to remove from the body the filth accumulated there through faulty habits of living. It is a beneficent process which should not be checked lest its arrest harm the organism and leave it in its state of filth. The primary cause of fever is error of diet, lack of exercise, etc.

"Let us contrast the two. A recent discussion of this question among a group of twelve Chiropractors, from at least six schools, brought out the fact that every one seeks to suddenly check, or abort a fever by adjustment; that all believe that less damage is done to the body, that there is less liability of unpleasant sequelæ when the fever is checked as soon as possible. Are they all wrong? If the Nature Cure theory is correct, then every Chiropractor should avoid 'breaking up' a fever. Logically, he should aid elimination and do as much as possible to give vitality to the patient, but the fever should run until the body is thoroughly 'cleansed'. Literally, we must be 'purged by fire'.

"Here are some facts of common experience, verifiable by all. The most frequent reduction of temperature in pneumonia is two degrees in from five to ten minutes following the adjustment. It is the rule that all acute fevers disappear in from a few minutes to two days after adjustment is commenced.

. . . "If the Chiropractic theory is correct, we check the fever by reversing the process of its causation."

I shall not comment at length upon the above quoted utterances of Dr. Loban. This entire volume constitutes my answer to this and other critics of Nature Cure philosophy.

In this connection I shall only say that, in the first place, I do not believe acute diseases of a serious character such as scarlet fever, diphtheria, typhoid fever, pneumonia, cerebrospinal meningitis, etc., after they once have a good and well defined start, can be suppressed in a few days' time by osteopathic, chiropractic, naprapathic or manipulative treatment.

In the second place, if such suppression were possible it should not be permitted because it would surely result in serious harmful after effects and pave the way to chronic disease as do other forms of suppression of Nature's acute reactions. I am justified in expressing an opinion in this matter because for over fifteen years graduates of the best osteopathic, chiropractic and (of late) naprapathic schools have been working and teaching in our institutions.

Suppose a person should develop a good healing crisis in the form of a diarrhea, acute catarrhal elimination, skin eruption, boils, carbuncles or some other inflammatory feverish form of elimination. What would happen to such a purifying, healing effort of Nature under Dr. Loban's care? According to his own statement, he would arrest it as quickly as his adjustments would enable him. Thereby he would undoubtedly throw the patient back into the chronic condition. Such may be considered good chiropractic treatment, but it is certainly not in harmony with the fundamental law of cure and the law of crises.

I do not wish to convey the impression that manipulation, properly applied, may not be very helpful in the treatment of acute diseases. But I do insist that the inflammatory processes, after they have once started, must not be checked or suppressed—that the most essential part of the natural treatment in such cases consists in fasting and hydrotherapy. These promote the elimination of morbid matter more thoroughly than does any other method of treatment.

The underlying causes of disease must be removed before we can bring about a normal condition of the organism. Suppose the chiropractor, osteopath or naprapath should succeed in suddenly stopping a fever. The patient would continue to ''load up'' more morbid materials (especially since these schools do not teach the importance of natural living), and it would be only a matter of time until the morbid accumulations in the body would excite new acute reactions, necessitating more adjustments. This may be all right for the practitioner, but what about the patient? In the long run it can have but one result, and that is chronic disease.

Massage

Massage has very much the same effects upon the system as the coldwater treatment. It accelerates the circulation, draws the blood into the surface, relaxes and opens the pores of the skin, promotes the elimination of morbid matter and increases and stimulates the electromagnetic energies in the body.

We have learned that one of the primary causes of chronic disease is the accumulation of waste matter and systemic poisons in the tissues of the body. These morbid encumbrances obstruct the circulation, interfere with osmosis and prevent the normal activity of the organs of elimination, especially the skin.

The deep going massage, the squeezing, kneading, rolling and stroking, actually **squeezes the stagnant blood and morbid accumulations out of the tissues** into the venous and lymphatic circulation, speeds this return circulation, charged with waste products and poisons, on its way to the lungs and other organs of elimination and enables the arterial blood with its freight of oxygen and nourishing elements to flow more freely into the less obstructed tissues.

Thorough manipulation of the deeper tissues draws the blood to the surface of the body, and in this way greatly facilitates the elimination of morbid matter through the relaxed and opened pores of the skin.

Very important are the electromagnetic effects of good massage upon the system. The positive magnetism of the masseur stirs up and intensifies the latent electromagnetic energies in the body of the patient, very much as a piece of iron or steel is magnetized by rubbing it with a magnet. The more normal and positive, morally and mentally as well as physically, the masseur, the more marked will be the good effects of the treatment upon the weak and negative patient.

CHAPTER XXXIV

MAGNETIC TREATMENT

During the first years of my work as a practitioner of Natural Therapeutics I administered magnetic treatment in addition to the regular manipulative movements and corrections. The ordinary magnetic treatment is administered by laying the hands on the affected parts or by making passes over the body while at the same time exerting the power of therapeutic faith, will and sympathy. I soon discovered, however, that by some patients the nature and meaning of the treatment was misunderstood, that they looked upon it with suspicion and fear as a sort of witchcraft or hypnotic process. Such apprehension is unfounded. Hypnotic and magnetic treatments differ decidedly in method and effect.

Through the hypnotic process the operator or hypnotist benumbs and paralyzes temporarily or, in extreme cases, permanently the highest faculties and powers of his subject, namely, reason, will and selfcontrol. While these higher attributes of the soul are temporarily benumbed and paralyzed the hypnotist, through the concentrated exertion of his imagination and will power, dominates the subconscious mind and by suggestion controls and directs the physical, mental and emotional activities of his subject. This process is, indeed, to be feared because it is destructive in its effects upon both operator and subject. It involves the usurpation of the highest functions of mind and soul. As explained in the volume on Eugenics, it results in soul murder and has been called the great psychological crime.

425

The magnetic healer does not attempt to subdue and control the will power and mental and emotional faculties of his patient. The latter remains during the treatment fully conscious and self possessed. The magnetic treatment affects only the purely vital conditions of the subject. It arouses, strengthens and harmonizes his weakened, negative and discordant vibrations. As has been demonstrated in other chapters disease is negative, health positive. The one is discordant the other harmonious vibration of the parts and particles composing the human entity on the physical, mental and psychical planes of being.

As the life force enters the human organism it is transmuted on the lower planes into electromagnetic and vitochemical energies. The ordinary electric cell contains two plates of opposite polarity immersed in acidulated water. For instance, one of the plates may be zinc which is positive, the other copper which is negative. The vessel is partly filled with a weak solution of sulphuric acid.

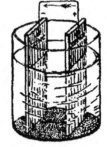

Fig. 3

The plates of zinc and copper are connected by copper wires at the bottom and at the top. (See Fig. 3.) The positive current flows from the zinc to the copper within the fluid and from the copper to the zinc through the wire connecting the upper ends of the plates above the fluid. The arrows in the illustration indicate the complete voltaic circuit of the current.

The positive electricity of the zinc traverses the liquid to the copper over which it flows through the copper wire to the zinc. The effect is that the part of the wire attached to the copper is positive (+) and is called the positive pole or electrode, while the end attached to the zinc is negative (—) and is called the negative pole or electrode.

The generation of this current is accompanied by chemical action in the cell. Experiment shows that the mere contact of dissimilar materials such as copper and zinc electrifies them, zinc being positive and copper negative; but contact alone does not yield a continuous current of electricity. When we plunge the two metals, still in contact either directly or indirectly through a wire, into water, preferably acidulated, a chemical action is set up, the water is decomposed and the zinc is consumed. Water, as is well known, consists of oxygen and hydrogen. The water combines with the zinc to form oxide of zinc and the hydrogen is set free as gas on the surface of the copper plate. So long as this process continues, that is to say so long as there is zinc and water left, we get an electric current in the circuit.

The existence of such a current may be proved by a very simple experiment. Place a penny above and a dime below the tip of the tongue, then bring the edges into contact and you will feel an acid taste in the mouth.

A living body is a great electric battery for the production of electromagnetic and vitochemical energies. Every minute cell in the body is an electric cell. Cell substance or protoplasm, as we have learned, is made up of hydrogen plus negative substances. Protoplasm is, therefore, negative in character. Under the microscope the cells appear like tiny islands surrounded by moving streams of blood and lymph.

The blood is highly charged with positive mineral elements and also contains small amounts of acids. Here, then, we have all the constituents present in an electric cell or battery, the negative elements in the protoplasm in contact with the positive mineral elements in the blood, and the acid constituents of blood and lymph correspond-

ing to the acid fluid in the cell. Acting through these cells
and batteries in living bodies, the life force is transmuted
into electromagnetic and vitochemical energies.

All the tissues and organs of the body are electromagnetic batteries made up of innumerable minute electric
cells. The internal and external membranes of the various organs and tissues, like the two elements in an electric
cell, are of opposite polarity. In some organs the inner
membranes are electromagnetically positive while the
outer membranes are negative. In other organs, the electromagnetic conditions are reversed. The secretions of
these membranes, also of opposite polarity, mingle and
promote the liberation of electromagnetic and vitochemical energies. I use the word "liberation" advisedly because these energies cannot be permanently produced by
the physical material elements of the body.

Vital force is transmuted through the electric cells and
batteries which make up the living body into electromagnetic and vitochemical energies. When vital force leaves
the body at death the production of vital energy ceases,
although the physical material alkaline and acid elements
are still present in the rapidly disintegrating body. For
these reasons we should not say the body produces but
rather the body **liberates** vital energy.

According to the ancient vedic teachings, vital force
enters the body through the pituitary bodies and is distributed through the sympathetic and central nervous systems. Modern physiology affirms that the involuntary
functions and activities of the body are controlled through
the sympathetic nervous system.

The brain is the most powerful and active electromagnetic battery in the body. In its infinite multitude of
glandular structures and minute cells and batteries, vital
force is transmuted into nervous, intellectual and emotional energy. The brain and nervous system are **the**

central power stations whose batteries and dynamos supply all the organs with the various forms of vital energy. The nerves and their ramifications are the wires which conduct and transmit vital energy.

Health, which is normal activity of the vital functions, depends upon the perfect balance of the positive and negative elements and energies, and this, in turn, depends largely upon the correct combination of food elements.

Electricity and magnetism produced by inanimate objects such as electric batteries or machinery belong to the mineral kingdom. These forms of electromagnetic energy are three kingdoms removed from the human. Their vibratory activities are, therefore, too slow and coarse for human bodies and not suitable for the treatment of disease. (Chap. XXVIII, "What is Positive, What Negative.")

In each higher kingdom of nature, under the influence of the life elements, all forms of matter and energy undergo constant refinement and assume higher velocity of vibration and greater complexity of structure and function.

It is for the foregoing reasons that in our work we have discarded electromagnetic treatment by means of electric contrivances. Several years of experimentation convinced me that this kind of treatment in the long run did more harm than good. In place of these dangerous agencies we apply through the various forms of manipulative and magnetic treatment the healing and harmonizing influences of the vital energies of the human plane.

As these vital energies are expended in the organism in the forms of physical, nervous, mental and emotional energy, they are thrown off and form around the body the multicolored aura which corresponds somewhat to the exhaust of an engine.

The aura is visible only during the hours of wakeful

activity. It disappears entirely during sound sleep and reappears on awakening with the beginning of physical and mental activity. The weaker and more negative a person is, the weaker the aura; the healthier and stronger and more active mentally, the more voluminous the aura. It varies from dark and muddy colors to the most beautiful tints of the rainbow. The more harmonious the vibratory conditions on the ascending planes of being, the brighter and more beautiful the color effects of the aura.

The vital energies manifest in higher or lower ranges of color according to their higher or lower degree of vibratory velocity and refinement. Thus purely vital energy, that which has been called "animal magnetism", appears close to the body as a vivid red, the color of blood. Red represents the lowest vibratory range in the color scale. The higher the degree of velocity and refinement of the vital activity, the higher it manifests in the vibratory range of the color scale. The finer shades of red express activity of sex passion; the higher love nature produces beautiful effects in pink and lavender; emotions of a religious character appear in shades of blue; intellectual activity, in shades of yellow. Violet and purple indicate intellectual and moral development of a high degree. They are the badge of mastership and royalty. We are told that on the spiritual planes of life angelic beings of a high order of spiritual development appear surrounded by a golden aura. This is the significance of the golden halo with which painters surround the heads of saints and angelic beings.

It is the vibratory quality of the aura of a person which affects us pleasantly or otherwise. This constitutes attraction or repulsion, sympathy or antipathy. Likewise the vibratory quality of the aura determines the therapeutic effect of magnetic and manipulative treatment. The purer and more powerful the magnetic vibrations, the greater the healing power. The more passive and sensitive the vibratory condition of a person, the more amenable he is to the tonic and harmonizing influences of a pure and powerful aura. This explains why certain persons have a soothing effect upon children and sick people, while others have a disturbing effect. It is a problem with which we have to deal in the selection of our operators.

The belief in a healing power emanating from spiritual or celestial planes of life may not be as superstitious as it appears to the worldly wise. Since we understand the possibilities of the wireless telephone, why should it be impossible for the powerful auras of angelic or divine beings to affect those who open themselves to their healing influence? Why should it not be possible for the emanations of the highest spiritual and celestial spheres, filled with beings of godlike nature and divine power, to penetrate into the lower planes of this planetary universe? As we connect our mental and emotional wireless with the higher spiritual and celestial planes of life or with the hells and purgatories, so will be the character of the influx —harmonizing or discordant, constructive or destructive.

Since spiritual love is the highest possible vibratory activity of the human soul, it is therefore the most powerful element in magnetic, mental and spiritual healing. The sympathy healers among the peasantry in European countries rightfully name sympathy as one of the basic elements in occult healing, the other two being absolute faith and the positive will. To these I would add a vivid imagination.

The secret of the healing power of Jesus undoubtedly lay in His great love for and sympathy with suffering humanity. Those who give manipulative and magnetic treatment shoulder a great responsibility. On the purity and power of their own physical, mental and moral vibrations depends the therapeutic effect of their treatment.

I am often asked the question, "Is there danger of losing my vitality and becoming negative by giving manipulative and magnetic treatment?"

It is true that manipulative and magnetic work, like everything else, can be overdone and that thereby it may produce harmful effects upon the operator. But within reasonable limits, massage and magnetic treatments will not deplete the power of the person giving them, providing he keeps his system in good condition. His own vibrations must be harmonious on all planes of being—the physical, mental, moral and spiritual. He must be inspired and actuated by the **faith** that he CAN heal, by the **positive will** to heal and by **sympathy** with the suffering of the one he is trying to heal.

Such an operator makes himself an instrument for the **transmission** of life force, which is healing force, from the source of all life. As he gives, so he receives, for this is the basic law of the universe, the law of compensation. If he gives the treatments in the right spirit **he will gain vital force instead of losing it.** He will actually **feel** his own intensified life vibrations and after treating he will experience a feeling of buoyancy and elation which nothing else can impart to him. "He who loses his life shall find it."

Like a musician who tunes up (puts in harmonious vibration) the relaxed strings of his instrument, so the magnetic healer "tunes up" and harmonizes the weakened and discordant vibrations of his patient.

The basic law of this universe is the law of compensation. It manifests in the relationships of human life in giving and receiving. "Give, and ye shall receive." "With what measure ye mete, it shall be measured unto you."

These are not merely the expressions of a religious enthusiast. They are scientific truths.

Give, give, give—not necessarily of money and precious stones, but of treasures far beyond these in value—sympathy, good cheer and loving service. Giving Himself freely and unceasingly, the Creator has accumulated innumerable solar systems with myriads of man-bearing planets, until the abyss of space sparkles with stars as thickly as the morning grass with dewdrops. From the great central sun, rays of light shoot outward until they become solidified and individualized in the ultimate forms of matter. In these the oversoul loses its self-consciousness. The Creator becomes the created: the positive becomes the negative. When man becomes the master, the angel and the God, the great snake of the Cosmos swallows its tail —the circle of being is completed. Involution and evolution have run their course.

The majority of people on this earth plane recognize and apply only one aspect of the law of giving and receiving—the receiving. They are only too willing to take, to acquire and to hold, but very reluctant to give a fair equivalent for that which they receive and most unwilling to render service without expectation of reward.

From this one-sided application of the law of compensation in social life arises all the injustice, cruelty and suffering which partakes of the nature of hell on this earth plane or on any other sphere; for all there is of hell anywhere in the universe is selfishness and all there is of heaven is unselfish service.

The keynote of the higher life here and on the higher spiritual spheres is that of unselfish, loving service, while that of the lower spheres is selfish taking and withholding.

Our present day social, commercial and political customs and usages are dictated by selfishness and greed.

These breed extreme poverty and privation on the one hand and excessive wealth and luxury on the other. They are the causes of constant strife between capital and labor and of the great calamity which is now destroying the white race in internecine conflict.

All this I have discussed in "The Unity of Disease in the Physical and Social Body", "The Spirit of Christmas", and "The Spirit of Hades". (Vol. 4, "Eugenics.")

In all commercial pursuits the interests of seller and buyer are hostile. Good business policy dictates that each take from the other as much as he may and give as little as possible. Only too often the servant is the paid enemy of him who hires. The mistress treats her servant with contempt or supercilious condescension; the clerk and saleswoman suffer from arrogance and lack of consideration on the part of those whom they serve.

More harmonious and congenial is the relationship between physician and nurse, on the one hand, and the patient on the other. No matter how selfish and inconsiderate a person may be, he usually shows the best side to those from whom he expects the healing of his ailments. The best and most successful physicians and nurses are those who are able to establish between themselves and their patients a sympathetic understanding and on this basis mutual faith and confidence. Thus the practice of healing brings out the best and finest qualities of human nature. The more each gives to the other of consideration and confidence, the greater the benefit to patient and physician. There is no greater work than that of healing; it is the work of the Master.

Every institution for the healing of the sick should be a center for spiritual power. Who can doubt that the many physicians, operators, nurses, students and patients in such a place, working together in unity of purpose and in perfect harmony of faith, can establish a spiritual center radiating healing power? Such is the meaning of the "Holy Grail".

There is no better method for generating and concentrating healing power than by daily meetings and lectures in which the principles of true healing are discussed and demonstrated. Many grateful guests have said to me, "The daily lectures are the best part of your work". I doubt not that our success in treating so called incurable chronic ailments depends to a large extent upon the operation of these higher and finer forces.

Many of our patients who leave for home before they are cured, thinking that they can eat and drink, bathe and exercise just as well at home, find that "something" is lacking, that the physical methods alone are not sufficient to attain the desired results. This something is the intellectual, magnetic and spiritual atmosphere of a center conducted in the right spirit for the healing of human ailments.

Nervous, mental and psychical ailments are especially influenced and benefited by the operation of these higher and finer forces.

To surround people suffering from various phases of abnormal psychism and obsession with these vitalizing, harmonizing and protecting influences is the most effective part of the treatment.

It is on this basis only that I have been able to explain to myself and to others the rapid cures of such cases which could not possibly result from physical treatment alone. This seems to be confirmed by the fact that in psychical cases as a rule we are not able to obtain satisfactory results in the ordinary home surroundings.

The nature and treatment of psychical disorders is described fully in the second and fourth volumes of this series.

The weakness in chronic disease and the inability of the organism to arouse itself to acute activity is caused by a deficiency of vital energy. The beneficial effect of magnetic treatment is not so much due to the transmission of vital force from operator to patient as to the arousing and stimulating of the latent positive electromagnetic and vitochemical energies of the sufferer—in the polarizing of his magnetic forces.

The positive magnetism of the operator stirs up and intensifies the inactive vital energies in the body of the patient, very much as a piece of iron is magnetized by rubbing it with a magnet. The magnet does not impart its own magnetism to the piece of iron, but the active electromagnetic energy in the magnet arouses the latent vibratory activity in the iron. This is proved by the fact that the magnetized iron retains its power as long as it is used for magnetizing other substances and that its magnetic qualities will diminish and disappear entirely with disuse.

A healthy person, animated by lofty ideals and the earnest desire to allay pain and suffering, is constantly radiating healing power whether he be aware of it or not. Use of this power for the healing of the sick cannot deplete and weaken the physician; on the contrary, the more he gives of these higher and finer energies, the more he receives from the inexhaustible storehouse of life and healing power. However, the work of the healer will gain in effectiveness in direct proportion to the conscious and concentrated effort he makes to benefit his patients.

The electromagnetic energies of the organism can be controlled by the will and either concentrated in or sent away from any part of the body, just as the circulation of the blood can be controlled. The latter I saw done by a hypnotist who made the blood flow into and out of the arms and hands of one of his subjects by the power of his will. While this was accomplished by means of a destructive process, it taught a most valuable lesson regarding the power of the will to control the physical conditions and vital energies.

I have frequently noticed in my own manipulative work how much the conscious and concentrated effort of the will has to do with the effectiveness of treatment. Often when I had given the usual massage or neurotherapy treatment and the patient still complained of pain in a certain locality of the body, I would lay my hands on the affected area and **concentrate my will** upon dissolving the congestion in that particular part and upon harmonizing its discordant vibrations. Very shortly, usually within a few minutes, the congestion would be relieved and the pain lessened.

Try it yourself. Next time you have one of your annoying headaches, recline comfortably in a chair or on a couch, relax completely and then **will the blood to flow away from the brain** in order to relieve the congestion and the attendant pain. Many of our patients have learned to treat themselves or members of their family in this way.

It is obvious that magnetic treatment will not permanently remove pain if the latter be due to irritation caused by a luxated bone, by some foreign body or by local accumulation of morbid matter and poisons in any part or organ. In all such cases the local cause of the irritation must be removed before the pain can subside or disappear.

The Practice of Magnetic Healing

Mesmer, a French physician, was the first to experiment scientifically with human magnetism and to use it for healing purposes. For him this method was called Mesmerism. Unfortunately, the term is also used to designate hypnotism and has thus contributed to the confusion as to the true nature and meaning of these greatly differing practices.

Mesmer made his discoveries toward the end of the eighteenth century. About the middle of the nineteenth century Baron von Reichenbach, a German scientist, took up the work where Mesmer had left it and brought actual proof of the existence of the electromagnetic energies and of their manifestation in the aura.

He conducted his experiments in a dark chamber impervious to light rays from without. Psychically sensitive persons, after remaining in the dark chamber for a short time, were able to perceive the aura more or less distinctly in the form of light or bluish vapor emanating from living objects placed before them. Clairvoyant psychics, or "sensitives" as he called them, were able to distinguish various colors of the aura.

Von Reichenbach was one of the greatest chemists of his or any other age. He first prepared from coal tar, paraffin and some of the analin dyes. The latter part of his life he devoted almost entirely to the study of the electromagnetic fluids emanating from living bodies. He called this emanation Od-Kraft, after Odin, the highest deity of Scandinavian mythology. He wrote a number of valuable treatises on this subject. The title of one booklet is "Who is Sensitive and Who is Not?" In this he gives many rules and methods for determining the degree of psychic sensitivity of a person.

I ascribe this sensitivity to a high degree of refinement of the sensory organs of the physical body or to the functioning of the sensory organs of the spiritual body. Matter on the physical plane is perceived by the sensory organs of the physical body only, while spiritual matter and its emanations of light, color, sound, etc., are perceived by the sensory organs of the spiritual body only.

The following simple experiments will make the purely

physical emanations of the aura visible to ordinary sight: In a room dark enough to leave the hands just visible, alternately approach and separate the finger tips. If a person is in good, healthy physical condition streaks of bluish light or vapor will appear between the finger tips. The bluish streams can be stretched out and moved in various directions like rubber bands.

If you wish to see the aura emanating from the body, prepare a room containing one window in the following manner: On the wall opposite the window hang a curtain of dull, black cloth. The window should have a shade which can be raised or lowered as may be required. Cover the lower part of the window with some fabric impervious to light and in front of the black curtain place a person nude to the waist. The observers stand in front of and with their backs turned to the window. The transition between daylight and darkness is the best time of day for this experiment. The inflow of light into the dark chamber is regulated by pulling the window shade down to a narrow slit so as to admit just enough light to leave the room in semi-darkness. When the condition of light, or rather of darkness, in the room is perfectly adjusted, the observers, with their backs to the window and their gaze fixed upon the subject, will soon see around the nude body a bluish light or vapor. The emanation will be more or less strong and distinct according to the positive or negative condition of the subject. The healthier and stronger physically, intellectually and morally the person, the more voluminous and distinct will be his aura.

This bluish vapor, visible to the physical eye, represents the purely physical emanation of the subject. The higher and finer intellectual, emotional and moral emanations are visible only to clairvoyant sight. I found that about eight or nine persons in ten were capable of seeing the physical aura when the conditions were right. To spiritual sight the physical emanation appears, as before explained, red —the color of blood.

I have elsewhere explained that the aura disappears entirely during sound sleep and reappears with the awakening of consciousness, with the beginning of physical and mental activity; and that during the hours of sleep the body acts as a storage battery for the accumulation of vital energy. When this is exhausted in the daily work the tired feeling makes its appearance and there is a desire for rest and sleep. Sleep is the only restorer of vital energy.

Magnetic Treatment

Vital energy is active not only through the laying on of hands, or magnetic passes, but also through the eyes, the sound of the voice and, most of all, through the breath.

The principal rule to be observed by the physician when administering magnetic treatment is to place himself in such a position to the subject that opposite parts of their bodies come into juxtaposition, that is the right hand must touch or pass over the left side of the patient, and vice versa.

Magnetic passes must proceed from the head downward over the body, the hands returning in a sweeping outward, circular movement so as not to counteract the downward passes. If you should treat a person from behind or while he is lying on his stomach, your hands must be crossed and passed over the body in that way from the head downward in order to cover the opposite poles in the body of the patient.

Magnetic Treatment for Poor Circulation in the Extremities

Have the patient lying on a couch or bed with shoes and stockings removed; lay your hands flat against the soles of his feet or grip his feet firmly around the ankles. Slight friction will aid reaction. While thus applying your magnetic current, will the vital fluids to flow into the extremities and to warm them with the glow of life.

I have cured in this manner many cases of chronic cold feet and always advise our nurses and operators to apply this natural treatment in place of the hot water bottle, which brings about a cold reaction and in the long run makes the circulation more inactive.

When giving the magnetic passes in a sitting position the subject should remain in a comfortable, relaxed and receptive condition. The more receptive and sensitive the subject, the more distinctly he will feel the magnetic vibrations like a mild current from an electric battery.

A simple experiment to test the existence and strength of the magnetic emanations of a person, is the following: The subject stretches out his hands horizontally while the operator approaches them from below, his finger tips approaching each other and turned upwards. As he slightly moves the finger tips in close proximity to the palms of the subject the latter will feel the magnetic vibrations, according to his degree of sensitiveness, as a slight breath of air or as a more or less powerful electric current. The degree of sensation will vary according to the negativity or sensitivity of the subject and the positivity of the operator.

One of the best ways of administering magnetic treatment is through magnetized water. Water may be charged with positive or negative magnetism as required by the character of the ailment. Positive magnetism has an astringent effect upon the tissues of the body, while negative magnetism has a relaxing effect. Positive magnetism, therefore, would be in order for the treatment of chronic diarrhea, while negative magnetism is most effective for the treatment of constipation.

In order to charge water or any other fluid positively the left hand is placed under the vessel, while the right hand with fingers pointing downward and in close proximity to the fluid makes circular passes. If a substance is to be magnetized negatively, the process would be reversed, that is the fingers of the left hand must do the charging. In like manner, fabrics and other substances may be charged magnetically.

In every family a person possessed of good, healthy magnetism should train for giving this valuable method of treatment. It will be found very valuable and helpful in many forms of acute and chronic diseases.

I have been asked the question whether there is not danger of suppressing crises by the administration of magnetic treatment. There is no danger in this respect because the right kind of magnetic treatment arouses and stimulates the vital energies, and as healing crises are manifestations of increased vital activity magnetic treatment will help to produce them and to increase their constructive activity.

Sympathy Healing

This is a form of healing practiced among the country population of Northern Europe. It is an occult science handed down from father or mother to son or daughter in certain families known for their probity and piety. While I was studying Nature Cure in Europe my attention was repeatedly called to the seemingly mysterious and miraculous results obtained by these healers. This led me to investigate their methods and after convincing one of these healers of my sincerity of purpose, he confided to me the secrets of his art.

Their remedies consist in prayers, charms and similes. Some plant or object that in some way resembles the disease is given to the sick person. In this connection it is interesting to remember that Jesus many times made use of material similes when performing works of healing, as when he told the leper to bathe in the River Jordan; when he rubbed the eyes of the blind man with spital.

The mystical remedies become efficient only when administered with faith, will and sympathy. The healer must have absolute faith that he can heal with the aid of the higher powers and he must have the positive will to heal and sympathy with the sufferings of the one he is trying to benefit.

The work of healing must be done in silence, without reward and without vain boasting. While going and coming on the errand of mercy the healer does not utter a word unless it be of prayer. He does not accept any material reward for his services nor does he ever speak of his cures. To break any of these sacred obligations would be sacrilegious and would in his opinion bring about the loss of his power.

I have had plenty of proof that their methods are sometimes strangely successful but at other times they fail equally mysteriously.

The villagers in Northern Europe to a large extent depend upon these occult healers for treatment and undoubtedly in most cases with more lasting results than under orthodox poison treatment. These primitive methods date back to the time when the Germanic matron, the Druid or the tribal priest combined in their ministrations the holy offices of physician, prophet and priest.

This shows that mental and spiritual methods of healing did not originate with leaders of modern mental healing cults. One cannot help but observe how infinitely more unselfish, pure and spiritual are the methods of these simple country folk than the commercialized, self-advertising practices of certain modern mental healers. If simony or trading in the gifts of the Holy Spirit and in the power of the Holy Ghost was branded as a sin and a crime by the disciples of Jesus, why is it "Christian" science now?

The specious arguments of our modern healers as to "the necessity of making a living" and "the laborer is worthy of his hire" are effectively contradicted by the unselfish ministrations of the sympathy healers.

CHAPTER XXXV

THE LEGITIMATE SCOPE AND NATURAL LIMITATIONS OF MENTAL AND METAPHYSICAL HEALING

DURING the last generation people have perceived more or less clearly the fallacies of old school medicine and surgery. They have grown more and more suspicious of orthodox theories and practices. From allopathic "overdoing" the pendulum has swung to the other extreme of metaphysical nihilism, to the "underdoing" of mental and metaphysical systems of treating human ailments.

Some of these systems and cults of metaphysical healing have met with success and wide popularity, and this is looked upon by their followers as a proof that all the claims and teachings of these cults and "isms" are based upon absolute truth.

However, a thorough understanding of the fundamental laws of cure, as I have explained them in this volume, will reveal in how far their teachings and their practices are based upon truth and in how far they are inspired by erroneous assumptions.

Let us then apply the weights and measures of Nature Cure philosophy in testing the true value of the claims of metaphysical healers.

For ages people have been educated in the belief that almost every acute disease will end fatally unless the patient is drugged or operated on. When they find to their surprise that the metaphysical formulas or prayers of a mental healer or Scientist will cure baby's measles or father's smallpox just as well as and possibly better

445

than Dr. Dopem's pills and potions, they are firmly convinced that a miracle has been performed in their behalf and straightway they become blind believers in and fanatical followers of their new idols.

They simply exchange one superstition for another: the belief in the efficacy of drugs and surgical operations for the belief in the wonder working power of a metaphysical formula, a selfappointed savior, or a reason stultifying and will benumbing cult. They have not been taught that **every acute disease is the result of a healing effort of Nature** and therefore fail to see that it is **vital force**, the "physician within", that under favorable conditions cures measles and smallpox as easily as it repairs the broken blade of grass or heals the wounded deer of the forest.

"That is exactly what we say!" exclaim healer and Scientist. "Have unlimited faith in the God within and all will be well!"

True, Brother, faith is good—but faith and works are better. Though we cannot heal and give life we can in many ways assist the healer within. We can teach Nature's laws, we can remove obstructions and we can make the conditions within and around the patient more favorable for the action of Nature's healing forces.

When the Great Master said: "Go forth and sin no more, lest worse things than these befall you," he acknowledged sin, or the transgression of natural laws, to be the primary cause of disease and made health dependent upon compliance with the law. The necessity of compliance with the law, in all respects and on all the planes of being, is still more strongly emphasized in the following:

"For whosoever shall keep the whole law and yet offend in one point, he is guilty of all."

The skeptic and the superficial reader may reply: "This saying is utterly unreasonable. Stealing a penny is not committing a murder; overeating does not break the law of chastity; how, then, is it possible to break all laws by breaking any single one of them?''

There is, however, a deeper meaning to this seeming paradox which makes it scientifically true.

Selfcontrol the Whole Law

Obedience to all laws on all planes of being depends primarily on selfcontrol. Selfcontrol is, therefore, in a sense ''the whole law'', for man cannot break any one law unless he breaks first this fundamental ''law of all laws''. This implies that the demoralizing effect of sinning or lawbreaking on any one of the planes of being does not depend so much upon the enormity of the deed as upon the loss of selfcontrol. Continued weakening of selfcontrol in trivial things may therefore, in the end, prove more destructive than a murder committed in the heat of passion. If there is not selfcontrol enough to resist a cup of coffee or a cigar, whence shall come the will power to resist greater temptations?

Truly, lack of selfcontrol in small things is the ''dry rot'' of the soul.

Is it not, then, somewhat unreasonable to expect God or Nature to strain and twist the immutable laws of Nature at the request of every ''healer'' in order to save us from the natural consequences of overeating, meat eating, whisky drinking, smoking, tobacco chewing, drugging, and a thousand and one other transgressions of natural laws?

In spite of the finest spun metaphysical sophistries, we continue to burn our fingers in the fire until we know enough to leave it alone. Herein lies the corrective purpose of that which we call evil—suffering and disease. The rational thing to do is not to deny the existence of Mother Nature's punishing rod, but to escape her salubrious spankings by conforming to her laws.

What About the "Cures"?

As in medicine, so also in metaphysical healing, men judge by superficial results, not by the real underlying causes. The usual answer to any criticism of Christian Science or kindred methods of cure is: "That may be all right; but see the results! Nobody can deny their wonderful cures," etc.

Let us see whether there really is anything wonderful or supernatural about these cures or whether they can be explained on simple, natural grounds.

In another chapter we explain the difference between functional and organic disease and show how in diseases of the **functional** type the life force or healing force, which always endeavors to establish normal conditions and the perfect type, may work unaided up to the reconstructive healing crises and through these eliminate the morbid encumbrances from the system and reestablish normal structure and function.

It is in cases like these that metaphysicians attain their best results simply because **Nature helps herself.**

On the other hand, in cases of the true **organic** type, where the vitality is low and the destruction of vital parts and organs has progressed to a considerable extent, the system is no longer able to rouse itself to selfhelp.

In such cases faith alone is not sufficient to obtain results. It must be backed and assisted by all the natural methods of treatment at our command.

"Healers" Work with Laws Which They Do Not Understand

In our critical analysis of old school methods we found that by far the greater part of all chronic ailments is due to drugging and to surgery. People commence doctoring for little troubles which are aggravated by every dose of medicine and every surgical operation until they end in big troubles.

Is it marvelous that such patients improve and that many are cured when they are weaned from drugs and the knife?

Metaphysical healers unconsciously do their best and most beneficial work because they induce their followers not to suppress acute diseases and healing crises by drugs and surgical operations, thus allowing them to run their natural course in harmony with the fundamental law of Nature Cure; namely, that every acute disease is the result of a cleansing and healing effort of Nature. People will refrain from the suppressive drug treatment under the influence of metaphysical teachings which appeal to the miracle loving element in their nature, when they cannot be convinced by common sense Nature Cure reasoning.

Thus metaphysicians assist Nature **indirectly** by non-interference and **directly** by soothing fear and worry, by instilling faith, hope and confidence. Frequently they also aid Nature by prohibiting the use of tobacco, alcohol and pork, and by otherwise regulating the life and habits of their followers.

Let us consider the problem from another point of view. Let us assume, for argument's sake, that the average person passes in the course of a lifetime through a dozen different diseases. He recovers from eleven of these no matter what the treatment. It is only the twelfth to which he succumbs. Yet whosoever happened to treat the first eleven diseases claims to have **cured** them and, perhaps, to have saved the patient's life when, very often, the recovery was in spite of the treatment and not because of it.

These explanations account for the seemingly miraculous results of metaphysical healing. If healers and Scientists were to explain their cures by the laws and principles of Nature Cure philosophy, mystery and miracle would be taken out of their business.

"Faith Without Works" Dangerous

To believe that God or Nature will overcome the natural effects of our ignorance, laziness and viciousness by wonders, signs and metaphysics, or to deny the existence of sickness, sin and suffering, must lead inevitably to intellectual and moral stagnation and degeneration. I am a thorough and consistent optimist and New Thought enthusiast, but I do not overlook the fact that in this, as in everything else, there lurks always the danger of overdoing and of exaggerating virtue into fault.

The greatest danger of this revulsion from old time pessimism to modern optimism lies in the fact that the "higher thought" enthusiast may cut from under his feet the solid ground of reality; that he may become a dreamer instead of a thinker and doer; and that he may mistake selfish, emotional sentimentalism for practical charity and altruism.

This unhealthy "all-is-good, there-is-no-evil" emotionalism leads only too often to weakening of personal effort, a deadening of the sense of individual responsibility and thereby to mental and moral atrophy; for any of our voluntary functions, capacities and powers which we fail to exercise will in time become benumbed and paralyzed. Unprejudiced observers who come in close contact with metaphysicians cannot help perceiving the pernicious effect of their subtle sophistries on reason and character.

A chronic invalid who had been under the treatment of a faith healer for several years exclaimed, when we gave her our various instructions for dieting, bathing, breathing exercises, etc.: "How glad I am that you give me something to do! **I fear I have been imposing too long on the goodness of the Lord, expecting Him to do my work**

for me.'' Often afterwards, while recovering from life-long ailments, she expressed her happiness and contentment in that she herself was doing something which in her opinion was rational and helpful because it assisted Nature's healing efforts.

We believe firmly and fully in the influence of mind over matter, in the fact that vibrations of the physical plane by continuity create corresponding vibrations on the mental and psychical planes and vice versa. We know that, in accordance with this law, anything which affects the mind or the moral life of a person affects also his physical condition; but instead of hypnotizing the minds of our patients by law-defying, reason-and-will-benumbing dogmas and formulas, we strengthen and harmonize their mental vibrations by appealing to reason, by teaching and explaining natural laws instead of obscuring and denying them.

The more intelligent the patient, the more amenable he will be to such normal suggestions based on scientific truth and on the dictates of reason and common sense.

While nonresistance to Nature's healing efforts is better than suppression by drugs or the knife, there is something still more helpful and rational than the mere negative attitude toward disease on the **physical** plane assumed by metaphysical cults. That ''something'' is intelligent cooperation with Nature's cleansing and healing efforts.

Where the old school fails by sins of commission the faith schools fail by sins of omission. Daily many patients are sacrificed through fanatical inactivity when their lives might be saved by the wet pack or cold sponge bath, by the internal bath, rational diet, judicious fasting, scientific manipulation, or other simple yet powerful natural remedy. To permit a patient to perish in a burning fever, depending solely upon the efficacy of prayers, **formulas** and self induced mental attitude, when wet packs and cold sponging would in a few minutes reduce the temperature below the danger point, is manslaughter even though it be done in the name of religion.

Incidents like the following are common in our practice: A little girl in the neighborhood of our institution contracted diphtheria. The mother, an ardent Christian Scientist, called in several healers of her cult but the child grew worse day by day until the false membranes in the throat began to choke her to death.

A boarder in the house, who was a follower of Nature Cure, finally induced the mother to call upon us for advice by threatening to notify the City Health Department. Within an hour after the application of the whole-body packs and the cold ablutions, the blood was sufficiently drawn away from the local congestion in the throat into the surface of the body so that the child breathed easily and freely and from then on made a splendid recovery.

Another instance: A man had been suffering from sciatic rheumatism for fifteen years. He had swallowed poisonous drugs to no avail. For several years he had been under Mental Science treatment but the suffering had grown more intense.

When he applied to us for help we found that the right hip bone (the innominate) had slipped upward and backward. A few manipulative treatments replaced the bone where it belonged and the "sciatic rheumatism" was cured.

In this case, the combined "concentration" and prayers of all the metaphysical healers on earth would not have succeeded in replacing the dislocated hip bone, which required the full strength of a trained manipulator.

Metaphysicians could not have accomplished this feat any more than they could have moved, by their mental efforts, a hundred-pound weight from one place to another.

Mechanical lesions of that kind (and there are many of them) require mechanical treatment.

Another factor which makes converts to metaphysical healing cults by the hundreds and thousands is the "get-rich-quick" instinct in human nature, the desire to get "something for nothing" or for as little effort as possible. Herein lies the seductive pull of old-time drugging and of modern metaphysics. "It does not matter how you live, when you get into trouble, a bottle of medicine or a metaphysical formula will make it all right." That sounds very easy and promising, but the trouble is—it does not always work.

Our forefathers were too pessimistic; "higher thought" enthusiasts are often too optimistic. While the former poisoned their lives and paralyzed their God-given faculties and powers by dismal dread of hell's fire and damnation, our modern healers and Scientists have drifted to the other extreme. They tell us there is no sin, no pain, no suffering. If that be true, there is also no action and reaction, our modern healers and Scientists have drifted to the no need of self control, selfhelp nor personal effort.

The ideal of the faith healer is the ideal of the animal. The animal trusts implicitly, it has absolute faith. Guided by instinct, God or Nature, it follows the promptings of its appetites and passions without worrying about right or wrong. It acts today as it did ten thousand years ago.

In man, **reason** has taken the place of instinct. We must think and manage for ourselves. We are free and responsible moral agents. If we deny this, we deny the very foundations of equity, justice and right. It behooves us to use the talents which God has given us, to study the laws of our being and to comply with them to the best of our ability so that enlightened reason may take the place of animal instinct and guide us to physical, mental and moral perfection.

CHAPTER XXXVI

THE DIFFERENCE BETWEEN FUNCTIONAL AND ORGANIC DISEASE

MUCH confusion concerning the curability of chronic diseases by the various methods of treatment arises through failure to understand the difference between **functional** and **organic** chronic disease.

For instance, there is a close resemblance between pseudo and true locomotor ataxia. Often it is difficult to distinguish functional lung trouble from the organic type of the disease. In our practice, several cases of mental derangement which had been diagnosed as "true paresis" proved to be of the functional type and under natural treatment recovered rapidly.

Functional diseases may present a very serious appearance, may be labeled with awe inspiring Greek or Latin names and yet yield readily to natural methods of living and treatment.

In diseases of an **organic** nature, however, right living and self treatment are usually not sufficient to insure satisfactory results. In such cases all forms of active and passive treatment must be applied and even then it is frequently difficult and sometimes impossible to produce a cure.

Chronic diseases of a functional nature develop when an otherwise healthy organism becomes saturated and clogged with food and drug poisons to such an extent that these encumbrances interfere with the free circulation of the blood and nerve currents and with the normal functions of the cells, organs and tissues of the body.

Such cases resemble a watch which is losing time because its works are filled with dust. All that such a waste encumbered watch or body needs, in order to restore normal functions, is a good cleaning. Natural diet, fasting, systematic exercise, deep breathing, cold bathing and the right mental attitude are usually sufficient to accomplish this physical house cleaning and to restore perfect health.

Functional disorders yield readily to the various forms of metaphysical treatment. Remove such patients from the weakening and destructive effects of poisonous drugs and of surgical operations, supplant fear and worry by courage and faith, and the results often seem miraculous to those who do not understand the power of the purifying and stimulating influence of clean living and of the right mental attitude.

In diseases of the **organic** type, however, good results are not so easily achieved. A body affected by organic disease resembles a watch whose mechanism has been injured and partly destroyed by rust and corrosive acids. If such be the case, cleaning and oiling alone will not be sufficient to put the timepiece in good working order. The watchmaker has to replace the damaged parts.

That is easy enough in the case of the watch but it is not so easily accomplished in the human body. Besides, in many instances the corroding acids are the very medicines which were given to cure the disease, and the injury and destruction of vital parts and organs is only too often the direct or indirect result of surgical operations.

The watchmaker may remove those parts of the watch which are suffering from "organic" trouble and replace them by new ones. This the surgeon cannot do. He can extirpate but he cannot replace. Operative treatment leaves the organism forever after in a mutilated and therefore unbalanced condition and often prevents or seriously interferes with Nature's cleansing and healing crises.

The Limitations of Metaphysical Healing

It is often claimed by metaphysical healers that they can cure organic diseases as easily and as quickly as functional ailments. If they better understood the difference between functional and organic disorders as explained in the foregoing pages, they would not make such deceptive and extravagant claims. They would then realize the natural limitations of metaphysical healing.

When waste matter, ptomains or poisonous alkaloids and acids produced in the body as a result of wrong diet and other violations of Nature's laws have brought about destruction and corrosion in vital parts and organs—when dislocations and subluxations of bony structures or new growths and accumulations in the forms of tumors, stones or gravel obstruct the blood vessels and nerve currents, shut off the supply of the vital fluids, and thus cause malnutrition and gradual decay of the tissues—when in addition to this the organism has been poisoned or mutilated by drugs and surgical operations, then its purification and repair becomes a tedious and difficult task.

Not only must the mechanism of the body be cleansed and freed from obstructive and destructive materials, but the injured parts must be repaired, morbid growths and abnormal formations dissolved and eliminated, and lesions in the bony structures corrected by manipulative treatment.

In organic diseases the vitality is usually so low and destruction so great that the organism cannot arouse itself to selfhelp. Even the cessation of suppressive treatment and the stimulating influence of mental and metaphysical therapeutics are not sufficient to bring about the reconstructive healing crises. **This can only be accomplished by the combined influences of all the natural methods of living and of treatment.**

It is in cases like these that metaphysical healing and hygienic living find their limitations. Such organic defects require systematic treatment by all the methods, active and passive, which the best Nature Cure sanitariums can furnish. It may be slow and laborious work to obtain satisfactory results and if the vitality be too low or the destruction of vital parts and organs have too far advanced, even the best and most complete combination of natural methods of treatment may fail to produce a cure.

However, this can be determined only by a fair trial of the natural methods. The forces of Nature are ever ready to react to persistent, systematic effort in the right direction and when there is enough vitality to keep alive there is likely to be enough to purify and reconstruct the organism and in time to bring about improvement and cure.

This explains why, in the organic types of diseases, metaphysical methods of treatment alone are insufficient. At least one half of the patients who come to the Nature Cure physician have faithfully tried these methods without avail, but the failures are easily excused by "lack of faith", "wrong mental attitude", or "something wrong with the patient or his surroundings".

In our experience with patients who had formerly tried metaphysical methods of healing faithfully but without results, we sometimes come face to face with a curious and amusing phase of human nature. As our patients improve under the natural regimen and treatment they gradually return to their "first love" and ascribe the good effects of natural treatment to a better understanding of Science. As health and strength return they say: "Formerly I did not know just how to apply Science, but now I know and that is why I am growing better".

I suppose this form of selfdeception which we have frequently observed is due to the fact that people feel flattered by the idea that Providence has taken a special interest in their case and cured them by miraculous intervention, or that the cure has been effected by a mysterious metaphysical principle. It is so much more interesting to be cured by some occult principle than by simple diet and cold water.

Undoubtedly it is this miracle loving element in human nature that makes metaphysical healing so much more popular than plain, common-sense Nature Cure.

Not long ago Professor Münsterberg investigated the claims made by Christian Scientists that they were "constantly curing diseases of the organic type". He reported his findings in a series of articles in McClure's Magazine (1908), stating that he inquired personally into one hundred cases said to have been cured by Christian Science and found that ninety-two of them had been of the functional type, while eight were claimed to have been organic but that in no instance could this be proved beyond doubt.

CHAPTER XXXVII

THE TWOFOLD ATTITUDE OF MIND AND SOUL

THE following is an extract from a letter sent to me in response to one of my articles in The Nature Cure Magazine.

"Sometimes you say we must rely on our own personal efforts and at other times you teach dependence upon a higher power. This to me is contradictory and confusing. I cannot understand how, consistently, we can do both at the same time. Which is right? Is it best to rely upon our own power and our personal efforts or upon the 'Higher Power'?"

There is nothing contradictory or incompatible in the teachings of Nature Cure philosophy concerning the physical and metaphysical methods of treating human ailments. Both the independent and the dependent attitudes of mind and soul are good and true and may be entertained at the same time. It is necessary for us to rely on our own personal efforts in carrying out the dictates of reason and of common sense. But this need not prevent us from praying for and confidently expecting a larger inflow of vital power and intuitional discernment from the source of all intelligence and power in the innermost parts of our being.

This twofold attitude of mind and soul is justified not only by reason and intuition, but also by the anatomical structure of the human organism and its physiological and psychological faculties, capacities and powers.

The activities of the human organism are governed by

two different systems of nerves, the sympathetic and the motor. The sympathetic nervous system is the conveyor of vital force to the organs and cells of the body. Just what this vital force is and where it originates we do not know. It is a manifestation of that which we term God, Nature, Life, the Higher Power or the Divine Within.

Heart action, the circulation of the blood, respiration, digestion, assimilation of food, elimination and all other involuntary activities and functions of the human organism are controlled by means of the sympathetic nervous system. The nature of the controlling force itself is not known to us. We do know that it is supremely powerful, intelligent and benevolent.

The more we study the anatomy, physiology and psychology of the human organism, the more we wonder at its marvelous complexity and ingenuity of structure and function. Every moment there are enacted in our bodies innumerable mechanical, chemical and psychological miracles. Who or what performs these miracles? We do not know. Yet every moment of our lives depends upon the infinite care and wisdom of this unknown intelligence and power.

Why, then, should we not trust the one so faithful? Why should we not ask aid from one so powerful? Why not seek enlightenment from one who is so wise and so benevolent?

However, not all of the human entity is dependent upon a controlling power, nor are all its functions involuntary. Within the house prepared by the Divine Intelligence there dwells a sovoreign in his own right and by his own might. He is endowed with freedom of desire, of choice and of action. He creates in his brain the nerve centers which control the voluntary activities of the body and from these brain centers he sends his commands through the fibres of the motor nerves to the voluntary muscles and makes them do his bidding; some he commands to walk, others to laugh, to eat, to speak, etc.

This independent principle in man we call the ego, the individual intelligence. It imagines, desires, reasons, plans and works out, by the power of free will and independent choice, its own salvation or destruction, physically, mentally, morally and spiritually. By means of the motor nervous system this thinker and doer directs and controls from the headquarters in the brain all the voluntary functions, capacities and powers of the human organism.

This part of the human entity can evolve and progress only through its own conscious and voluntary personal efforts.

In this Man differs from the animal creation. The animal is able to take care of itself shortly after birth. It inherits, fully developed, those brain centers for the control of the bodily functions which the new born human must develop slowly and laboriously through patient and persistent effort in the course of many years.

Of voluntary capacities and powers the new born infant possesses little more than the simplest unicellular animalcule, about all it can do is to scent and swallow food. Its cerebral hemispheres are as yet blank slates to be inscribed gradually by its conscious and voluntary exertions. Before it can think, reason, speak, walk or do anything else it must first develop in its brain special centers for each and every one of these voluntary faculties and functions.

Through these persistent personal efforts, reason, will and selfcontrol are gradually evolved and developed; while the animal, being hereditarily endowed with the faculties and functions necessary for the maintenance of life, has no occasion for the development of the **higher** faculties and powers and therefore remains an irresponsible automaton which cannot be held accountable for its actions.

To recapitulate: Freedom of choice and of action distinguish the human from the animal. In the animal kingdom, reasoning power and freedom of action move in the narrow limits of heredity and instinct, while Man through his own personal efforts is capable of unlimited development physically, mentally, morally and spiritually, both here and hereafter. We say physically advisedly, for in the spiritual realms in the life after death the physical (spiritual material) body also is capable of deterioration or of ever greater refinement and beautification.

Through the right use of his voluntary faculties, capacities and powers Man is enabled to become the master of himself and of his destiny.

Thus we find that the human organism consists of two distinct parts or departments, the one acting independently of the ego and deriving its motive force from an unknown source and the other under the conscious and voluntary control of the ego.

This twofold nature of the human entity justifies the twofold attitude of mind and soul—on the one hand the prayerful and faithful dependence upon that mysterious power which flows into us and controls us through the sympathetic nervous system and on the other hand the conscious and voluntary dominion over the various faculties, capacities and powers with which Nature has endowed us.

It is our privilege and our duty to maintain both attitudes, the dependent as well as the independent. The desire and the will to plan, to choose and to perform are ours, but for the power to execute we are dependent upon a higher source.

CHAPTER XXXVIII

THE SYMPHONY OF LIFE

HUMAN LIFE appears to me as a great orchestra in which we are the players. The great composition to be performed is the "Symphony of Life", its infinitude of dissonances and melodies blending into one colossal tone picture of harmony and grandeur. We players must study the laws of music and the score of the great symphony and we must practice diligently and persistently until we can play our parts unerringly in harmony with the concepts of the Great Composer. At the same time we must learn to keep our instrument, the body, in the best possible condition; for even the greatest artist, endowed with a profound knowledge of the laws of music and possessed of the most perfect technique, cannot produce musical and harmonious sounds from an instrument with strings relaxed or over tense, or with its body filled with rubbish.

The artist must learn that the instrument, its material, its construction and its care are just as much subject to law as are the harmonics of the score.

In the final analysis, everything is vibration acting in and on the universal ethers which are held to be the primordial substance. Possibly the ethers themselves are modes of vibration.

That which is constructive is harmonious vibration. That which is destructive is inharmonious or discordant vibration.

Against this it may be urged that devolution has its harmonics as well as evolution, that every symphony is made up of dissonances as well as of harmonies. To this

463

I answer, "Unadulterated harmony may, solely from lack of change, become monotonous; but discords alone never create harmony, health or happiness".

As the artist seeks vibratory harmony between his instrument and the harmonics of the universe of sound, so the health seeker must endeavor to establish vibratory unison between the material elements of his body and Nature's harmonics of health in the physical universe.

The atoms and molecules in the wood and strings of the violin, as well as the sounds produced from them, are modes of motion or vibration. In order to bring forth musical and harmonious notes, the vibratory conditions of the physical elements of the violin must be in harmonious vibratory relationship with Nature's harmonics in the universe of sound.

The elements and forces composing the human body are also vibratory in their nature. They also must be kept in a certain well balanced chemical combination, mechanical adjustment and physical refinement, if they are to vibrate in unison with Nature's harmonics in the physical universe and thus produce the harmonies of health and strength and beauty.

If our instrument is out of tune or if we ignorantly or wilfully insist on playing in our own way regardless of the score, we create discords not only for ourselves but also for our fellow artists in the great orchestra of life.

Sin, disease, suffering and evil are but discords produced by the ignorance, indifference or malice of the players. Therefore we cannot attribute the discords of life to the Great Composer. They are of our own making and will last as long as we refuse to learn our parts and to play them in tune with the Great Score. For in this way only can we ever hope to master the art and science of right living and to enjoy the harmonies of peace, self-content and happiness.

CHAPTER XXXIX

THE THREEFOLD CONSTITUTION OF MAN

THE following diagram and accompanying explanations will serve to illustrate the Three Planes of Being, the corresponding Threefold Constitution of Man, and their analogy to the artist and his instrument.

The Threefold Constitution of Man

Planes of Being	Threefold Constitution of Man	Analogy
Moral or Psychic	Soul	Music, Laws of Harmony
Mental	Mind	Player
Material	Bodies (Physical and Spiritual)	Violin

Man lives and functions on three distinct planes of being: the physical material and spiritual material, the mental and the soul (psychical or moral) planes.

He may be diseased upon any one or more of these planes. The true physician must look for causes of disease and for methods of treatment upon all three planes of being.

The purely materialistic physician concentrates all his study and effort upon the physical material plane of being. To him mental, spiritual, psychical and moral phenomena are merely "chemical and physiological actions and reactions of brain and nerve substance". He has nothing but

465

contempt and derision for the man who believes in or knows of a spiritual body or a soul.

He is like an artist who says: ''My violin is all there is to music. The musician's art consists in keeping his instrument in good condition. Technique and the laws of harmony are matters of imagination and of superstitious belief.''

On the other hand, mental healers, Christian Scientists and faith healers concentrate all their efforts upon either the mental or the soul plane, frequently making no distinction between the two. In the treatment of disease they ignore the conditions and needs of the physical body and some of them even deny its existence.

These metaphysicians are like the artist who devotes all his time and energy to the study and practice of technique, counterpoint and harmony, neglecting his instrument and taking no heed whether its mechanism is out of order or its interior filled with rubbish. His knowledge of the laws of harmonics and his execution may be ever so perfect; but with his instrument out of tune and out of order he will produce discord instead of harmony.

The true artist realizes that **MIND**, the **player**, must study **SOUL**, the **harmonics**; and that the mind must also have its **instrument**, the **BODY**, in perfect condition in order to interpret perfectly and artistically the harmonies of the ''Symphony of Life''.

Likewise, the Nature Cure physician will look for causes of disease and for means of cure upon the material, mental and psychical planes of being.

Thus will higher civilization and greater knowledge lead back to the natural simplicity of primitive races, where physician and priest are one.

After all, physical health is the best possible basis for the attainment of mental, moral and spiritual health. All building begins with the foundation. We do not first suspend the steeple in the air and then build the church under it. So also the building of the temple of human character should begin by laying the foundation in physical health.

We have known people who have attained high intellectual, moral and spiritual development and then suffered utter shipwreck physically, mentally and in every other way, because ignorantly they had violated the laws of their physical natures.

There are others who believe that the possession of occult knowledge and the achievement of mastership confer absolute control over Nature's forces and phenomena on the physical plane. These people believe that a man is not a master if he does not miraculously heal all manner of disease and raise the dead.

If such things were possible, they would overthrow the laws of cause and effect and of compensation. They would abolish the basic principles of morality and constructive spirituality. If it is possible in one case to heal disease and to overcome death through the fiat of the will of a master, then it must be possible in all cases. If so, then we can ignore the existence of Nature's laws, indulge our appetites and passions to the fullest extent and when the natural results of our transgressions overtake us, we can go to a healer or master and have our disease "instantly and painlessly" removed, like a bad tooth.

I say this with all due reverence for and faith in the efficacy of true prayer, and with full knowledge of the healing power of therapeutic faith; but I do not believe that God, or Nature, or a master, or metaphysical formulae can or will make good in a miraculous way for the inevitable results of our transgressions of the natural laws that govern our being.

If such miraculous healing were possible and of common occurrence, what occasion would there be for the exercise of reason, will and selfcontrol? What would become of the scientific basis of morality and constructive spirituality?

All this leads us to the following conclusions:

If there is in operation a constructive principle of Nature on the ethical, moral and spiritual planes of being with which we must align ourselves and to which we must conform our conscious and voluntary activities in order to achieve individual completion and happiness, then this constructive principle must be in operation also in our physical bodies and in their correlated physical, mental and emotional activities. If the constructive principle is active in the physical as well as in the moral and spiritual realms, then the established harmonic relationship of the physical to the constructive law of its being must constitute the morality of the physical; and from this it follows that the achievement of health on the physical plane is as much under our conscious and voluntary control as the working out of our individual salvation on the higher planes of life.

To recapitulate: **First,** our well being on all planes and in all relationships of life depends upon the existence, recognition and practical application of the great fundamental laws and principles just explained.

Second: Physical health as well as moral health is of our own making. We are personally responsible not only for our own physical and mental health, but we are also morally responsible for the hereditary tendencies of our offspring toward health or disease.

Third: The attainment of physical health through compliance with Nature's laws is just as much our duty as is our ethical, moral and psychical development.

The Unity and Continuity of the Law

That which we call God, Nature, the Creator or the Universal Intelligence is the great central cause of all things, and the vibratory activities produced by or proceeding from this central or primary cause continue through all spheres of life, as the light waves of the sun, moon and fixed stars penetrate through the intervening spheres of life to our plane of earth. Therefore all powers, forces, laws and principles which manifest on our plane, proceed and continue from the innermost Divine to the outermost external plane in physical nature. This explains the continuity, stability and correspondence on all planes of being of that which we call "National Law." In others words, "Natural Law is the established harmonic relationship of effects and phenomena to their causes, and of all particular causes to the one great primary cause of all things."

CHAPTER XL

MENTAL THERAPEUTICS

THE new psychology and the science of mental and spiritual healing teach us that the lower principles in man stand or should stand under the dominion of the higher. The physical body with its material elements is dominated and guided by the mind. The mind is inspired through the inner consciousness which is an attribute of the soul. The soul of man is in communion with the over-soul which is the source of all life and all intelligence animating the universe.

Wherever this natural order is reversed there is discord or disease. Too many people think and act as though the physical body were all in all, as though it were the only thing worth caring for and thinking about. They exaggerate the importance of the physical and become its abject slaves.

The physical body is the lowest and least intelligent of the different principles making up the human entity. Yet people allow their minds and their souls to become dominated and terrified by the sensations of the physical body.

When the servants in the house control and terrify the master, when the master becomes their slave and they can do with him as they please, there can be no order and harmony in that house.

We must expect the same results when the lower principles in man lord it over the higher. When physical weakness, illness and pain fill the mind with fear and dismay, reason becomes clouded, the will atrophied and selfcontrol is lost.

Every thought and every emotion has its direct effect upon the physical constituents of the body. The mental and emotional vibrations become physical vibrations and structures. Discord in the mind is translated into disease in the body, while the harmonies of hope, faith, cheerfulness, happiness, love and altruism create in the organism the corresponding health vibrations.

Have you ever noticed how the written or printed notes of a tone piece or the perforations on the paper music roll of an automatic player are arranged in symmetrical and geometrical figures and groups? Dry sand strewn on the top of a piano on which harmonious tone combinations are produced shows a tendency to arrange itself in symmetrical patterns.

In this you have a visual illustration of the translation of harmonious sound vibrations, which express "the harmonics of the soul's emotions", into correspondingly harmonious arrangements and configurations in the physical material of the paper roll.

A jumble of discords of sound, if reproduced on a music roll, would present a chaotic jumble of perforations.

Thus the purely mental and emotional is translated into its corresponding discords or harmonies in the physical.

As the perforations on the paper music roll arrange themselves either symmetrically or without symmetry and order, in strict accordance with the harmonies or discords of the composition, so the atoms, molecules and cells in the physical body group themselves in normal or abnormal structures of health or of disease in exact correspondence with the harmonious or the discordant vibrations conveyed to them from the mental and emotional planes.

Another illustration: Two violins, as they leave the shop of the maker, are exactly alike in material, structure and quality of tone. One of the two instruments is constantly used by beginners and persons incapable of producing pure notes. The other passes into the hands of an artist who understands how to use the instrument to the best advantage and who draws from it only musical tones that are true in pitch and quality.

After a few years compare the two violins again. You will find that the one used by the tyros in music has deteriorated in its musical qualities, while the one in the hands of the artist has greatly improved in quality and purity of tone. What is the reason? The atoms and molecules in the wood of the two instruments have grouped themselves according to the discords or the harmonies that have been produced from them.

If this rearrangement of atoms is possible in "dead" wood, how much easier must be this adjustment of atoms, molecules and cells to discordant or harmonious vibratory influence in the living, plastic and fluidic human organism!

What harmony is to music, hope, faith, cheerfulness, happiness, sympathy, love and altruism are to the vibratory conditions of the human entity. These emotions are in alignment with the constructive principle in Nature. They harmonize the physical vibrations, relax the tissues and open them wide to the inflow of the life force.

Swedenborg truly says: "The warmth of life is the heat of the divine love permeating and animating the universe". The more we possess of hope, faith, love and kindred emotions, the more we open ourselves to the inflow and action of the vital energies. The good natured, cheerful, sympathetic person is more alive than the crabbed, morose, selfish individual.

It has been proved over and over again by everyday experience that **mental and emotional conditions positively affect the chemical composition of the tissues and secretions of the body.** The destructive emotions of fear, worry, anger, jealousy, revengefulness, envy, etc. actually poison the fluids and tissues of the body. The bite of an angry man may cause blood poisoning, and prove as fatal as the bite of a mad dog. Sudden fear, anger or any other destructive emotion in the nursing mother may cause illness or even death of the infant.

In psychological laboratories it has been found by scientifically conducted experiments that under the influence of destructive mental and emotional conditions, the secretions and excretions of the body show an increase of morbid and poisonous elements.

Selfishness, fear and worry contract and congeal the blood vessels, the nerve fibres and the other channels through which the life forces are conveyed from the innermost source of life to different parts and organs of the physical body. The flow of the life currents is impeded and diminished. Such are the actual physiological effects of fear, anxiety and egotism on the physical organism.

A man under the influence of great fear and one exposed to freezing present the same outward appearance. In both cases death may result through the congealing of the tissues and the shutting out of the life currents. The person afflicted with the worry habit may not die suddenly like one overcome by great and sudden fear. Nevertheless, fear and worry vibrations constantly maintained will surely obstruct and diminish the inflow of the life force, lower the vitality and therewith the resistance to the encroachment of influences inimical to the health of the organism.

The cells in the body are negative, or at least they should be negative to the positive mind. The relationship of the mind to the cell should be like that of hypnotist to subject. If the mind could not exert such absolute control over the cells and cell groups, it would be impossible for us to walk, talk, write, dodge danger, etc. with almost automatic ease.

The cells are not able to reason upon the truth or

untruth of the suggestions conveyed to them from the mind. They accept its promptings unqualifiedly and act accordingly.

Thus, if the mind constantly thinks of, say, the stomach as being in a badly diseased condition, unable to do its work properly, the mental images of weakness and disease with their accompanying fear vibrations are telegraphed over the efferent nerves to the cells of the stomach, and these become more and more weakened and diseased through the destructive vibrations sent to them from the mind.

I often advise my patients to procure a book on anatomy and physiology and to study and keep constantly before their mind's eye the **normal** structure and functions of a **healthy** stomach or liver or whatever organ may be involved in any particular case.

Positive Affirmations

The foregoing explains why affirmations of health are justifiable in the face of disease. The health conditions must be first established in the mind before they can be conveyed to and impressed upon the cells.

The wellbeing of the human body as a whole depends upon the health of the billions of minute cells which compose it. These cells are so small that they have to be magnified several hundred times under a powerful microscope before we can see them. Yet they are independent living beings which grow, assimilate food, work and die like the big cell, Man.

These little cells are congregated in communities which form the organs and tissues of the body and in these communities they carry on the complicated activities of citizens living in a large city. Some are carriers, bringing food materials to the tissues and organs or conveying waste and morbid matter to the excretory channels of the body. Other cells manufacture chemical substances, such as sugar, fats, ferments, etc. for the production of which complicated factories are required.

The marvelous work performed by these minute organisms, as well as observations made in the dissecting room and under the microscope, strongly indicate that these cells are endowed with some sort of individual intelligence. They do their work without our aid or conscious volition. Nevertheless, they are greatly influenced by the varying conditions of the mind. While their activities seem to be controlled through the sympathetic nervous system, they stand in direct telegraphic communication with "headquarters" in the brain and every impulse of the mind is conveyed to them.

If there be dismay and confusion in the mind, this condition is telegraphically conveyed over the nerve trunks and filaments to every cell in the body, and as a result these little workers become panic-stricken and incapable of rightly performing their manifold duties.

The cell system of the body resembles a vast army. The mind is the general at the head of it. The cells are the soldiers, divided into groups for special work.

Much of the work of an army is carried on through well established departments, as the commissariat, hospital service, scouts and pickets, etc. Though the life and the activities of the army are so well regulated that they seem automatic, nevertheless much depends upon the commander.

The vital processes of the human organism, digestion, assimilation, elimination, respiration, circulation of the blood, etc., are going on without our volition whether we be awake or asleep. These involuntary activities are impelled by the **sympathetic** nervous system, while the voluntary functions of the body are controlled through the **motor** nervous system. This division, however, is not a sharp one, the two departments frequently overlapping one another.

The sympathetic nervous system resembles the commissarial department of the army which attends to the material welfare of the soldiers, while the motor nervous system, with headquarters in the brain, corresponds to the commander with his executive staff, the nerve centers in the spinal cord and other parts of the body being the subordinate officers in the field.

While the physical wellbeing of the army depends upon the almost automatic work of its various departments, its mind and soul is the man commanding it. He determines the spirit, the energy and the efficiency of the vast organization.

If the commander-in-chief lack insight, force and determination, the discipline of the army will be lax and its efficiency greatly impaired. If he be a craven, without faith in himself and in the cause he represents, his lack of courage, his doubt and indecision will communicate themselves to the whole army, resulting in discouragement and defeat.

The most successful commanders have been those who were possessed of absolute confidence in themselves and in the efficiency of their army, who in the face of grave danger and discouraging situations pressed on to the predetermined goal with dogged courage and resolution. Determination and pertinacity of this kind create the magnetic power which imparts itself to every individual soldier in the army and makes him a willing subject, even unto death, to the will of his commander.

When the pest was invading Napoleon's army, that great general entered the hospitals where the victims of the plague were lying, took them by the hand and conversed with them. He did this to overcome the fear in the hearts of his soldiers and thus to protect them against the dread disease. He said: "A man whose will can conquer the world, can conquer the plague".

To my mind, this was one of the greatest deeds of the Corsican. At a time when "New Thought" was practically unknown, the genius of this man had grasped its principles and was making them factors in his apparent success. "Apparent" because, while we admire his genius we deplore the ends to which he applied his wonderful powers.

At times when the battle seemed lost, Napoleon would go to the front where the danger was greatest, and by the mere sight of him the hard pressed soldiers under his command were inspired to superhuman effort and final victory.

As long as the glamour of invincibility surrounded him Napoleon **was invincible**, because he infused into his soldiers a faith and courage which nothing could withstand. But when the cunning of the Russian broke his power and decimated his ranks on the icebound steppes, the hypnotic spell was broken also. Friends and enemies alike recognized that, after all, he was but a man, subject to chance and circumstance. From that time on he was vulnerable and suffered defeat after defeat.

The power of the mind over the physical body and its involuntary functions (the functions which are regulated and controlled through the sympathetic nervous system) may be illustrated by the demonstrated facts of hypnotism. Through the exertion of his own imagination and his willpower, the hypnotist can so dominate the brain and through the brain the physical body of his subject, as to influence not only the sensory functions but also heart action and respiration. By the power of his will the hypnotist is able to retard or accelerate pulse and respiration and even to subdue the heart beat so that it becomes hardly perceptible.

If it is possible thus to control by the power of will the vital functions in the body of another person, it must be possible also to control these functions in our own bodies. Many Hindoo fakirs and yogi have developed this power of the mind over the physical body to a marvelous extent.

Here lies the true domain of mental therapeutics. We can learn to dominate and regulate the vital activities and the life currents in our bodies so that they will do their work intelligently and serenely even under the stress of illness or danger. We can by the power of will direct the vital currents to those parts and organs which need them most, and we can relieve congested areas by equalizing the circulation, by drawing therefrom the surplus of blood and nerve currents and distributing the vital fluids over other parts of the body.

We must be careful, however, to use our higher powers in conformity with Nature's intent; that is, we must not endeavor to suppress Nature's cleansing and healing efforts. It is possible to do this by the power of will as well as by ice bags and drugs.

Mentally and emotionally as well as physically we must work with Nature, not against her. When we understand the fundamental laws of disease and cure we cannot well do otherwise.

CHAPTER XLI

HOW SHALL WE PRAY?

SHALL we say, "Father, give me this!"—"Father, do for me that!" Or, "Behold, I am perfect! Imperfection, sin and suffering are only errors of mortal mind!"?

Or shall we pray: "Father, give me of Thy strength that I may live in harmony with Thy law, for thus only will all good come to me!"?

The first is to beg, the second to steal, the third to earn by honest effort.

"Father, give me this!"—"Father, do for me that!" Thus prayed our fathers, not understanding the great law of compensation, the law of giving and receiving, which demands that we give an equivalent for everything we receive. To receive without giving is to beg.

The lily, in return for the nourishment it receives from the soil and the sun, gives of its beauty and fragrance. The birds of the air give a return for their sustenance by their songs, their beauty of plumage, and by destroying pests which are the enemies of plants and men. Every living thing gives an equivalent for its existence in some way or other.

With man the fulfillment of the law of service and of compensation becomes conscious and voluntary and his selfrespect refuses to take without giving.

"Behold, I am perfect! Imperfection, sin, and suffering are only errors of mortal mind!" Such is the prayer of certain metaphysical healers.

To assume the possession of goodness and perfection without an earnest effort to develop and to deserve these qualities is to steal the glory of the only Perfect One. The assumption of present perfection precludes the necessity of striving and laboring for its attainment. If I am already all goodness, all love, all wisdom and all power, what remains for me to strive for?

Herein lies the danger of metaphysical idealism. While it may dispel pessimism, fear and anxiety, it inevitably weakens the will power and the capacity for selfhelp and personal effort.

The ideal of the metaphysician is the ideal of the animal. The animal does not worry about right or wrong, nor, with few exceptions, does it make provision for the future. Its care and forethought extend only to the next meal. But this perfect, ideal, passive trust in Nature's bounty causes the animal to remain animal and prevents its rising above the narrow limitations of habit and instinct.

The inherent faculties, capacities and powers of the human soul can be developed only by effort and use. The savage, living in the most favored regions of the earth, depending for his sustenance in perfect faith and trust on Nature's bounty, has remained savage. Through ages he has risen but little above the level of the beasts that perish.

The great law of use ordains that those faculties and powers which we do not develop remain in abeyance and that those which we possess weaken and atrophy if we fail to exercise them.

The Master, Jesus, emphasized this law of use in many of his parables and sayings.

"For whosoever hath, to him shall be given, and he shall have more abundance: but whosoever hath not, from him shall be taken away even that he hath."

What does this mean? Those who have the desire and the will to work out their own salvation, acquire greater knowledge and power in exact proportion to their well directed efforts; but those who have neither the desire nor the will to help themselves, lose their natural endowments and the possibilities and opportunities which these would have conferred upon them.

The anatomy and physiology of the human brain reveal the fact that for every voluntary faculty, capacity and power of body, mind and soul which we wish to develop, we have to create new centers in the brain. In this respect, Nature gives us no more and no less than we deserve and work for. If we try to cheat by usurping the perfection and the power which we have not honestly earned and developed, then some time, somewhere, we shall have to balance the account.

The Right Way to Pray

After all, the only true prayer is personal effort and selfhelp. This does not mean that we should not invoke the help of the higher powers, of those who have gone before us, of the Great Friends and Invisible Helpers and of the Great Father, the giver of all life, all wisdom and all power. **We should pray for strength to do our work, not to have it done for us.** The wise parent will not do for the child the home tasks assigned him at school. Neither will the powers on high or the Great Friends perform our allotted tasks for us.

This life is a school for personal effort. If it were not so, life would be meaningless. From the cradle to the grave, our days are one continuous effort to learn, to acquire, to overcome difficulties. Only in this way can we develop our latent faculties, capacities and powers. These cannot be developed by having our tasks done for us, nor by assuming that we already know and possess everything.

The athlete must do his own training. No one else can do it for him. Therefore the **assumption** of **superiority** over his opponent will not develop his suppleness of body and strength of muscle. To be sure, faith and courage are essential to victory, but they must be backed by careful and persistent training. Vainglorious boasting alone will not win the contest.

So in the battle of life, the more faith we have in God, in the Great Friends and in our own powers, the wider do we open ourselves to the inflow of wisdom and strength from all that is good and true and powerful in the universe. But through persistent and well directed effort alone can we control the powers and fashion the materials which Nature has so lavishly bestowed upon us.

The creative will, actuated by desire and enlightened by reason, brings order and harmony out of chaotic forces and materials. And yet certain metaphysicians tell us that we ourselves must do nothing to overcome weakness, sin and suffering; that we must depend entirely upon the efficiency of metaphysical formulae; that the deity and the powers of Nature are jealous of our personal efforts; that we must not try to help ourselves lest we forfeit their good will.

Is it not blasphemous to assume that God would blame us and withhold his aid because we dared to use the faculties, capacities and powers with which he has endowed us? You say, "Nobody is foolish enough to claim such things." But this is the teaching of a popular healing cult. Its members are forbidden, on penalty of expulsion, to use in the treatment of human ailments the most innocent natural remedies. The giving of an enema or the common sense regulation of diet are regarded as sufficient to nullify the power of their metaphysical formulae and to prevent the working of Nature's healing forces.

One of our patients who had been under such treatment until she was in a dying condition told us afterwards that her bowels often did not move for a week and when she complained to her "healer" about this condition and asked permission to take an enema, he answered: "Pay no attention. The Lord is taking care of that in some other way."

This "healer" had been a prominent allopathic physician who, like so many others ignorant of Nature's simple laws, had swung from one extreme to the other, from allopathic overdoing to metaphysical underdoing. In this instance, the Lord "took care" of the patient's bowels until she was down with a severe attack of appendicitis and peritonitis.

Amidst all the extremes, Nature Cure points the common sense middle way. Basing its teachings and its practices on a clear understanding of the laws of health, disease and cure, it refrains from suppressing acute diseases with poisonous drugs or the knife, knowing that they are in reality Nature's cleansing and healing efforts. Neither does it sit idly by and expect the Lord or metaphysical formulae or the medicine bottle and the knife to do our work and to make good for our violations of Nature's laws.

Understanding the Law, Nature Cure believes in co-operating with the law; in giving the Lord a helping hand. It teaches that "God helps him who helps himself," that He will not become angry and refuse His help if His children use rightly the reason, the will power and the selfcontrol with which he has endowed them so that they may achieve their own salvation.

Nature Cure from beginning to end is one grand, true prayer. It teaches the law on all planes of being—the physical, the mental, the moral and the spiritual; and it insists that the only way to attain perfect health of body, mind and soul is to comply with the law to the best of our ability. **When we do that we place ourselves in alignment with the constructive principle in Nature, and in exact** proportion to our intelligent and voluntary cooperation with the laws of our being all good things will come to us.

Therefore we pray: "Father, give me Thy strength that I may live in harmony with Thy law, for thus only will all good come to me."

CHAPTER XLII

SCIENTIFIC RELAXATION AND NORMAL SUGGESTION

UNDER the strain of workaday hurry and worry, your nerve vibrations are apt to become more and more intense and excited. They run away with you until, as the saying goes, you are "flying all to pieces".

A good illustration of this condition of the nervous system may be found in a team of horses shying at some object in the path. The driver, panic stricken, drops the reins, the frightened horses take the bits between their teeth and dash headlong down the road, until their master regains control, checks the animals in their maddened course and compels them to resume their ordinary pace.

So the highstrung, oversensitive individual must gain control over his nervous system and must subdue his runaway mental and emotional activities into restful, harmonious vibrations.

This is done by **insuring sufficient rest and sleep** under the right conditions and by **practicing scientific relaxation** at all times.

The nervous person gets easily excited. Comparatively little things will cause an outbreak of intense irritation or emotional hyperactivity.

Usually, the victim of unbalanced nerves is of the highstrung, sensitive type, naturally inclining to more rapid vibrations on all planes, capable of greater achievement than the stolid, heavy, slow-vibrating person who "doesn't know that he has any nerves", but also is in greater danger of mental and emotional overstrain and physical deple-

485

tion as a result of the excessive and uncontrolled expenditure of life force and nervous energy.

Watch your nervous friend while performing some trivial task, picking up something from the floor or putting a book in its accustomed place. The fitful, jerky movements betray the inner impatience and irritability. Worry, hurry and flurry do not hasten the task in hand. They only retard it. They cause neglect and bungling, which require more time to straighten out than deliberate and patient work in the first place.

Watch him while he is resting or sleeping. Instead of "letting go" of the body his muscles are drawn and tense. The body is screwed up into all sorts of awkward positions and acrobatic distortions. He nervously clutches the arm chair, or strenuously clings to the bed, as though these aids to rest and comfort were trying to escape from under him. The sleep is fitful and disturbed, as are the physical and mental vibrations.

To the sensitive the aura is visible, indicating continuous expenditure of nerve force. This interferes with the accumulation of vital energy in the millions of tiny storage batteries in the brain, the spinal cord and the sympathetic ganglia, with the result that during sleep not sufficient reserve force is stored for the work of the following day.

Such an one expends as much vitality while sleeping as another who has learned the art of restful relaxation expends while working. No wonder he feels all fagged out in the morning—as tired as when he went to bed!

Relaxation While Working

At first glance this expression may seem paradoxical. However, experience proves that it is not only possible but absolutely necessary that we perform our work in a relaxed and serene condition of body and mind. The most strenuous physical or mental labor will then not cause as much exhaustion as light work done in a state of nervous tension, irritability, fretfulness or worry.

Relaxation while working necessitates plan and system. Most nervous breakdowns result not so much from overwork as from the vitality wasted through lack of orderly procedure.

Therefore, take some time to plan and arrange your work and form the habit of doing certain things that have to be done every day as nearly as possible in the same way (making sure that it is the right way) and at the same time of the day. Orderly system will soon become habitual and result in saving much valuable time and energy.

Always cultivate a serene and cheerful attitude of mind and soul, taking whatever comes as "part of the day's work", doing your best under the circumstances but absolutely refusing to worry and fret about anything. Do not "cross a bridge before you get to it" and do not waste time regretting something that cannot be undone.

Relaxation While Sitting

Sit upright in a comfortable chair without strain or tension, spine and head erect, the legs forming right angles with the thighs (the chair should be neither too high nor too low), feet resting firmly upon the floor, toes pointing slightly outward, the forearms resting lightly upon the legs with the hands upon the knees. This must be accomplished without effort, for effort means tension.

Dismiss all thoughts of hurry, care, worry or fear and dwell upon the following thoughts:

I am now completely relaxed in body and mind. I am receptive to Nature's harmonious and invigorating vibrations—they dispel the discordant and destructive vibrations of hurry, worry, fear and anger. New life, new

health, new strength are entering into me with every breath, pervading my whole being.

Repeat these thoughts mentally, or if it helps you say them aloud several times quietly and forcefully, impressing them deeply upon your inner consciousness.

After practicing relaxation in this manner, lie down for a few minutes' rest if circumstances permit, or practice rhythmical breathing (Vol. II). Then return to your work and endeavor to maintain a calm, trustful, controlled attitude of mind.

If you are inclined to be irritable, suspicious, jealous, fault-finding, envious, etc. dwell on the following thought pictures:

I am now fully relaxed, at rest and at peace. The world is an echo. If I send forth irritable, suspicious, hateful thought vibrations, the like will return to me from other minds. I shall think such thoughts no longer. God is love, love is harmony, happiness, heaven. The more I send forth love, the more I am like God; the more of love will God and men return to me; the more shall I realize true happiness, true health, true strength, and true success.

Relaxation Before Going to Sleep

When ready to go to sleep lie flat on your back so that as nearly as possible every part of the spine touches the bed, extend the arms along the sides of the body, hands turned upward, palms open, every muscle relaxed.

Dismiss all thoughts of work, annoyance or anxiety. Say to yourself: I am now going to sleep soundly and peacefully. I am master of my body, my mind and my soul. Nothing evil shall disturb me. At .... a. m., neither earlier nor later, I shall awaken rested and refreshed, strong in body and mind. I shall meet tomorrow's tasks and duties promptly and serenely.

Simple as this formula may seem, it has helped cure many a case of persistent insomnia and nervous prostration.

Having thus set your "mental alarm clock", with a few times' practice you will be able to wake up, without being called, at the appointed time and to demonstrate to yourself the power of your mind over your body.

The quality of your sleep and its effect upon your system depend on the character of the mental and psychic vibrations carried into it. If you harbor thoughts of passion, worry or fear, these destructive thought vibrations will disturb your slumbers and you will awaken in the morning weak and tired.

If, however, you repeat mentally a formula like the above, suggesting harmonious, constructive thoughts, until you lose consciousness, you will carry into your slumbers vibrations of rest, health and strength, producing corresponding effects upon the physical organism.

After a perfectly relaxed condition of body and mind has been attained, it is not necessary to remain lying on the back. Any position of the body may then be assumed which seems most restful.

My patients frequently ask what position the body is best during sleep. It is not good to lie continuously in any one position. This tends to cause unsymmetrical development of the body and to affect unfavorably the functions of various organs. It is best to change occasionally from one position to another, as bodily comfort seems to indicate and require.

Many persons fret and worry if sleep does not come as quickly as desired. They picture to themselves in darkest colors the dire results of wakefulness.

Such a state of mind makes sleep impossible. If persisted in, it will inevitably lead to chronic insomnia.

Instead of indulging in hurtful worry, say to yourself:

"I do not care whether I sleep or not! Though I do not sleep I am lying here perfectly relaxed, at rest and at peace. I am strengthened and rested by remaining in a state of peaceful relaxation."

However, the "I do not care" must be actually meant and felt, must not be merely a mechanical repetition of words.

Nothing is more conducive to sleep, even under the most trying circumstances, than such an "I-don't-care" attitude of mind. Try it and the chances are that just because you do not care you will fall fast asleep.

CHAPTER XLIII

MAN'S DEMANDS ARE GOD'S COMMANDS

UR critics say: "If Nature Cure is all that you claim for it, why is it not more generally accepted by the medical profession and the public?"

The greatest drawback to the spreading of the Nature Cure idea is **the necessity of selfcontrol which it imposes.** If our cures of socalled incurable diseases could be made without asking the patients to change their habits of living, without the demand for effort on their own part, Nature Cure sanitariums could not be built fast enough in this country.

No matter how marvelous the results of the natural methods—when investigators learn that the treatment necessitates the control of indiscriminate appetite and self-indulgence and the persistent practice of "natural" living and all that this involves, they exclaim: "The natural regimen may be all right, but who can live up to it? You are asking the impossible. You are looking for a perfection which does not exist. Your directions call for an amount of willpower and selfcontrol which nobody possesses."

Fortunately, however, this is not true. Human nature is good enough and strong enough to comply with Nature's laws. Furthermore, the natural ways must be the most pleasant in the end or Nature is a fraud and a cheat. True enjoyment of life and happiness are impossible without perfect physical, mental and moral health, and these depend upon **natural** living and **natural** treatment of human ailments.

491

The Strengthening of Willpower and Selfcontrol

If I were asked the question: "What do you consider the greatest benefit to be derived from the Nature Cure regimen?" I should answer: "**The strengthening of willpower and selfcontrol.**"

This is the very purpose of life. Upon it depends all further achievement. Selfcontrol is the "master's key" to all higher development on the mental, moral and spiritual planes of being; but before we can exercise it on the higher planes, we must have learned to apply it on the lower plane in the management and control of our physical appetites and habits. When we have learned to control these, "higher development" will come easily.

A good method for strengthening the willpower is autosuggestion. The most opportune moments in the twenty four hours of the day for practicing this "mental magic" are those before dropping to sleep. At this time there is the least disturbance and interference from outside influences, the mind is most passive and susceptible to suggestion, and impressions made under these favorable conditions upon the "phonograph records" of the subconscious mind are the most lasting and the most powerful to control physical, mental and moral activities.

When thoroughly relaxed, at rest and at peace, say to yourself: "Whatever duties confront me tomorrow I shall execute them promptly without wavering or hesitation. I shall not give in to this bad habit which has been controlling me. I shall do that only which reason and conscience approve."

In order to be more specific and systematic and to obtain results more surely and quickly, **concentrate upon one weakness at a time.** When that has been overcome, take up another, until in this way you have attained perfect control over your thoughts, feelings and actions.

Suppose you have acquired the habit of remaining in bed and dozing after your mental alarm clock has given its signal to arise, and you dread the effort of going through your morning exercises and ablutions. Then, the night before impress upon the subconscious mind deeply and firmly the following suggestions: "Tomorrow morning on awakening I shall jump out of bed without hesitation and go through my morning exercises with zest and vigor."

Or, suppose you are subject to the fear and worry habit. Say to yourself: "Tomorrow or any time thereafter when depressing, gloomy thoughts threaten to control me, I shall overcome them with thoughts of hope and faith and with absolute confidence in the divine power of the will within me to overcome and to achieve."

Or, when in need of strengthening guidance, "Almighty Love, Creative Love, purify, strengthen, enlighten me."

In this manner you may give the subconscious mind suggestions and impressions for overcoming bad habits and for establishing and strengthening good habits.

If a serious problem is confronting you and you are unable to solve it to your satisfaction, think upon it just before you are dropping off to sleep and confidently demand that the right solution come to you during the hours of rest. The inner consciousness is always awake. It is the watchman who awakens you at the appointed time in morning. It will work upon your problem while your the morning. It will work upon your problem while your justification for the popular phrase: "Before I decide the matter I'll sleep over it."

In the practice of mental magic, as in everything else, success depends upon patience and perseverance. It would be entirely useless to go through these mental drills occasionally and in a desultory fashion; but if persisted in faithfully and intelligently, they will prove truly magical in their effects upon the development of willpower and selfcontrol, and on these depend the mastery of conditions within and without, the conquest of fate and destiny.

Constructive Affirmations

Desire and will are the open doors to heaven and hell.

I am spirit: I rejoice in an abundance of life, health, strength, wisdom and divine love.

Selfcontrol—the only key to mastership.

I am thy child created in thy likeness. Help me to know the power that Thou hast given me.

I radiate Faith, Power, Goodness and Love.

I am thankful because Faith has taken the place of fear, and knowledge the place of ignorance and superstition. All good will come to me as I obey the laws of my being.

I am Harmony; I radiate Health and Happiness.

I am now drinking from the well of Everlasting Life within me.

Giving is God's way of accumulating.

Thou art my physician: Thou renewest my body with the waters of Life, of Health and of Strength.

I am made whole through the renewing of my mind.

My soul is a magnet which draws to itself the vitality and healing currents of Nature.

I am now living in harmony with the Law, and the Law will make me whole.

"The Kingdom of Heaven is within you."

I sow words of Life and reap Health and Happiness.

The Divine Energy within me harmonizes and puts in order the material elements of my body.

Only as I live above the attraction and discord of mortal things and fill my mind with immortal truth do I realize the peace and perfection of divine being.

All good comes to me because I am learning to live in harmony with the laws of my being.

Infinite Love and Faith fill my mind and thrill my body with Healing Life.

"Omnipotent Goodness and Love, we are now in Thy sacred presence. By Thy breath the whole Universe is created. By Thy love the whole Universe leaps with joy and gladness."

My mind now rests from all material activity. I am at Peace in the health and strength-giving life of the Spirit.

My flesh is alive with the Life, Strength and Intelligence of the Healing Spirit.

My doubts and fears are dissolved and dissipated. I rest in confidence and peace in Thy unchangeable law.

"Through Faith I am quickened into life. My faith makes me whole."

The Divine Will within me rises victorious over disease and death. I am the Master of my fate.

My soul is radiant with Divine Peace. Every cell in my body is vibrant with Divine Harmony and Power.

I will be what I will to be.

I now vibrate in unison with all that is good and true and perfect on the Higher Planes of Being.

All forces are against us until we learn to conquer them, then they become our obedient servants.

My mind my kingdom is: my will the King!

The more I live in harmony with things spiritual the more I am freed from the bondage of things physical.

I am an instrument sounding forth the harmonics of health and happiness.

Health is the natural state of man. Do not allow any thought opposed to this to dominate your mind. Say with positive assurance "The Peace and Harmony of Divine Mind makes me perpetually whole."

I am one with God, I am one with the Great Life Principle, I am one with Eternal Vitality—I am almighty Energy.

By Faith I transmute evil into good.

With every breath I absorb Infinite Omnipotent Life.

Through a deeper understanding of the mysteries of life my entire being is regenerated.

I am an intelligent soul power searching through the depths of Nature's storehouse of life for healing essence, for vitalizing power, for the mystic medicines of healing with which God has stored his Universe.

Faith and Will are the Master Keys which unlock to us the treasures of the Universe.

The more I give the more I receive from the Infinite and Everlasting Storehouse of riches and power.

Mighty Spirit: In Thy strength I am strong; in Thy healing atmosphere I am realizing health; from Thy vital spirit flows the vigor that my body needs.

I am a center for the concentration and radiation of spiritual power; as I give so I receive.

Fear destroys. Through Faith I am quickened into Life.

"Till one appears who hears
All Nature silent is—silent for evermore,
Beating its waves of force on an unanswering shore—
    Till one appears who hears."

"Men grumble because God put thorns with roses; would it not be better to thank God that He put roses with the thorns?"

"Talk Faith: The world is better off without your uttered ignorance and morbid doubt. If you have Faith in God or man or self, say so; if not, push back upon the shelf of silence all your thoughts till Faith shall come; no one will grieve because your lips are dumb."

Ella Wheeler Wilcox.

"Resist not evil, but overcome evil with good."

"Faith opens wide the flood gates of life."

He who thinks he can, develops within himself the power that can.

Nature is full of music, as it exists through the laws of harmony. Man only is discordant and out of tune.

"He that believeth on Me, the works that I do he shall do also. And greater works shall he do."

"Where two or three are gathered together in my name, there am I in the midst of them."

Calm demand brings all good things in time; impatient demand drives them away.

Man is a macrocosm. As he learns to rule his Universe within he learns to master the Universe without.

"Father, give me of Thy strength and Thy wisdom that I may comply with Thy law in all things. Thus only can I come into the possession of the divine heritage which Thou hast prepared for me from the beginning."

I now assert my freedom and integrity as an independent individual, intelligence and free moral agent. Only as I grow and expand mentally and spiritually can I throw off the fetters of ignorance, poverty, disease and failure.

Evil is not a punishment, not a curse, but a necessary complement of good.

The active principle in my will is the force which creates and governs the Universe.

"All forces have been steadily employed to complete and to delight me. Now on this spot I stand with my robust soul."—Walt Whitman.

"Be still, my soul, and know that peace is thine; Be steadfast, heart, and know that strength divine belongs to thee; Cease from thy turmoil, mind, and thou the everlasting rest shall find."

Only as I give the best that is within me can I receive the best that is without me.

Suffering is often the greatest blessing to humanity. It compels us to search out and remove its cause and thus we learn the beauties of eternal law.

A vivid imagination, a positive faith **and a** powerful will are the workers of mental magic.

Health and happiness depend upon **the** attainment of poise and power.

Eagerness and indolence are both obstructive and result in weakness and suffering. Nothing can come to us except we draw it. Nothing can stay when we let go. Nothing can go till it has fulfilled its purpose.

Each man his prison makes. You are not bound but as you bind yourself. Within deliverance must be sought.

The way of peace is the way of power. It brings us repose without lethargy, activity without effort, love without anxiety, and joy without reaction.

> "Our lives are songs, God writes the words,
> And we set them to music at leisure,
> And the song is sad or the song is glad
> As we choose to fashion the measure."

We attract to ourselves whatever influences we choose.

The greatest force in the universe is the power of many minds united in purpose, faith and will. The higher and better the motive, the greater the power.

"As a man thinketh in his heart so is he."

The only death imaginable is stagnation.

I am today what my past thoughts and emotions have made me.

I am a free born citizen of this boundless Universe. Nothing can bind me, hold me or limit me but my own opinions and my own actions.

Almighty Love, creative Love, purify, strenghten, enlighten me!

"God of the granite and the rose,
Soul of the sparrow and the bee—
The mighty tide of being flows
Through every creature, Lord, from Thee.
It leaps to life in bird and flowers,
Through every grade of being runs,
Till from creation's radiant towers
Its glories flame in stars and suns.
Know that like bird and grass and flower.
The life within thee is divine;
Nor time, nor space, nor human power,
The God within thee can confine.
God of the granite and the rose,
Soul of the sparrow and the bee—
The mighty tide of being flows
From every creature back to Thee;
Thus round and round the circle runs—
A mighty sea without a shore—
While men and angels, stars and suns,
Unite to praise Thee evermore."

REFERENCE INDEX

501

DISEASE CRISES—see Crises.
DISEASE GERMS—see Bacteria.
DOUCHES—antiseptic for womb, 189.
DRINKS—see Coffee and Tea; fruit juice in diphtheria, 179; in fasting, 329; see Alcohol.
DRUGS—are destructive, 25; causes of disease, 39; poisonous, 63; reactions, 63, 65; suppression by, 69; proofs of presence in system, 80; after effects of drug treated typhoid, 119; anesthetics, results of, 122; vs. healing crises, 259; how laxatives act, 260; effects of digitalis, 262; Osler on use of, 289-293; Nature Cure in regard to, 294; cause chronic disease, 294; high potency doses, 307-313.
DUAL EFFECT—law of, see Action and Reaction.

ELECTRICITY—what is, 334; in re life force, 351; electric cell described, 426; produced by inanimate objects belongs to mineral kingdom, 429.
ELECTROMAGNETIC—life element, 336, 339; energies in body intensified by massage, 324; energy derived from life force, 426; brain most powerful electromagnetic battery in body, 428; treatment by electric contrivances discarded as harmful, 429; energies can be controlled by will, 436.
ELECTRONS—what electron is to atom, microzyma is to cell, 16; vibratory, 81; number in atom, atomic weight depends on, 273, 334.
ELIMINATION—methods of, 40, 72; process of, 94; through colds, 112; of hereditary taints through smallpox, 165-168; through tonsils, 181; leukorrhea, form of, 188; menses, form of, 198; by fevers, etc., 215; from cells, 248; in chronic disease, 251; experiments by Dr. Lahmann, sweating, etc., 263; of mineral poisons difficult, 303; effect of diet, 320; by fasting, 322; through natural organs of depuration, 346.
EMOTIONS—influence of, 46; effect of, 471; effect of blind faith, 386; influence of sex emotions of parents, 388; effects of food on, 391; effects of fear, 392; power of strong aspiration, 393; as healing power, 431, 436; unhealthy "all is good" emotionalism, 452; effect in the body, 472-476.
EPIDEMICS—explained, 54.
EPILEPSY—suppressed, not cured by bromids, 70; caused by vaccination, treatment, 160; caused by removal of tonsils, 184.
ERUPTIONS—sycotic, milk scurf, measles, etc., 72; as healing crises, 212.
EYE DIAGNOSIS—see Iridiagnosis.

FAITH—blind faith related to hypnotism, 386; without works dangerous, 450; rational faith justified, 459-462; increases inflow of vital force, 472.
FALLOPIAN TUBES—obstruction of, 190.
FASTING—in appendicitis, 138; fruit juice for drink in, 179; in typhoid, 292; when indicated, 323; induces abnormal psychism, 324; dangers of, 325; in chronic disease, 366; procedure before, 328; fear of unfounded, 329.
FEAR—and the germ theory, 52; effects of, 427.
FEMALE—see Woman.

APPENDIX

THE LINDLAHR SYSTEM OF NATURAL THERAPEUTICS

The Lindlahr Institutions were established, first, for the purpose of providing suitable environment and facilities for the care and treatment of patients desiring to be cured of acute and chronic ailments; second, to train young men and women in the arts of natural healing, to turn them out as qualified nurses and physicians; third, to publish and distribute literature for the purpose of educating the public in the proper care of body and mind, thus promoting the ideas of natural living; fourth, to establish local centers throughout the country to further the work of education.

The Lindlahr Institutes are essentially educational in character and bear the stamp of liberality in thought, consistent with the highest ideals of the age.

The work is divided into departments which are controlled by men and women of superior ability and breadth of vision. All departments are personally supervised by Dr. Lindlahr.

THE SANITARIUMS

In the Sanitariums facilities are provided for the thorough, conscientious treatment of those who are unable to undertake their treatment at home. There are many serious conditions which require supervision and treatment by experienced physicians and nurses. The Sanitariums provide the proper facilities and ideal environment for carrying out the natural regimen and for administering the various methods of natural treatment.

Diagnosis. To begin with, a careful analysis is made of every patient's condition to determine the exact nature of his ailments and the degree of his vitality and recuperative powers. For this purpose advantage is taken of all the latest and best methods of diagnosis. These include:

1. **Physical Diagnosis.** Each patient is subjected to a thorough physical examination.

2. **Laboratory Analysis.** Examinations are made of the patients' blood, sputum and urine and, if necessary, also of stomach contents and of feces. Records are kept and comparisons made from time to time with previous analyses in order to determine the degree of improvement.

3. **Diagnosis from the Eye.** The iris of the eye holds records of many abnormal changes in structure and function as they occur in the body. Upon the patient's entrance to our institution the records in the iris are carefully noted, and signs of improvement are recorded during the course of treatment.

4. **Spinal Analysis,** according to the various systems of manipulative treatment, offers a valuable addition to diagnostic science. It reveals mechanical interference with the circulation of vital fluids and of nerve currents and points out the best methods of correction.

5. **Basic Diagnosis.** In this we possess a valuable method for determining the general constitutional tendencies toward health or disease and for prognosing the chances of recovery in any given case. The findings are based on the relative strength and activity of the three principal organ systems of the body, viz., the digestive, respiratory and reproductive systems.

6. **X-Ray Diagnosis.** Wherever necessary the X-Ray is employed to show abnormalities of structure.

NATURAL THERAPEUTICS

The essential element in curative treatment is a natural environment in which the patient is provided with proper food and subjected to the beneficial influences of the great natural curative forces found in sunlight, air and intimate contact with mother earth. But these regenerative influences are not sufficient to bring about marked improvement or recovery in serious chronic cases. "Chronic" means that the system can no longer help itself, that the cells and organs have become so encumbered and weakened by pathogenic conditions that they cannot arouse themselves to acute curative effort. In such cases the purifying and tonic influences of the various methods of natural treatment are absolutely necessary to bring about the desired results. In many instances one kind or several kinds of treatment are not sufficient. The cure requires "the whole bill of fare" and then it is difficult and tedious enough to try to the uttermost both physician and patient.

For these reasons Natural Therapeutics selects and combines everything that is good in dietetic treatment, hydrotherapy, massage, osteopathy, chiropractic, naprapathy, neurotherapy, Swedish movements, curative gymnastics, breathing exercises, and in magnetic and mental therapeutics.

Thus everything is done to overcome the primary manifestations of disease, viz., lowered vitality, abnormal composition of vital fluid, accumulation of pathogenic materials, mechanical lesions and destructive mental and emotional activities. In this way only can we secure a more copious inflow of the Life Force, which is healing Force, and through this perfect health, happiness and greater efficiency.

EXTENSION DEPARTMENT

This department has been established for the benefit of t.1ose who are not sick enough to need institutional treatment or those who for some reason are not able to take advantage of it. These patients may receive advice and special instructions by mail or telegraph. Dr. Lindlahr takes entire charge of this work and daily dictates letters and telegrams to sufferers all over the country who are relying on his advice to make them whole again. Details regarding this department will be mailed on request.

Transient Treatment Department. Both in Elmhurst and in Chicago a department is maintained for transient patients. Besides their treatments these patients receive instructions in diet, home treatment and natural living.

COLLEGE DEPARTMENT

Exceptional opportunities are offered to young men and women desiring a vocational training.

The college department is maintained at the expense of the institution for the education of physicians, nurses and teachers.

For this purpose a number of courses of instruction have been arranged to meet the ever growing demand.

COLLEGE PREPARATORY COURSE

This course prepares students for college and at the same time they are given exceptional opportunities for earning their way.

THREE YEAR NURSES' TRAINING COURSE

Our sanitariums are open to young women who desire training in nursing. This is a wonderful chance to acquire a liberal education and vocational training while at the same time earning fair wages and in many instances high wages on the commission plan.

FOUR MONTHS' PRACTICAL TRAINING COURSE

This course makes it possible for every young man and woman to secure a practical knowledge of the laws and principles underlying the science of eugenics and the arts of natural living and healing. This constitutes the best preparation for the responsibilities and duties of marriage and of parenthood. It is an ideal course for parents or for others upon whom depends the care of a family.

FOUR YEAR PHYSICIANS' COURSE

Young men and women about to enter college in preparation for their life's work should carefully consider the new profession of Natural Therapeutics. This is the only college in the country offering a thorough course in all branches of drugless and bloodless therapy and natural healing. The minimum of time required for this course according to the provisions of the Medical Practice Act is forty months.

RESIDENCE POSTGRADUATE COURSES

To the graduates of other schools we offer finishing courses in all branches of Natural Therapeutics, ranging from a few weeks to four months.

POSTGRADUATE EXTENSION COURSES

For practicing physicians of all schools who are unable to take our Residence Postgraduate Course there has been instituted an Extension Course in which all the subjects of diagnosis and treatment are taught by correspondence. Many valuable books and charts are given free to students subscribing to this course. Without the payment of an additional tuition fee these students are allowed to attend our Postgraduate Residence Course.

PUBLISHING DEPARTMENT

This department is maintained for the purpose of spreading the New Gospel of Natural Living and Healing. Yearly thousands of tracts, booklets and other forms of literature are published and distributed to bring light to the ignorant and hope to the sufferer. Dr. Henry Lindlahr is now completing six most valuable volumes whose contents will cover the entire field of Natural Therapeutics.

The first book written by Dr. Lindlahr was entitled "Nature Cure Philosophy and Practice." It was a monumental work which gave for the first time a correct and scientific exposition of Nature Cure philosophy and practice in the English language. The subject matter of the first publication has been thoroughly revised and enlarged to such an extent as to make two volumes, one devoted entirely to philosophy and principles, and the other to treatment. The third volume of the series will be a revision of the Nature Cure Cook Book. Volume IV will be "Eugenics, or Man Building on the Physical, Mental and Moral Planes of Being", based on the principles of Natural Therapeutics. Volume V will present the nature and treatment of special diseases from the allopathic viewpoint and according to the principles of Natural Therapeutics. Volume VI will be an extensive treatise of Iridiagnosis and other methods of diagnosis and prognosis.

MAGNIFYING COMBINATION
LENS AND MIRROR

FOR

IRIDIAGNOSIS

Iridiagnosis is greatly facilitated by a lens of good magnifying power.

We are now prepared to supply a lens specially made for this purpose. It folds into a hard rubber case, and can be carried conveniently in the vest pocket or handbag. This instrument has, as an additional feature, a magnifying mirror lens. By means of this mirror you are enabled to study the changes in your own eyes.

To practicing physicians the mirror is of a special value for teaching the patients to observe the changes in their condition, as revealed in the iris.

Price for combination lens and mirror in hard rubber case, $5.00

LINDLAHR PUBLISHING CO. Not Inc.
515-529 South Ashland Boulevard   CHICAGO

LINDLAHR COLLEGE OF NATURAL THERAPEUTICS   LINDLAHR SANITARIUM

BUNGALOW, ELMHURST

TENT CITY, ELMHURST RESORT